Revenge

冨樫義博

TV shows from Osaka are hilarious!

Yoshihiro Togashi

Yoshihiro Togashi's manga career began in 1986 at the age of 20, when he won the coveted Osamu Tezuka Award for new manga artists. He debuted in the Japanese **Weekly Shonen Jump** magazine in 1989 with the romantic comedy **Tende Shôwaru Cupid**. From 1990 to 1994 he wrote and drew the hit manga **YuYu Hakusho**, which was followed by the dark comedy science-fiction series **Level E**, and finally this adventure series, **Hunter x Hunter**, available from VIZ Media's SHONEN JUMP Advanced imprint. In 1999 he married the manga artist Naoko Takeuchi.

HUNTER X HUNTER Volume 23
SHONEN JUMP ADVANCED Manga Edition

STORY AND ART BY
YOSHIHIRO TOGASHI

English Adaptation & Translation/Lillian Olsen
Touch-up Art & Lettering/Mark McMurray
Design/Matt Hinrichs
Editor/Yuki Murashige

HUNTERxHUNTER © POT (Yoshihiro Togashi) 2005. All rights
reserved. First published in Japan in 2005 by SHUEISHA Inc., Tokyo.
English translation rights arranged by SHUEISHA Inc.

The stories, characters and incidents mentioned in this publication are
entirely fictional.

Printed in the U.S.A.

Published by VIZ Media, LLC
P.O. Box 77010
San Francisco, CA 94107

10 9 8 7 6 5 4 3 2
First printing, November 2008
Second printing, May 2016

PARENTAL ADVISORY
HUNTER X HUNTER is rated T+ for Older Teen
and is recommended for ages 16 and up.
Contains realistic violence and mature language.
ratings.viz.com

www.viz.com

www.shonenjump.com

HUNTER × HUNTER

ハンター ✕ ハンター

Story & Art by
Yoshihiro Togashi

Volume 23

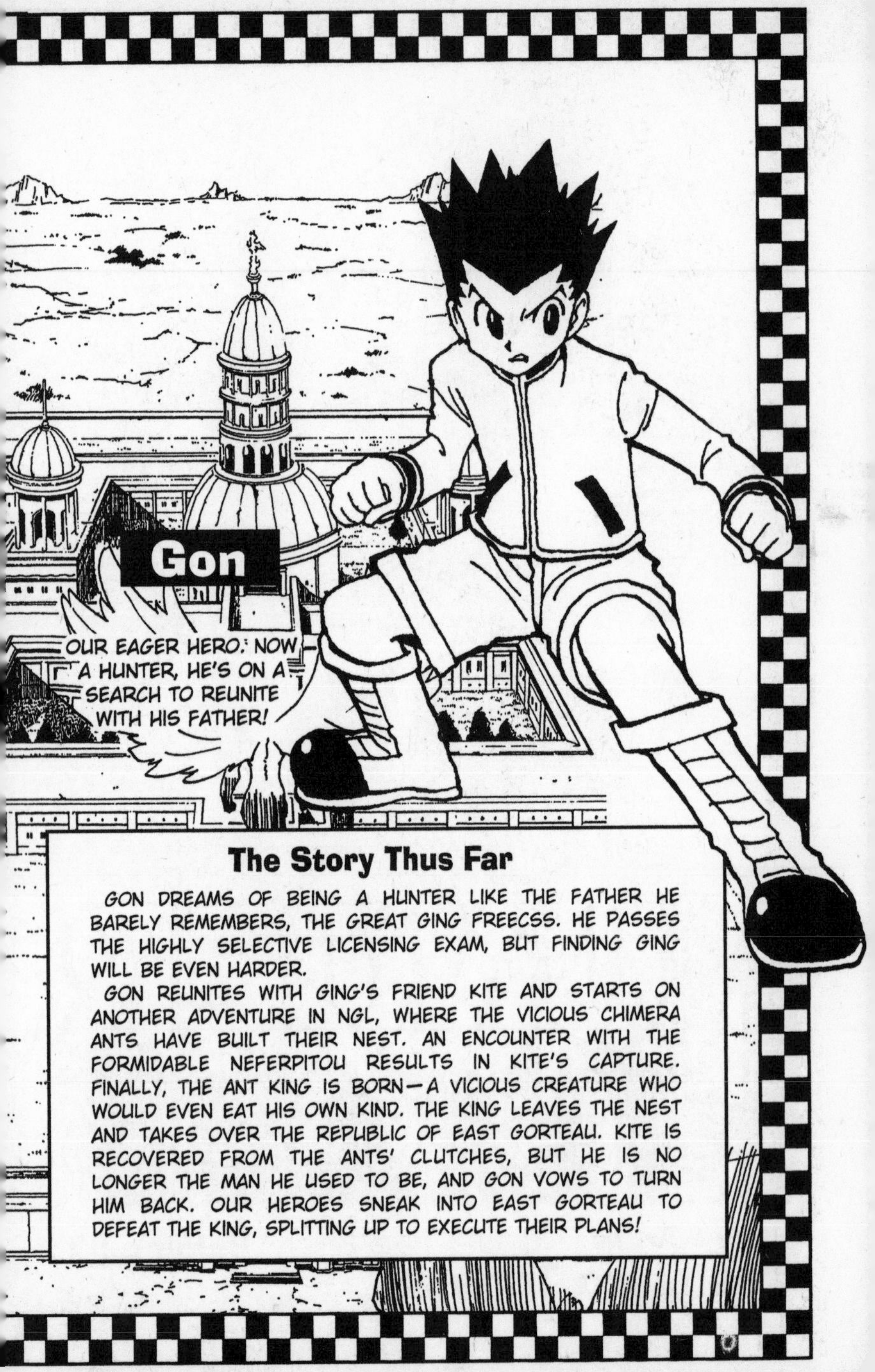
Gon
OUR EAGER HERO: NOW A HUNTER, HE'S ON A SEARCH TO REUNITE WITH HIS FATHER!

The Story Thus Far

GON DREAMS OF BEING A HUNTER LIKE THE FATHER HE BARELY REMEMBERS, THE GREAT GING FREECSS. HE PASSES THE HIGHLY SELECTIVE LICENSING EXAM, BUT FINDING GING WILL BE EVEN HARDER.

GON REUNITES WITH GING'S FRIEND KITE AND STARTS ON ANOTHER ADVENTURE IN NGL, WHERE THE VICIOUS CHIMERA ANTS HAVE BUILT THEIR NEST. AN ENCOUNTER WITH THE FORMIDABLE NEFERPITOU RESULTS IN KITE'S CAPTURE. FINALLY, THE ANT KING IS BORN—A VICIOUS CREATURE WHO WOULD EVEN EAT HIS OWN KIND. THE KING LEAVES THE NEST AND TAKES OVER THE REPUBLIC OF EAST GORTEAU. KITE IS RECOVERED FROM THE ANTS' CLUTCHES, BUT HE IS NO LONGER THE MAN HE USED TO BE, AND GON VOWS TO TURN HIM BACK. OUR HEROES SNEAK INTO EAST GORTEAU TO DEFEAT THE KING, SPLITTING UP TO EXECUTE THEIR PLANS!

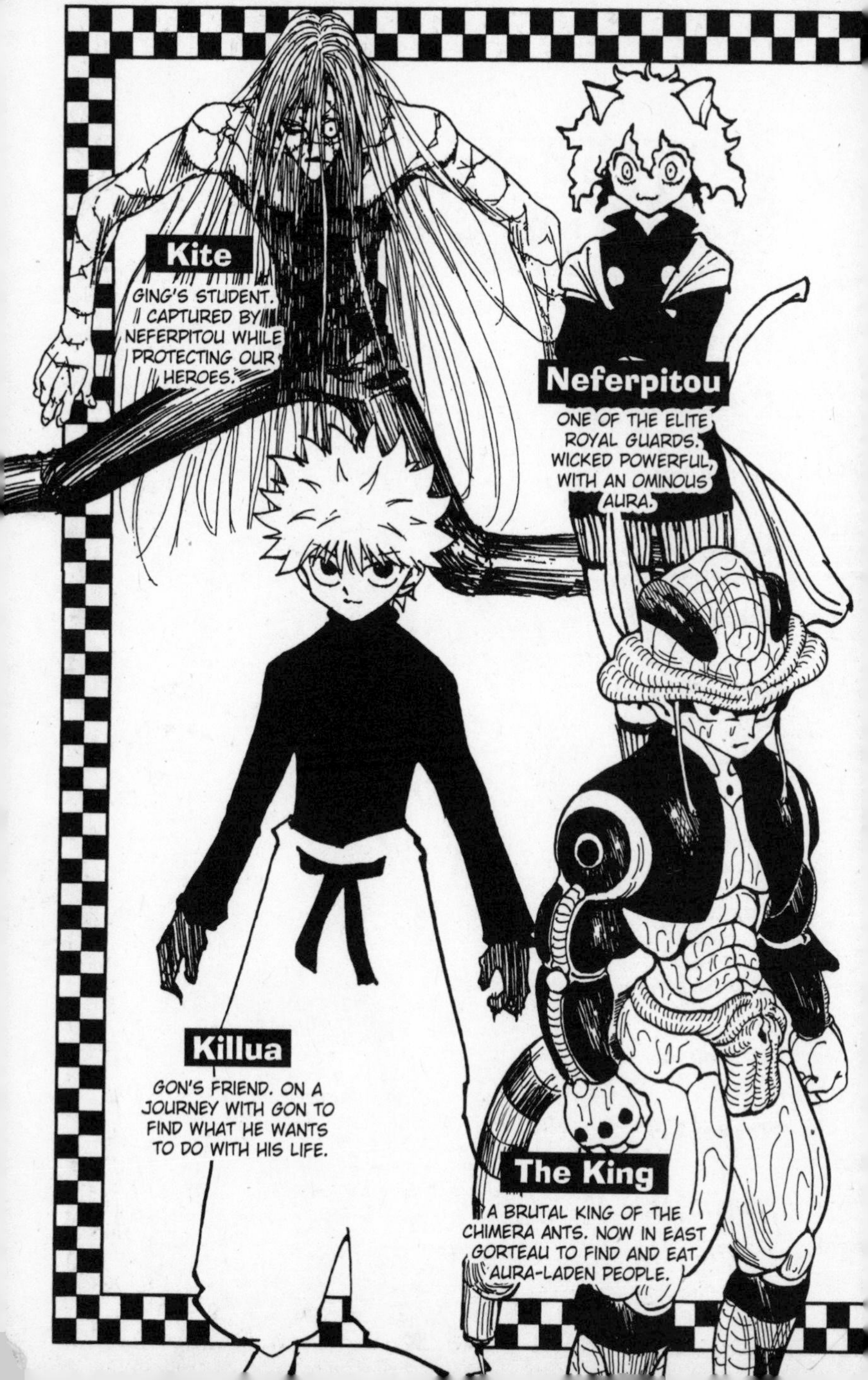
Kite
GING'S STUDENT. CAPTURED BY NEFERPITOU WHILE PROTECTING OUR HEROES.
Neferpitou
ONE OF THE ELITE ROYAL GUARDS. WICKED POWERFUL, WITH AN OMINOUS AURA.
Killua
GON'S FRIEND. ON A JOURNEY WITH GON TO FIND WHAT HE WANTS TO DO WITH HIS LIFE.
The King
A BRUTAL KING OF THE CHIMERA ANTS. NOW IN EAST GORTEAU TO FIND AND EAT AURA-LADEN PEOPLE.

HUNTER × HUNTER

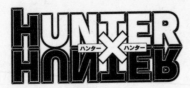

Volume 23

CONTENTS

Chapter 236: 8: Part 2

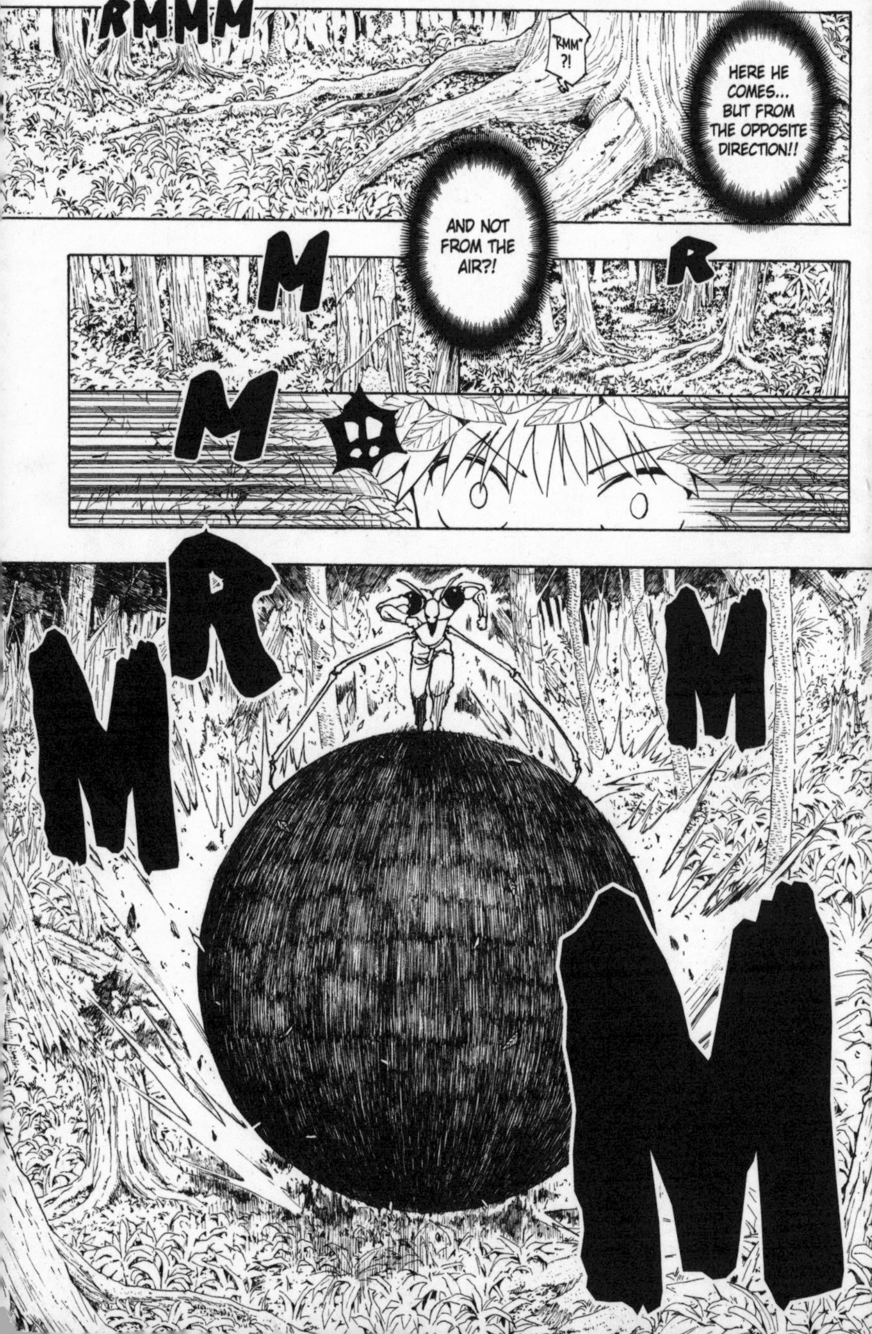
HERE HE COMES... BUT FROM THE OPPOSITE DIRECTION!!
"RMM" ?!
RMMMM
AND NOT FROM THE AIR?!
R
M
M
!!
M
R
M
M

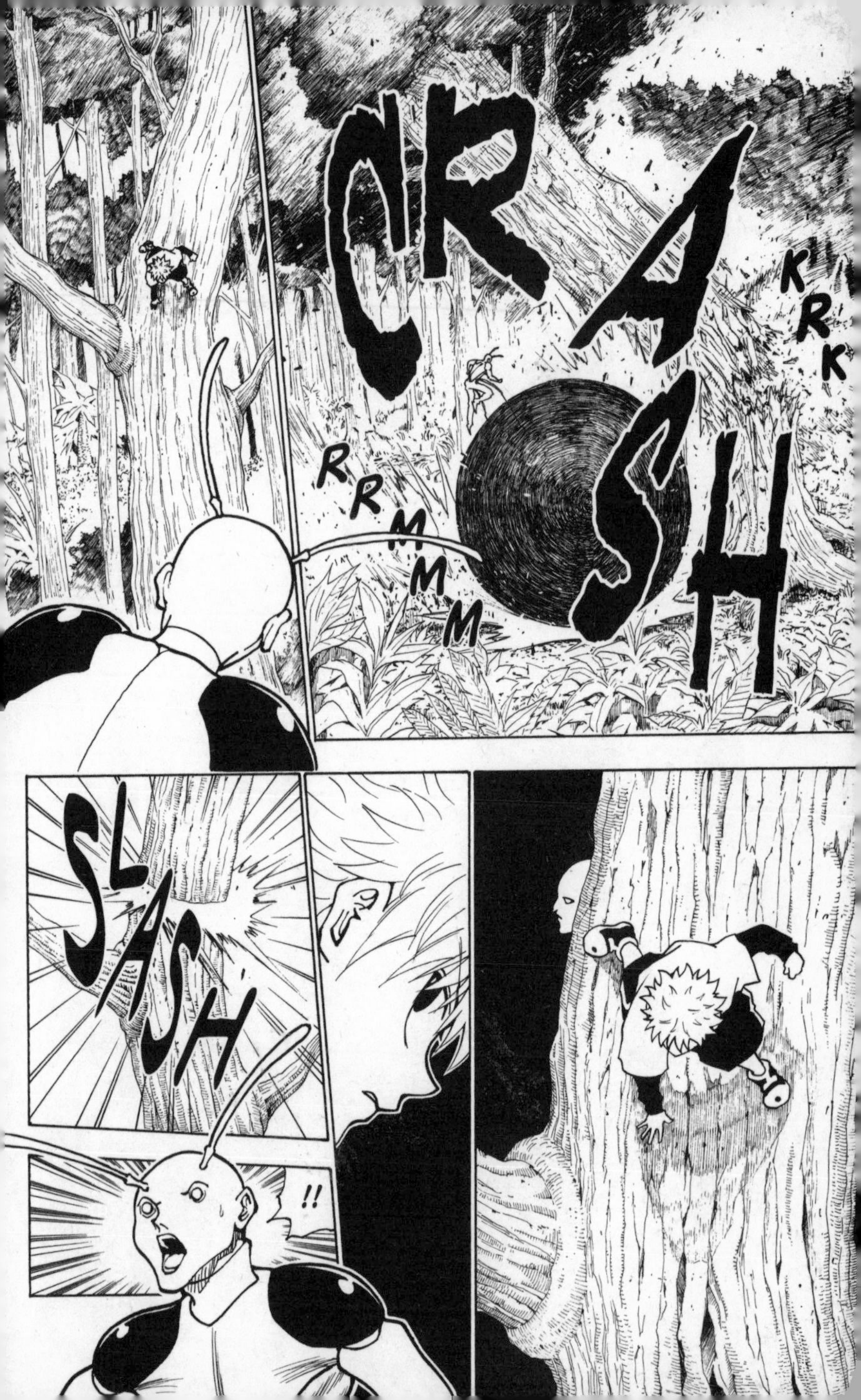
KRK
CRASH
RRMMMM
SLASH
!!

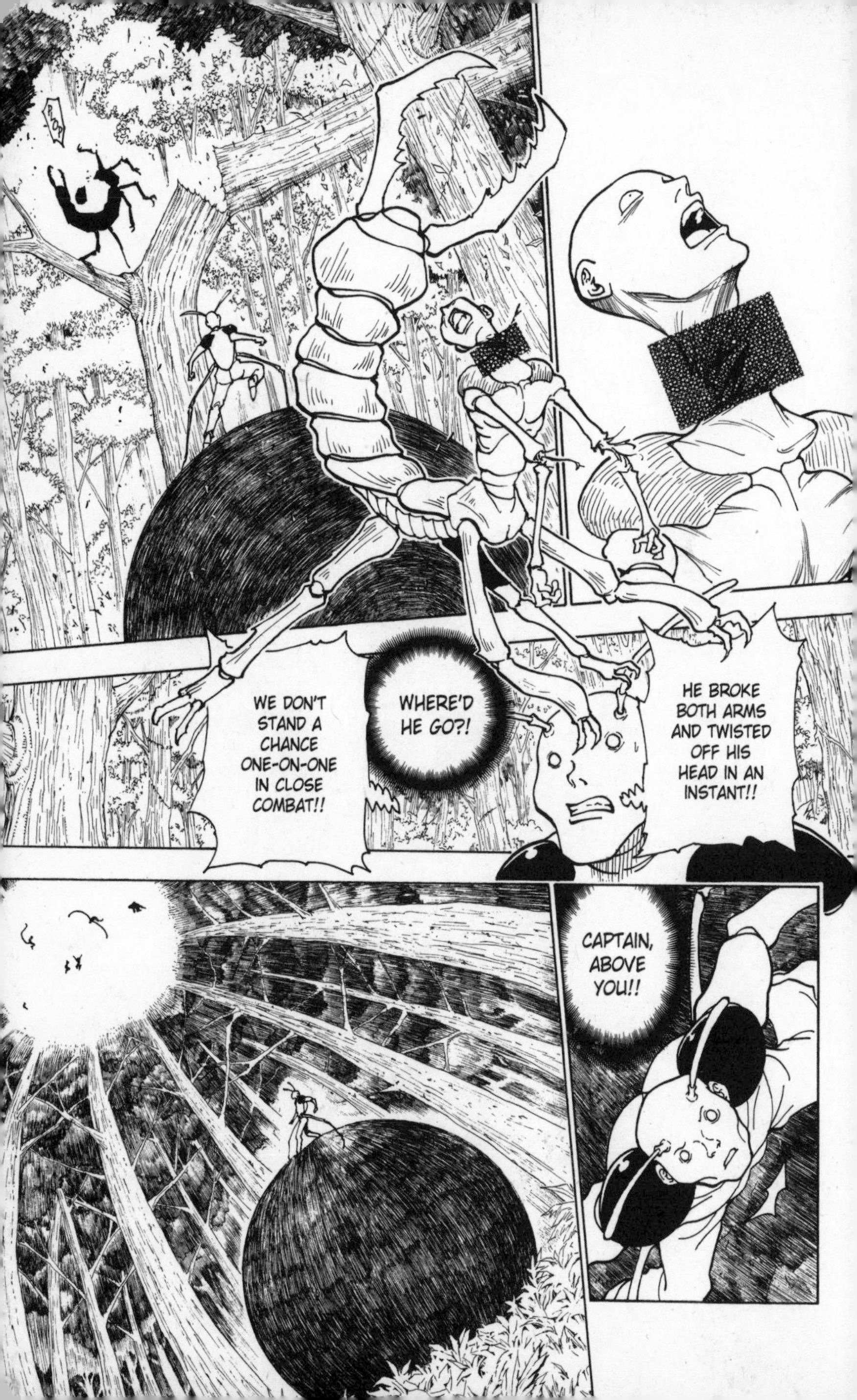
PLOP
HE BROKE BOTH ARMS AND TWISTED OFF HIS HEAD IN AN INSTANT!!
WHERE'D HE GO?!
WE DON'T STAND A CHANCE ONE-ON-ONE IN CLOSE COMBAT!!
CAPTAIN, ABOVE YOU!!

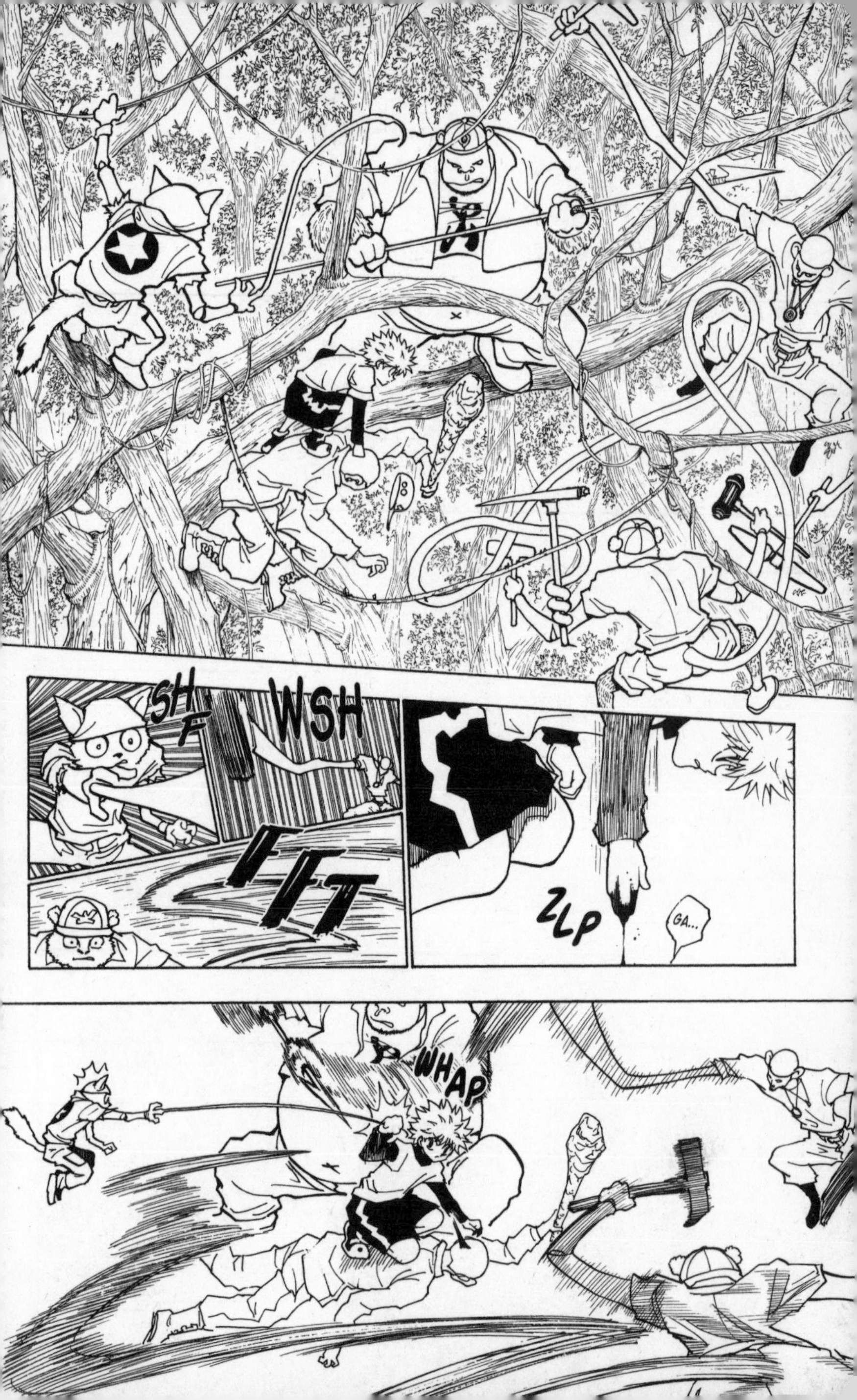
ZLP
GA...
SHF
WSH
FFT
WHAP

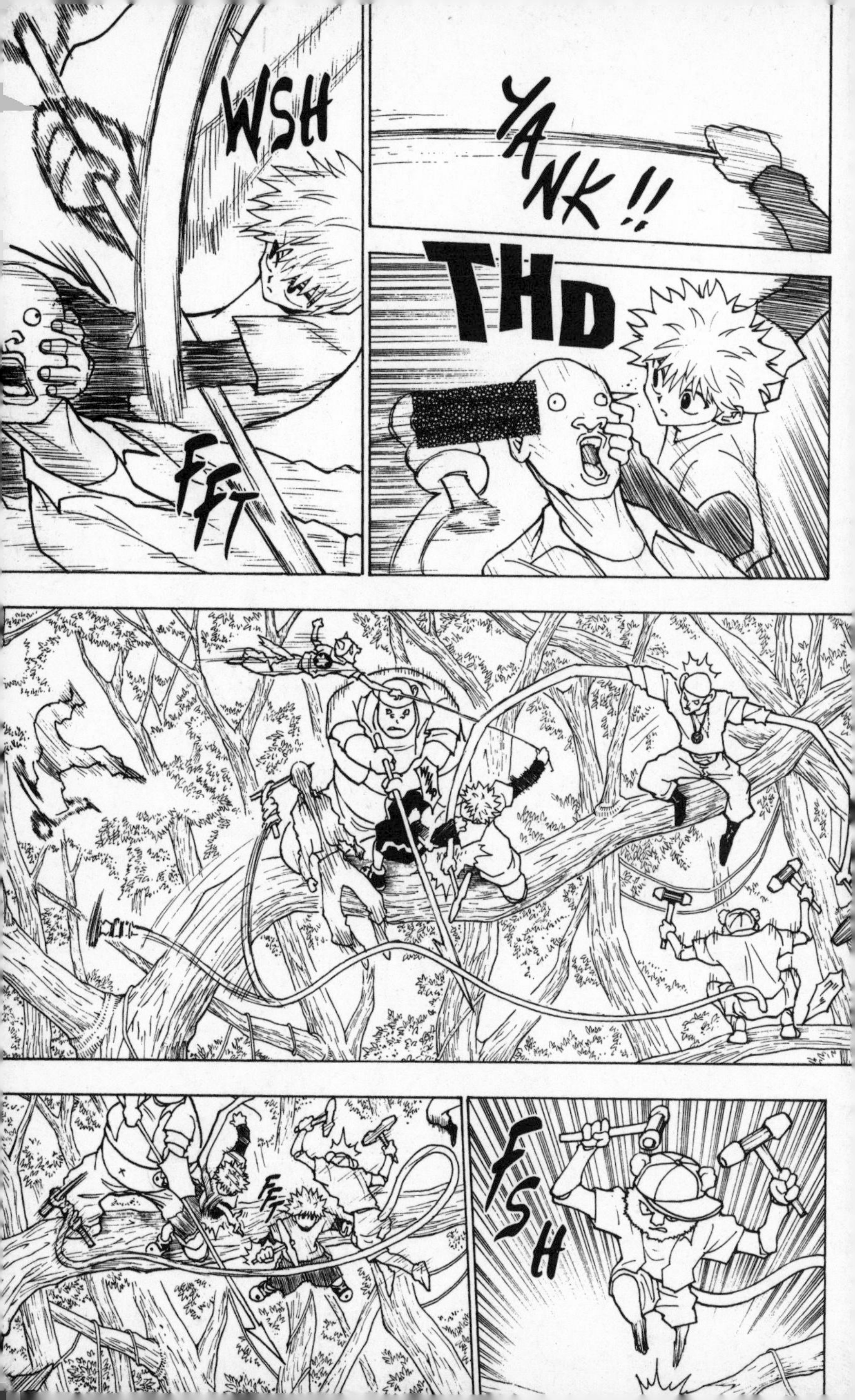
YANK!!
THD
WSH
FFT
FSH
FFT

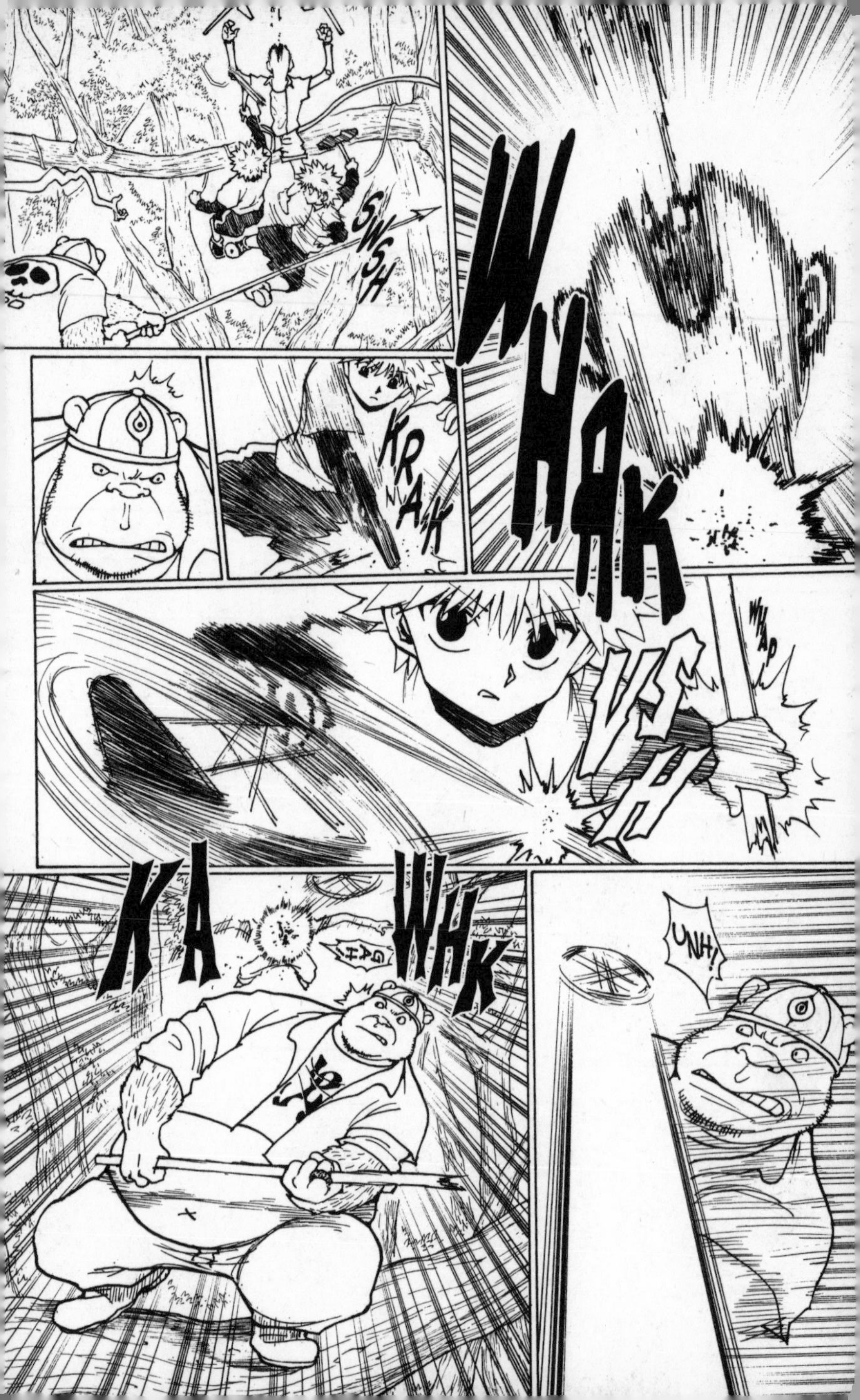

WHAK
SWSH
KRAK
WHAP
VSH
UNH!
KA WHK
GAH

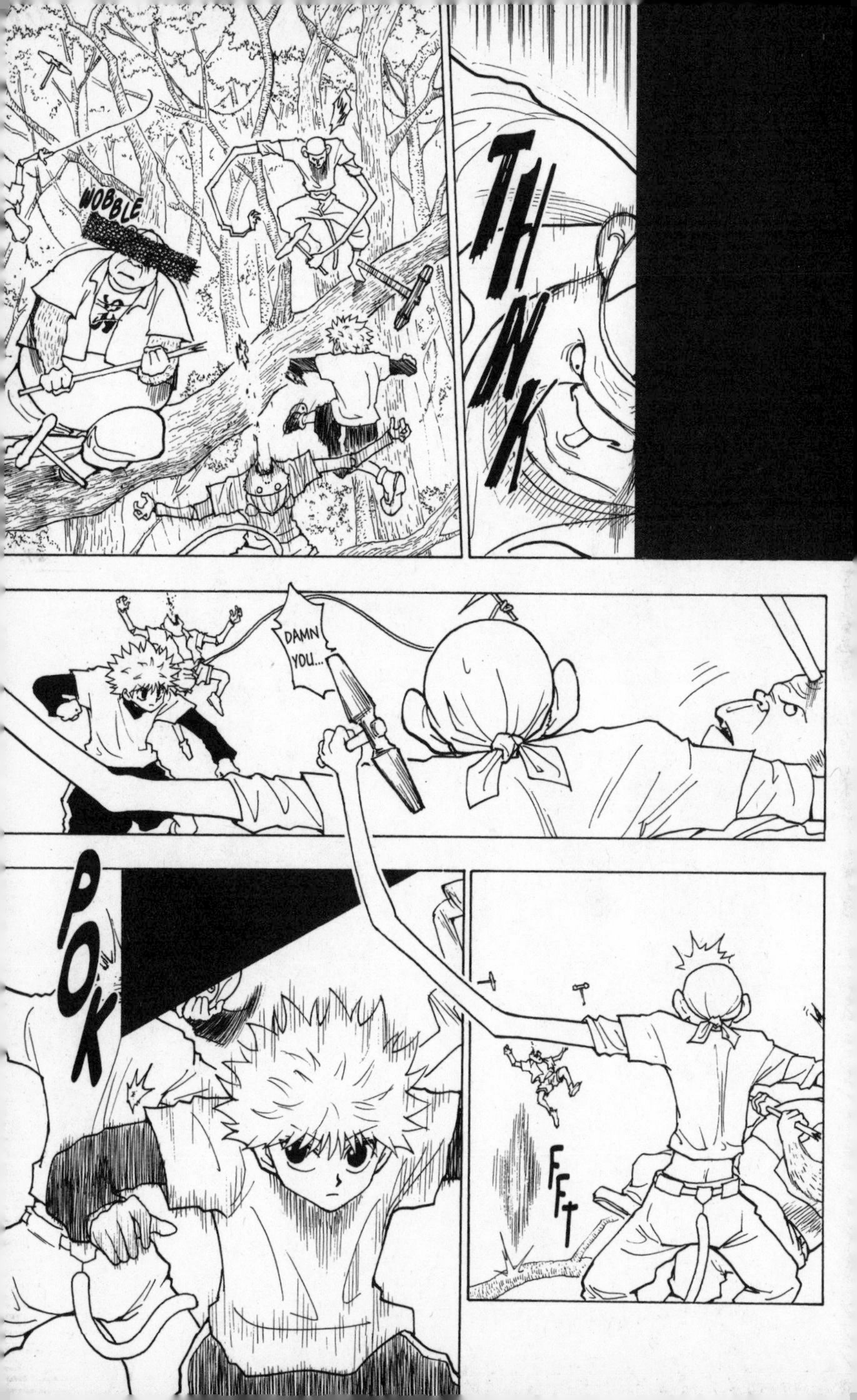
THNK
WOBBLE
DAMN YOU...
FFT
POK

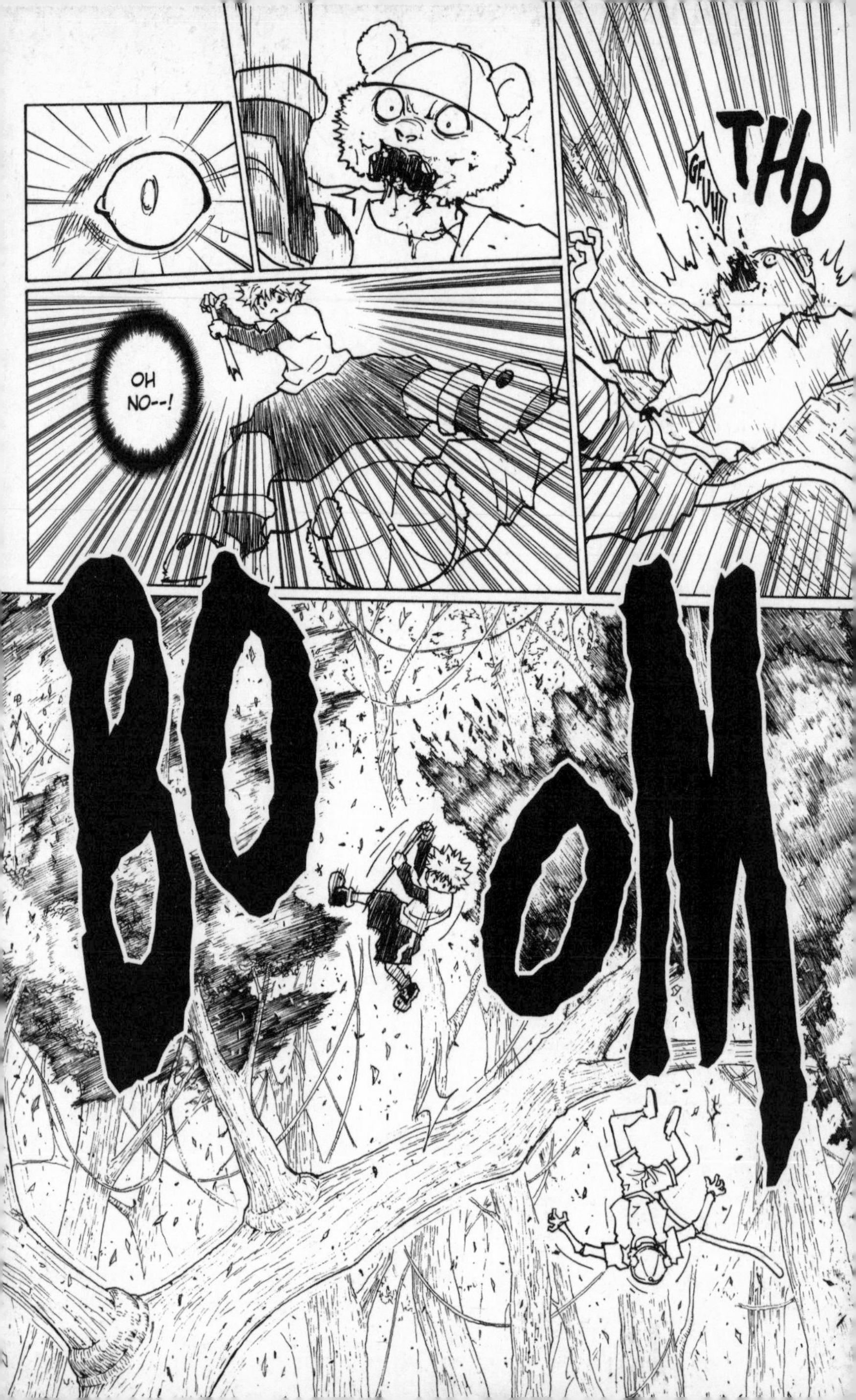
GFUH!
THD
OH NO--!
BOOM

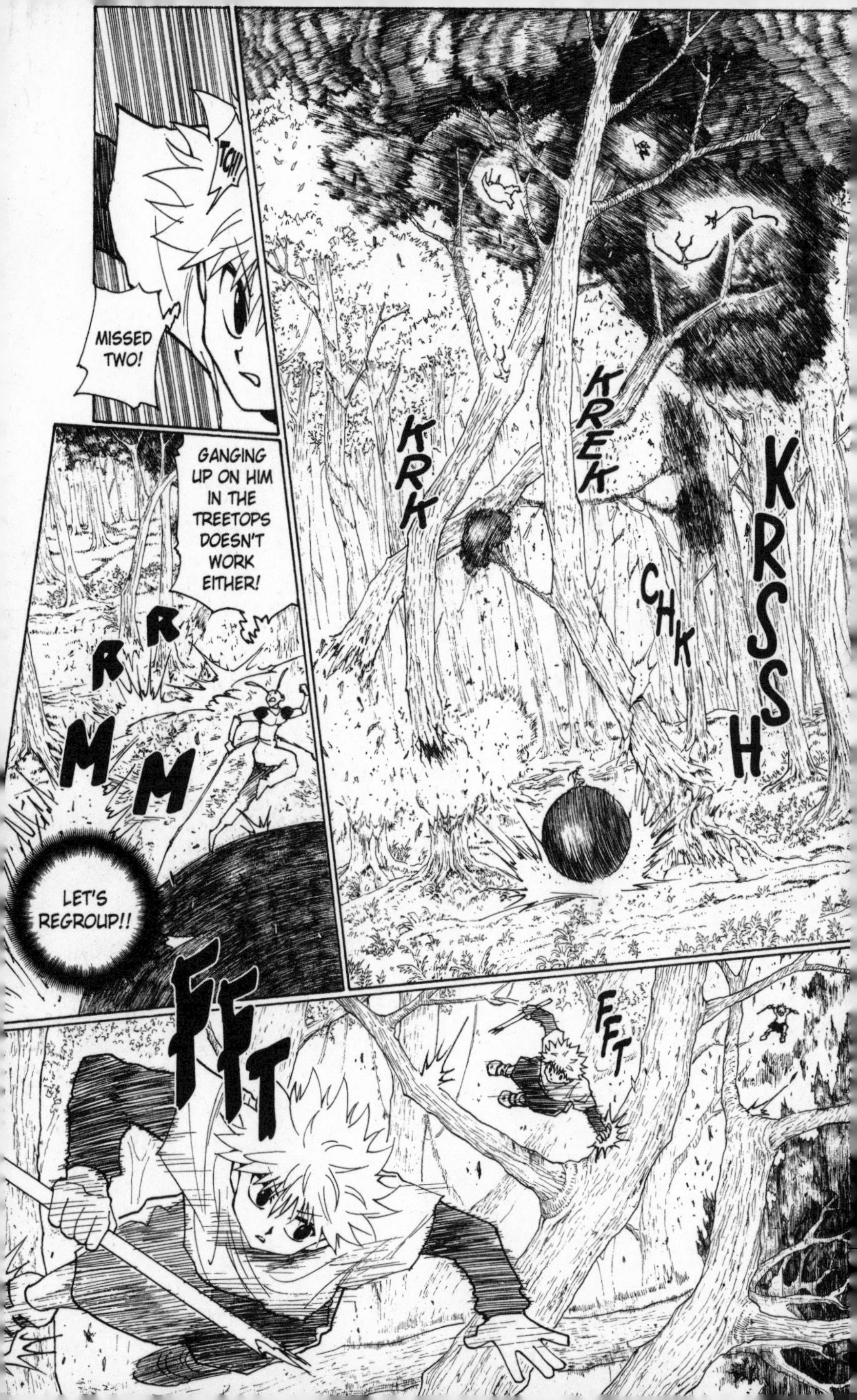
KREK
KRSSH
CHK
KRK
TCH!!
MISSED TWO!
GANGING UP ON HIM IN THE TREETOPS DOESN'T WORK EITHER!
RRMM
LET'S REGROUP!!
FFT
FFT

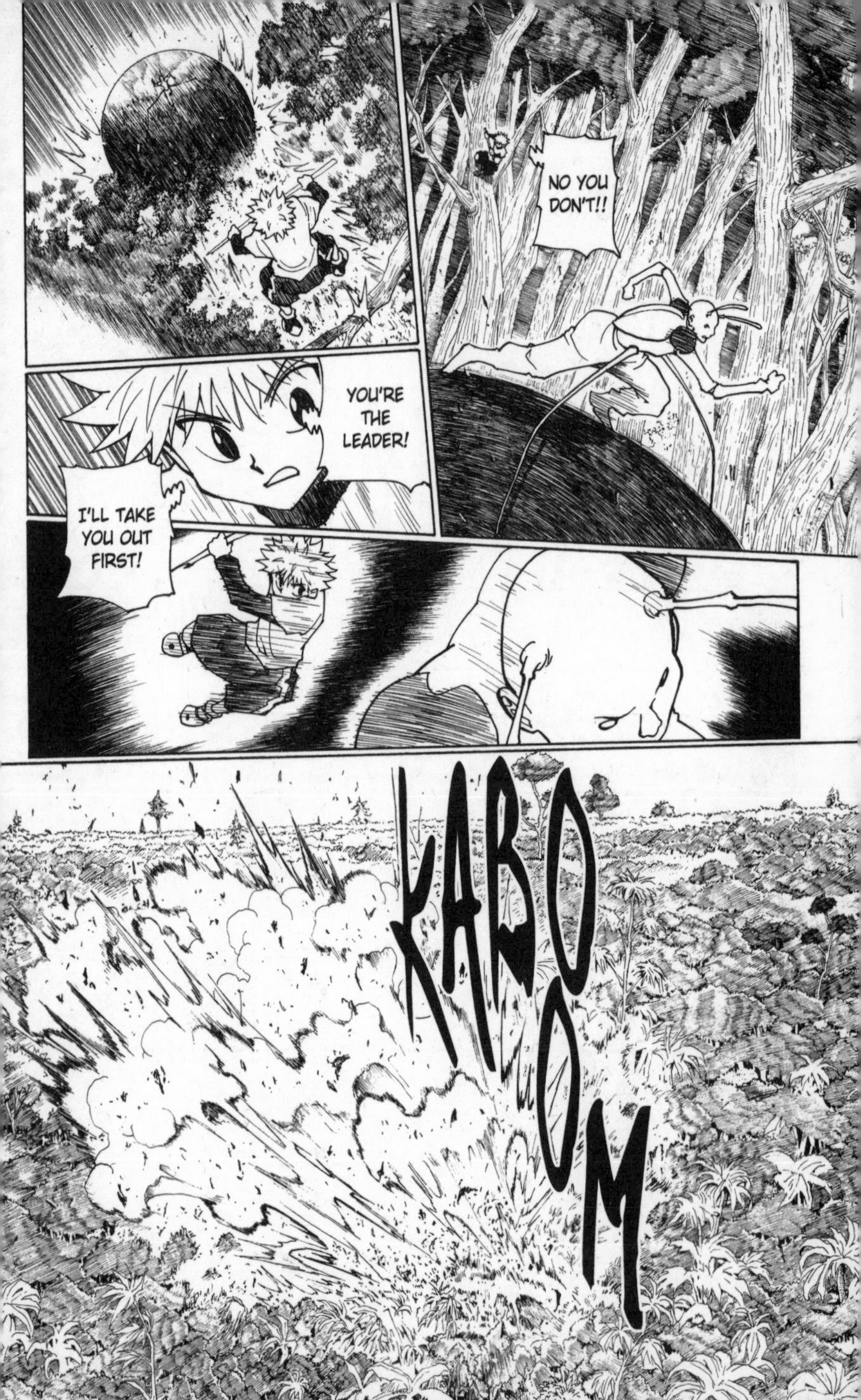
NO YOU DON'T!!
YOU'RE THE LEADER!
I'LL TAKE YOU OUT FIRST!
KABOOM

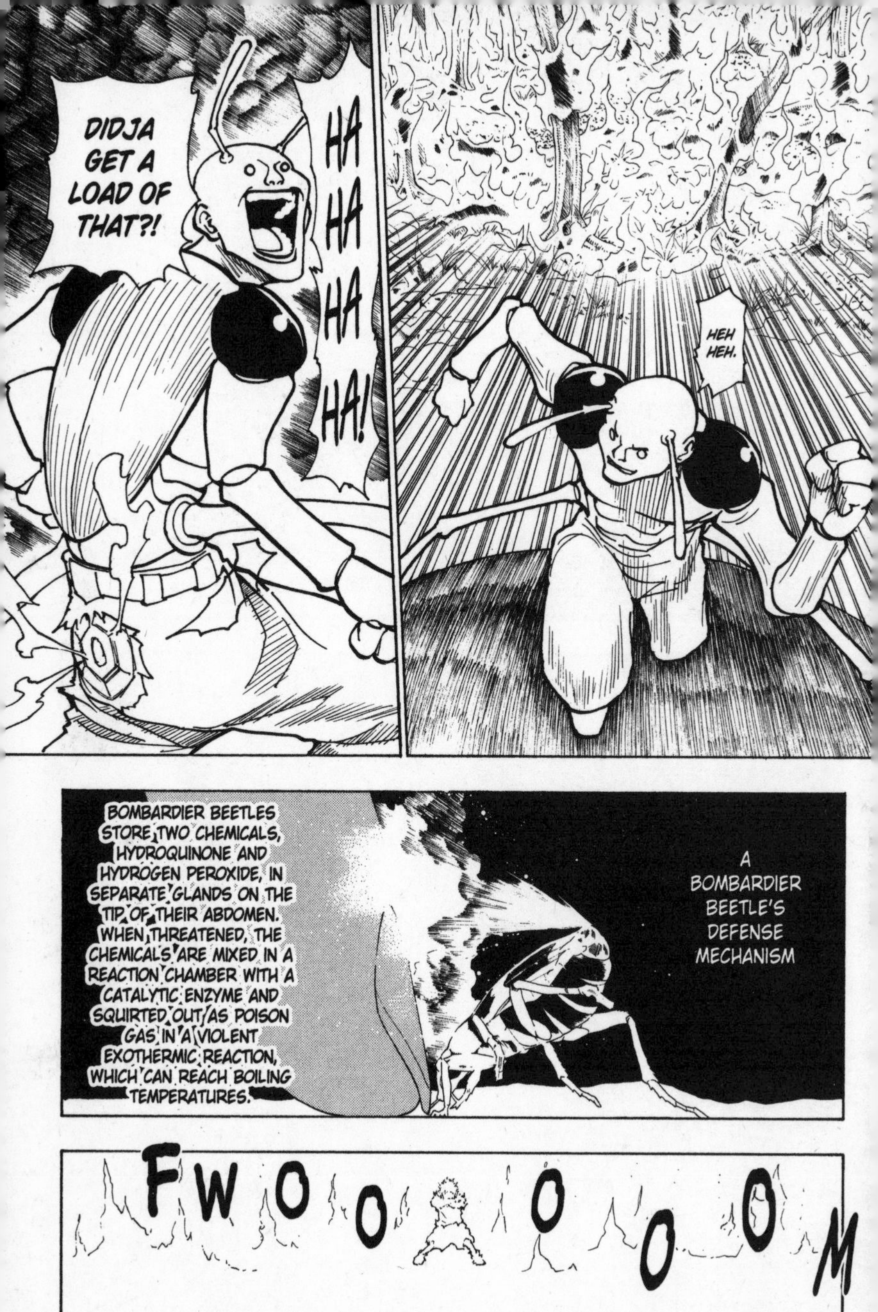
HEH HEH.
DIDJA GET A LOAD OF THAT?!
HA HA HA HA!
A BOMBARDIER BEETLE'S DEFENSE MECHANISM
BOMBARDIER BEETLES STORE TWO CHEMICALS, HYDROQUINONE AND HYDROGEN PEROXIDE, IN SEPARATE GLANDS ON THE TIP OF THEIR ABDOMEN. WHEN THREATENED, THE CHEMICALS ARE MIXED IN A REACTION CHAMBER WITH A CATALYTIC ENZYME AND SQUIRTED OUT AS POISON GAS IN A VIOLENT EXOTHERMIC REACTION, WHICH CAN REACH BOILING TEMPERATURES.
FWOOOOOOM

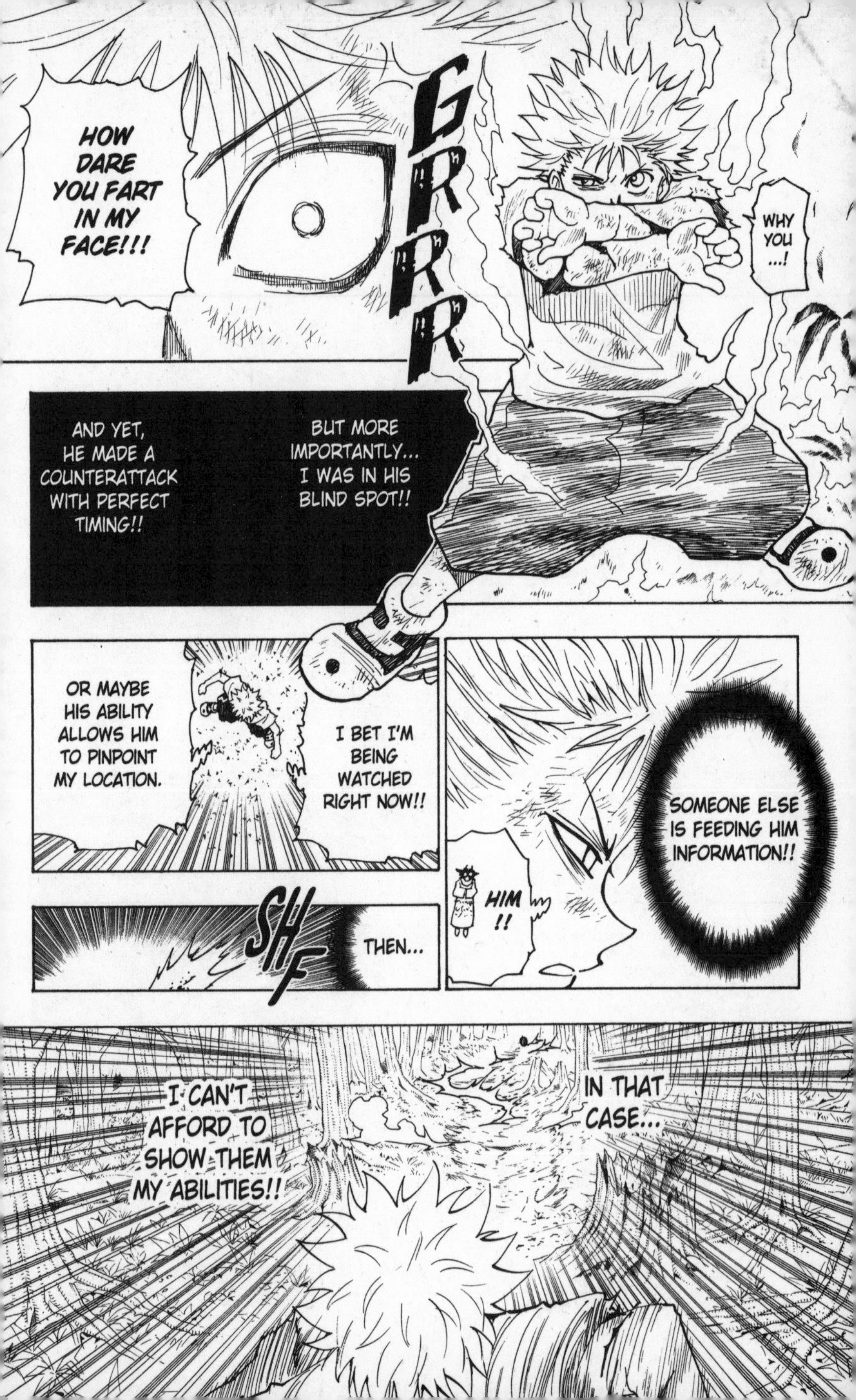
WHY YOU ...!
GRRR
HOW DARE YOU FART IN MY FACE!!!
BUT MORE IMPORTANTLY... I WAS IN HIS BLIND SPOT!!
AND YET, HE MADE A COUNTERATTACK WITH PERFECT TIMING!!
SOMEONE ELSE IS FEEDING HIM INFORMATION!!
HIM !!
I BET I'M BEING WATCHED RIGHT NOW!!
OR MAYBE HIS ABILITY ALLOWS HIM TO PINPOINT MY LOCATION.
THEN...
SHF
IN THAT CASE...
I CAN'T AFFORD TO SHOW THEM MY ABILITIES!!

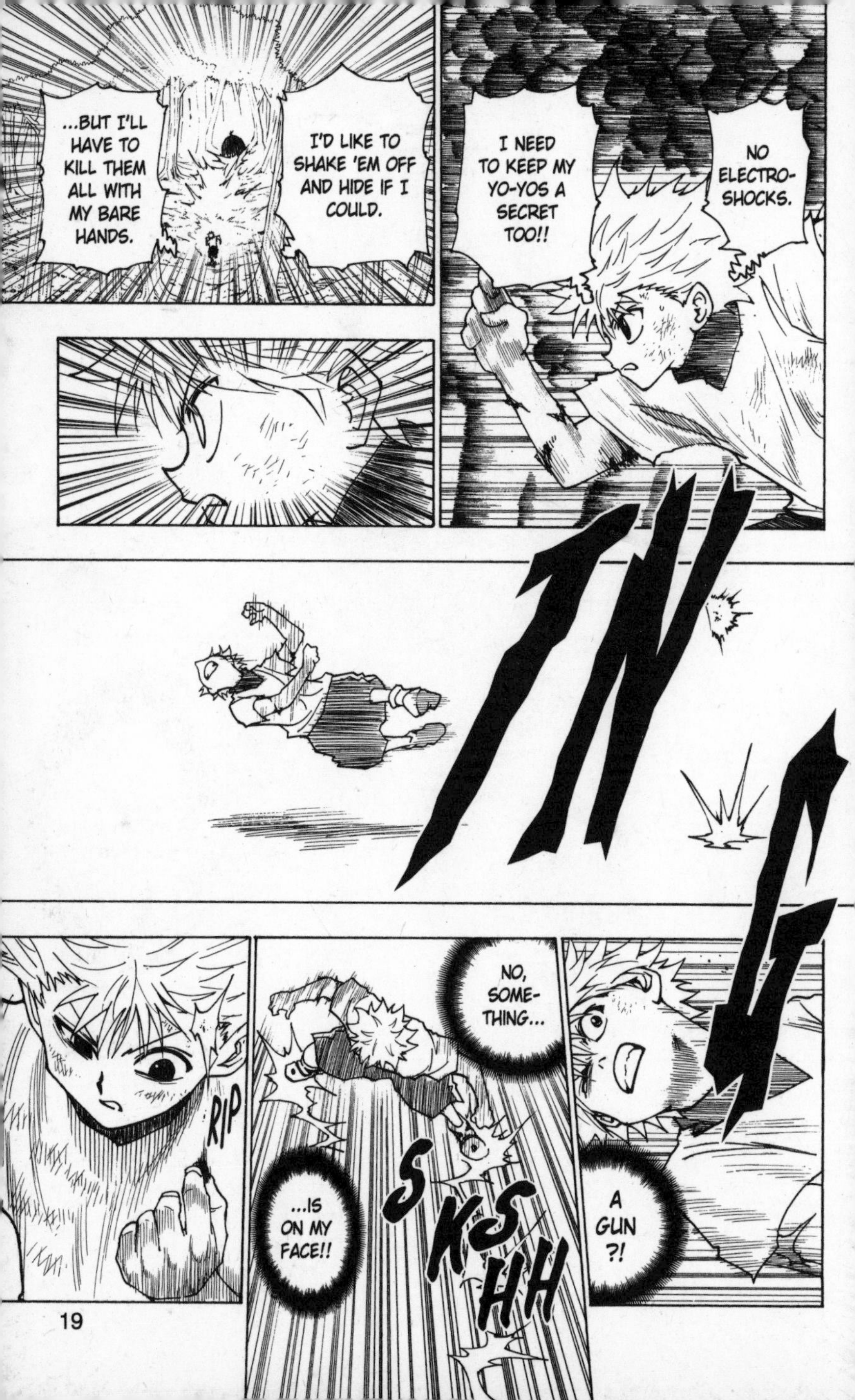
NO ELECTRO-SHOCKS.
I NEED TO KEEP MY YO-YOS A SECRET TOO!!
I'D LIKE TO SHAKE 'EM OFF AND HIDE IF I COULD.
...BUT I'LL HAVE TO KILL THEM ALL WITH MY BARE HANDS.
A GUN ?!
NO, SOMETHING...
SKSHH
...IS ON MY FACE!!
RIP

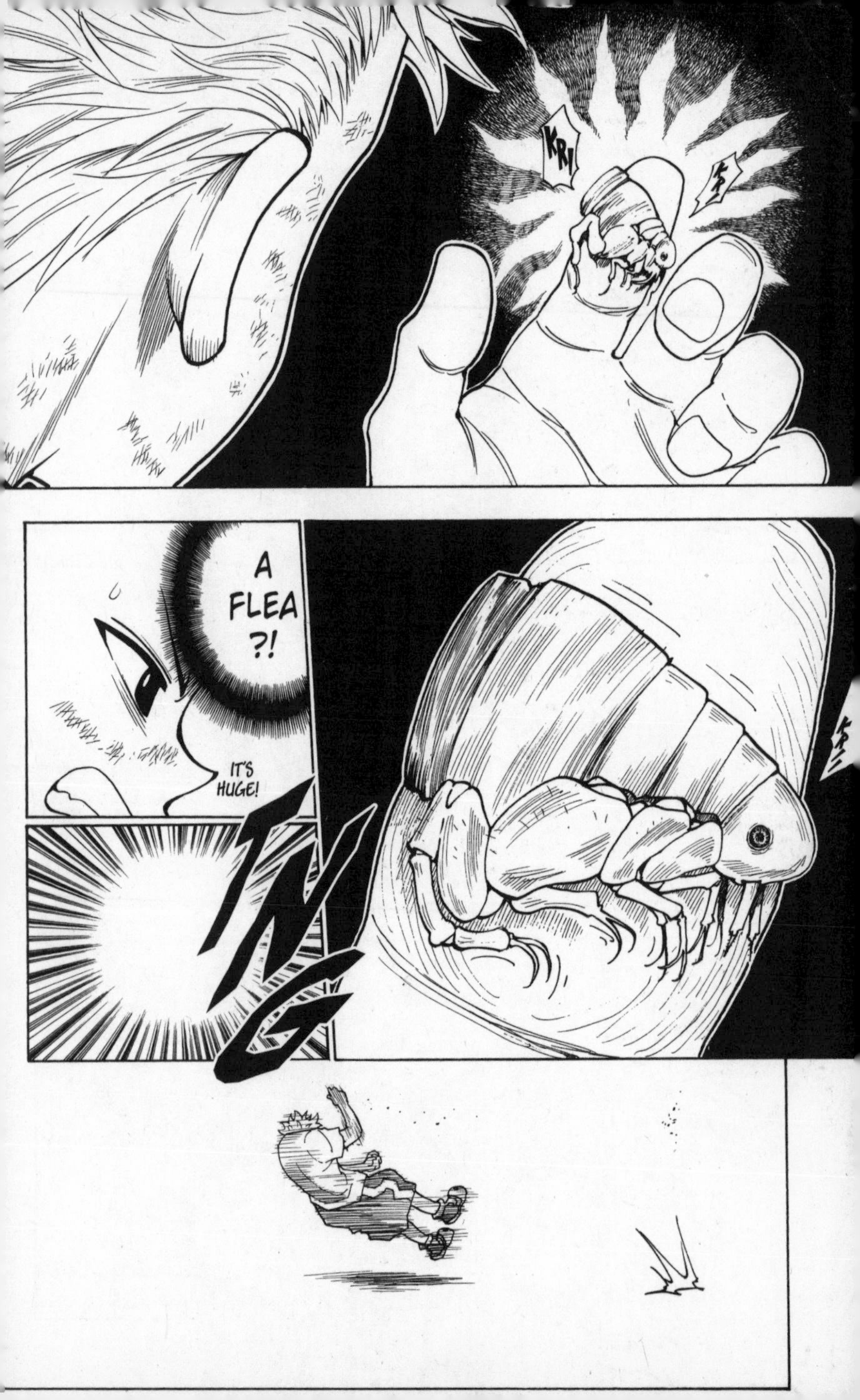
KRI
A FLEA ?!
IT'S HUGE!
TNG

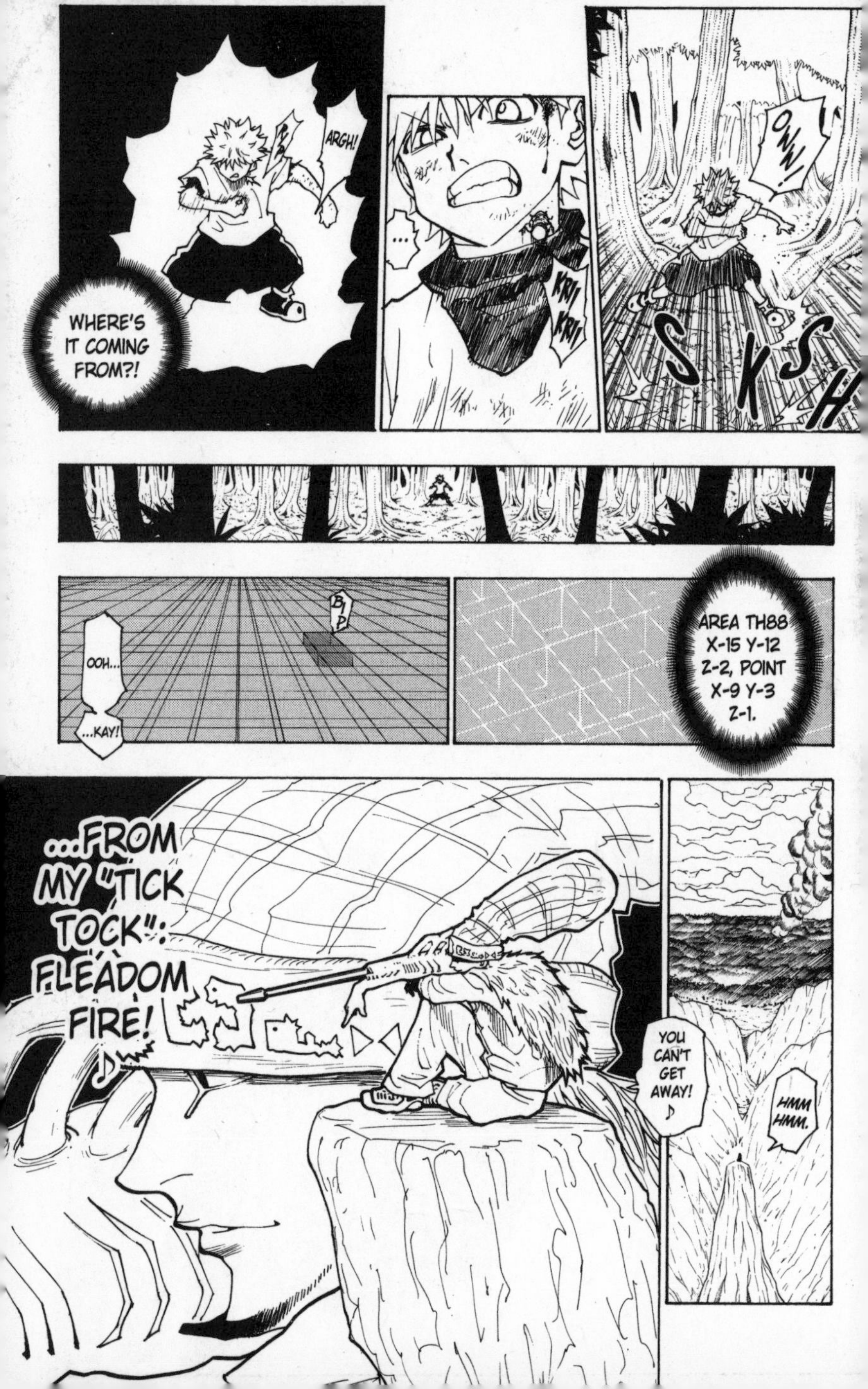
OWW!
SKSH
...
KRI KRI KRI
ARGH!
WHERE'S IT COMING FROM?!
AREA TH88 X-15 Y-12 Z-2, POINT X-9 Y-3 Z-1.
BIP
OOH...
...KAY!
HMM HMM.
YOU CAN'T GET AWAY! ♪
...FROM MY "TICK TOCK": FLEADOM FIRE! ♪

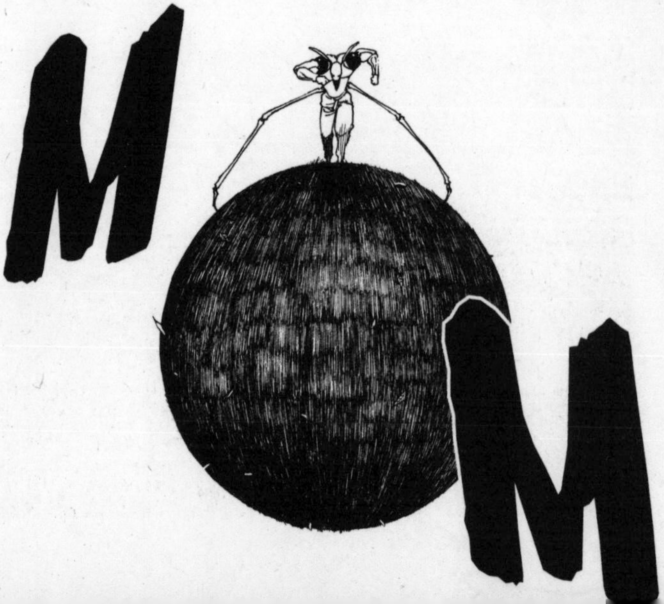
M
M

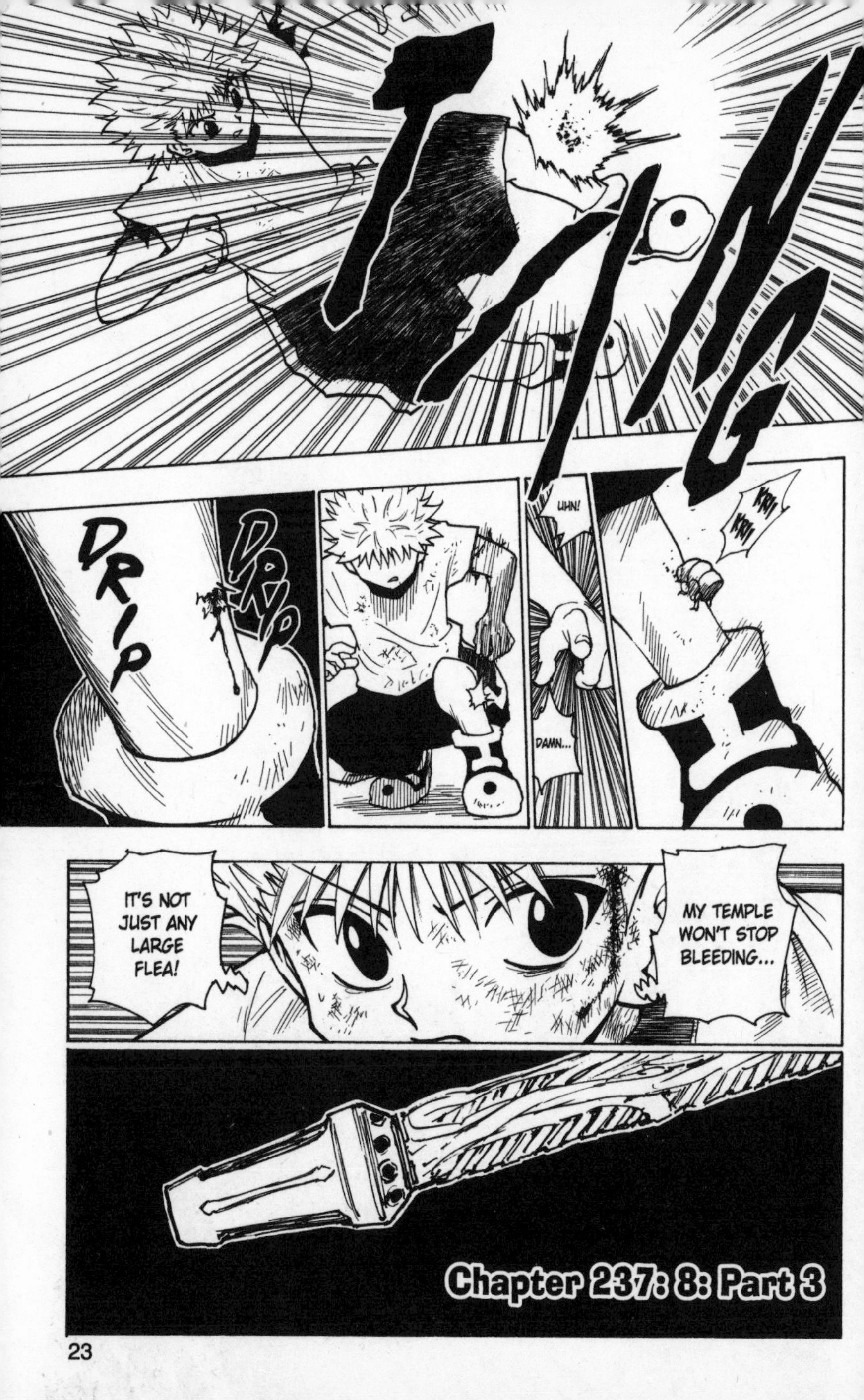
KRI KRI
UHN!
DAMN...
DRIP
DRIP
MY TEMPLE WON'T STOP BLEEDING...
IT'S NOT JUST ANY LARGE FLEA!
Chapter 237: 8: Part 3

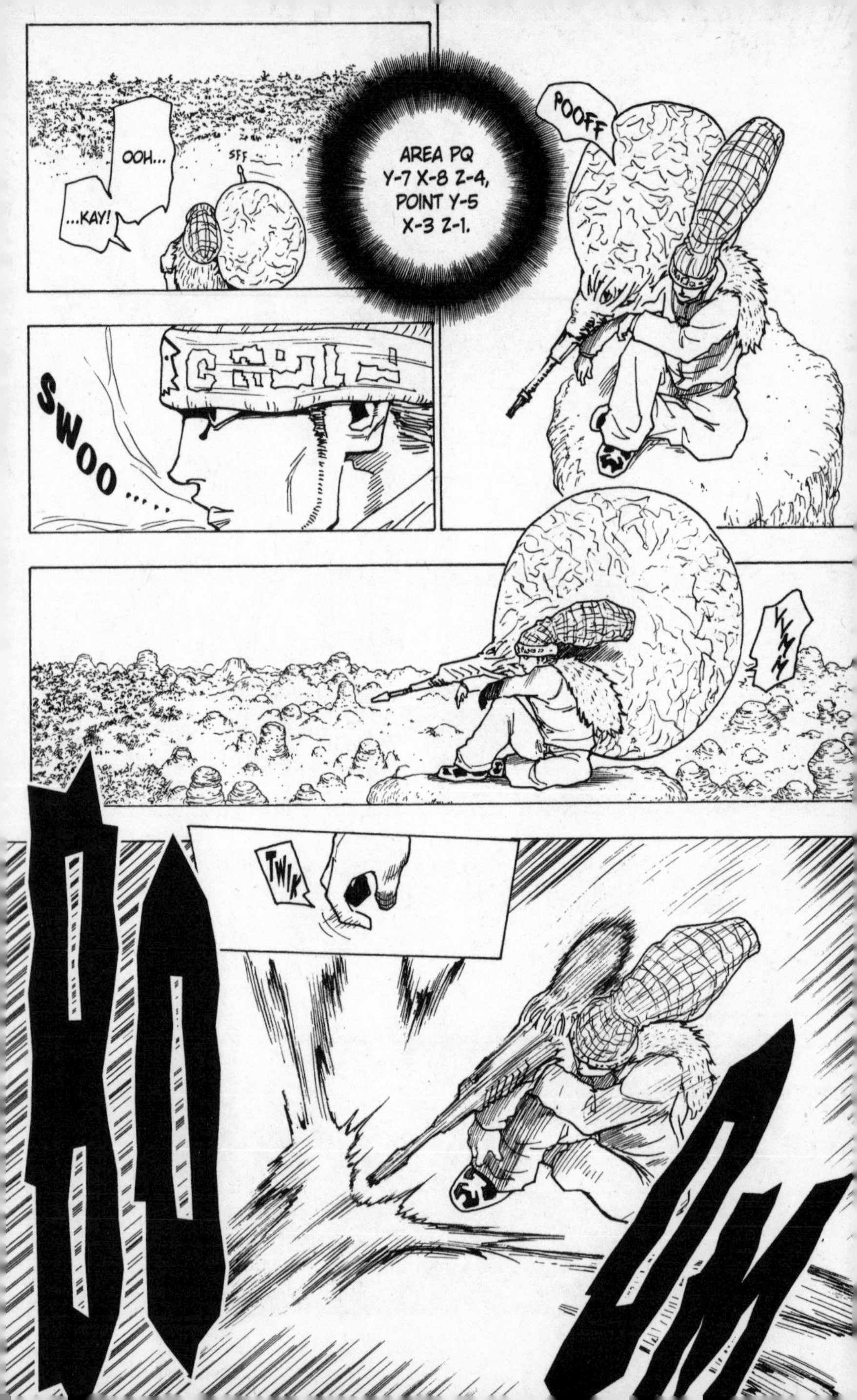
POOFF
AREA PQ Y-7 X-8 Z-4, POINT Y-5 X-3 Z-1.
OOH...
...KAY!
SFF
SWOO.....
TWIK

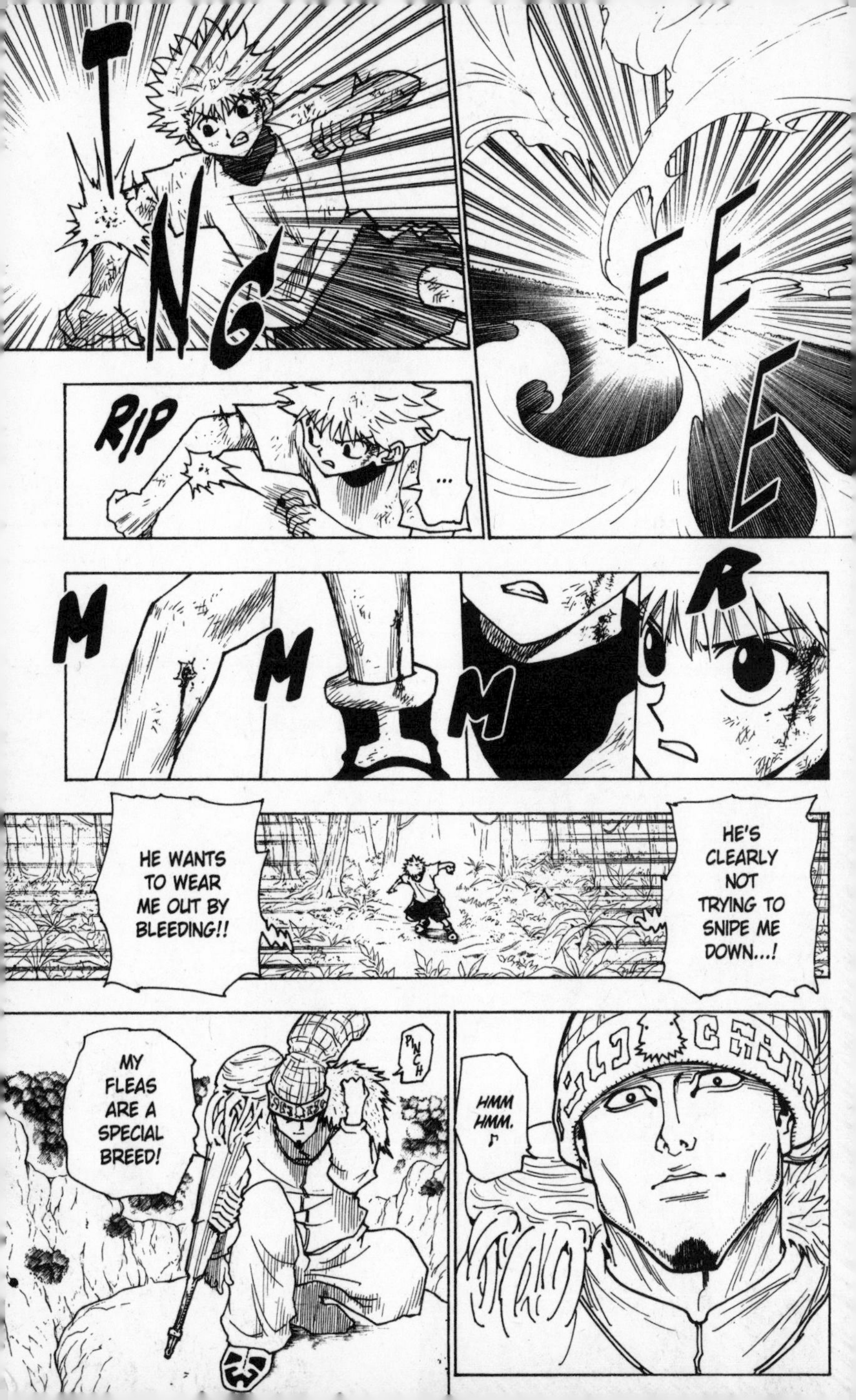
FEEE
TING
RIP
...
MMMR
HE'S CLEARLY NOT TRYING TO SNIPE ME DOWN...!
HE WANTS TO WEAR ME OUT BY BLEEDING!!
HMM HMM. ♪
PINCH
MY FLEAS ARE A SPECIAL BREED!

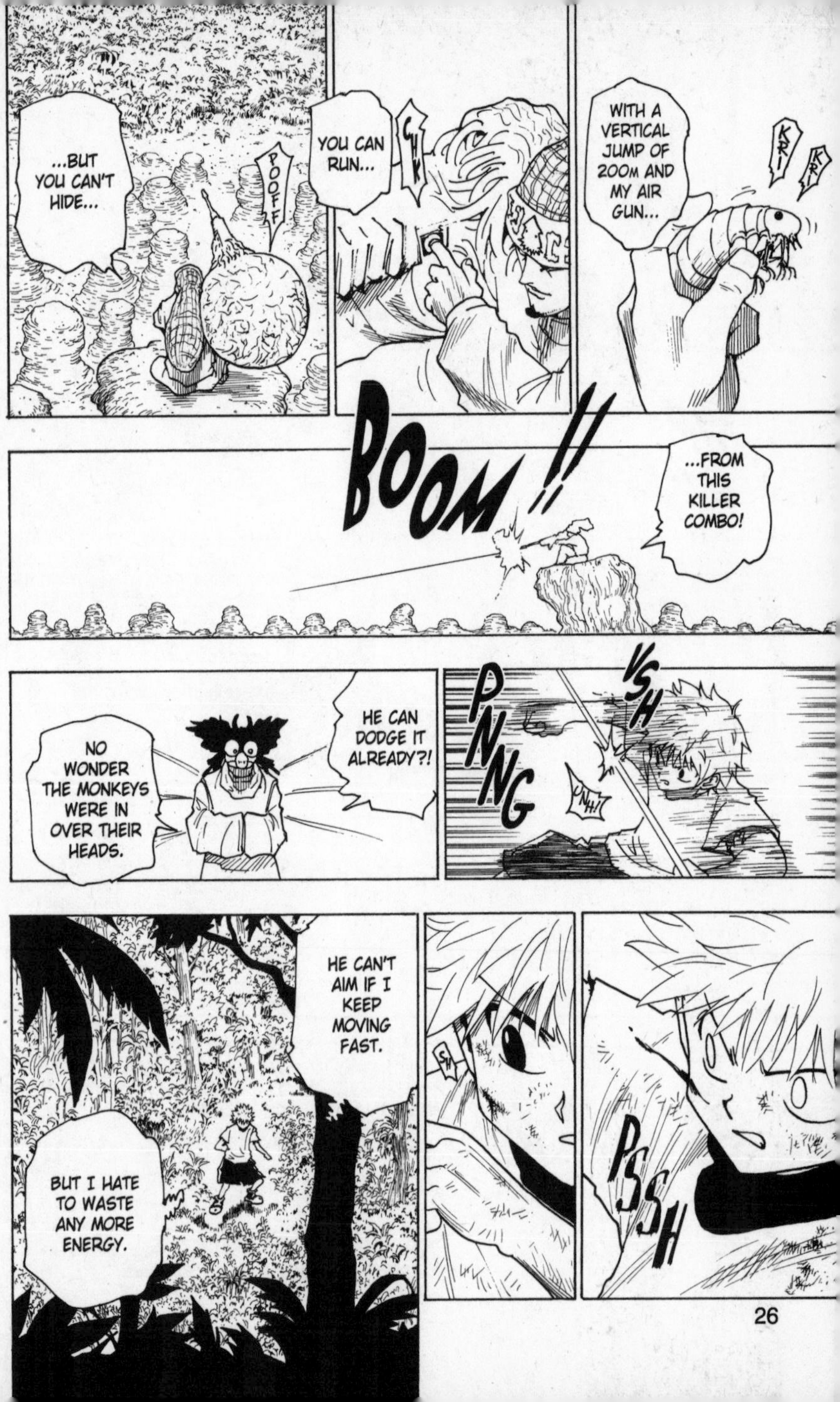
KRI KRI
WITH A VERTICAL JUMP OF 200M AND MY AIR GUN...
CHK
YOU CAN RUN...
POOFF
...BUT YOU CAN'T HIDE...
...FROM THIS KILLER COMBO!
BOOM!!
VSH
UNH!
PNNG
HE CAN DODGE IT ALREADY?!
NO WONDER THE MONKEYS WERE IN OVER THEIR HEADS.
PSSH
SH
HE CAN'T AIM IF I KEEP MOVING FAST.
BUT I HATE TO WASTE ANY MORE ENERGY.

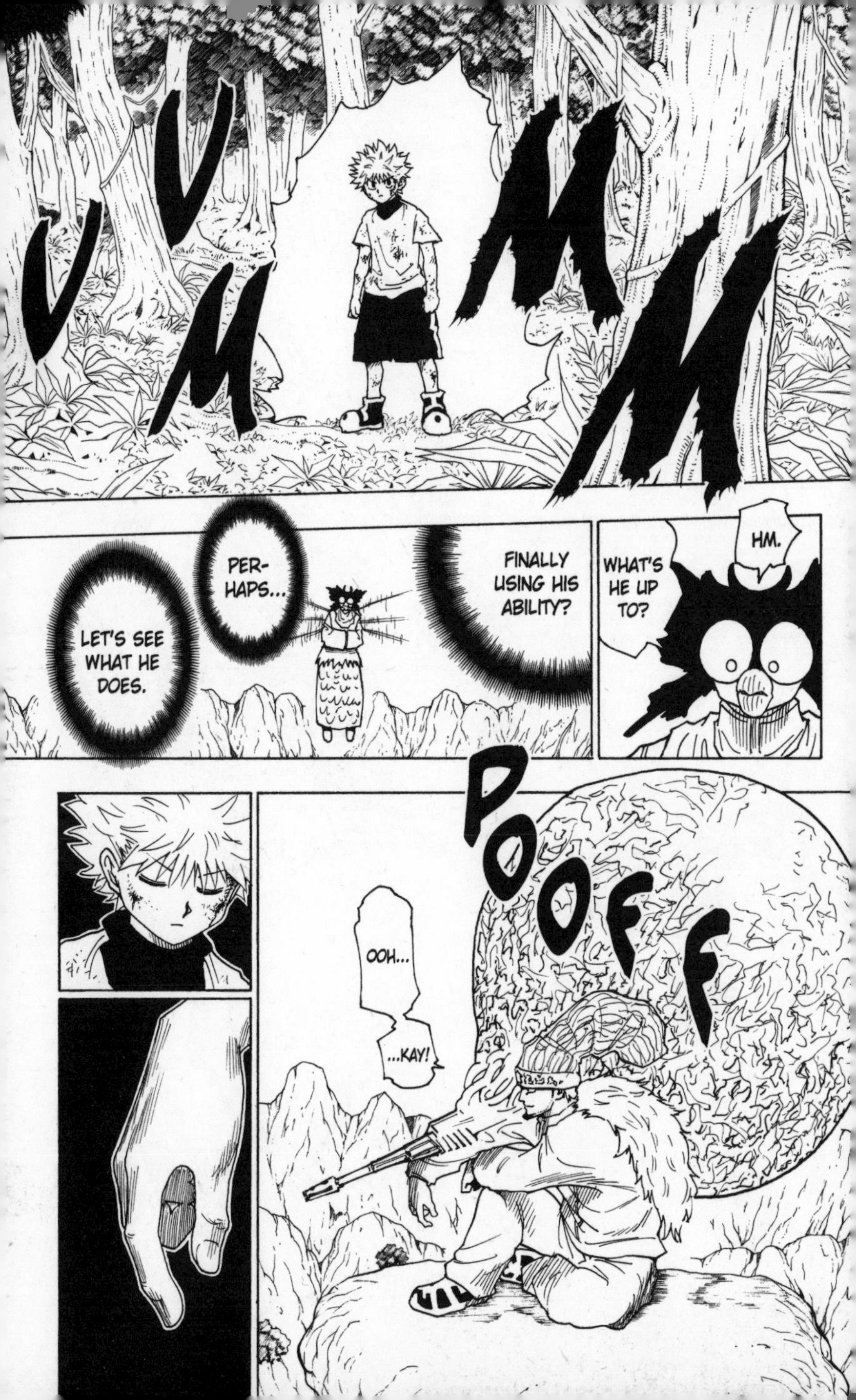
VVMMM
HM.
WHAT'S HE UP TO?
FINALLY USING HIS ABILITY?
PER-HAPS...
LET'S SEE WHAT HE DOES.
POOFF
OOH...
...KAY!

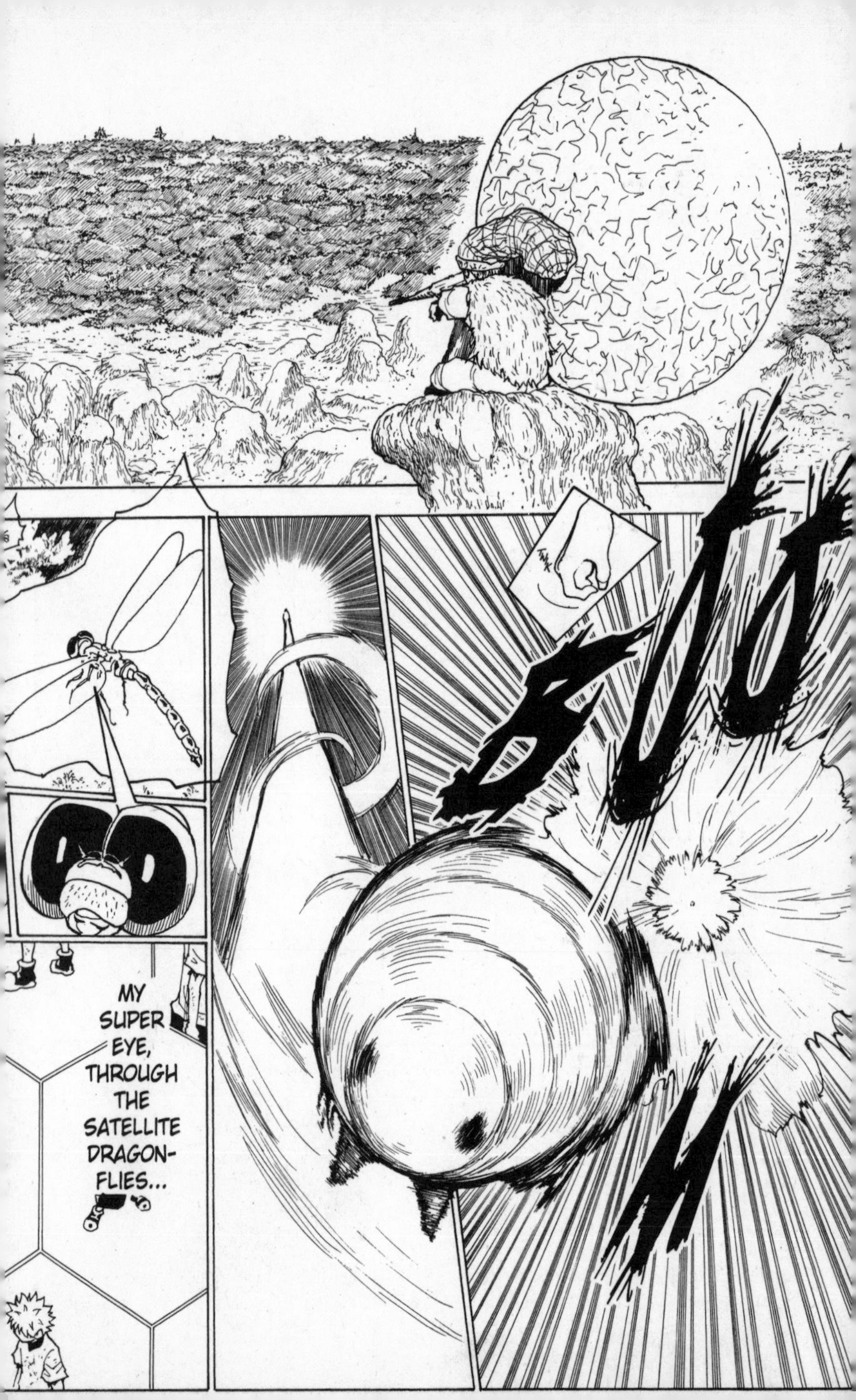
BLOOOM
MY SUPER EYE, THROUGH THE SATELLITE DRAGON-FLIES...

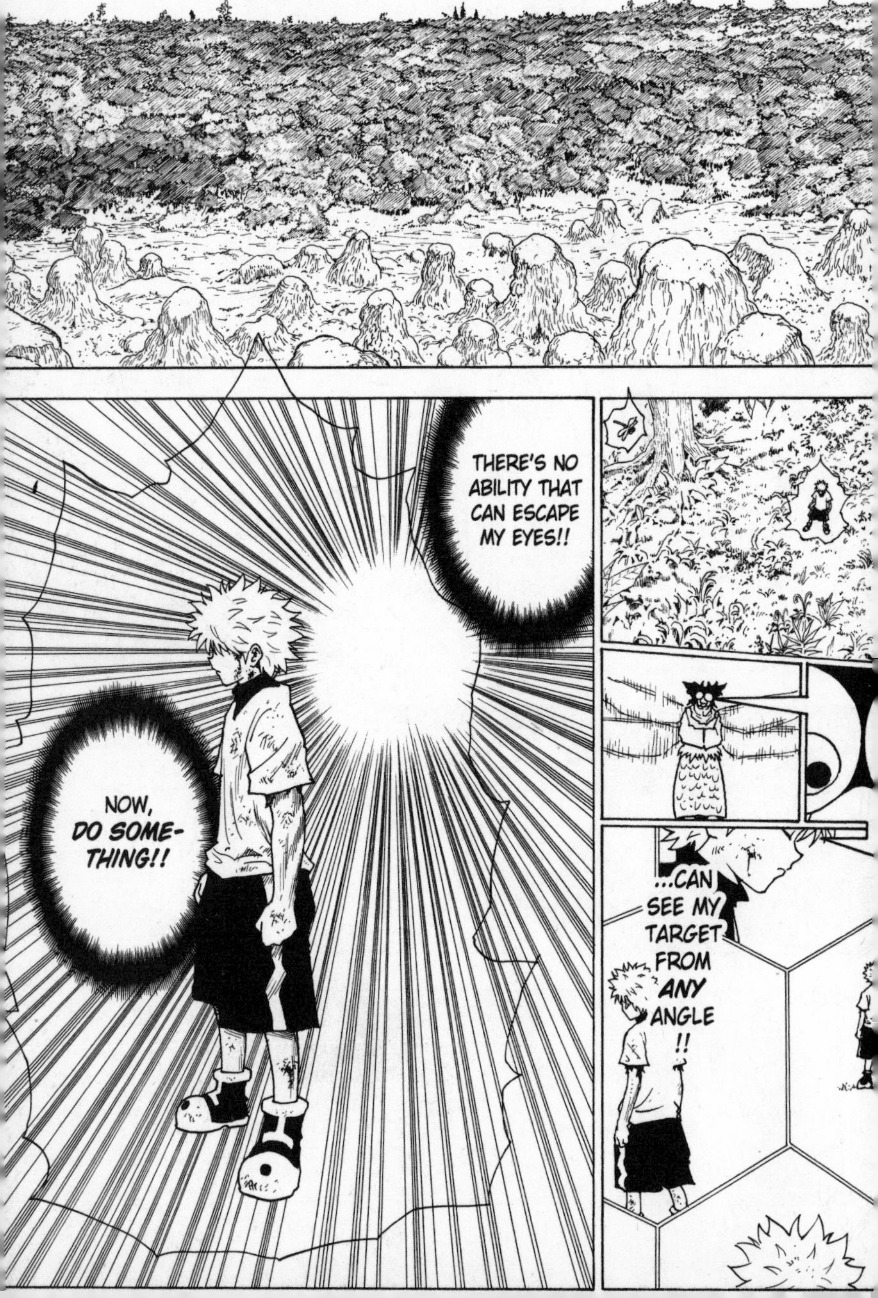
...CAN SEE MY TARGET FROM ANY ANGLE !!
THERE'S NO ABILITY THAT CAN ESCAPE MY EYES!!
NOW, DO SOME-THING!!

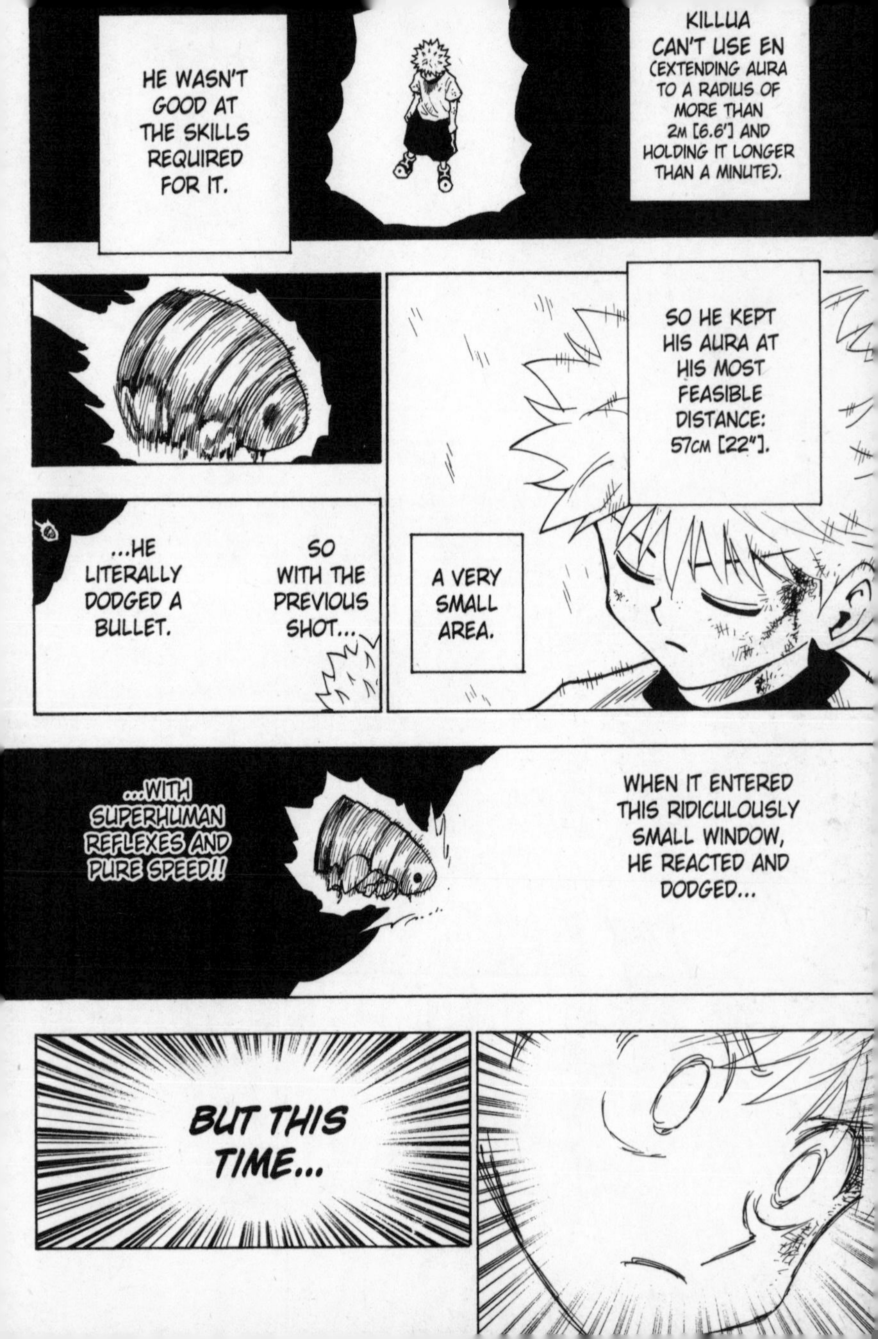
KILLUA CAN'T USE EN (EXTENDING AURA TO A RADIUS OF MORE THAN 2M [6.6'] AND HOLDING IT LONGER THAN A MINUTE).
HE WASN'T GOOD AT THE SKILLS REQUIRED FOR IT.
SO HE KEPT HIS AURA AT HIS MOST FEASIBLE DISTANCE: 57CM [22"].
A VERY SMALL AREA.
SO WITH THE PREVIOUS SHOT...
...HE LITERALLY DODGED A BULLET.
WHEN IT ENTERED THIS RIDICULOUSLY SMALL WINDOW, HE REACTED AND DODGED...
...WITH SUPERHUMAN REFLEXES AND PURE SPEED!!
BUT THIS TIME...

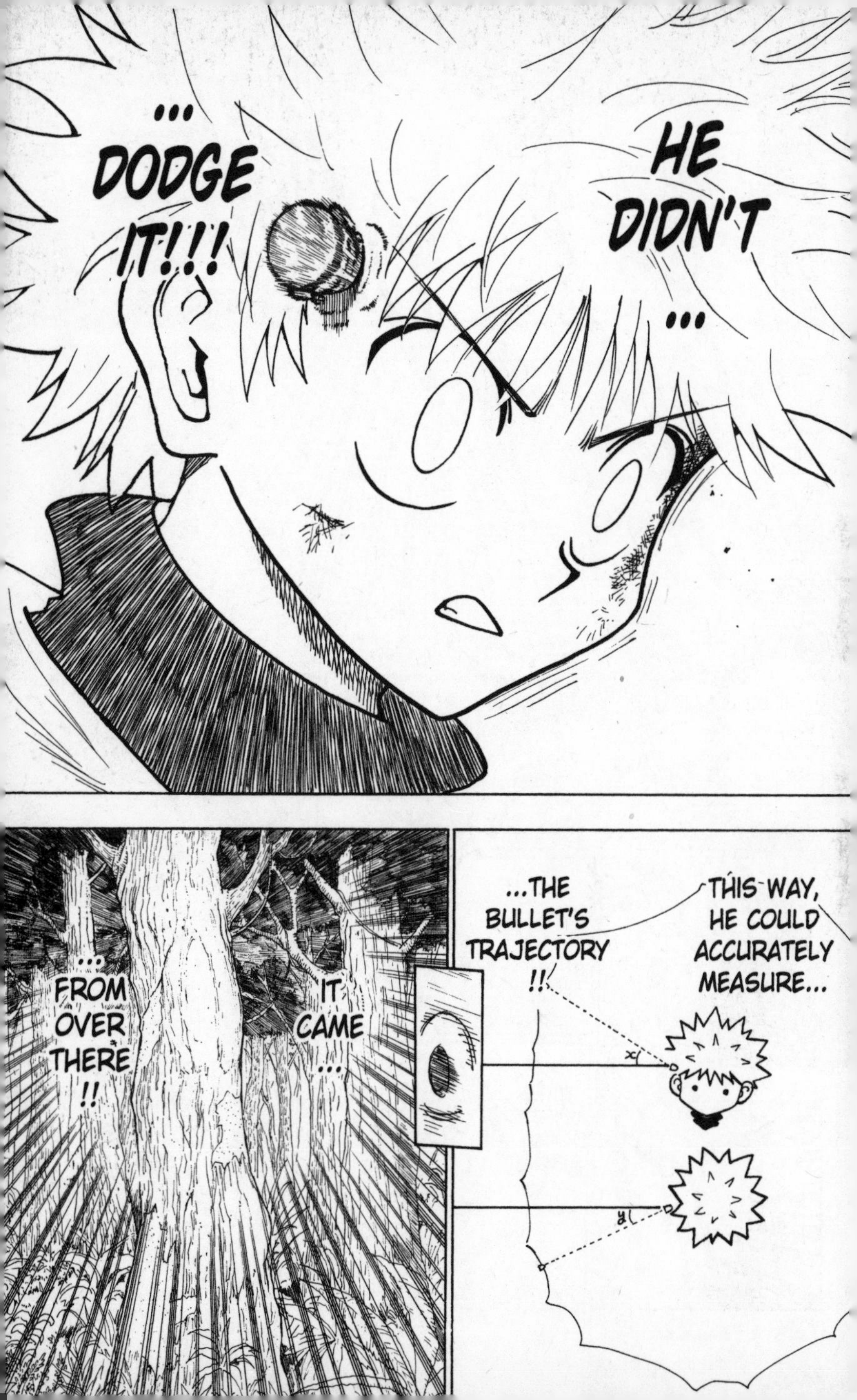
HE DIDN'T ...
... DODGE IT!!!
THIS WAY, HE COULD ACCURATELY MEASURE...
...THE BULLET'S TRAJECTORY!!
IT CAME ...
... FROM OVER THERE!!

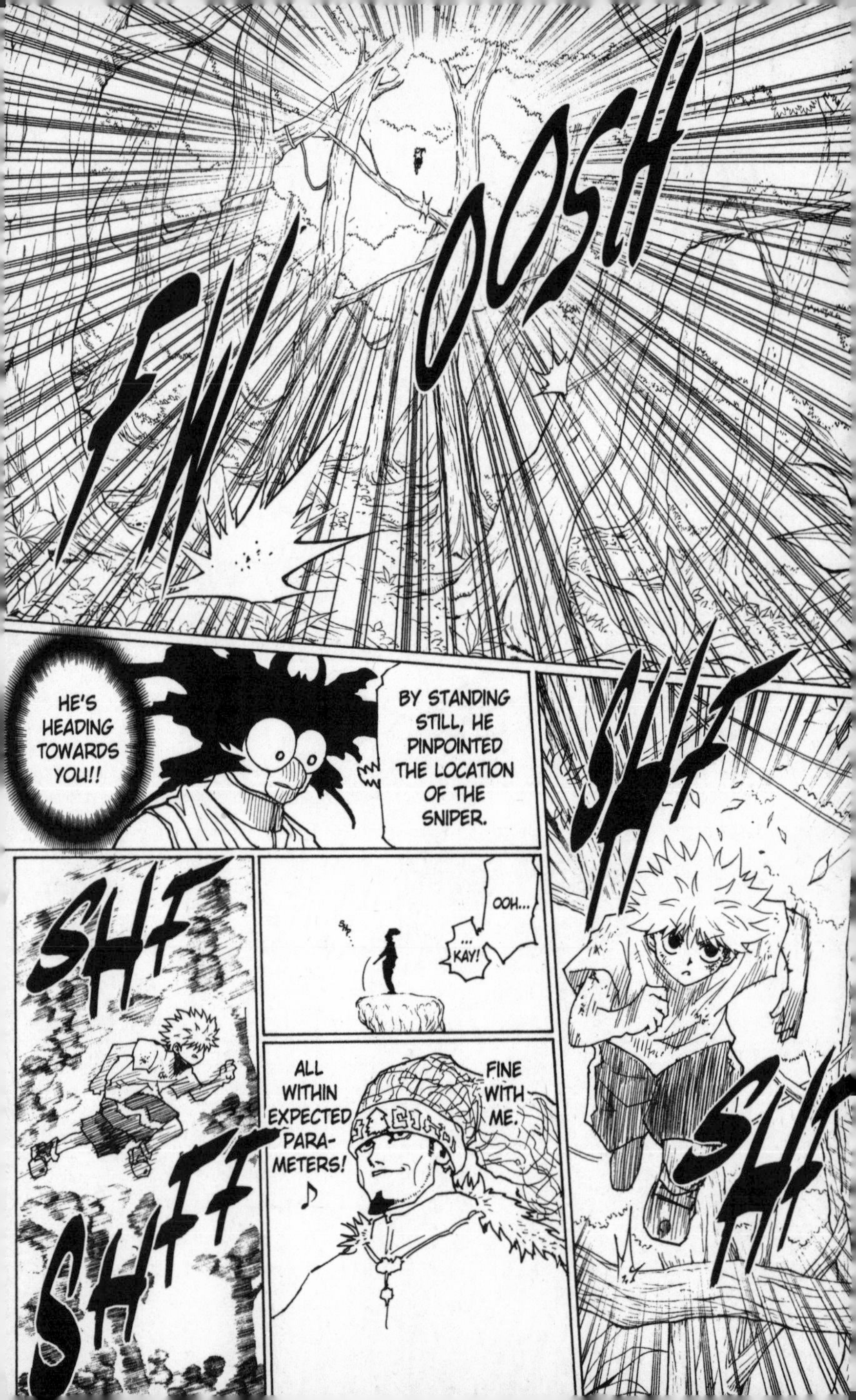
FWOOSH
SHF
SHF
BY STANDING STILL, HE PINPOINTED THE LOCATION OF THE SNIPER.
HE'S HEADING TOWARDS YOU!!
OOH...
...KAY!
FINE WITH ME.
ALL WITHIN EXPECTED PARA-METERS! ♪
SHF
SHFF

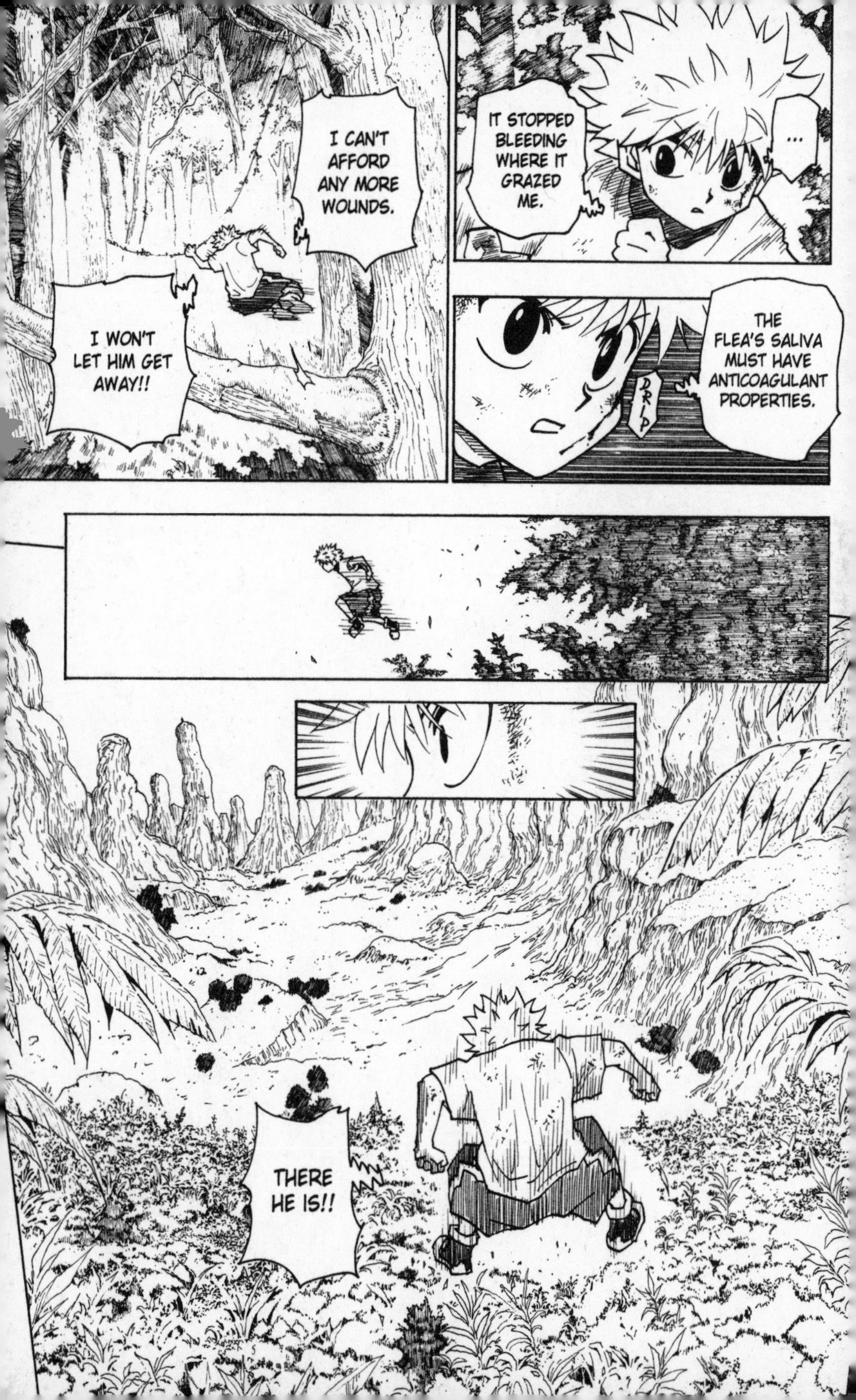
IT STOPPED BLEEDING WHERE IT GRAZED ME.
...
THE FLEA'S SALIVA MUST HAVE ANTICOAGULANT PROPERTIES.
DRIP
I CAN'T AFFORD ANY MORE WOUNDS.
I WON'T LET HIM GET AWAY!!
THERE HE IS!!

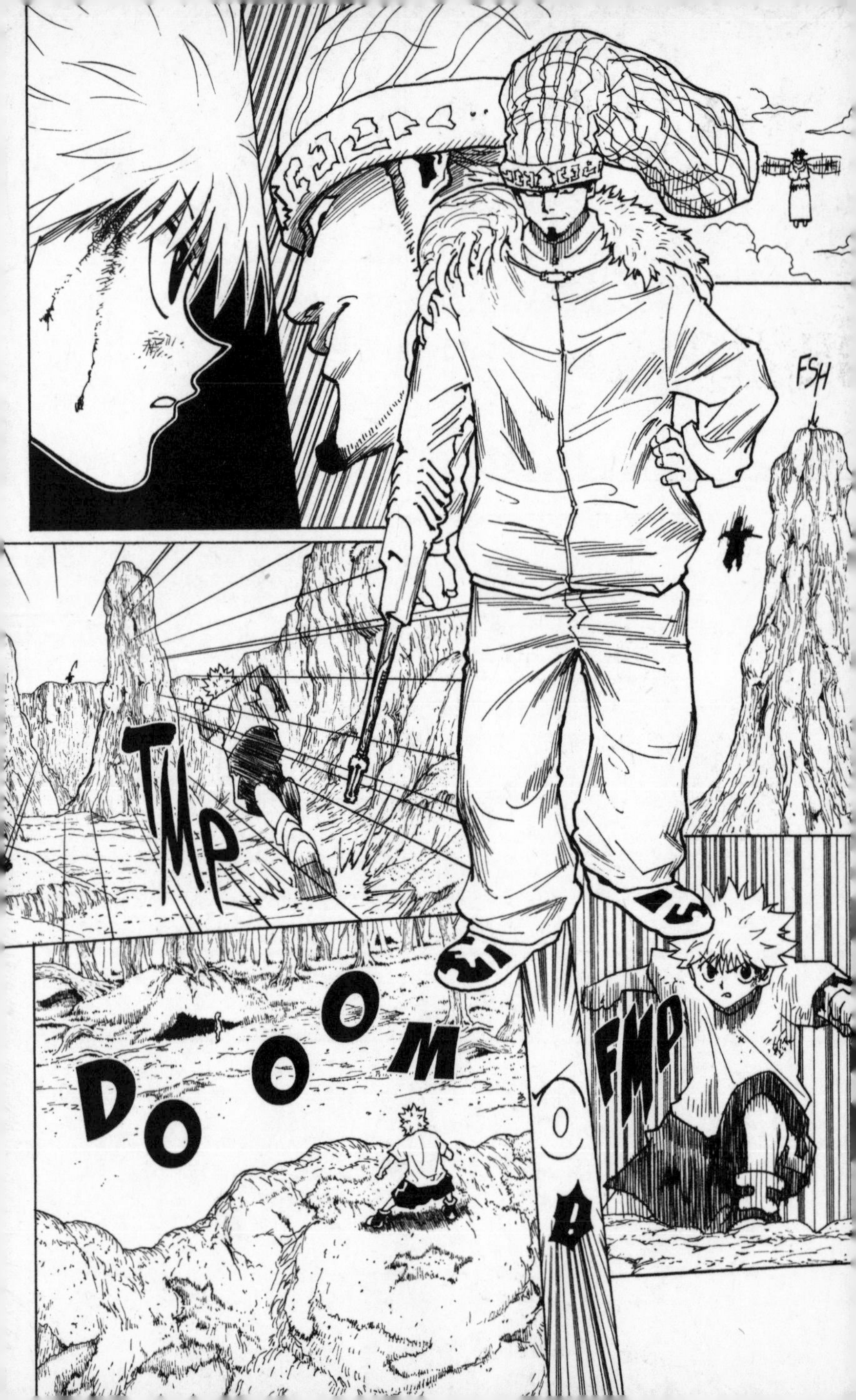
FSH
TMP
FMP
!
DOOOOM

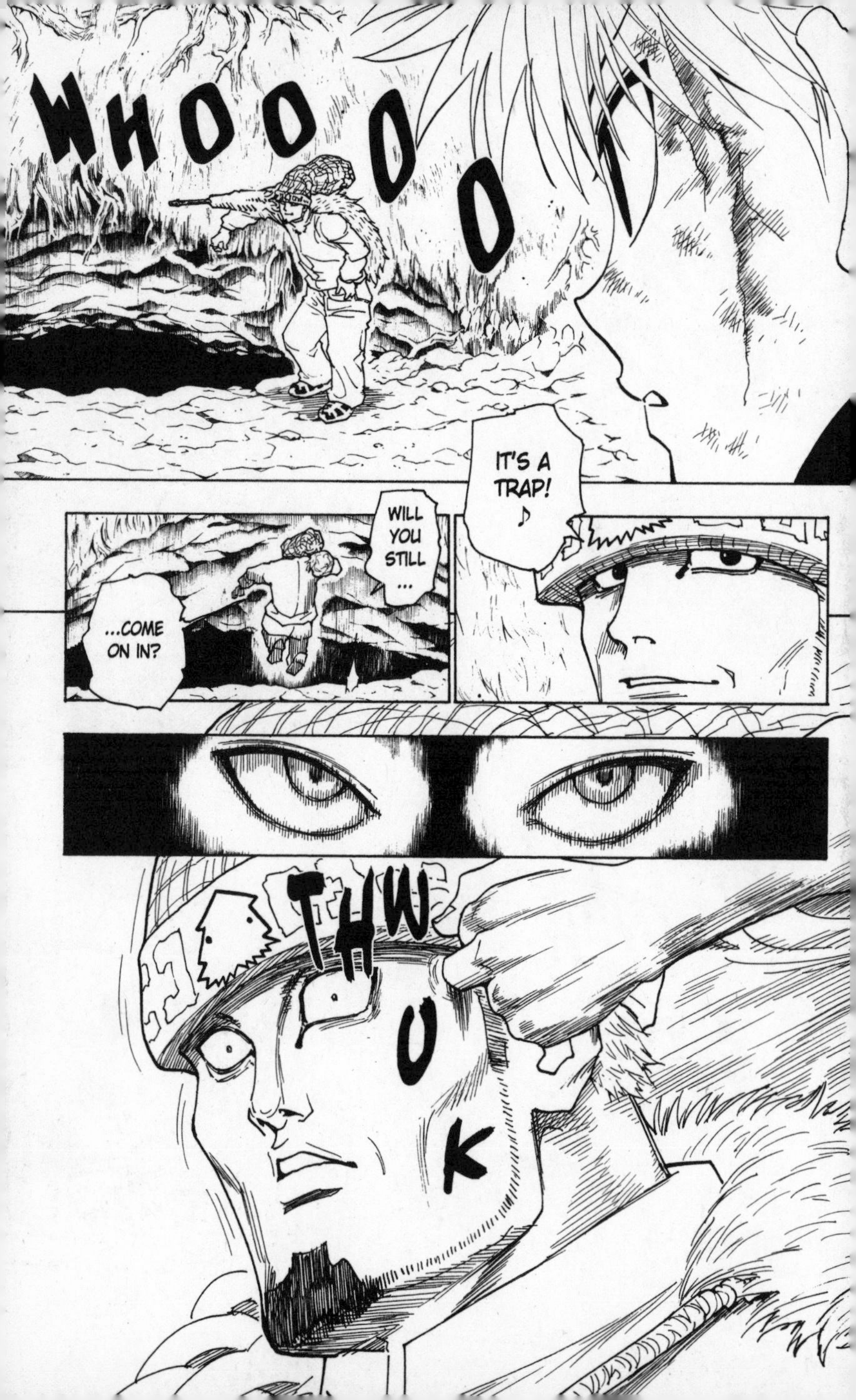
WHOOOOT
IT'S A TRAP! ♪
WILL YOU STILL ...
...COME ON IN?
THWUK

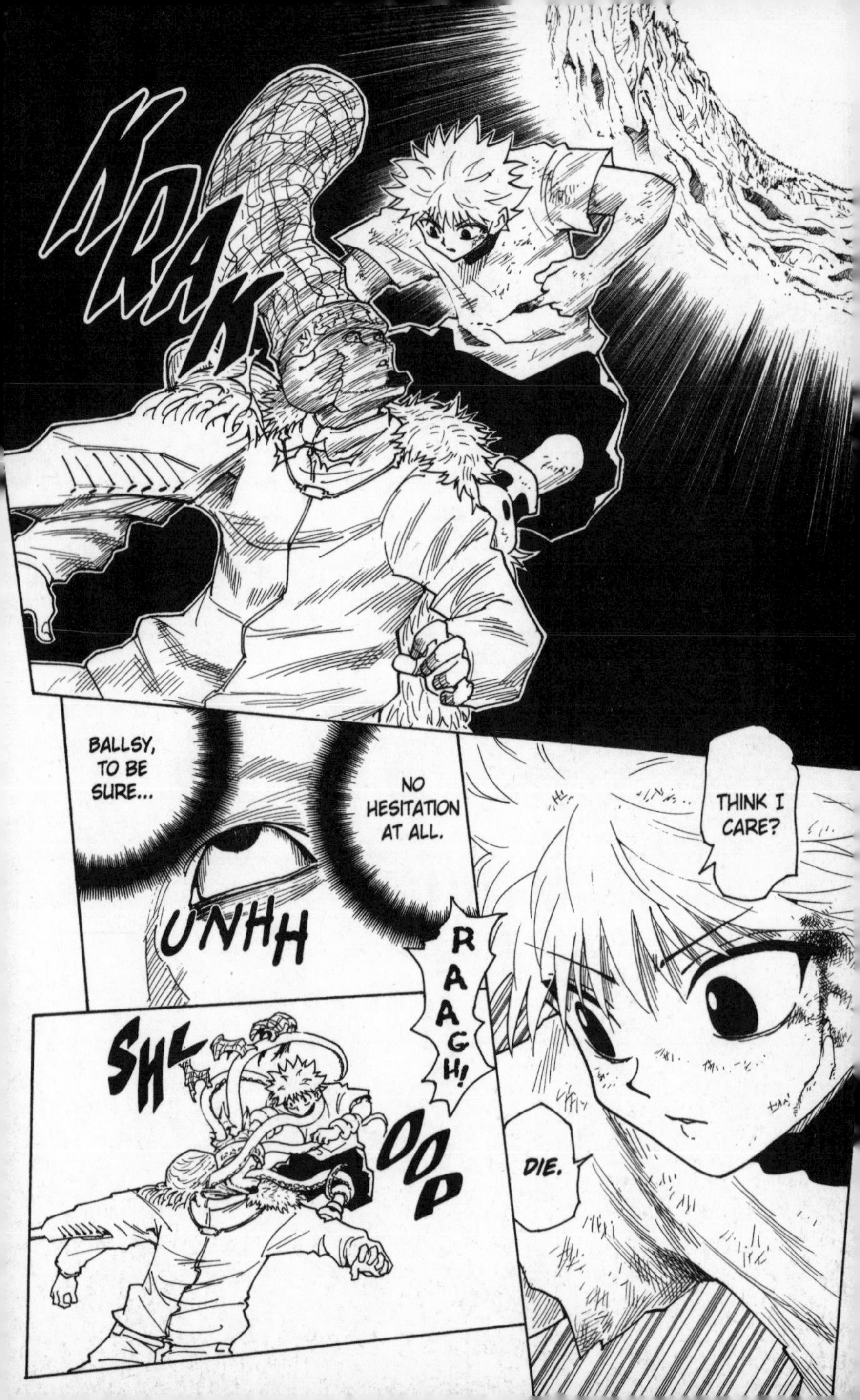
KRAK
THINK I CARE?
DIE.
BALLSY, TO BE SURE...
NO HESITATION AT ALL.
UNHH
RAAGH!
SHLOOP

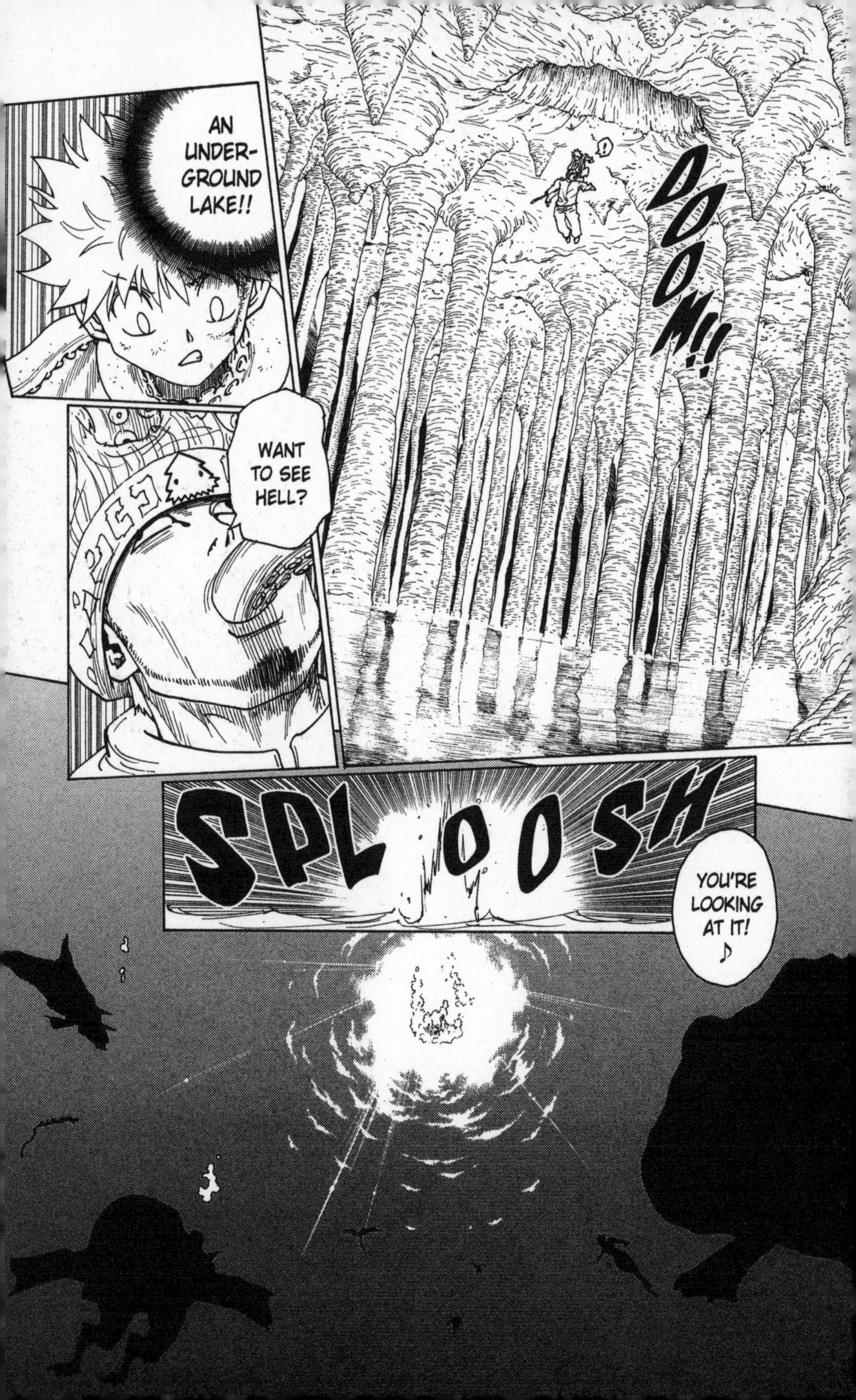
DOOOM!!
AN UNDER-GROUND LAKE!!
WANT TO SEE HELL?
SPLOOSH
YOU'RE LOOKING AT IT! ♪

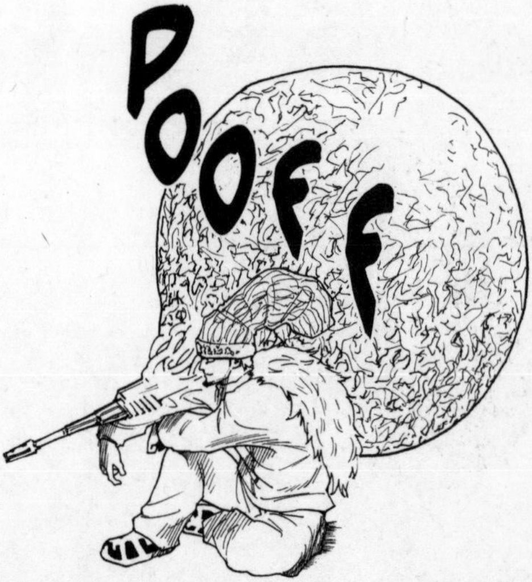
POOFF

Chapter 238: 8: Part 4

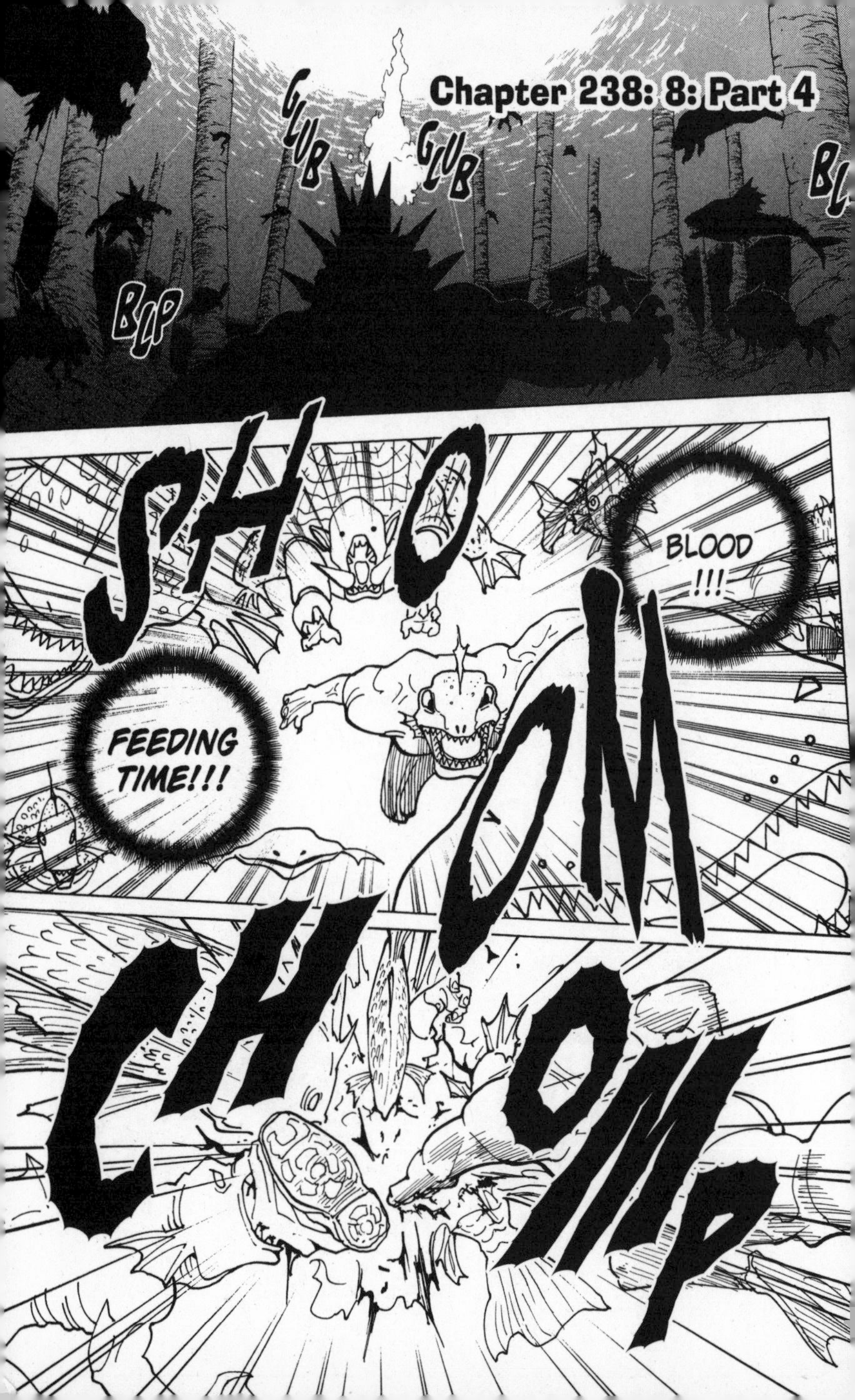
BL
GLUB GLUB
BLP
BLOOD!!!
FEEDING TIME!!!
SHOOM
CHOMP

FSSHH
HM?
WAIT...
THIS IS CAPT. IKALGO'S HOST!!
STOP EATING HIM!!
ARGH, I WANT TO STOP, BUT...
RRIP
RRIP
THE BLOOD IS CALLING US!!
RROMMM

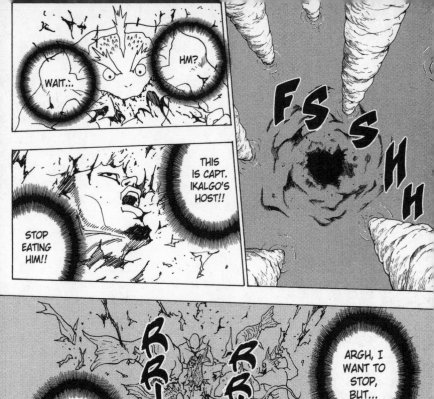

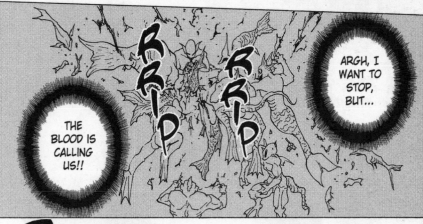

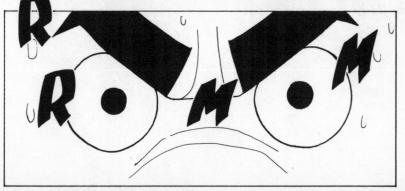

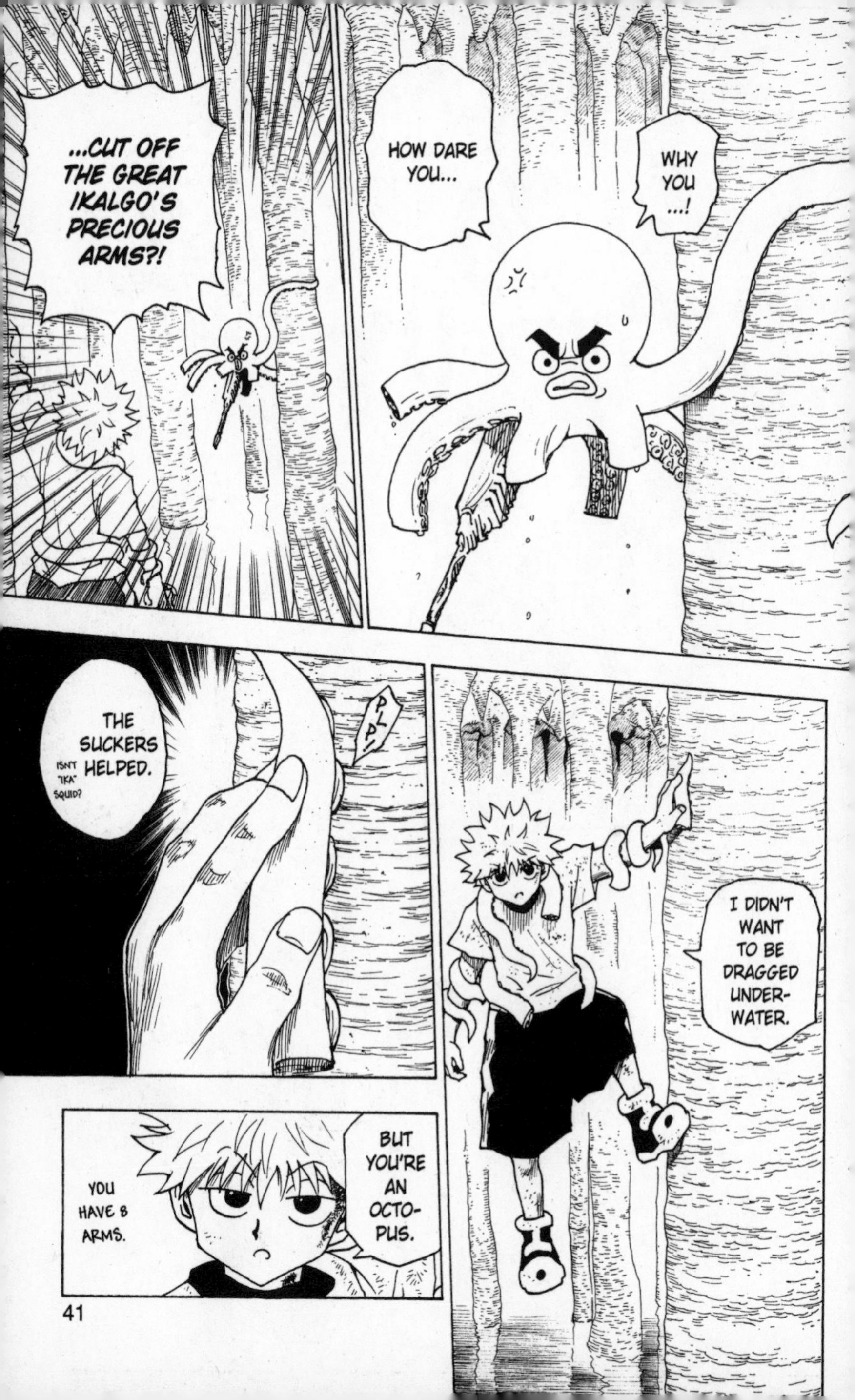
WHY YOU ...!
HOW DARE YOU...
...CUT OFF THE GREAT IKALGO'S PRECIOUS ARMS?!
I DIDN'T WANT TO BE DRAGGED UNDER-WATER.
PLP!
THE SUCKERS HELPED.
ISN'T "IKA" SQUID?
BUT YOU'RE AN OCTO-PUS.
YOU HAVE 8 ARMS.

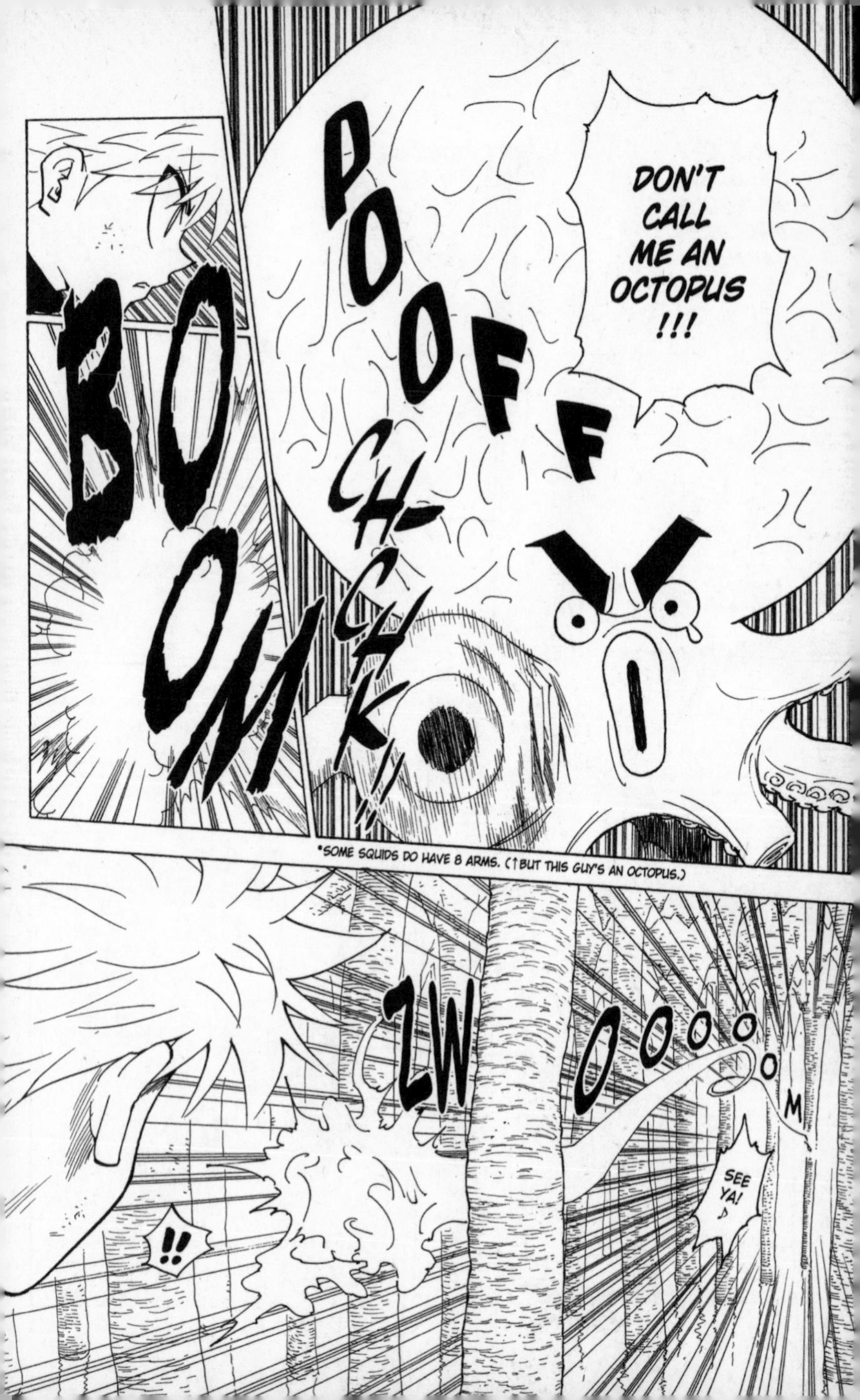
DON'T CALL ME AN OCTOPUS !!!
POOFF
CH-CHCHK!!
BOOM
*SOME SQUIDS DO HAVE 8 ARMS. (↑BUT THIS GUY'S AN OCTOPUS.)
ZWOOOOOOM
SEE YA! ♪
!!

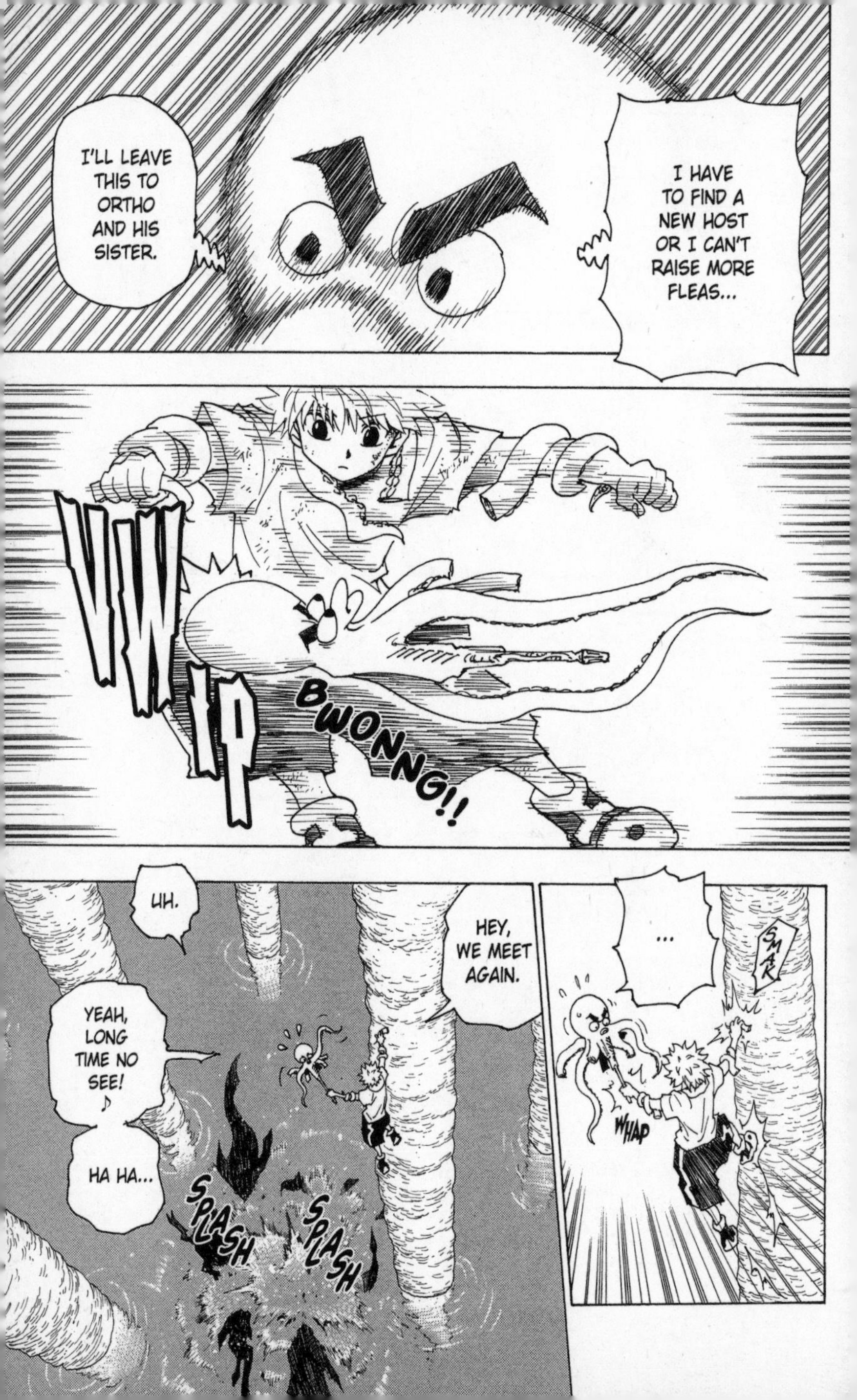
I HAVE TO FIND A NEW HOST OR I CAN'T RAISE MORE FLEAS...
I'LL LEAVE THIS TO ORTHO AND HIS SISTER.
VWIP
BWONNG!!
...
SMAK
WHAP
HEY, WE MEET AGAIN.
UH.
YEAH, LONG TIME NO SEE! ♪
HA HA...
SPLASH
SPLASH

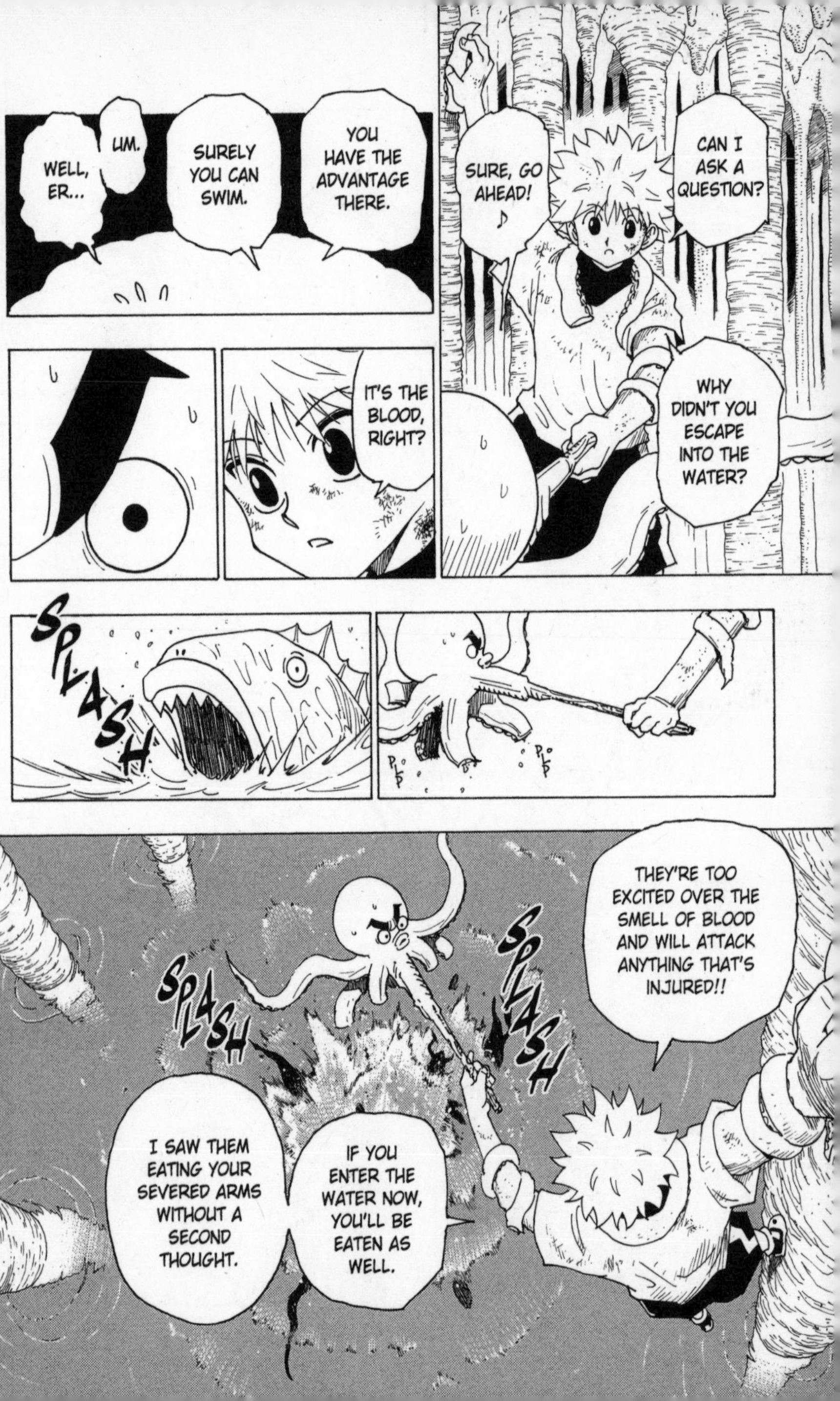
CAN I ASK A QUESTION?
SURE, GO AHEAD! ♪
WHY DIDN'T YOU ESCAPE INTO THE WATER?
YOU HAVE THE ADVANTAGE THERE.
SURELY YOU CAN SWIM.
UM.
WELL, ER...
IT'S THE BLOOD, RIGHT?
PLP
PLP
SPLASH
THEY'RE TOO EXCITED OVER THE SMELL OF BLOOD AND WILL ATTACK ANYTHING THAT'S INJURED!!
SPLASH
SPLASH
IF YOU ENTER THE WATER NOW, YOU'LL BE EATEN AS WELL.
I SAW THEM EATING YOUR SEVERED ARMS WITHOUT A SECOND THOUGHT.

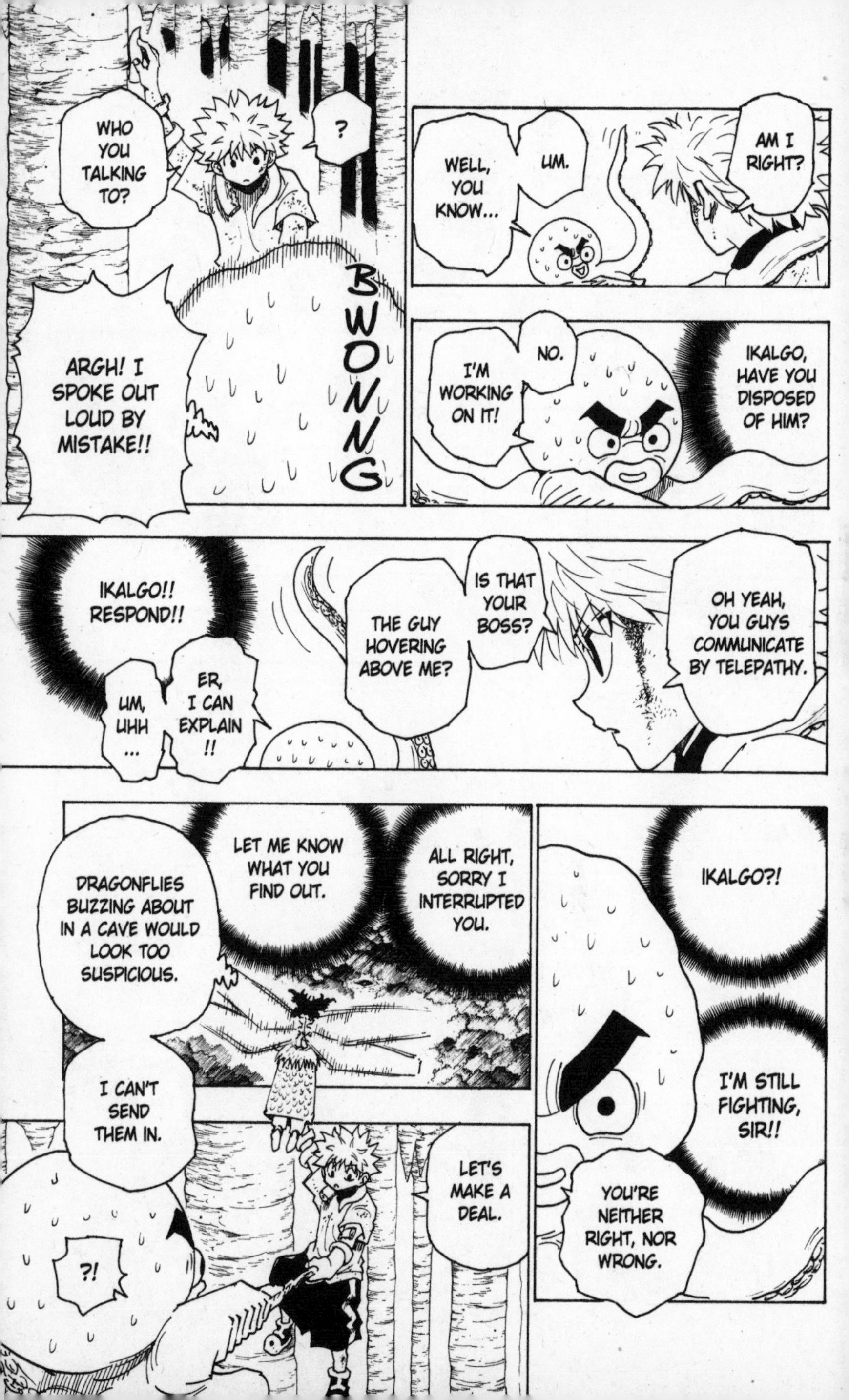
AM I RIGHT?
UM.
WELL, YOU KNOW...
IKALGO, HAVE YOU DISPOSED OF HIM?
NO.
I'M WORKING ON IT!
?
WHO YOU TALKING TO?
ARGH! I SPOKE OUT LOUD BY MISTAKE!!
BWONNG
OH YEAH, YOU GUYS COMMUNICATE BY TELEPATHY.
IS THAT YOUR BOSS?
THE GUY HOVERING ABOVE ME?
IKALGO!! RESPOND!!
ER, I CAN EXPLAIN!!
UM, UHH...
IKALGO?!
I'M STILL FIGHTING, SIR!!
YOU'RE NEITHER RIGHT, NOR WRONG.
ALL RIGHT, SORRY I INTERRUPTED YOU.
LET ME KNOW WHAT YOU FIND OUT.
DRAGONFLIES BUZZING ABOUT IN A CAVE WOULD LOOK TOO SUSPICIOUS.
I CAN'T SEND THEM IN.
LET'S MAKE A DEAL.
?!

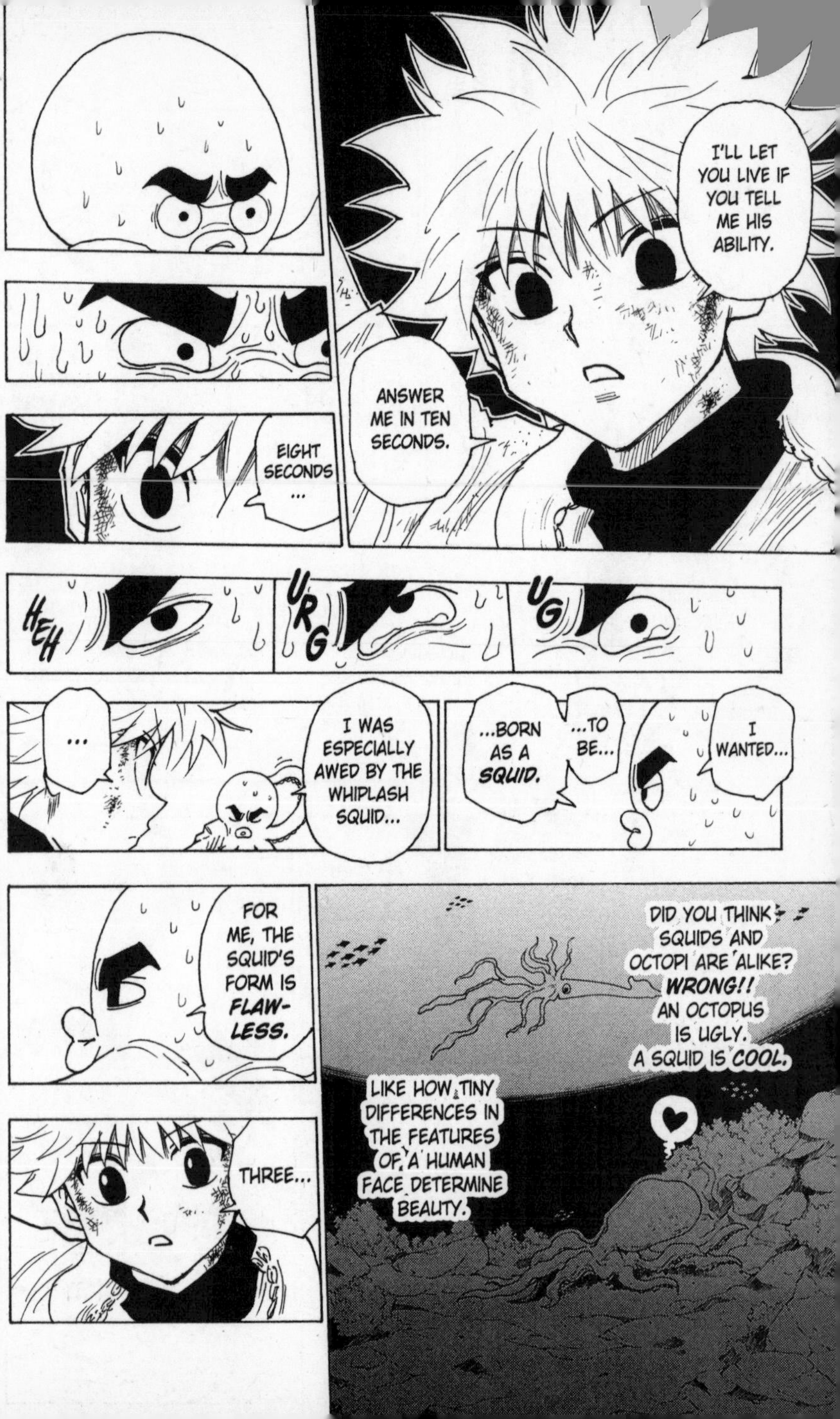
I'LL LET YOU LIVE IF YOU TELL ME HIS ABILITY.
ANSWER ME IN TEN SECONDS.
EIGHT SECONDS ...
UG
URG
HEH
I WANTED...
...TO BE...
...BORN AS A SQUID.
I WAS ESPECIALLY AWED BY THE WHIPLASH SQUID...
...
DID YOU THINK SQUIDS AND OCTOPI ARE ALIKE? WRONG!! AN OCTOPUS IS UGLY. A SQUID IS COOL.
LIKE HOW TINY DIFFERENCES IN THE FEATURES OF A HUMAN FACE DETERMINE BEAUTY.
FOR ME, THE SQUID'S FORM IS FLAWLESS.
THREE...

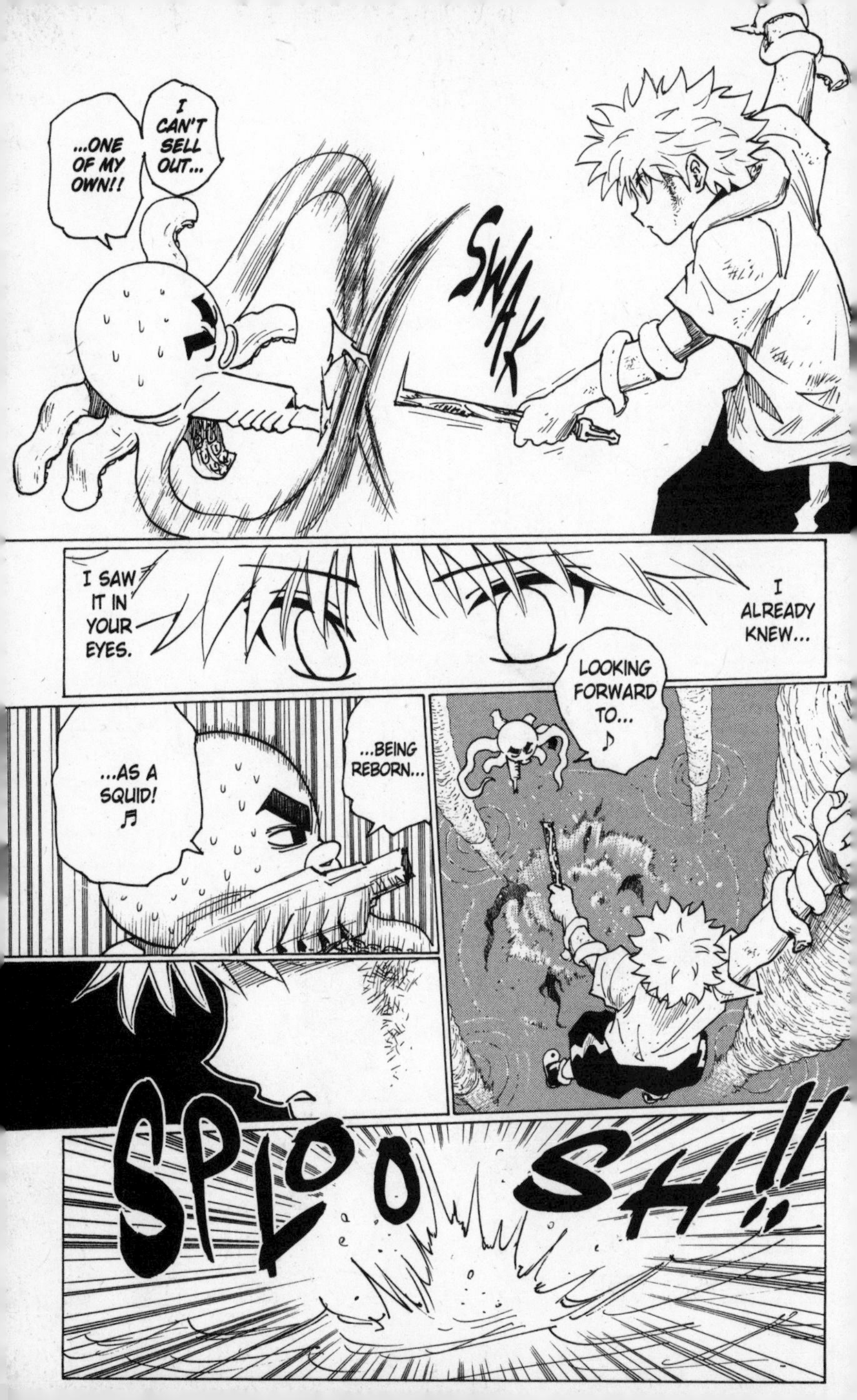
I CAN'T SELL OUT...
...ONE OF MY OWN!!
SWAK
I ALREADY KNEW...
I SAW IT IN YOUR EYES.
LOOKING FORWARD TO... ♪
...BEING REBORN...
...AS A SQUID! ♬
SPLOOSH!!

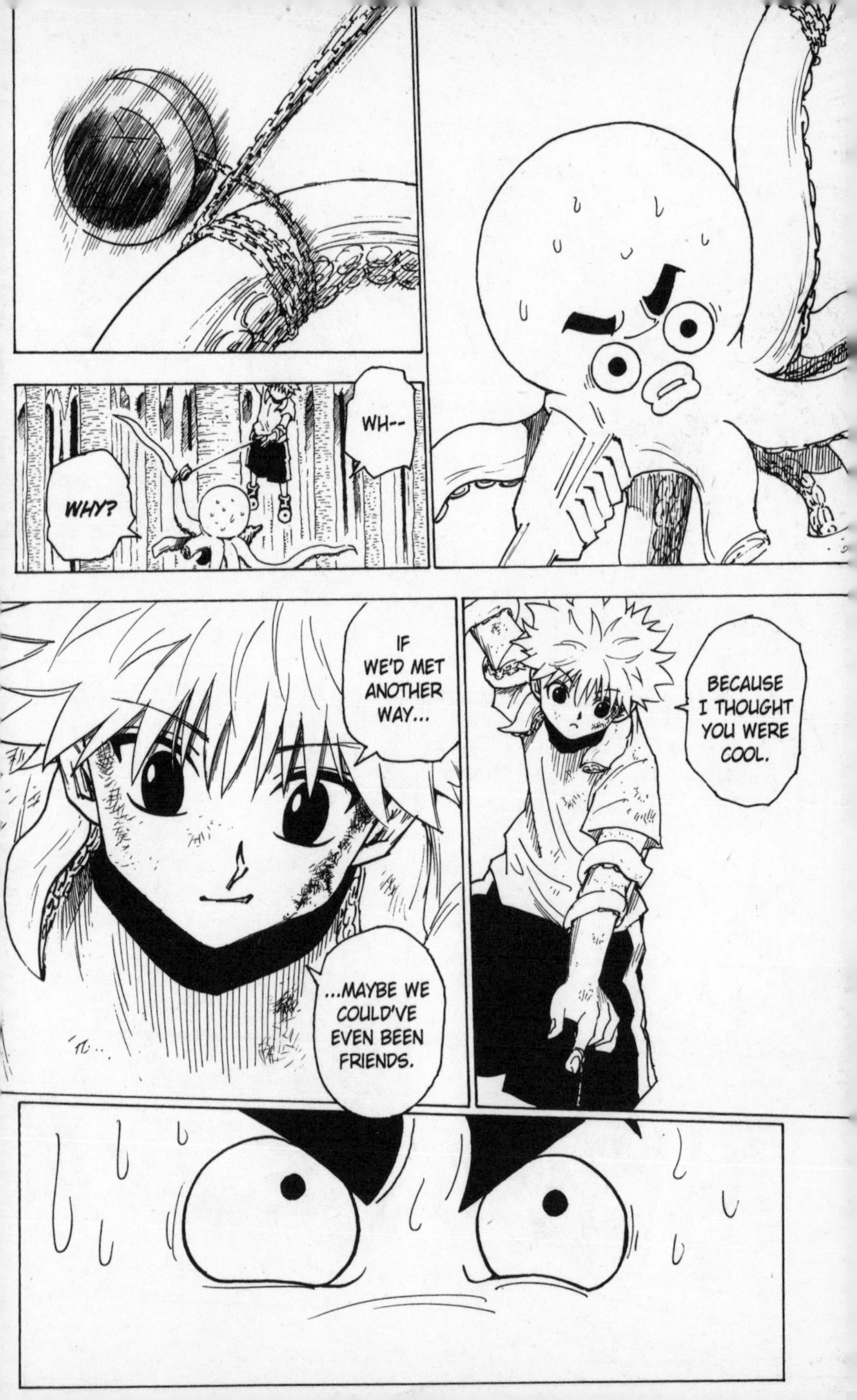
WH--
WHY?
BECAUSE I THOUGHT YOU WERE COOL.
IF WE'D MET ANOTHER WAY...
...MAYBE WE COULD'VE EVEN BEEN FRIENDS.

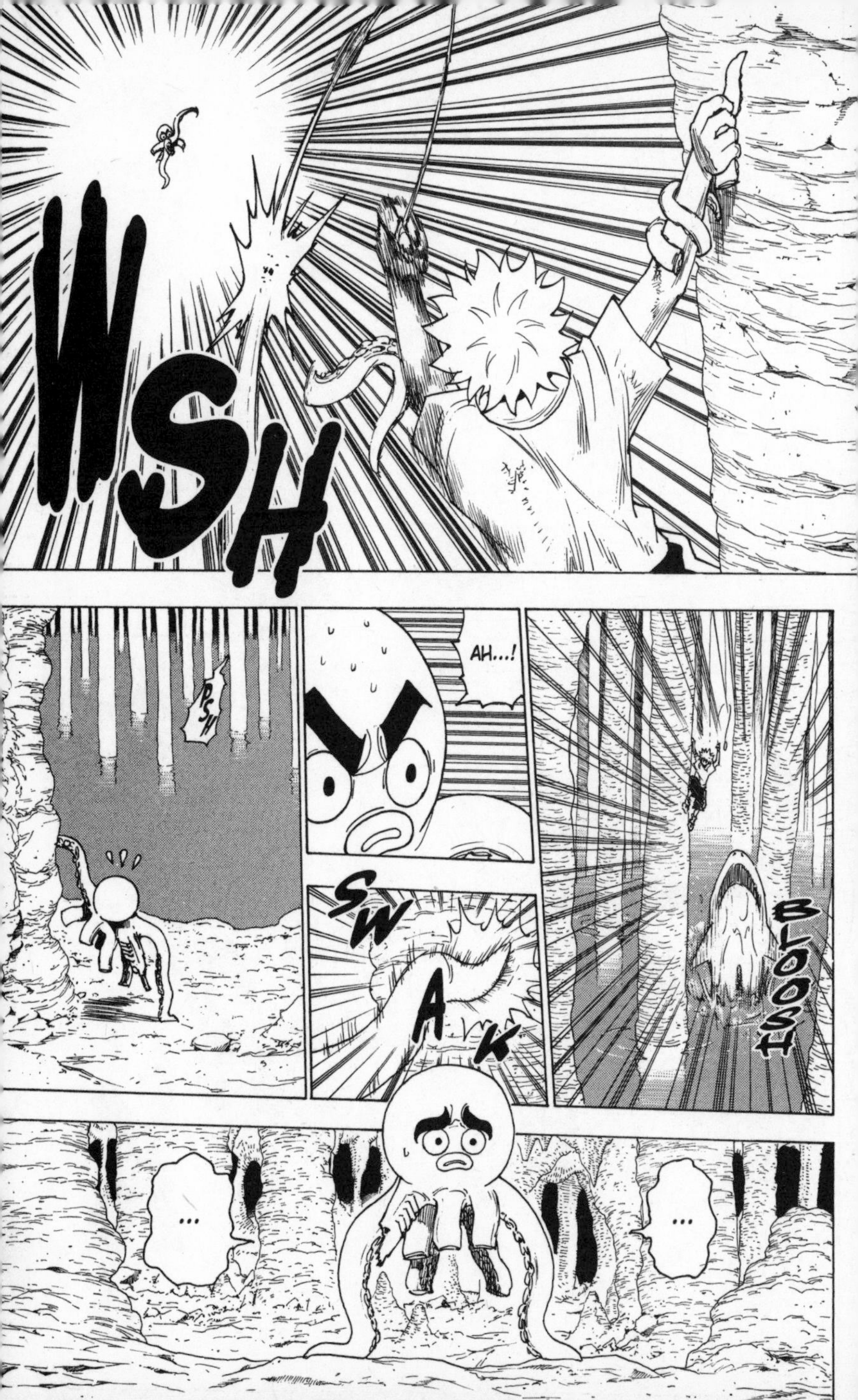
WSH
BLOOSH
AH...!
SWAK
PSH
...
...

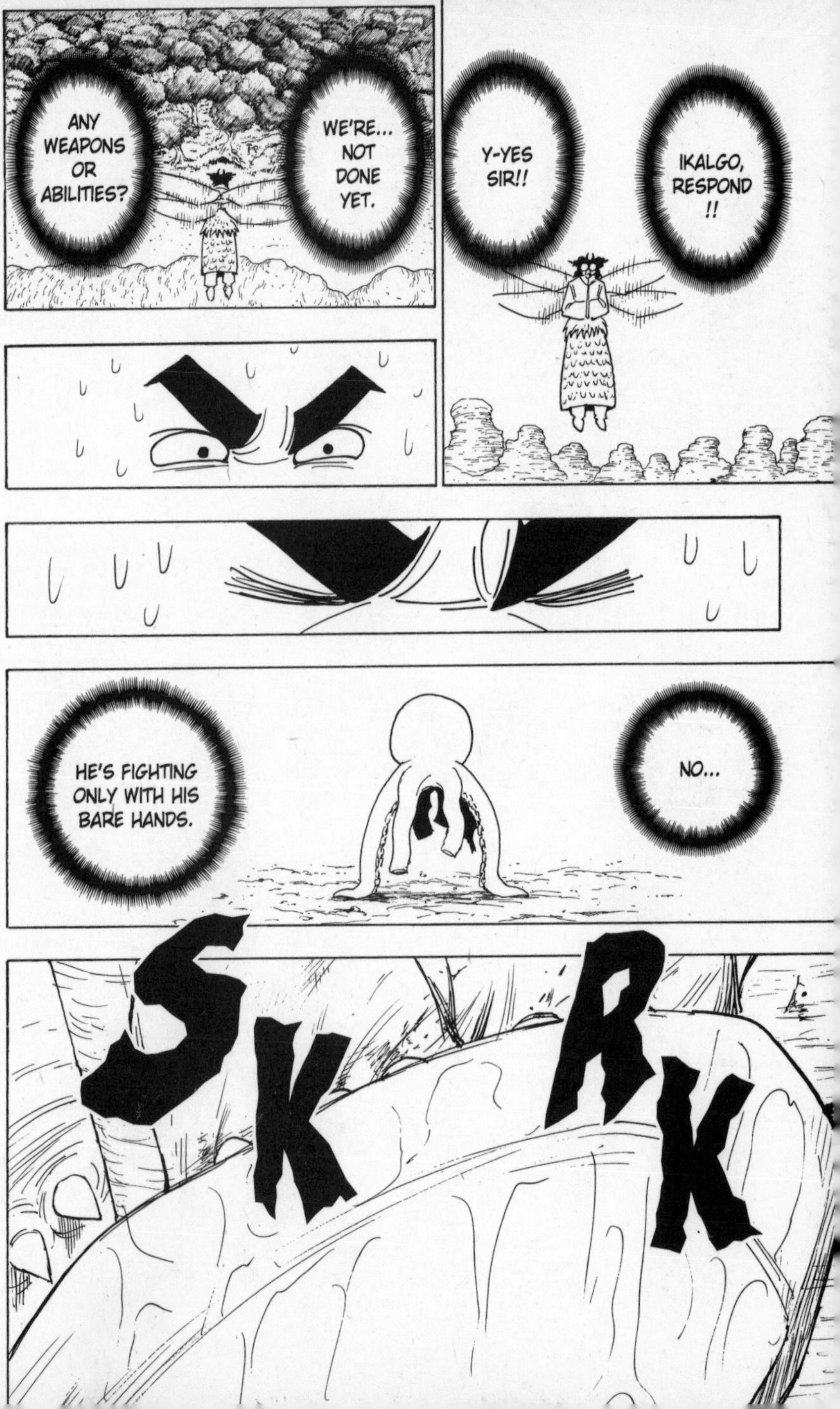
IKALGO, RESPOND!!
Y-YES SIR!!
WE'RE... NOT DONE YET.
ANY WEAPONS OR ABILITIES?
NO...
HE'S FIGHTING ONLY WITH HIS BARE HANDS.
SKRK

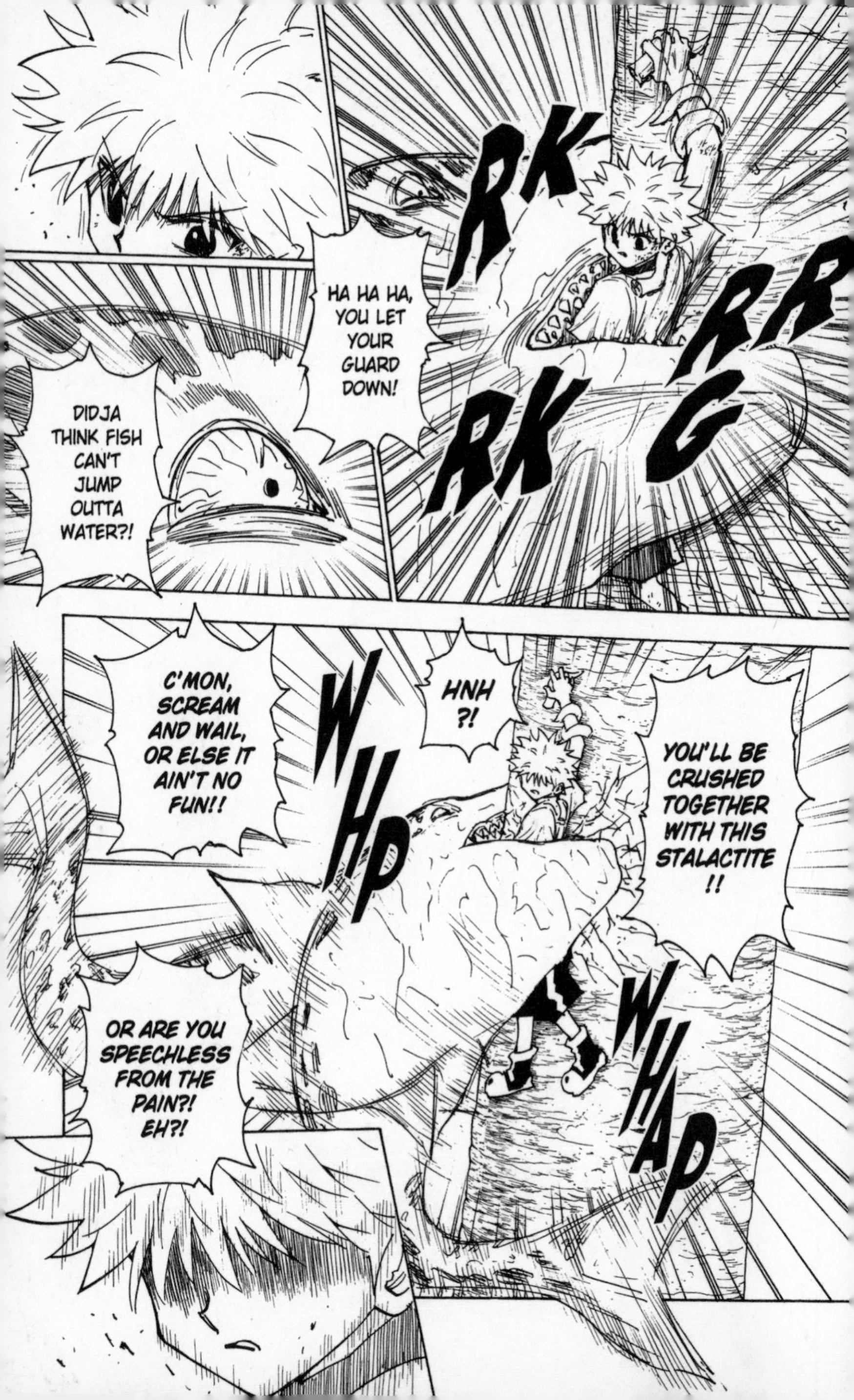
RK RR RK G
HA HA HA, YOU LET YOUR GUARD DOWN!
DIDJA THINK FISH CAN'T JUMP OUTTA WATER?!
YOU'LL BE CRUSHED TOGETHER WITH THIS STALACTITE!!
WHAP
HNH?!
WHP
C'MON, SCREAM AND WAIL, OR ELSE IT AIN'T NO FUN!!
OR ARE YOU SPEECHLESS FROM THE PAIN?! EH?!

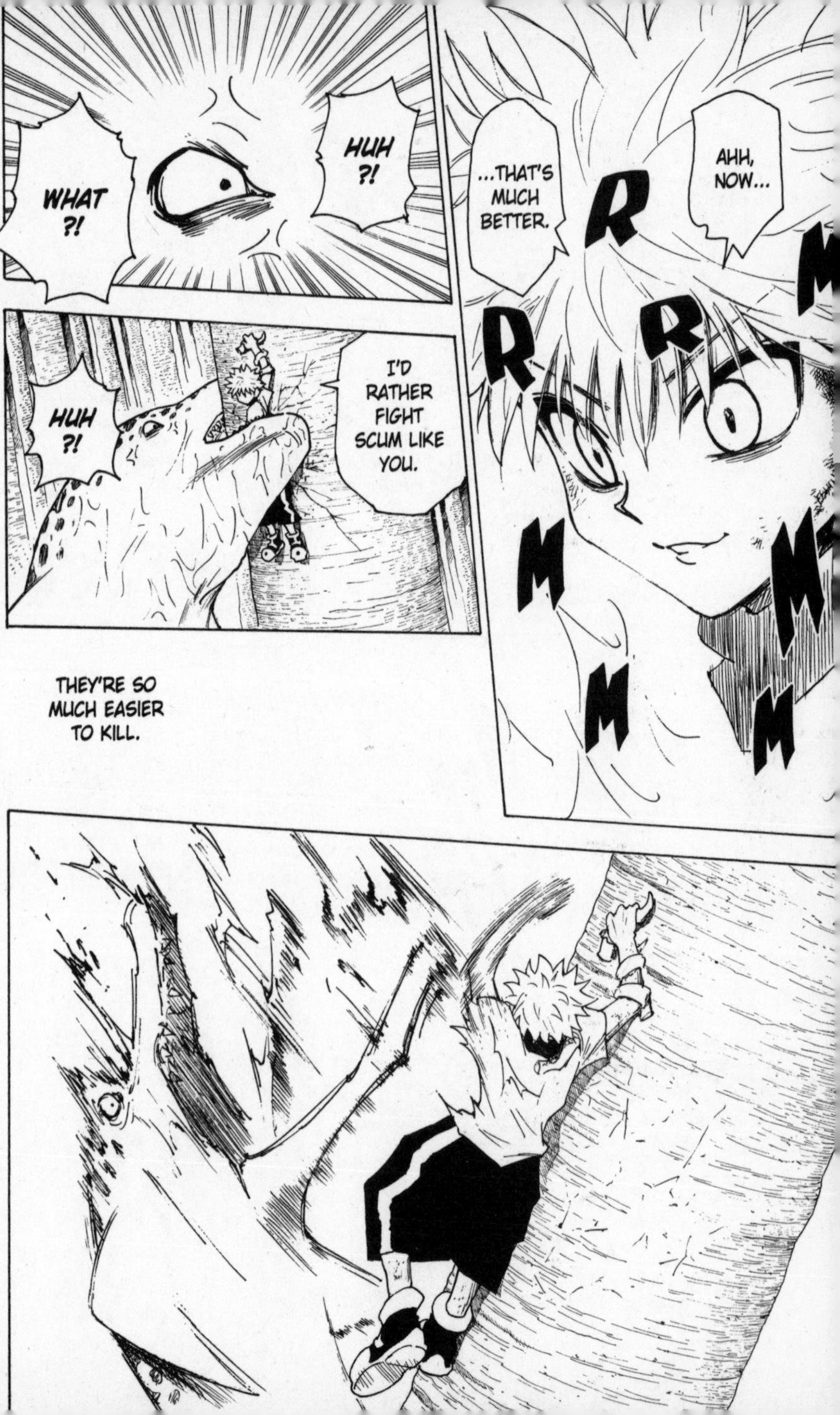
AHH, NOW...
...THAT'S MUCH BETTER.
HUH ?!
WHAT ?!
I'D RATHER FIGHT SCUM LIKE YOU.
HUH ?!
THEY'RE SO MUCH EASIER TO KILL.

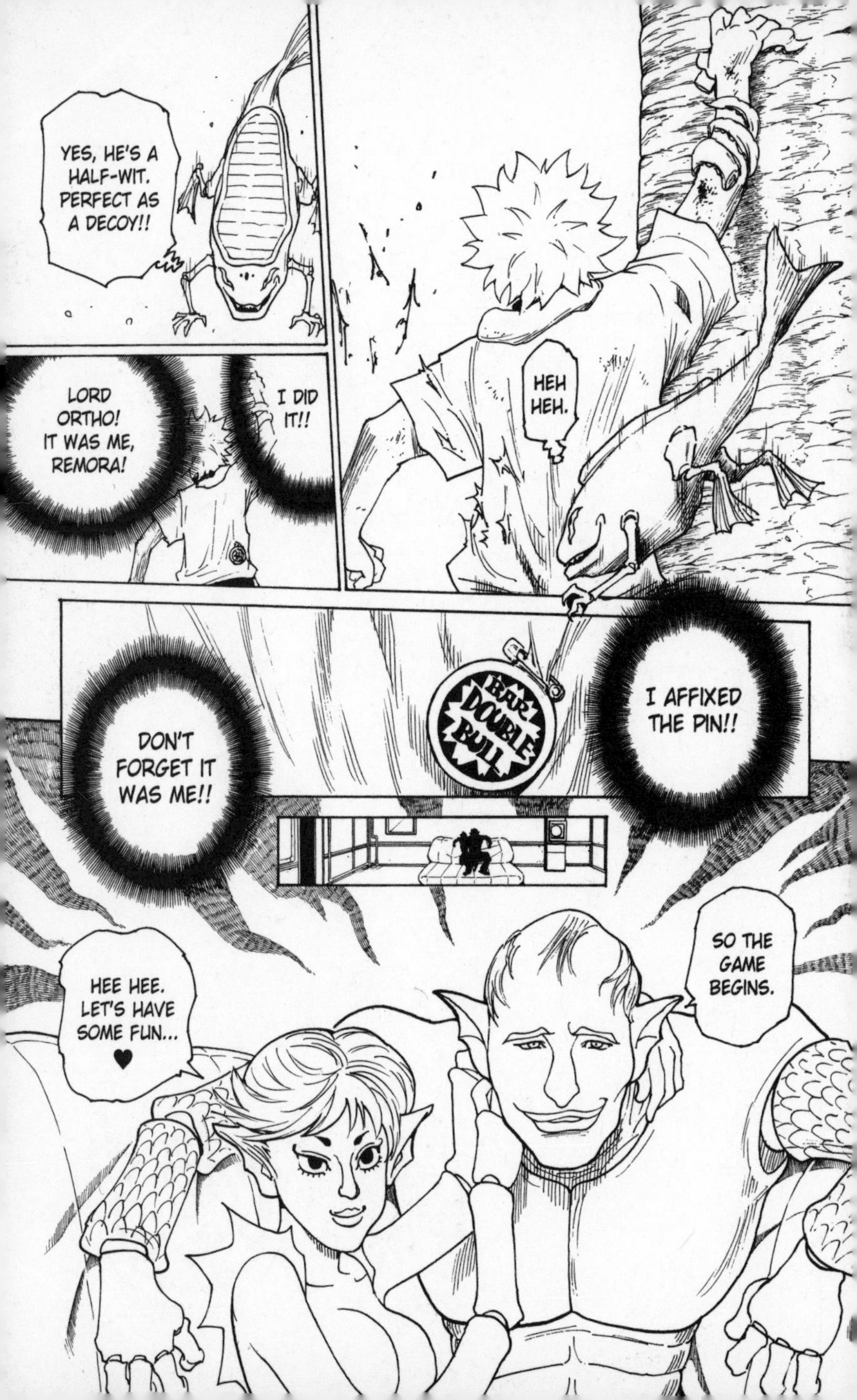
HEH HEH.
YES, HE'S A HALF-WIT. PERFECT AS A DECOY!!
I DID IT!!
LORD ORTHO! IT WAS ME, REMORA!
I AFFIXED THE PIN!!
DOUBLE BULL
DON'T FORGET IT WAS ME!!
SO THE GAME BEGINS.
HEE HEE. LET'S HAVE SOME FUN... ♥

BAR
DOUBLE
BULL

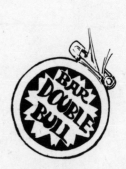

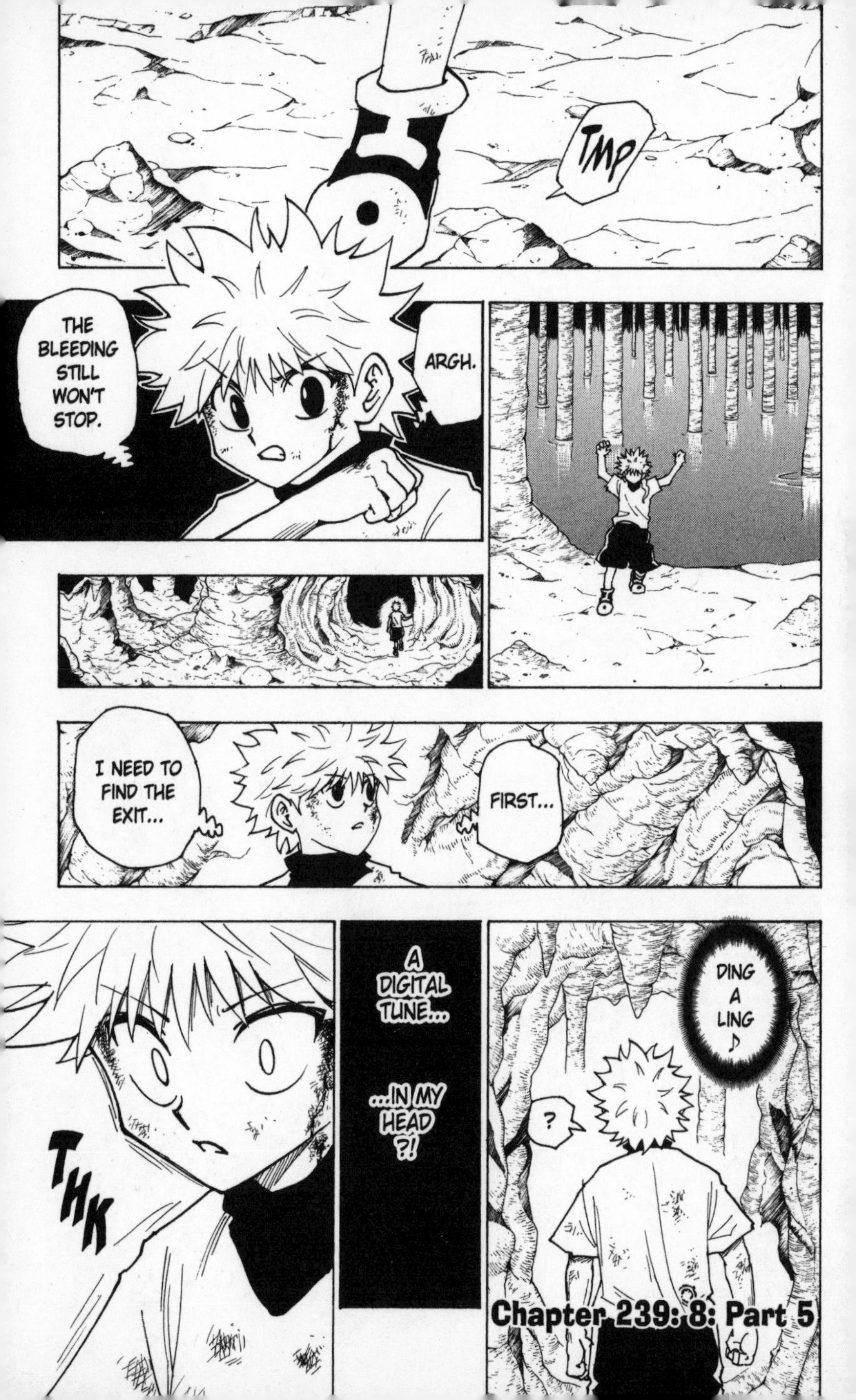
TMP
ARGH.
THE BLEEDING STILL WON'T STOP.
FIRST...
I NEED TO FIND THE EXIT...
DING A LING ♪
?
Chapter 239: 8: Part 5
A DIGITAL TUNE...
...IN MY HEAD ?!
THK

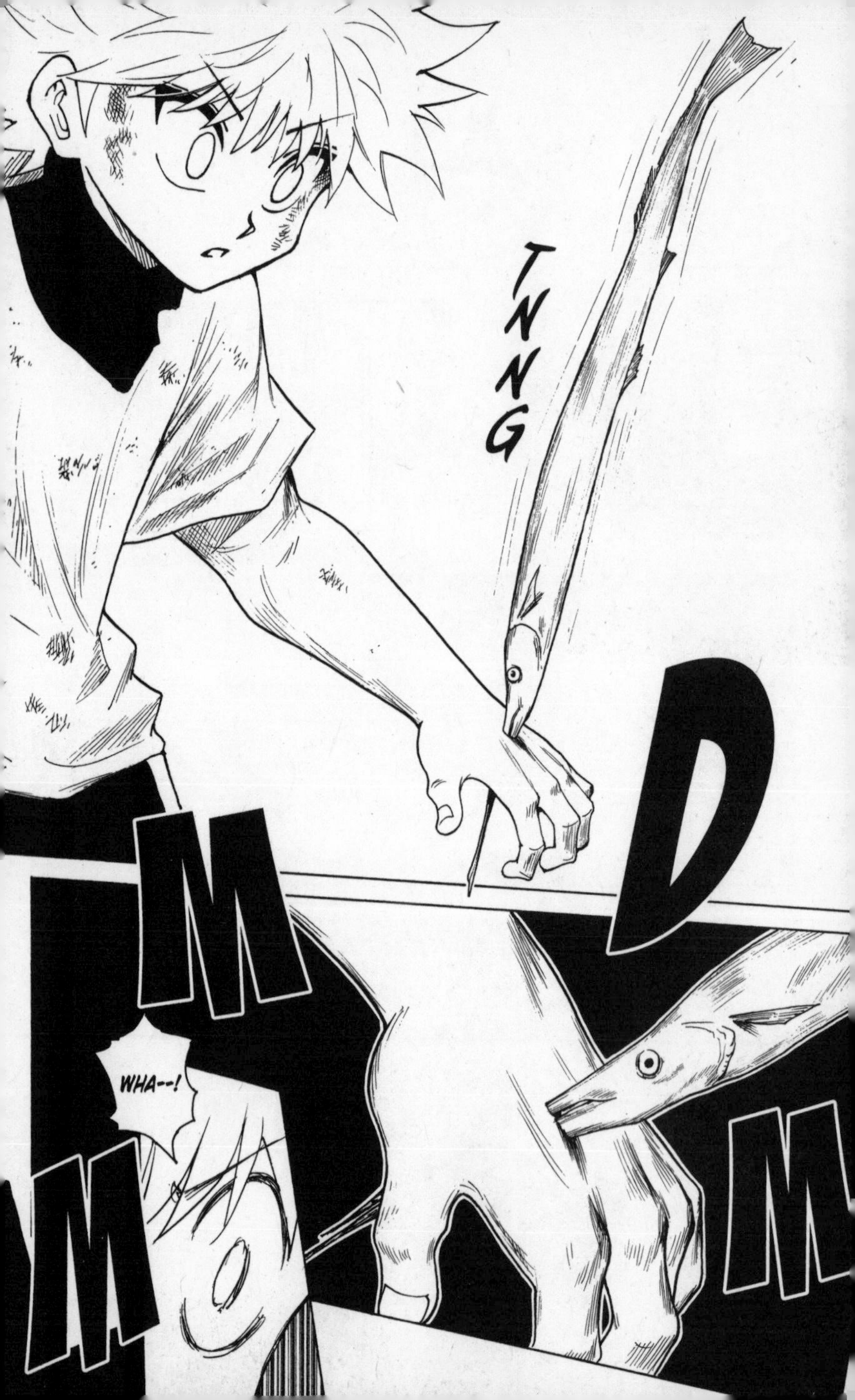
TNNG
D
M
WHA--!
M
M

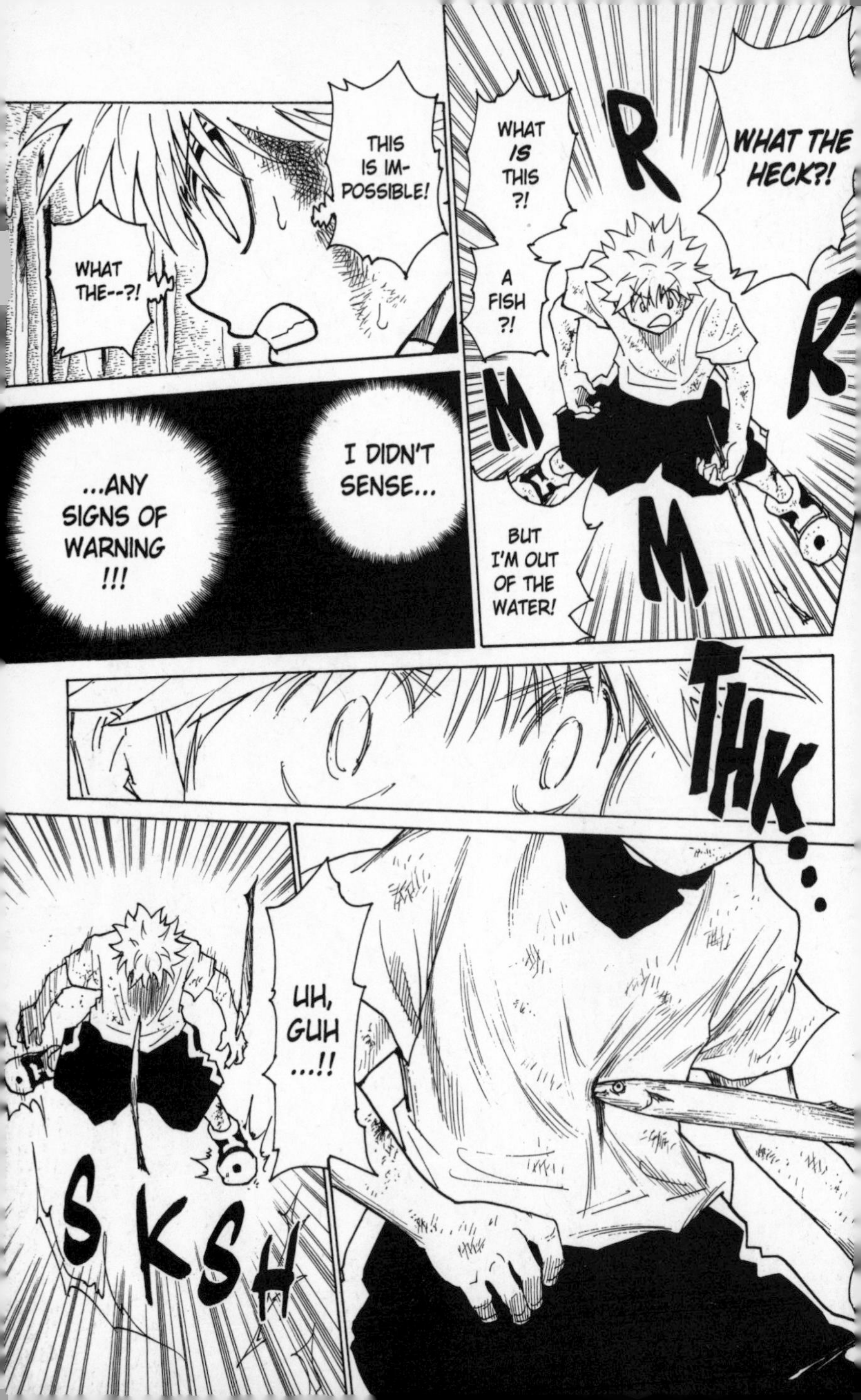

WHAT THE HECK?!
RRMM
WHAT *IS* THIS ?!
A FISH ?!
BUT I'M OUT OF THE WATER!
THIS IS IM-POSSIBLE!
WHAT THE--?!
I DIDN'T SENSE...
...ANY SIGNS OF WARNING !!!
THK...
UH, GUH ...!!
SKSH

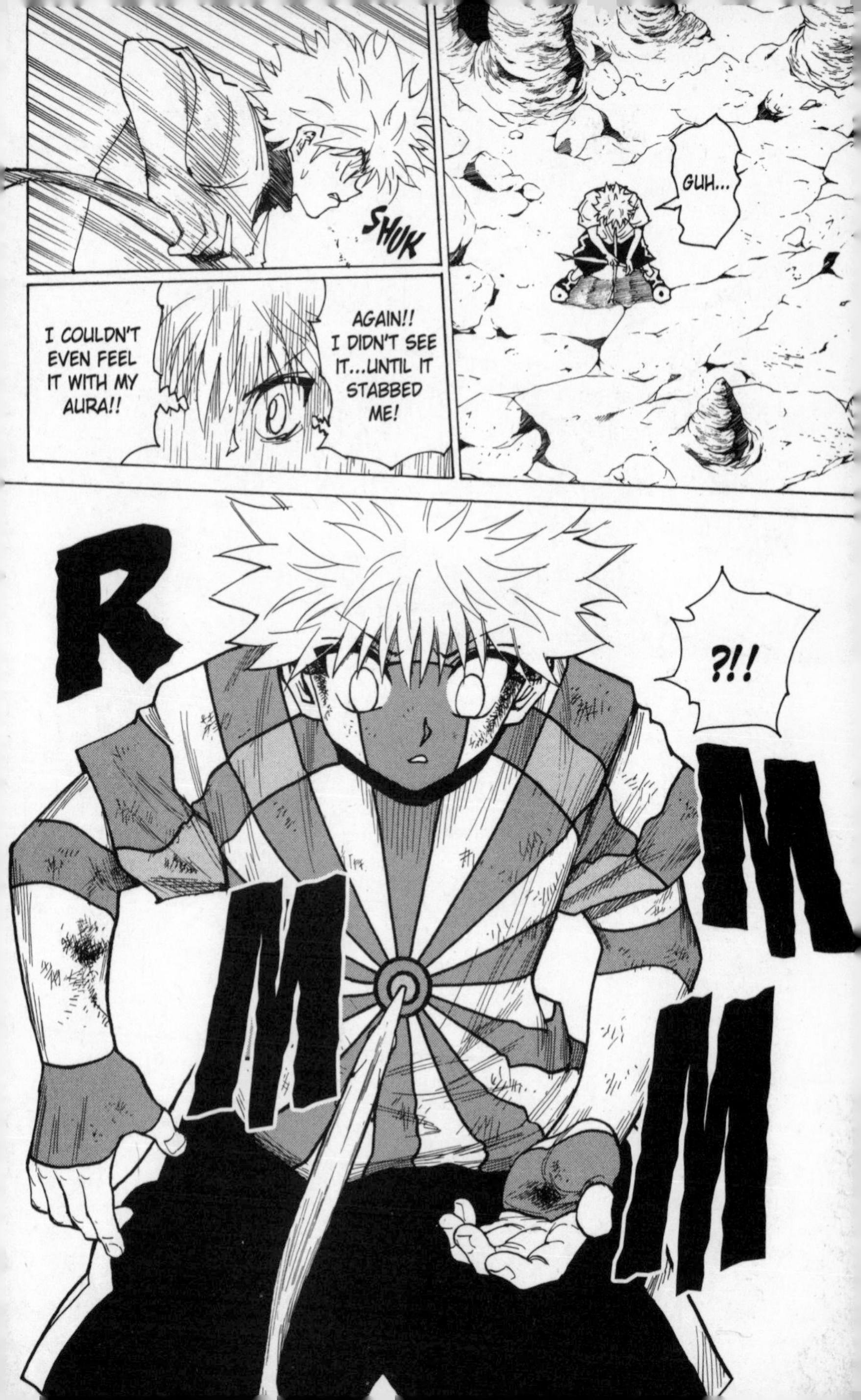
GUH...
SHUK
AGAIN!! I DIDN'T SEE IT...UNTIL IT STABBED ME!
I COULDN'T EVEN FEEL IT WITH MY AURA!!
?!!
RMMM

READ THIS WAY

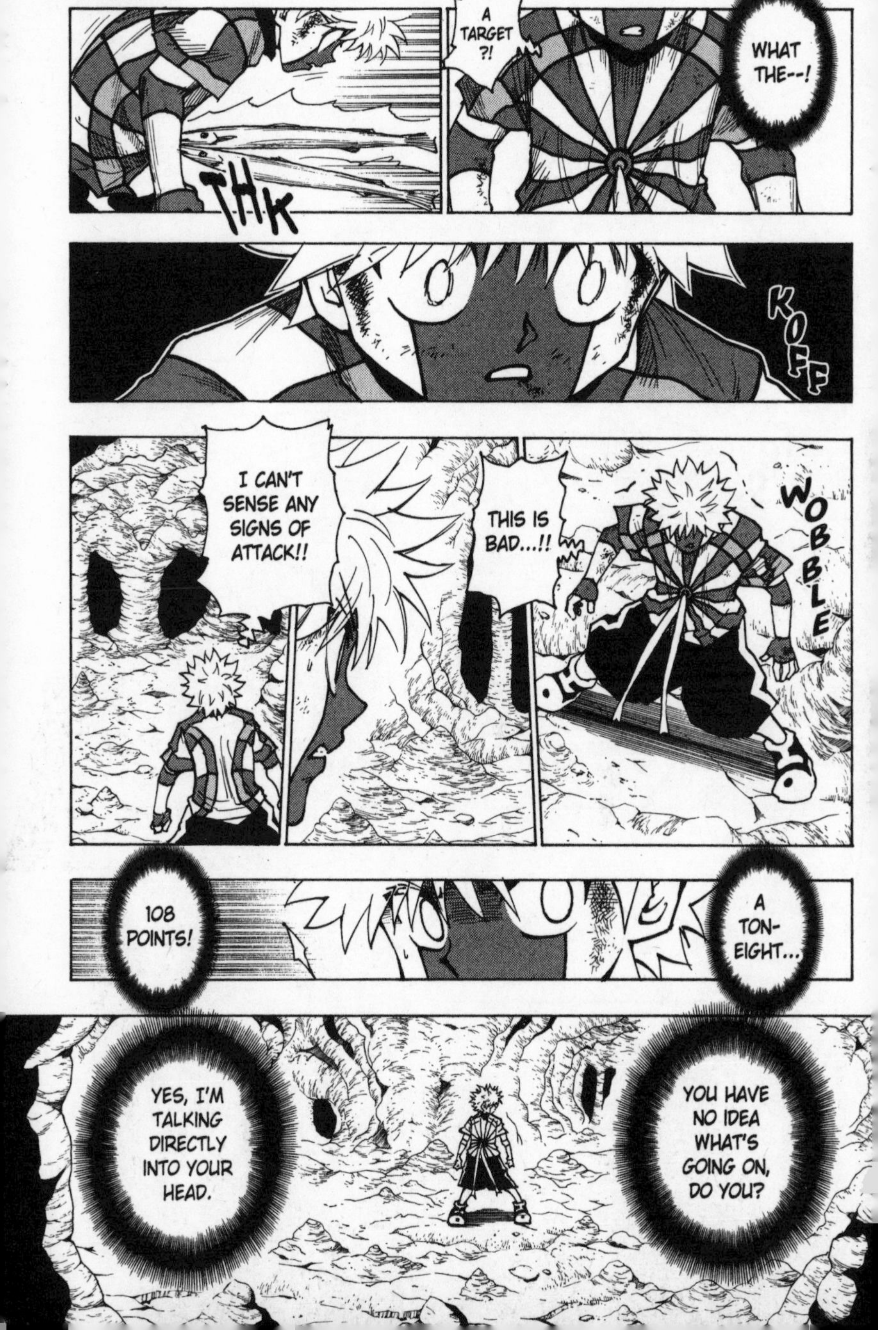
WHAT THE--!
A TARGET ?!
THK
KOFF
WOBBLE
THIS IS BAD...!!
I CAN'T SENSE ANY SIGNS OF ATTACK!!
A TON-EIGHT...
108 POINTS!
YOU HAVE NO IDEA WHAT'S GOING ON, DO YOU?
YES, I'M TALKING DIRECTLY INTO YOUR HEAD.

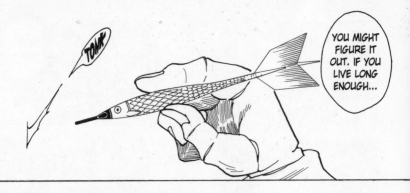

YOU MIGHT FIGURE IT OUT. IF YOU LIVE LONG ENOUGH...
TONK
TONK
!
FSSSH
OOZE
B-B-BMP
UNH...
BB-MP
SO THEY ARE NEN FISH!
BUT WHY COULDN'T I SENSE THEM?!
HIS ABILITY GOT ACTIVATED SOMEHOW!!
HOW ELSE ?!

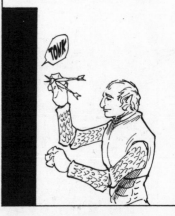

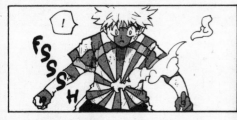

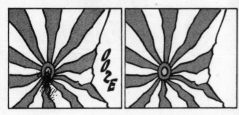

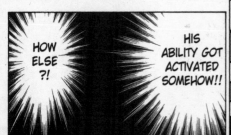

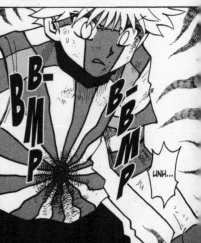

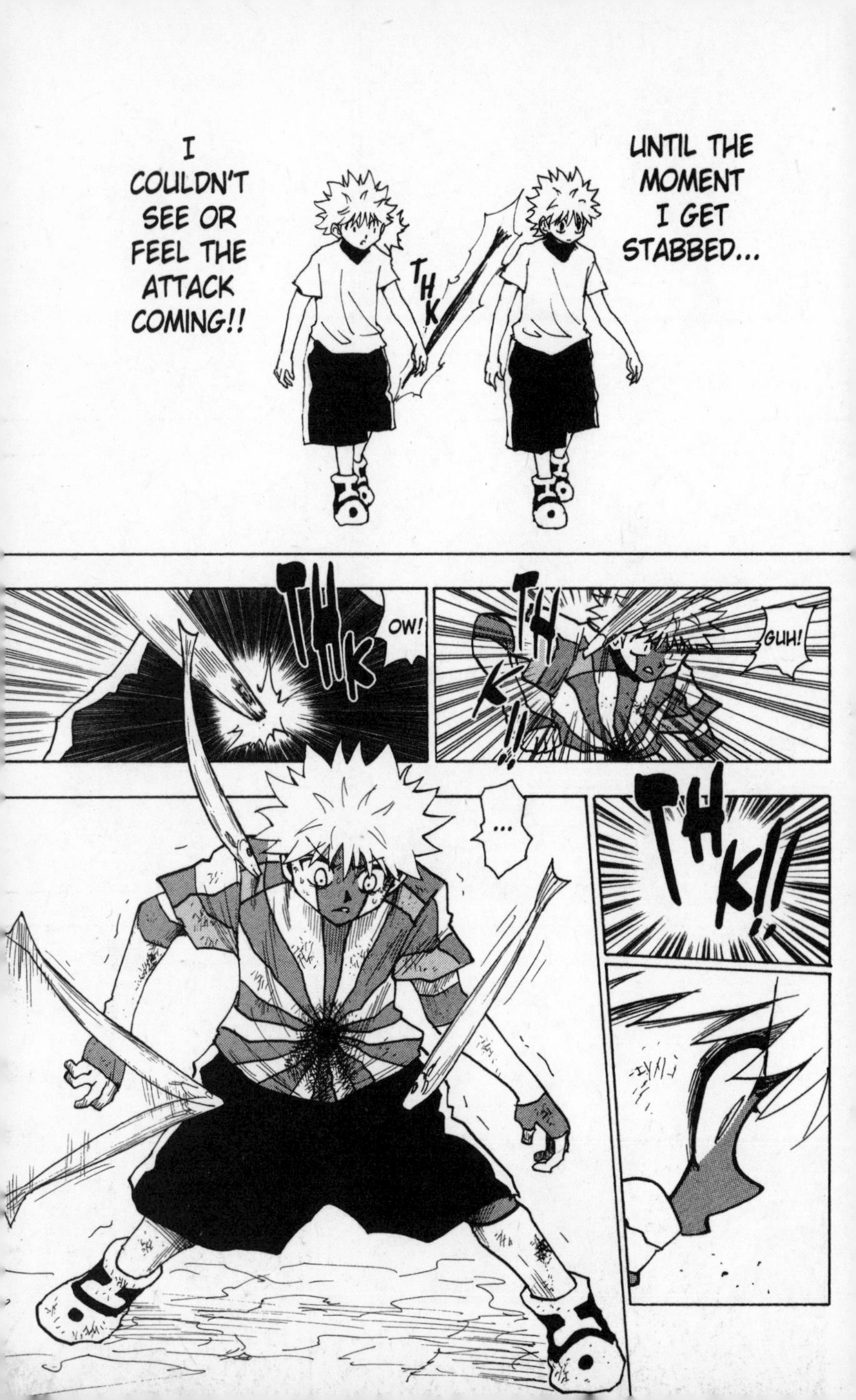
UNTIL THE MOMENT I GET STABBED...
THK
I COULDN'T SEE OR FEEL THE ATTACK COMING!!
THK!!
GUH!
THK
OW!
THK!!
...

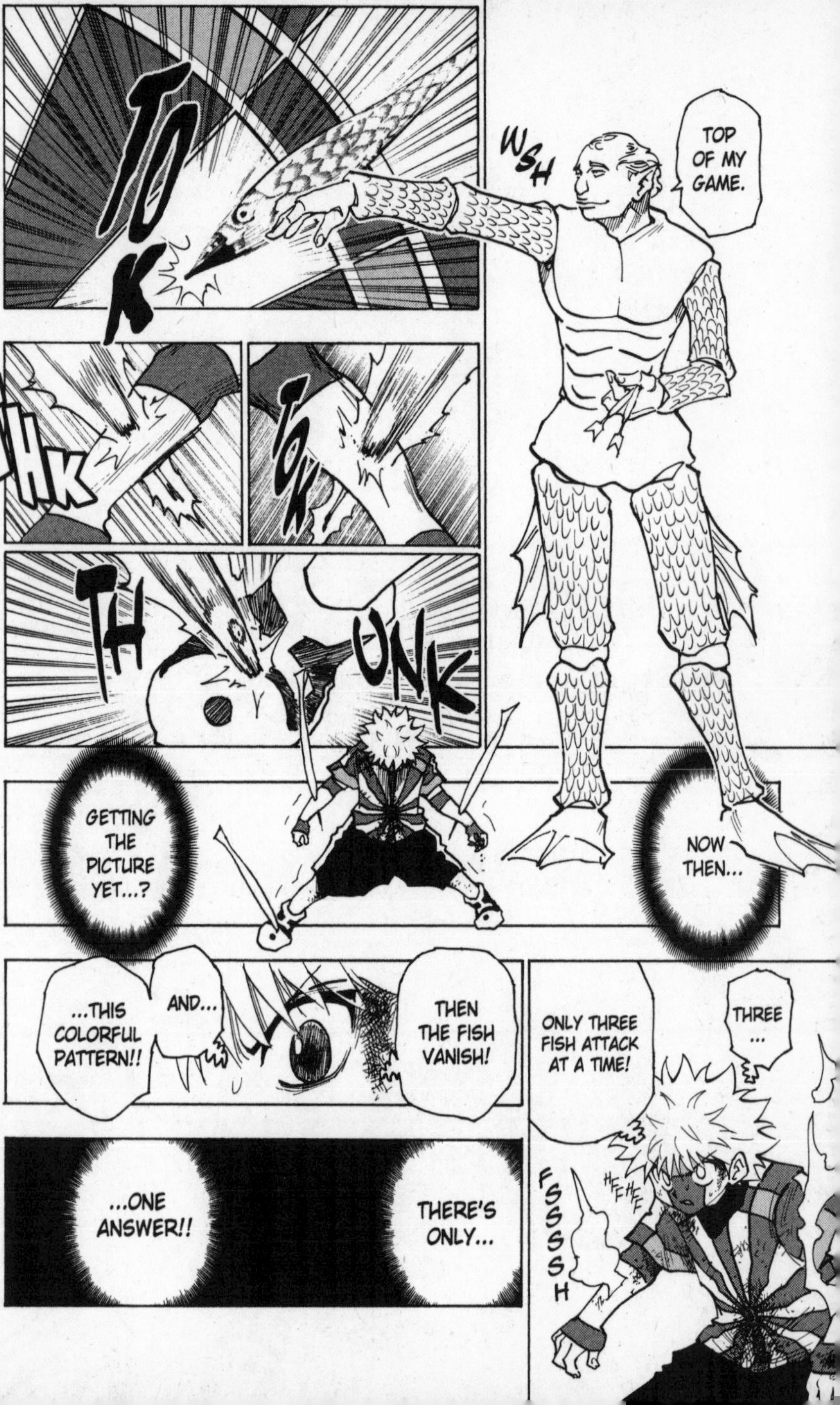
WSH
TOP OF MY GAME.
TOK
TOK
HK
THUNK
NOW THEN...
GETTING THE PICTURE YET...?
THREE ...
ONLY THREE FISH ATTACK AT A TIME!
HFF HFF
FSSSSH
THEN THE FISH VANISH!
AND...
...THIS COLORFUL PATTERN!!
THERE'S ONLY...
...ONE ANSWER!!

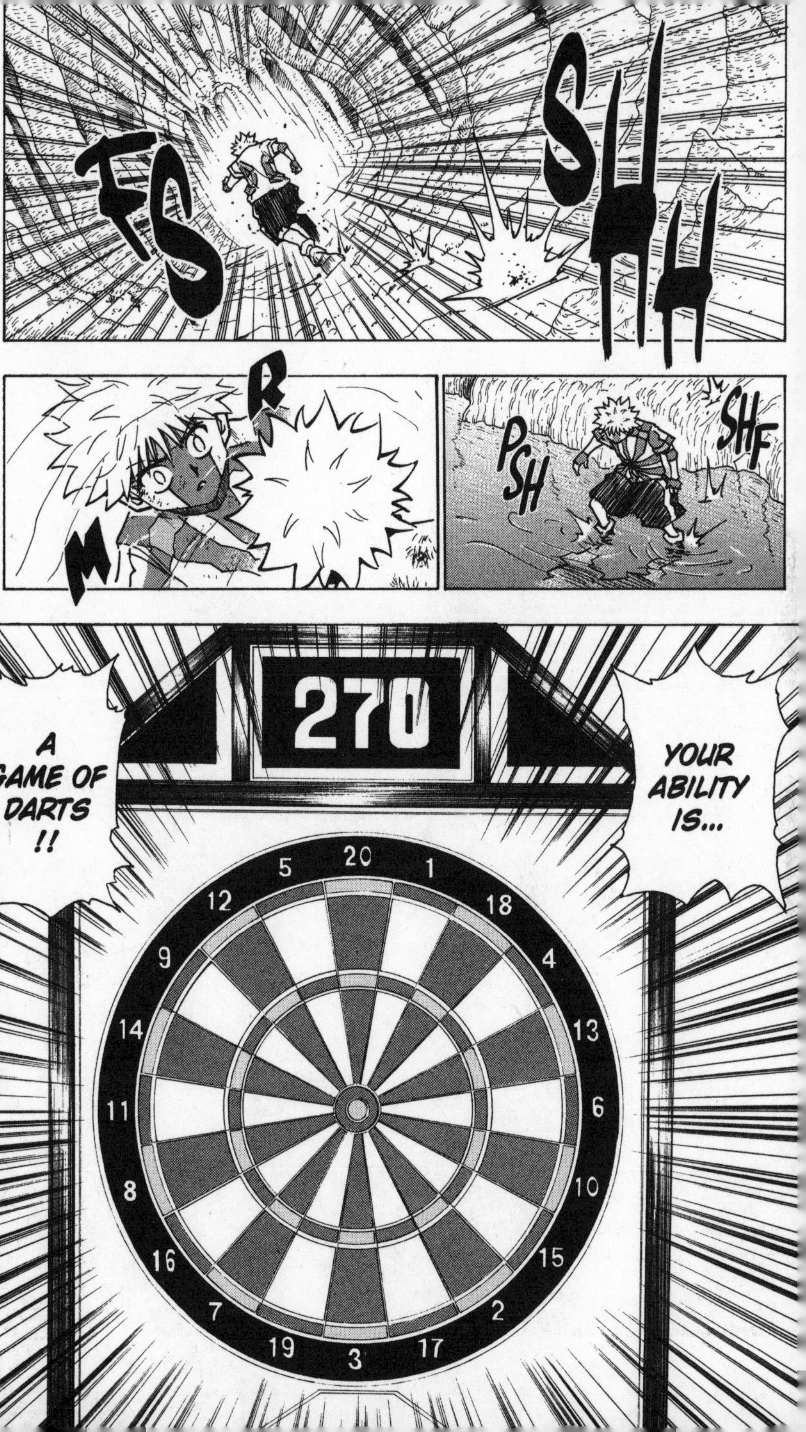
SHH
FS
SHF
PSH
R
M
YOUR ABILITY IS...
270
A GAME OF DARTS !!
20 1 18 4 13 6 10 15 2 17 3 19 7 16 8 11 14 9 12 5

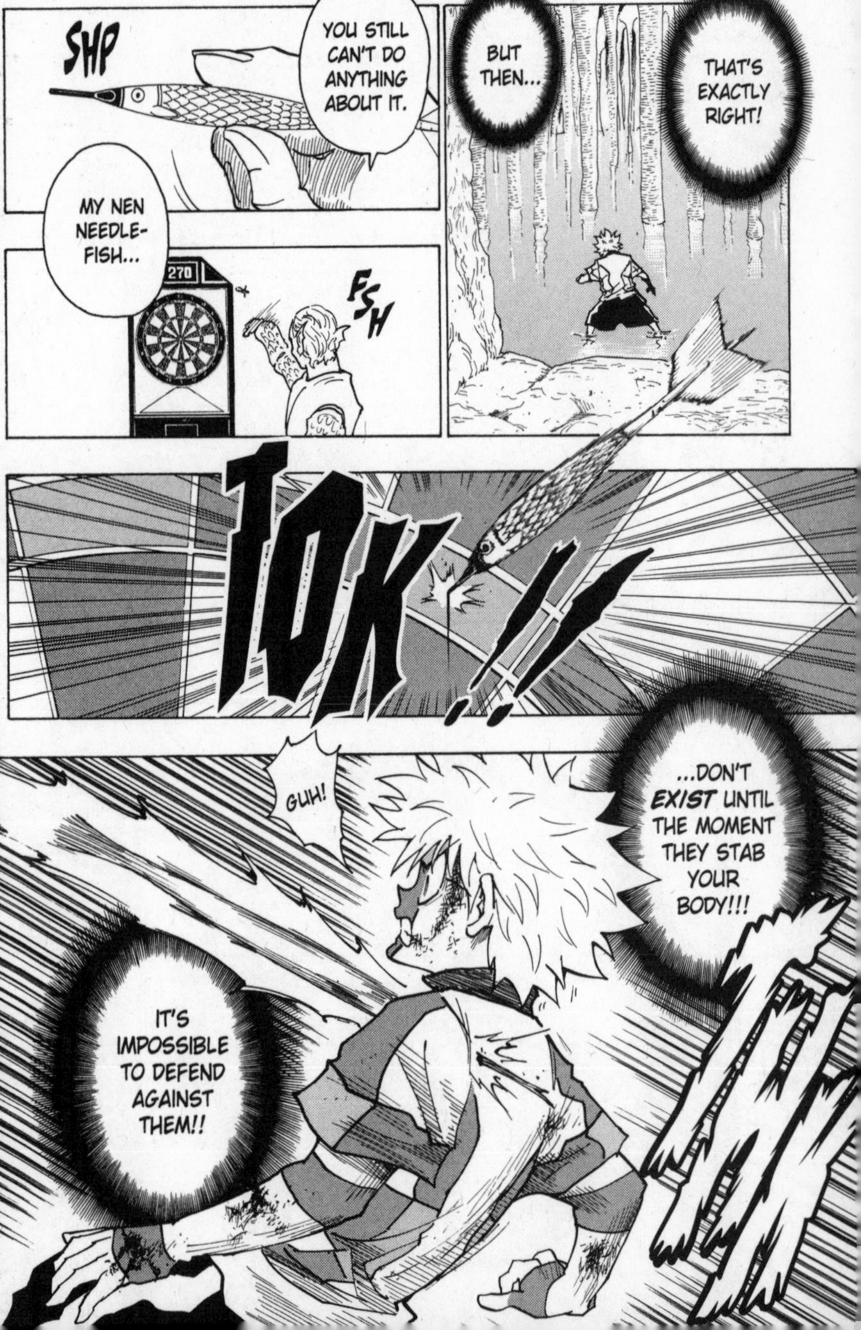
THAT'S EXACTLY RIGHT!
BUT THEN...
SHP
YOU STILL CAN'T DO ANYTHING ABOUT IT.
MY NEN NEEDLE-FISH...
270
FSH
TOK!!
...DON'T *EXIST* UNTIL THE MOMENT THEY STAB YOUR BODY!!!
GUH!
IT'S IMPOSSIBLE TO DEFEND AGAINST THEM!!

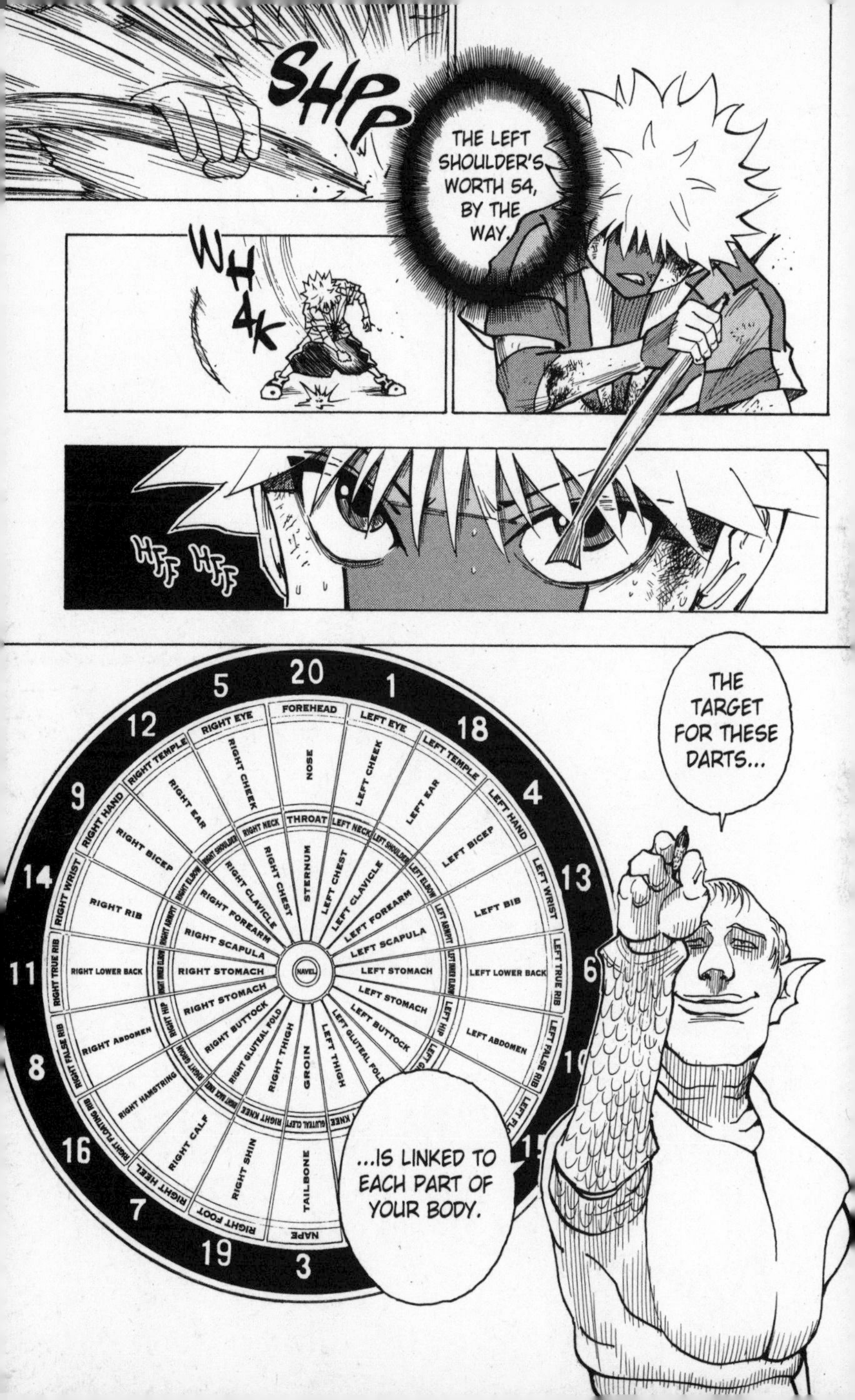
SHPP
THE LEFT SHOULDER'S WORTH 54, BY THE WAY.
WHAK
HFF HFF
THE TARGET FOR THESE DARTS...
20
1
18
4
13
6
11
14
9
12
5
8
16
7
19
3
FOREHEAD
LEFT EYE
LEFT TEMPLE
LEFT HAND
LEFT WRIST
LEFT TRUE RIB
LEFT FALSE RIB
RIGHT EYE
RIGHT TEMPLE
RIGHT HAND
RIGHT WRIST
RIGHT TRUE RIB
RIGHT FALSE RIB
RIGHT FLOATING RIB
RIGHT HEEL
RIGHT FOOT
NAPE
NOSE
LEFT CHEEK
LEFT EAR
LEFT BICEP
LEFT BIB
LEFT LOWER BACK
LEFT ABDOMEN
RIGHT CHEEK
RIGHT EAR
RIGHT BICEP
RIGHT RIB
RIGHT LOWER BACK
RIGHT ABDOMEN
RIGHT HAMSTRING
RIGHT CALF
RIGHT SHIN
TAILBONE
THROAT
LEFT NECK
LEFT SHOULDER
LEFT ELBOW
LEFT ARMPIT
LEFT INNER ELBOW
LEFT HIP
RIGHT NECK
RIGHT SHOULDER
RIGHT ELBOW
RIGHT ARMPIT
RIGHT INNER ELBOW
RIGHT HIP
RIGHT GROIN
RIGHT BACK KNEE
RIGHT KNEE
GLUTEAL CLEFT
LEFT KNEE
STERNUM
LEFT CHEST
LEFT CLAVICLE
LEFT FOREARM
LEFT SCAPULA
LEFT STOMACH
LEFT STOMACH
LEFT BUTTOCK
LEFT GLUTEAL FOLD
LEFT THIGH
GROIN
RIGHT THIGH
RIGHT GLUTEAL FOLD
RIGHT BUTTOCK
RIGHT STOMACH
RIGHT STOMACH
RIGHT SCAPULA
RIGHT FOREARM
RIGHT CLAVICLE
RIGHT CHEST
NAVEL
...IS LINKED TO EACH PART OF YOUR BODY.

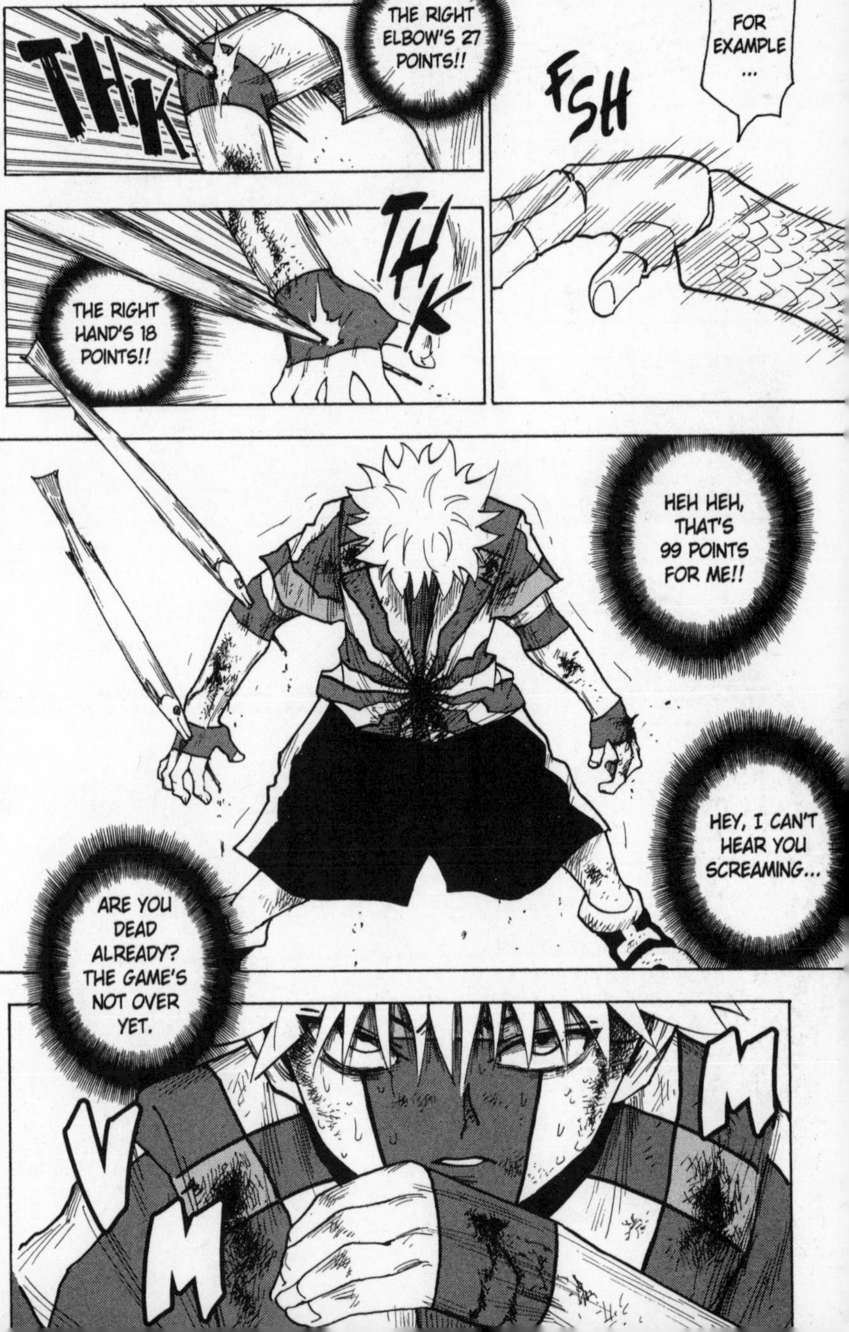
FOR EXAMPLE ...
FSH
THE RIGHT ELBOW'S 27 POINTS!!
THK
THK
THE RIGHT HAND'S 18 POINTS!!
HEH HEH, THAT'S 99 POINTS FOR ME!!
HEY, I CAN'T HEAR YOU SCREAMING...
ARE YOU DEAD ALREADY? THE GAME'S NOT OVER YET.
VMM
MM

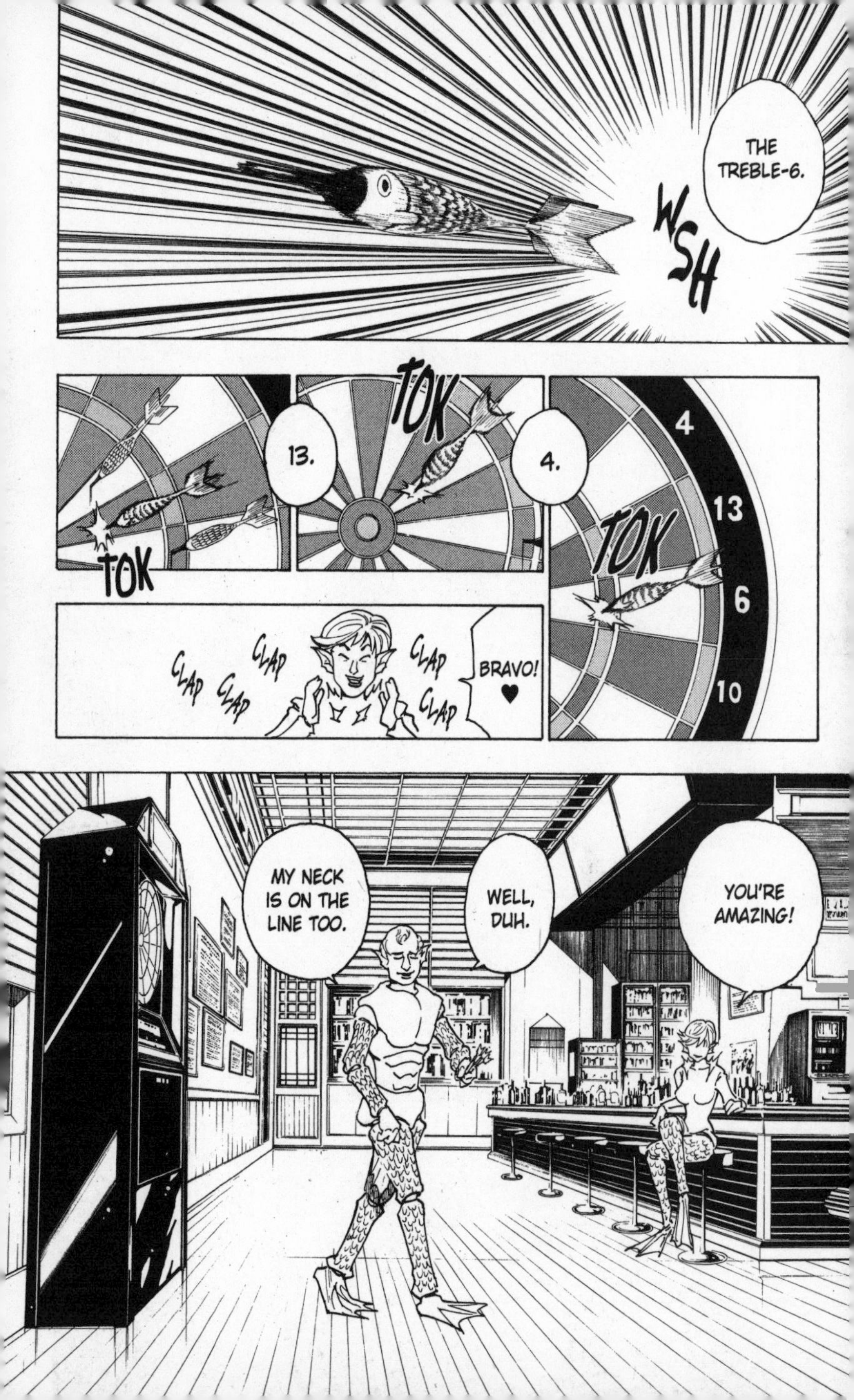
THE TREBLE-6.
WSH
4
13
6
10
TOK
4.
TOK
13.
TOK
BRAVO! ♥
CLAP CLAP
CLAP
CLAP CLAP
YOU'RE AMAZING!
WELL, DUH.
MY NECK IS ON THE LINE TOO.

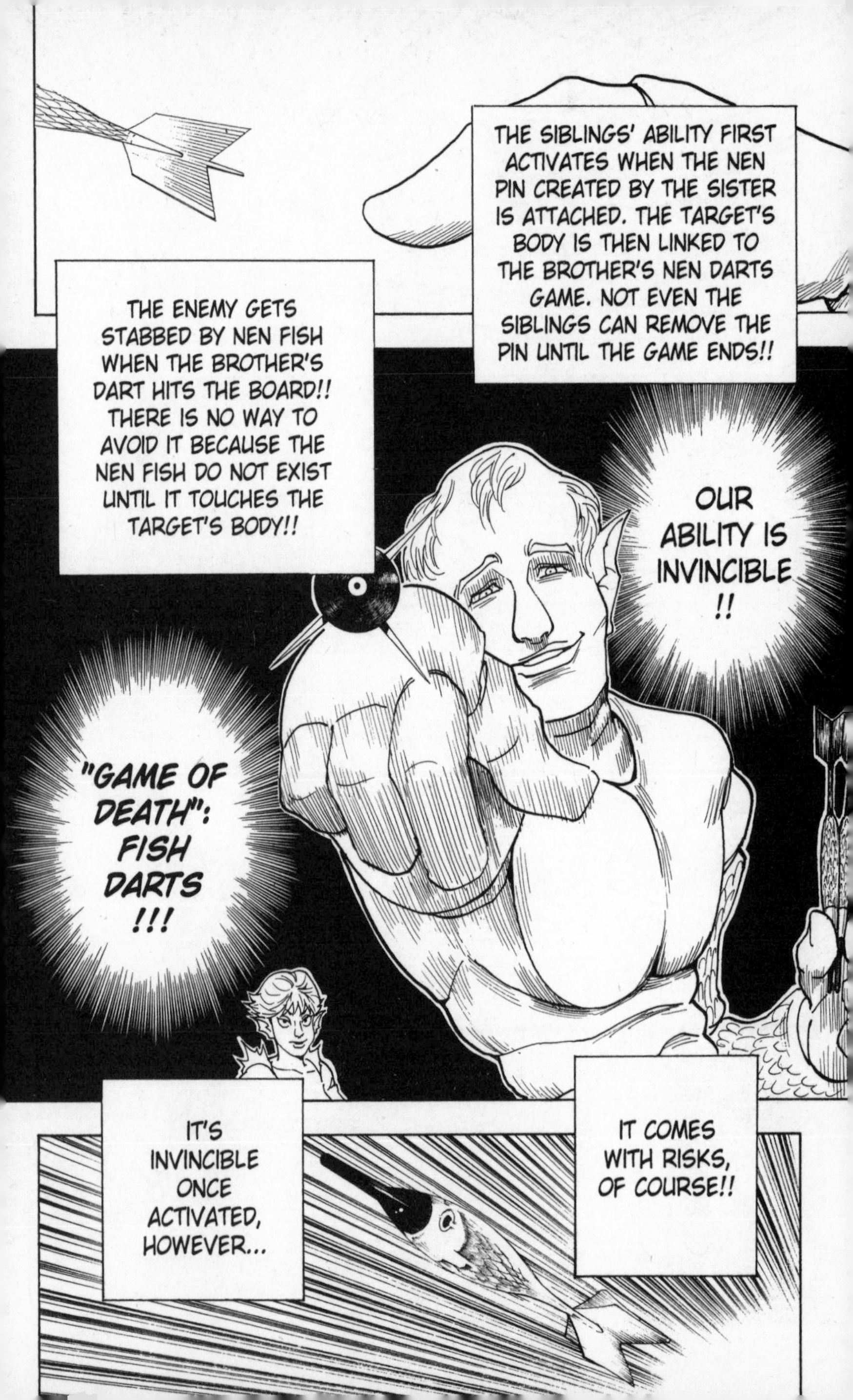
THE SIBLINGS' ABILITY FIRST ACTIVATES WHEN THE NEN PIN CREATED BY THE SISTER IS ATTACHED. THE TARGET'S BODY IS THEN LINKED TO THE BROTHER'S NEN DARTS GAME. NOT EVEN THE SIBLINGS CAN REMOVE THE PIN UNTIL THE GAME ENDS!!
THE ENEMY GETS STABBED BY NEN FISH WHEN THE BROTHER'S DART HITS THE BOARD!! THERE IS NO WAY TO AVOID IT BECAUSE THE NEN FISH DO NOT EXIST UNTIL IT TOUCHES THE TARGET'S BODY!!
OUR ABILITY IS INVINCIBLE !!
"GAME OF DEATH": FISH DARTS !!!
IT COMES WITH RISKS, OF COURSE!!
IT'S INVINCIBLE ONCE ACTIVATED, HOWEVER...

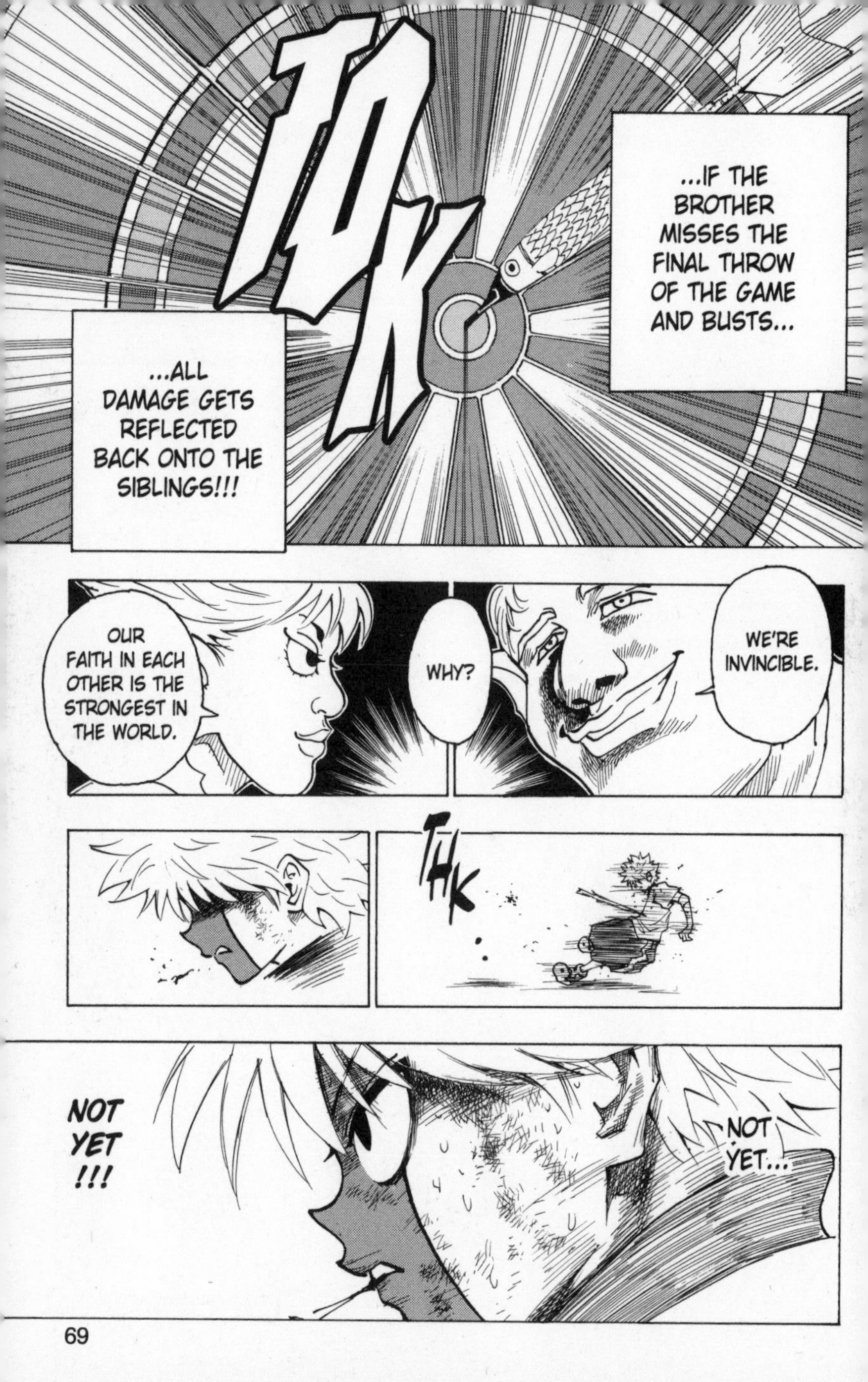
TOK
...IF THE BROTHER MISSES THE FINAL THROW OF THE GAME AND BUSTS...
...ALL DAMAGE GETS REFLECTED BACK ONTO THE SIBLINGS!!!
WE'RE INVINCIBLE.
WHY?
OUR FAITH IN EACH OTHER IS THE STRONGEST IN THE WORLD.
THK
NOT YET...
NOT YET!!!

Chapter 240: 8: Part 6

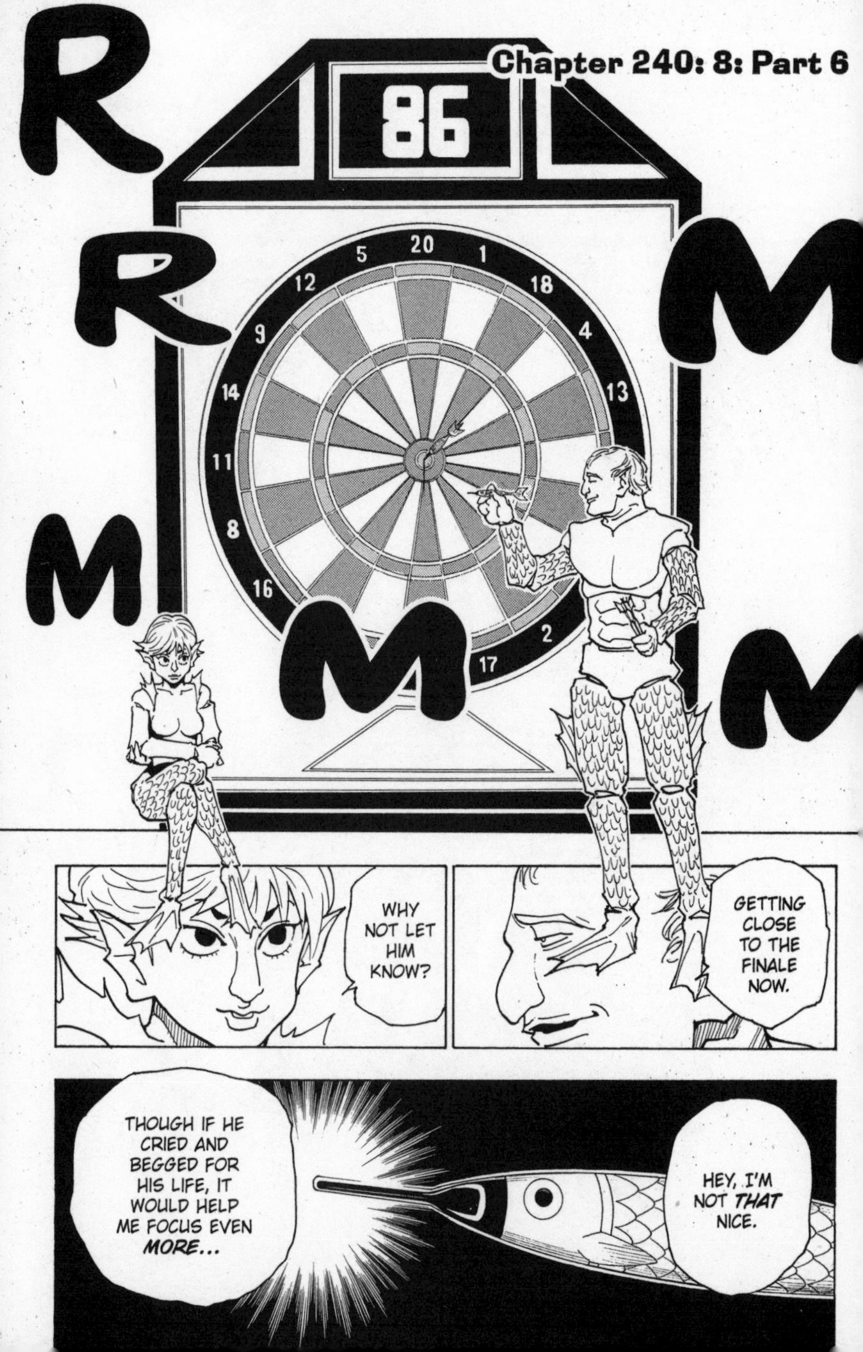
RRMMMM
86
GETTING CLOSE TO THE FINALE NOW.
WHY NOT LET HIM KNOW?
HEY, I'M NOT *THAT* NICE.
THOUGH IF HE CRIED AND BEGGED FOR HIS LIFE, IT WOULD HELP ME FOCUS EVEN ***MORE...***

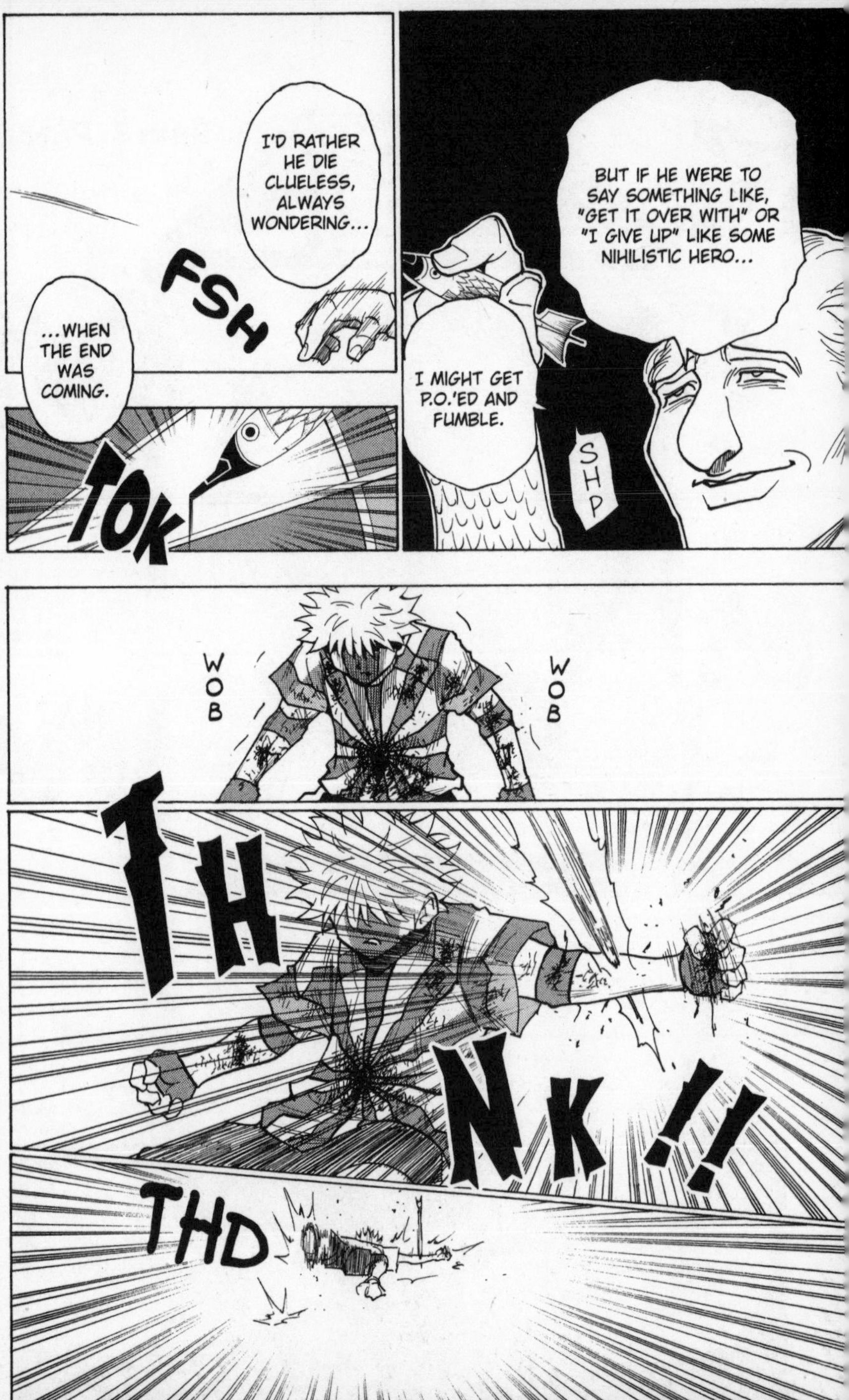
BUT IF HE WERE TO SAY SOMETHING LIKE, "GET IT OVER WITH" OR "I GIVE UP" LIKE SOME NIHILISTIC HERO...
I MIGHT GET P.O.'ED AND FUMBLE.
SHP
I'D RATHER HE DIE CLUELESS, ALWAYS WONDERING...
FSH
...WHEN THE END WAS COMING.
TOK
WOB
WOB
THNK!!
THD

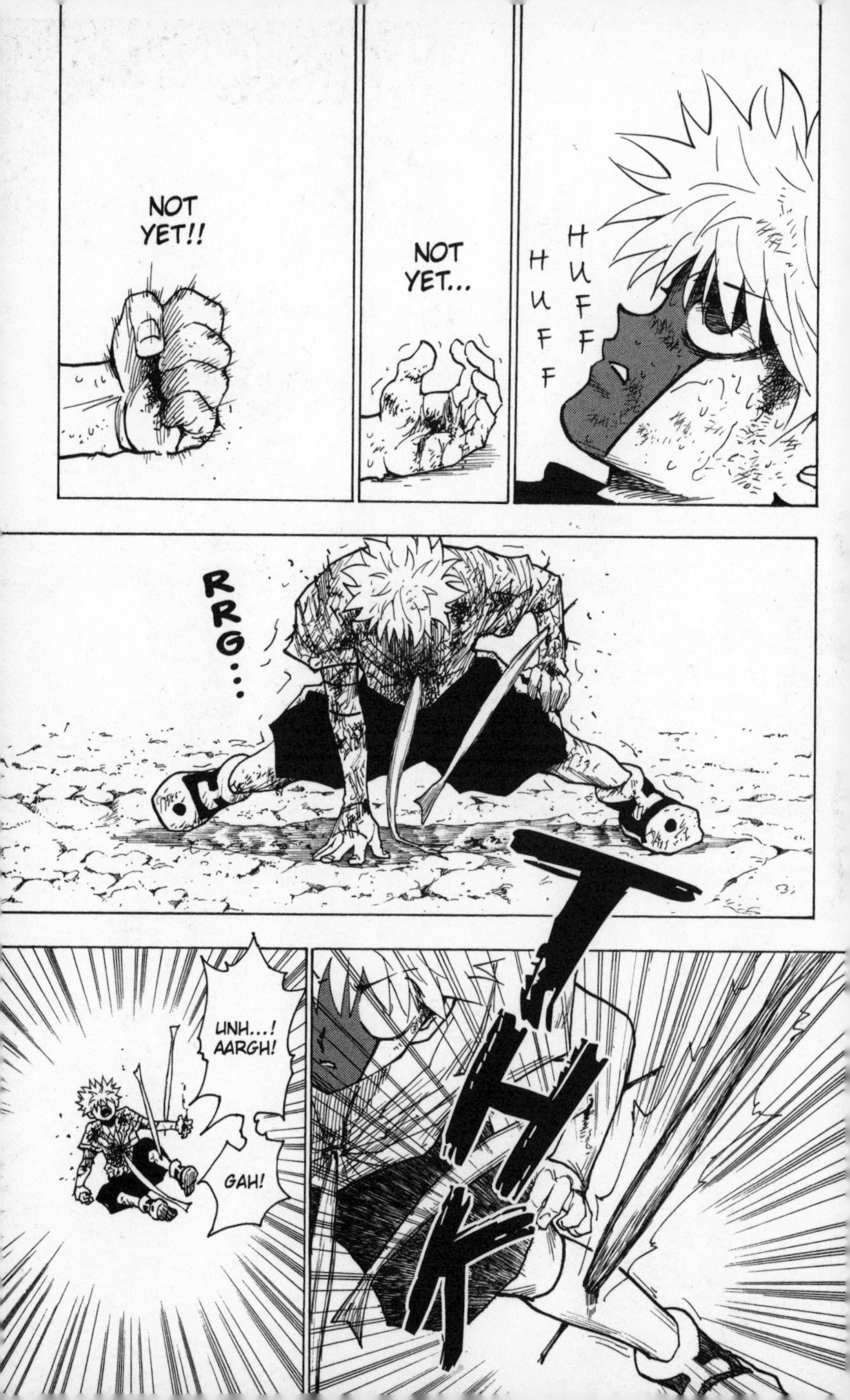
HUFF HUFF
NOT YET...
NOT YET!!
RRG...
THK
UNH...! AARGH!
GAH!

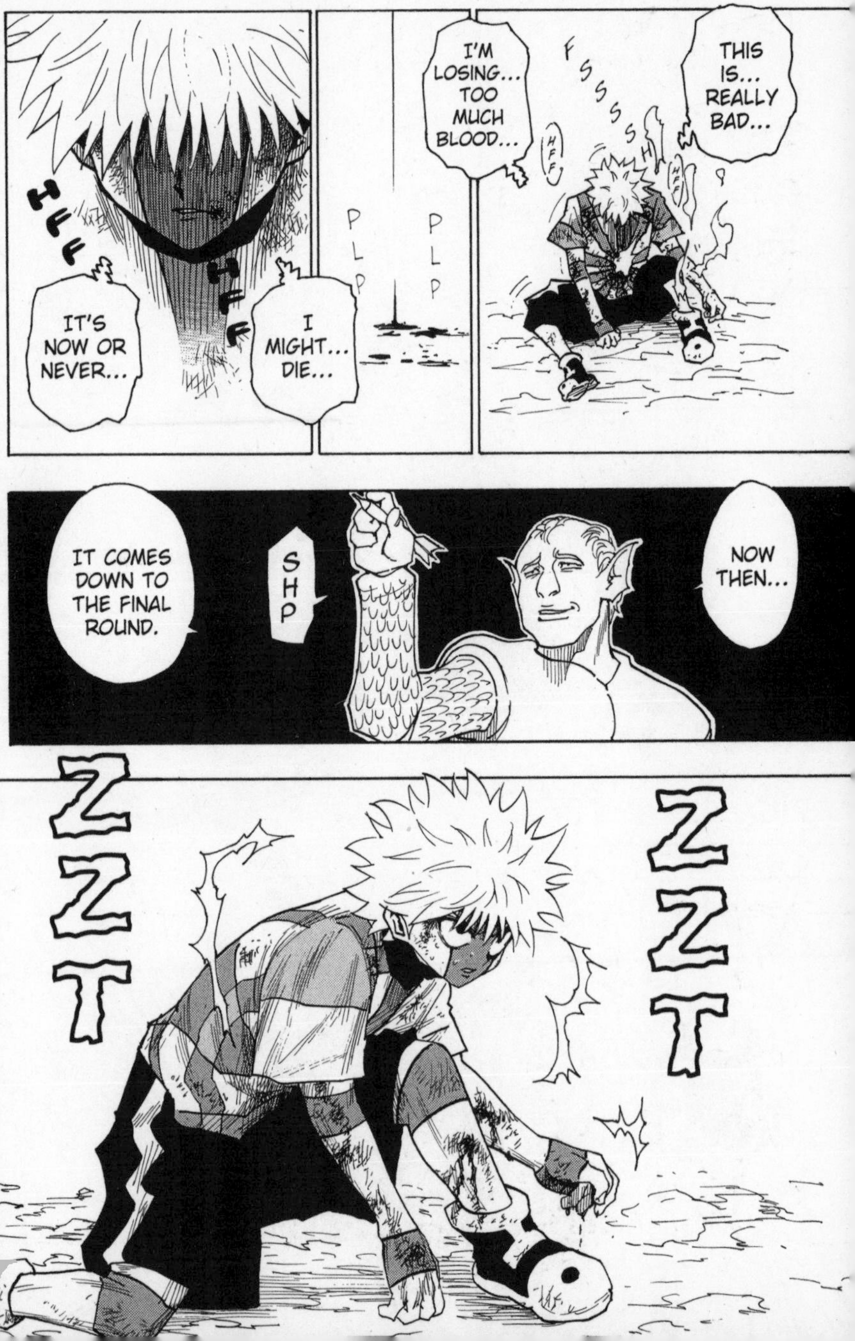
THIS IS... REALLY BAD...
FSSSSH
HFF
HFF
I'M LOSING... TOO MUCH BLOOD...
PLP
PLP
I MIGHT... DIE...
HFF
HFF
IT'S NOW OR NEVER...
NOW THEN...
SHP
IT COMES DOWN TO THE FINAL ROUND.
ZZT
ZZT

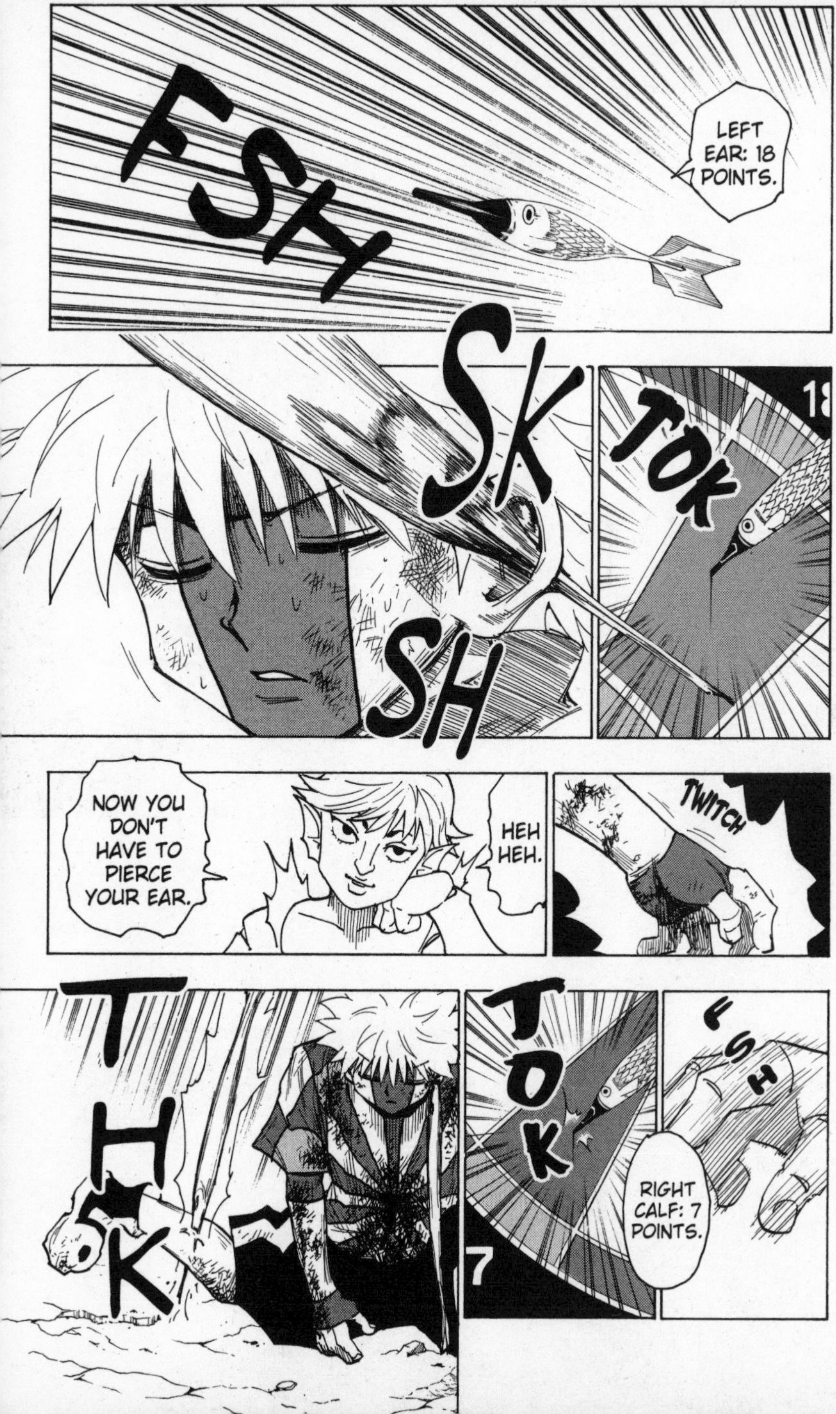
FSH
LEFT EAR: 18 POINTS.
18
TOK
SK
SH
TWITCH
HEH HEH.
NOW YOU DON'T HAVE TO PIERCE YOUR EAR.
FSH
RIGHT CALF: 7 POINTS.
TOK
7
THK

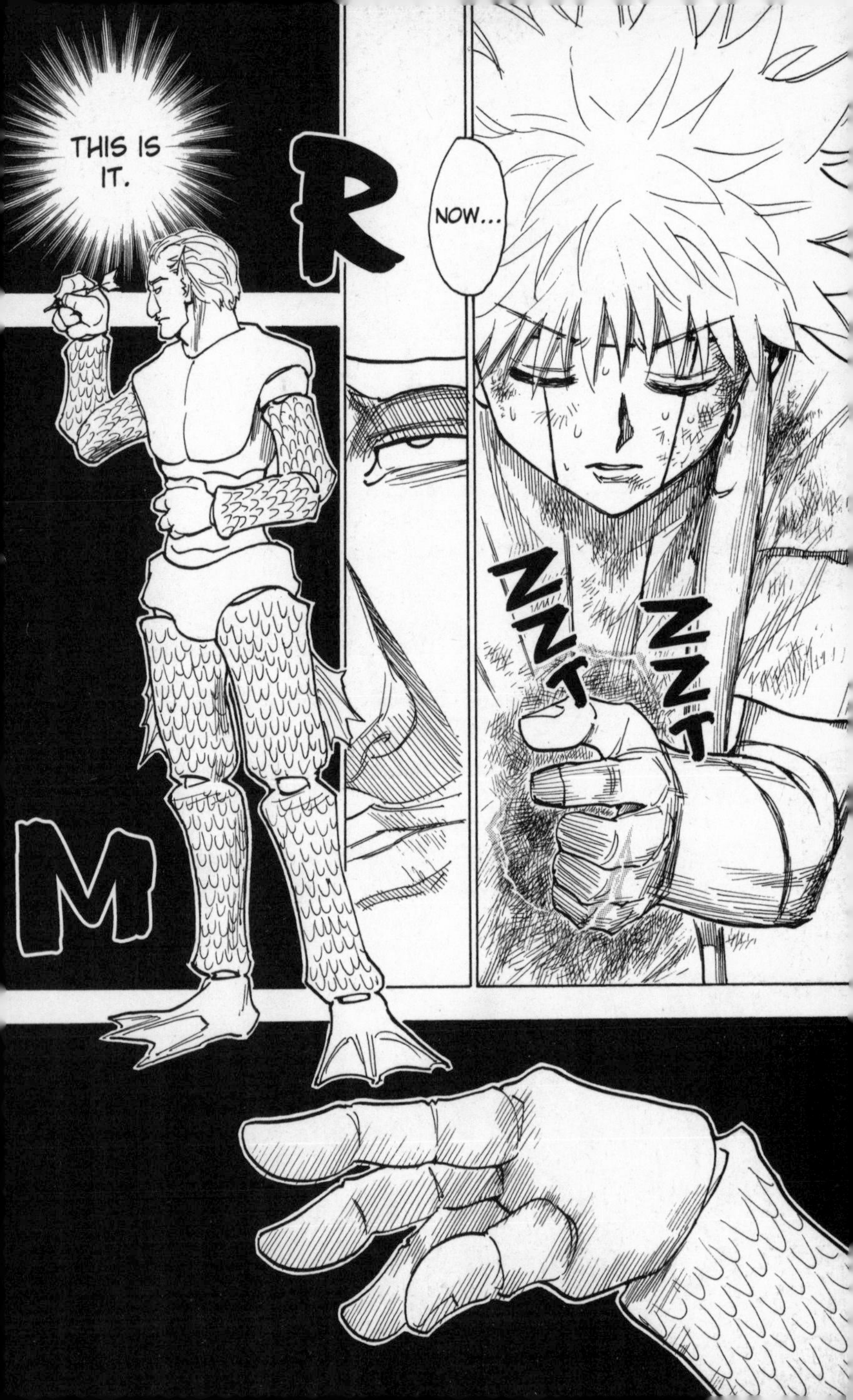
NOW...
ZZZT
ZZZT
R
THIS IS IT.
M

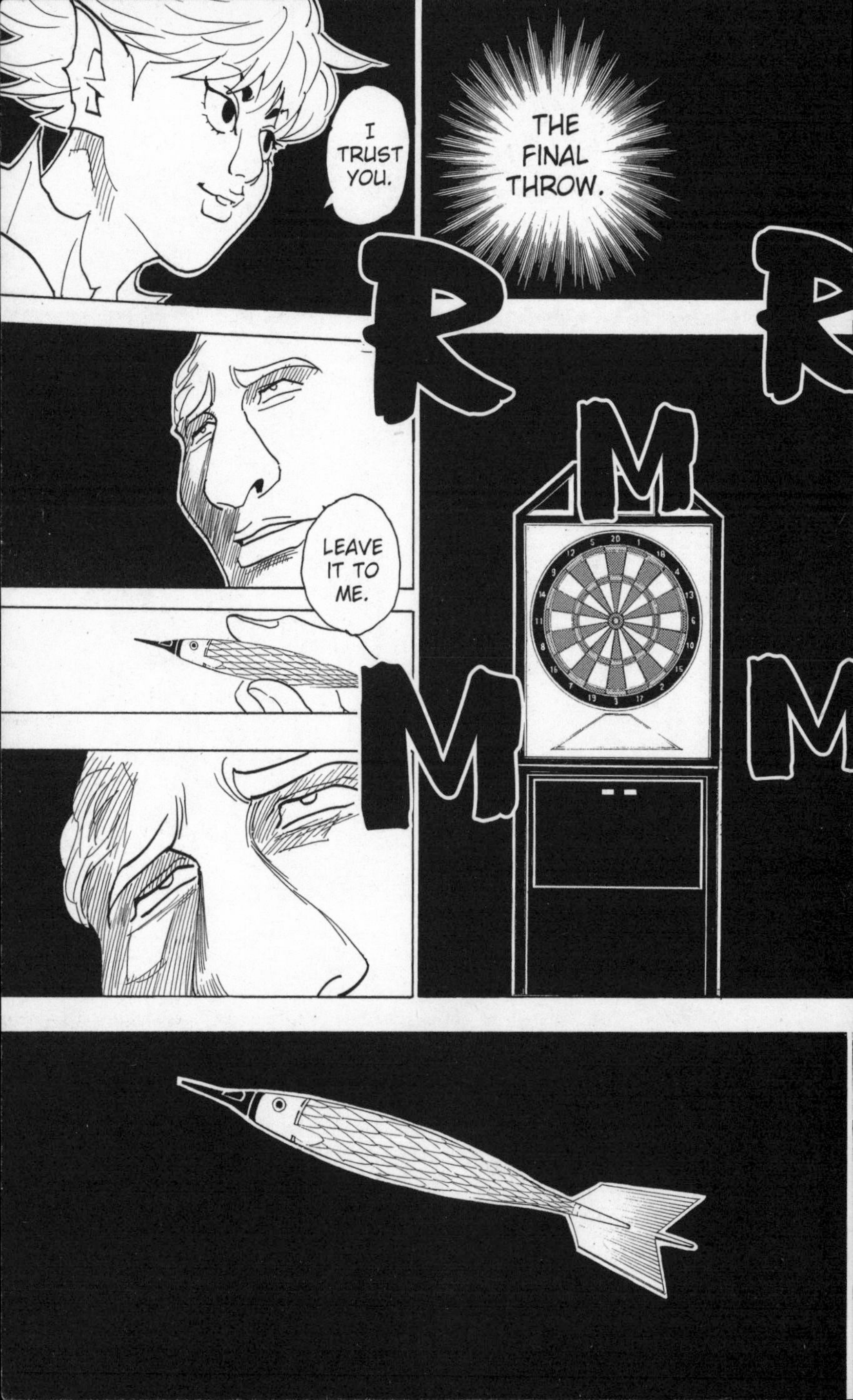
THE FINAL THROW.
I TRUST YOU.
RM
RMM
LEAVE IT TO ME.

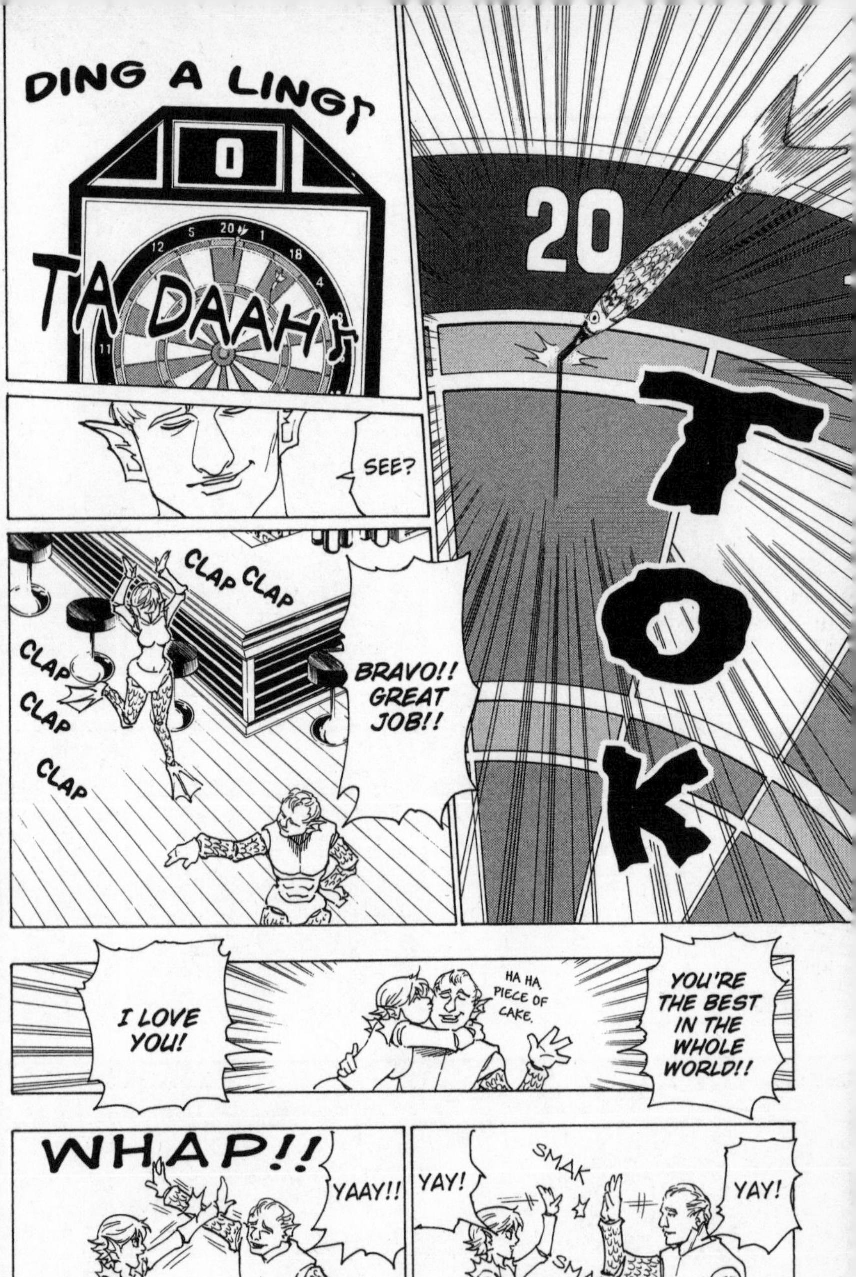
TOK
DING A LING♪
TA DAAH♪
SEE?
BRAVO!! GREAT JOB!!
CLAP CLAP
CLAP
CLAP
CLAP
YOU'RE THE BEST IN THE WHOLE WORLD!!
HA HA, PIECE OF CAKE.
I LOVE YOU!
YAY!
SMAK
YAY!
SMAK
YAAY!!
WHAP!!

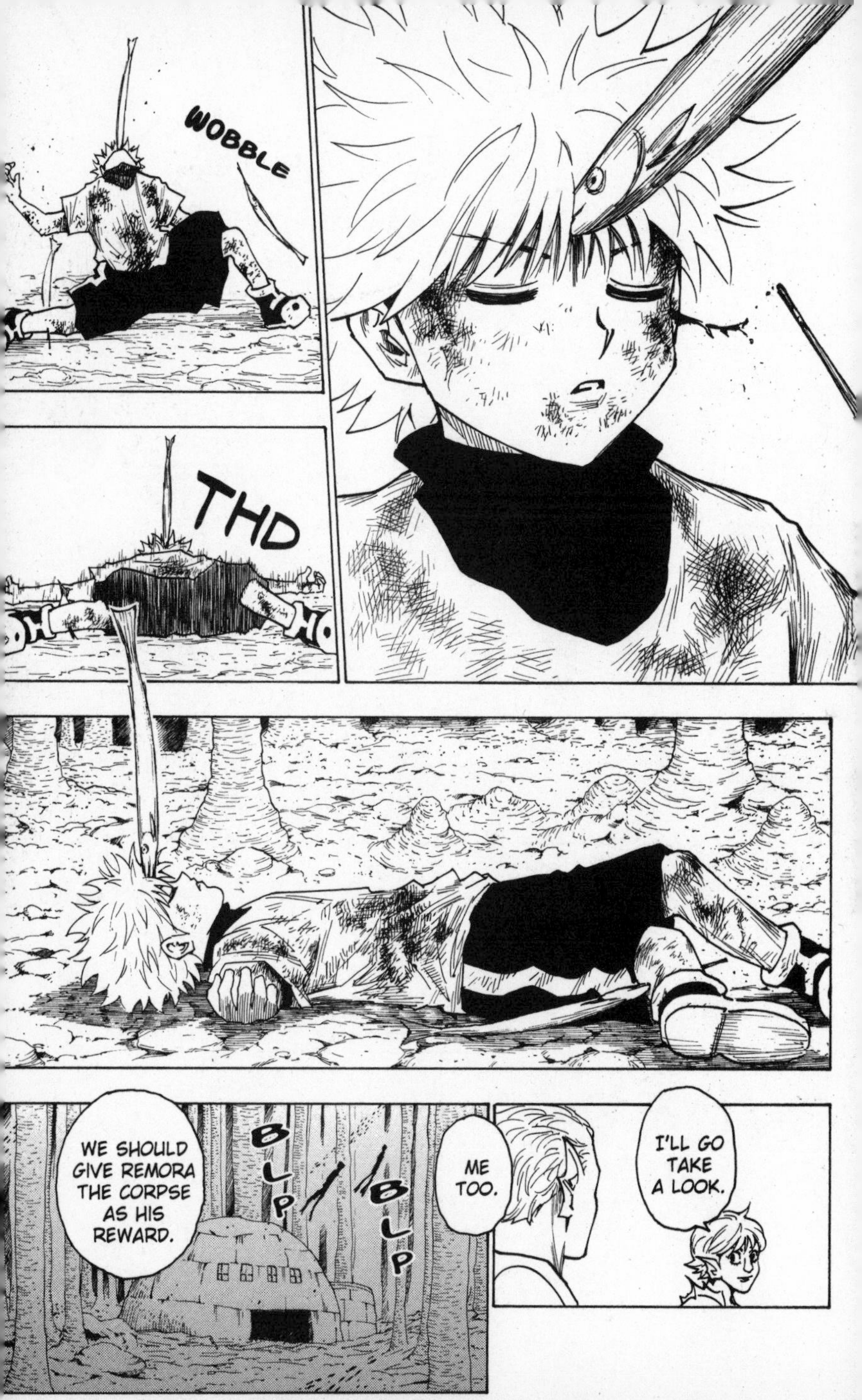
WOBBLE
THD
I'LL GO TAKE A LOOK.
ME TOO.
WE SHOULD GIVE REMORA THE CORPSE AS HIS REWARD.
BLUP
BLUP

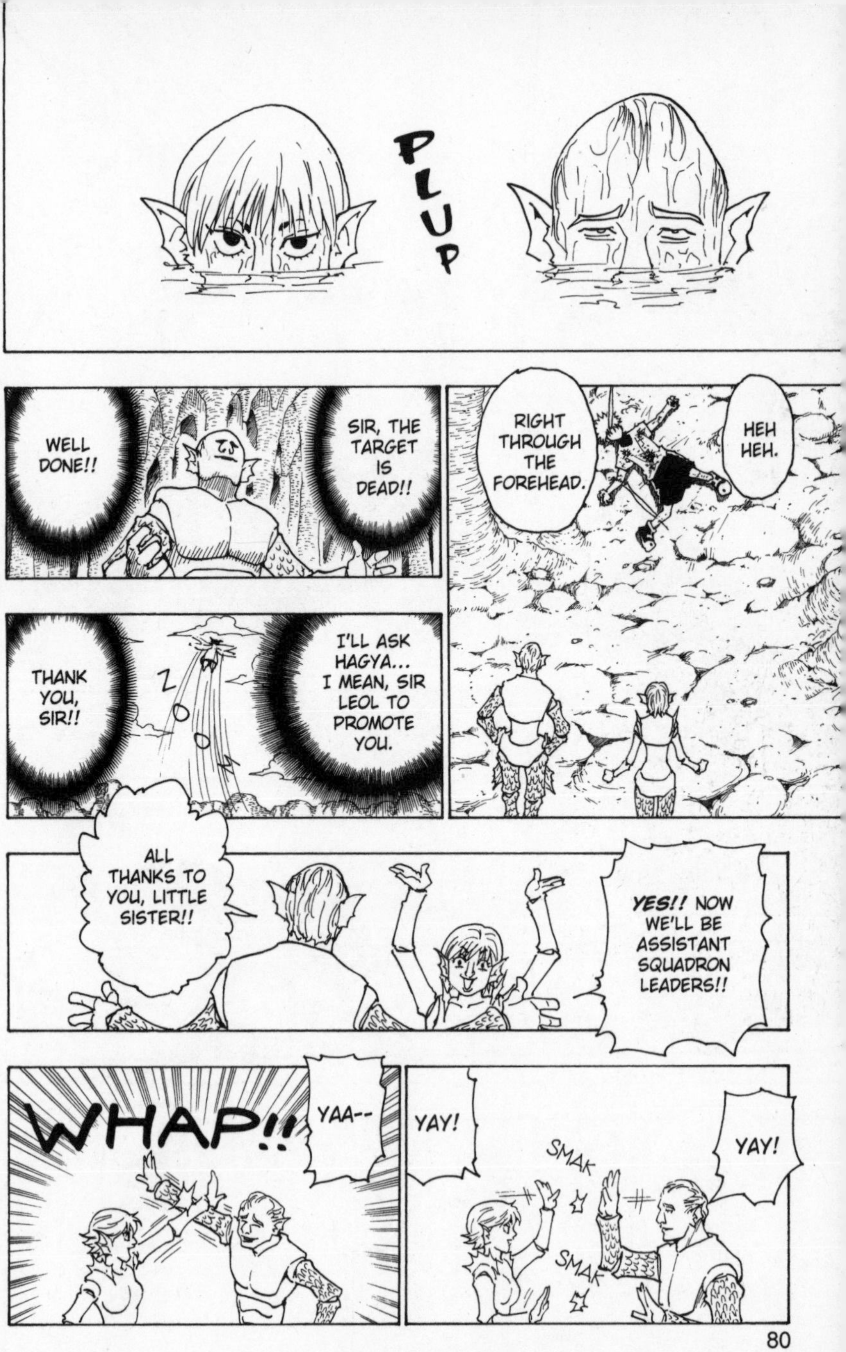
PLUP
HEH HEH.
RIGHT THROUGH THE FOREHEAD.
SIR, THE TARGET IS DEAD!!
WELL DONE!!
I'LL ASK HAGYA... I MEAN, SIR LEOL TO PROMOTE YOU.
ZOOO
THANK YOU, SIR!!
YES!! NOW WE'LL BE ASSISTANT SQUADRON LEADERS!!
ALL THANKS TO YOU, LITTLE SISTER!!
YAY!
SMAK
SMAK
YAY!
YAA--
WHAP!!

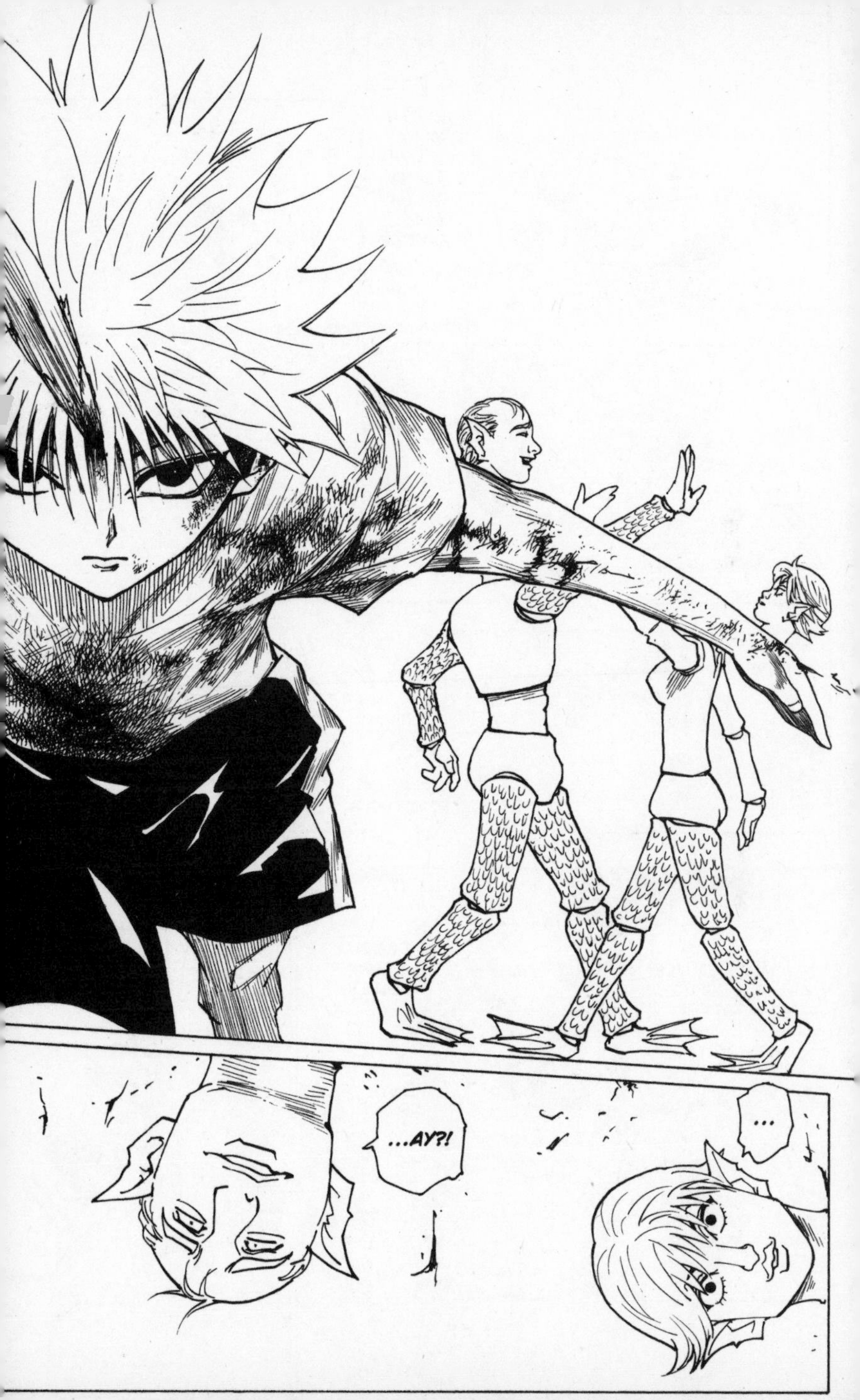
...
...AY?!

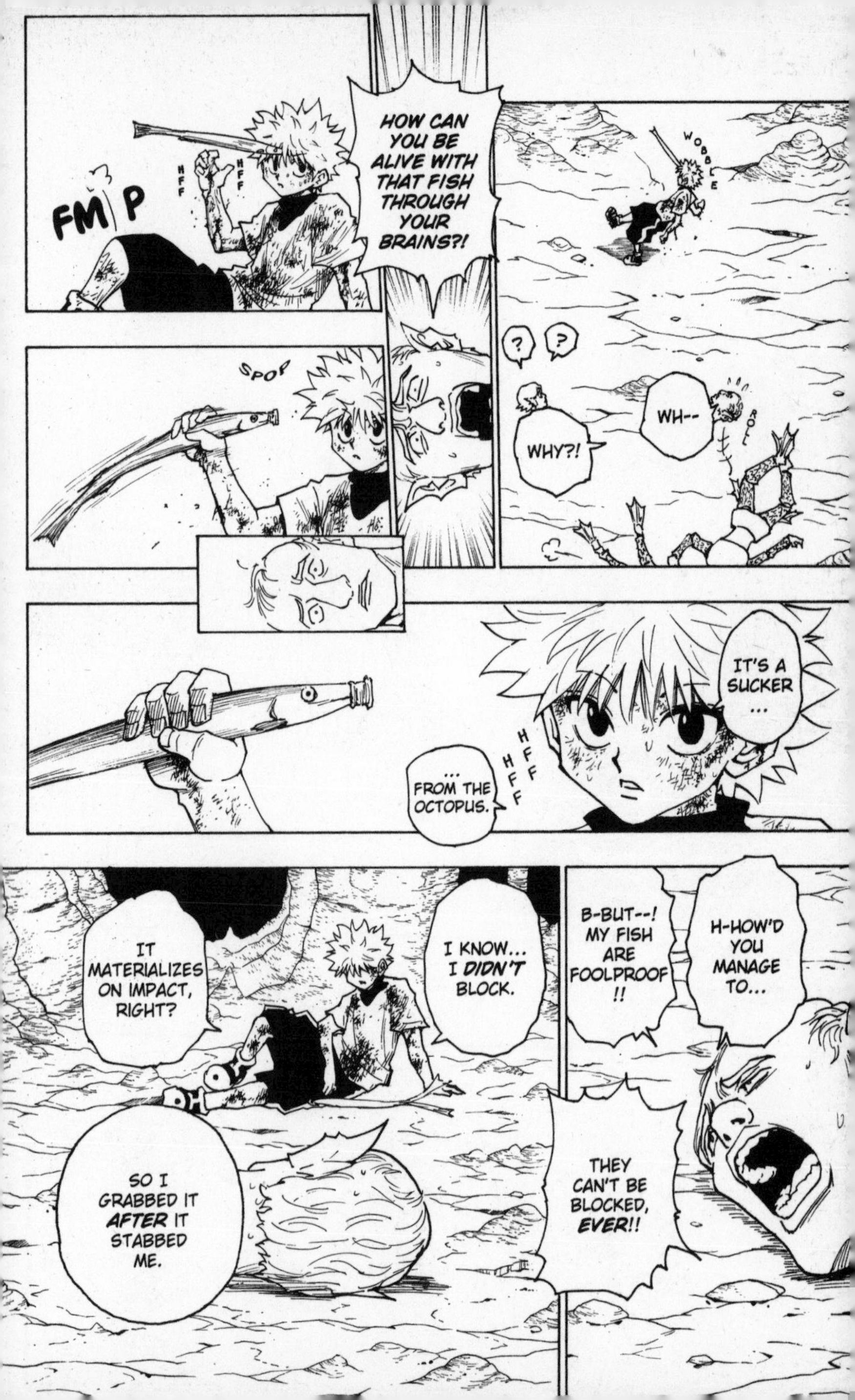
WOBBLE
?
?
WH--
ROLL
WHY?!
HOW CAN YOU BE ALIVE WITH THAT FISH THROUGH YOUR BRAINS?!
HFF HFF
FMP
SPOP
IT'S A SUCKER...
...FROM THE OCTOPUS.
HFF HFF
H-HOW'D YOU MANAGE TO...
B-BUT--! MY FISH ARE FOOLPROOF!!
THEY CAN'T BE BLOCKED, *EVER*!!
I KNOW... I *DIDN'T* BLOCK.
IT MATERIALIZES ON IMPACT, RIGHT?
SO I GRABBED IT *AFTER* IT STABBED ME.

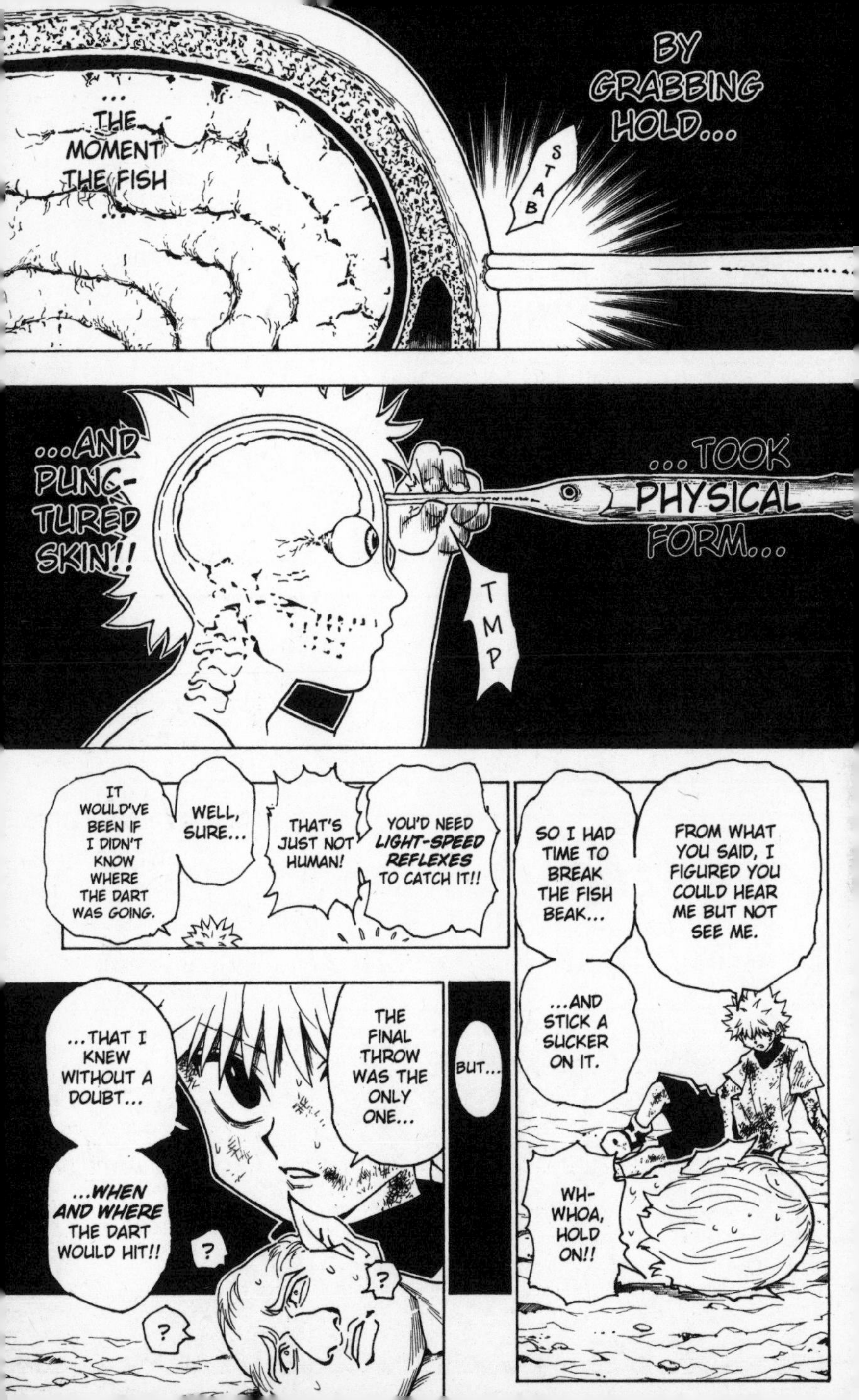
BY GRABBING HOLD...
STAB
...THE MOMENT THE FISH...
...TOOK PHYSICAL FORM...
TMP
...AND PUNCTURED SKIN!!
FROM WHAT YOU SAID, I FIGURED YOU COULD HEAR ME BUT NOT SEE ME.
SO I HAD TIME TO BREAK THE FISH BEAK...
...AND STICK A SUCKER ON IT.
WH- WHOA, HOLD ON!!
YOU'D NEED LIGHT-SPEED REFLEXES TO CATCH IT!!
THAT'S JUST NOT HUMAN!
WELL, SURE...
IT WOULD'VE BEEN IF I DIDN'T KNOW WHERE THE DART WAS GOING.
BUT...
THE FINAL THROW WAS THE ONLY ONE...
...THAT I KNEW WITHOUT A DOUBT...
...WHEN AND WHERE THE DART WOULD HIT!!
?
?
?

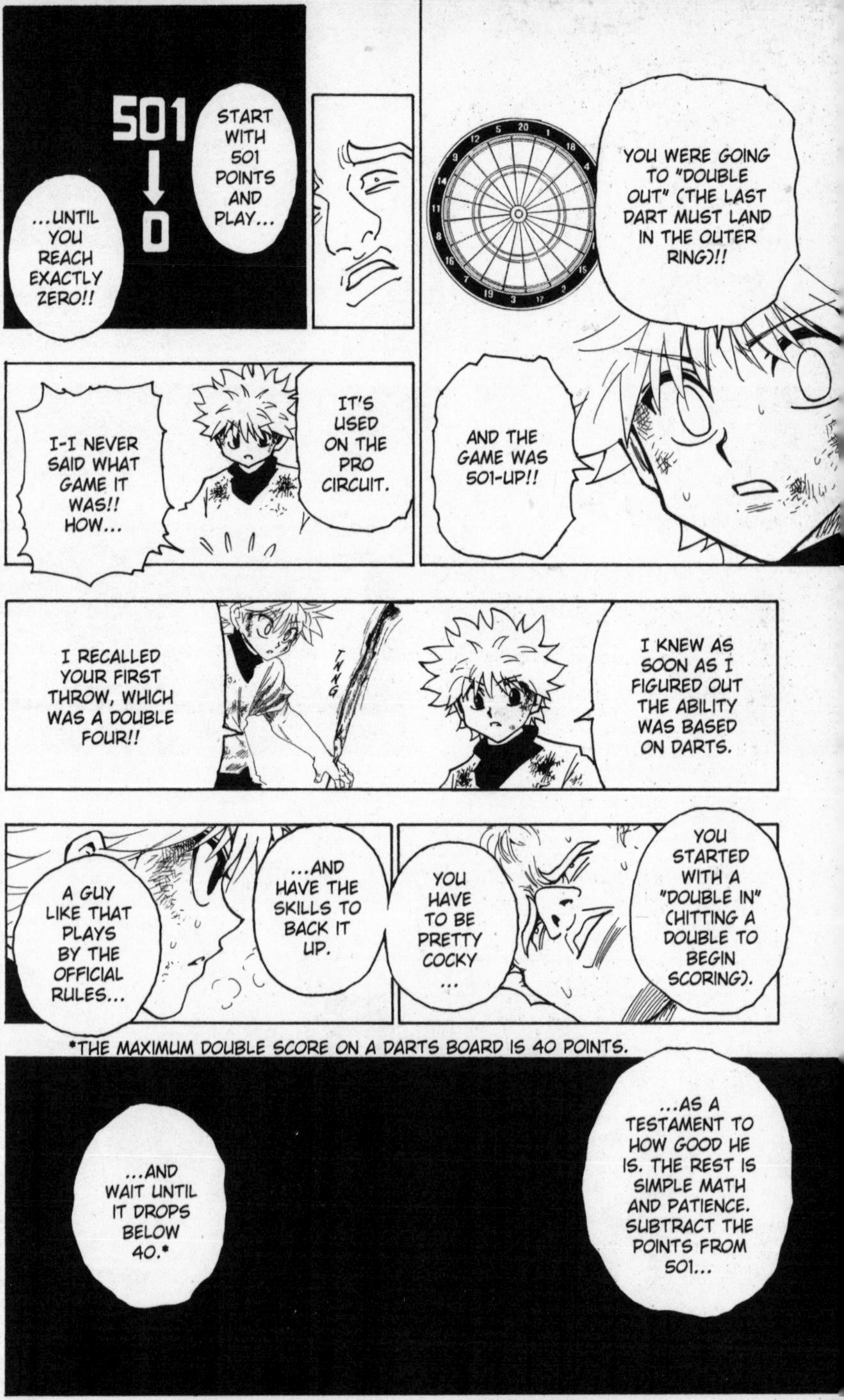
YOU WERE GOING TO "DOUBLE OUT" (THE LAST DART MUST LAND IN THE OUTER RING)!!
AND THE GAME WAS 501-UP!!
START WITH 501 POINTS AND PLAY...
501 → 0
...UNTIL YOU REACH EXACTLY ZERO!!
IT'S USED ON THE PRO CIRCUIT.
I-I NEVER SAID WHAT GAME IT WAS!! HOW...
I KNEW AS SOON AS I FIGURED OUT THE ABILITY WAS BASED ON DARTS.
TWNG
I RECALLED YOUR FIRST THROW, WHICH WAS A DOUBLE FOUR!!
YOU STARTED WITH A "DOUBLE IN" (HITTING A DOUBLE TO BEGIN SCORING).
YOU HAVE TO BE PRETTY COCKY ...
...AND HAVE THE SKILLS TO BACK IT UP.
A GUY LIKE THAT PLAYS BY THE OFFICIAL RULES...
...AS A TESTAMENT TO HOW GOOD HE IS. THE REST IS SIMPLE MATH AND PATIENCE. SUBTRACT THE POINTS FROM 501...
...AND WAIT UNTIL IT DROPS BELOW 40.*

*THE MAXIMUM DOUBLE SCORE ON A DARTS BOARD IS 40 POINTS.

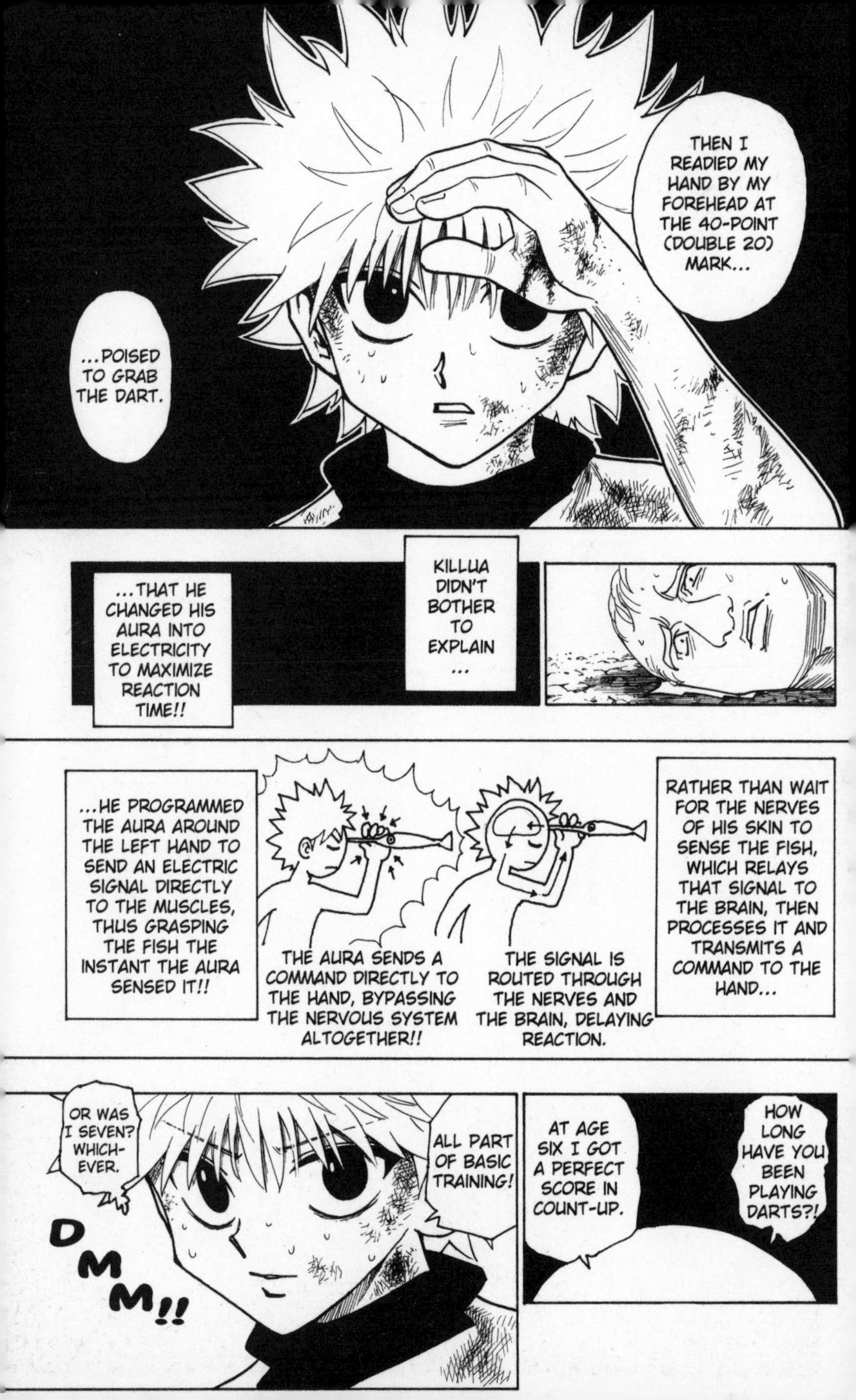
THEN I READIED MY HAND BY MY FOREHEAD AT THE 40-POINT (DOUBLE 20) MARK...
...POISED TO GRAB THE DART.
KILLUA DIDN'T BOTHER TO EXPLAIN ...
...THAT HE CHANGED HIS AURA INTO ELECTRICITY TO MAXIMIZE REACTION TIME!!
RATHER THAN WAIT FOR THE NERVES OF HIS SKIN TO SENSE THE FISH, WHICH RELAYS THAT SIGNAL TO THE BRAIN, THEN PROCESSES IT AND TRANSMITS A COMMAND TO THE HAND...
THE SIGNAL IS ROUTED THROUGH THE NERVES AND THE BRAIN, DELAYING REACTION.
THE AURA SENDS A COMMAND DIRECTLY TO THE HAND, BYPASSING THE NERVOUS SYSTEM ALTOGETHER!!
...HE PROGRAMMED THE AURA AROUND THE LEFT HAND TO SEND AN ELECTRIC SIGNAL DIRECTLY TO THE MUSCLES, THUS GRASPING THE FISH THE INSTANT THE AURA SENSED IT!!
HOW LONG HAVE YOU BEEN PLAYING DARTS?!
AT AGE SIX I GOT A PERFECT SCORE IN COUNT-UP.
ALL PART OF BASIC TRAINING!
OR WAS I SEVEN? WHICH-EVER.
DMM!!

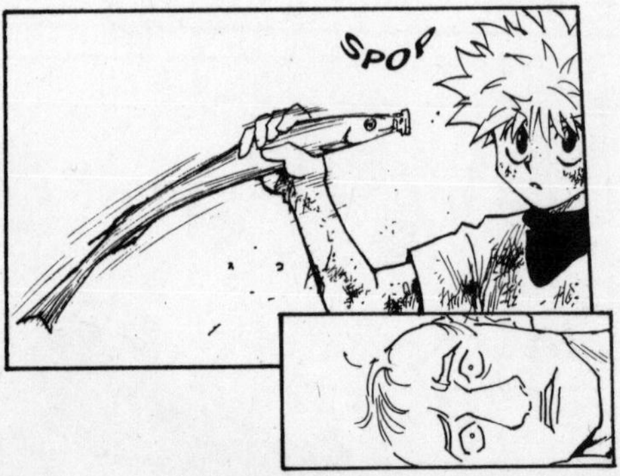
SPOP

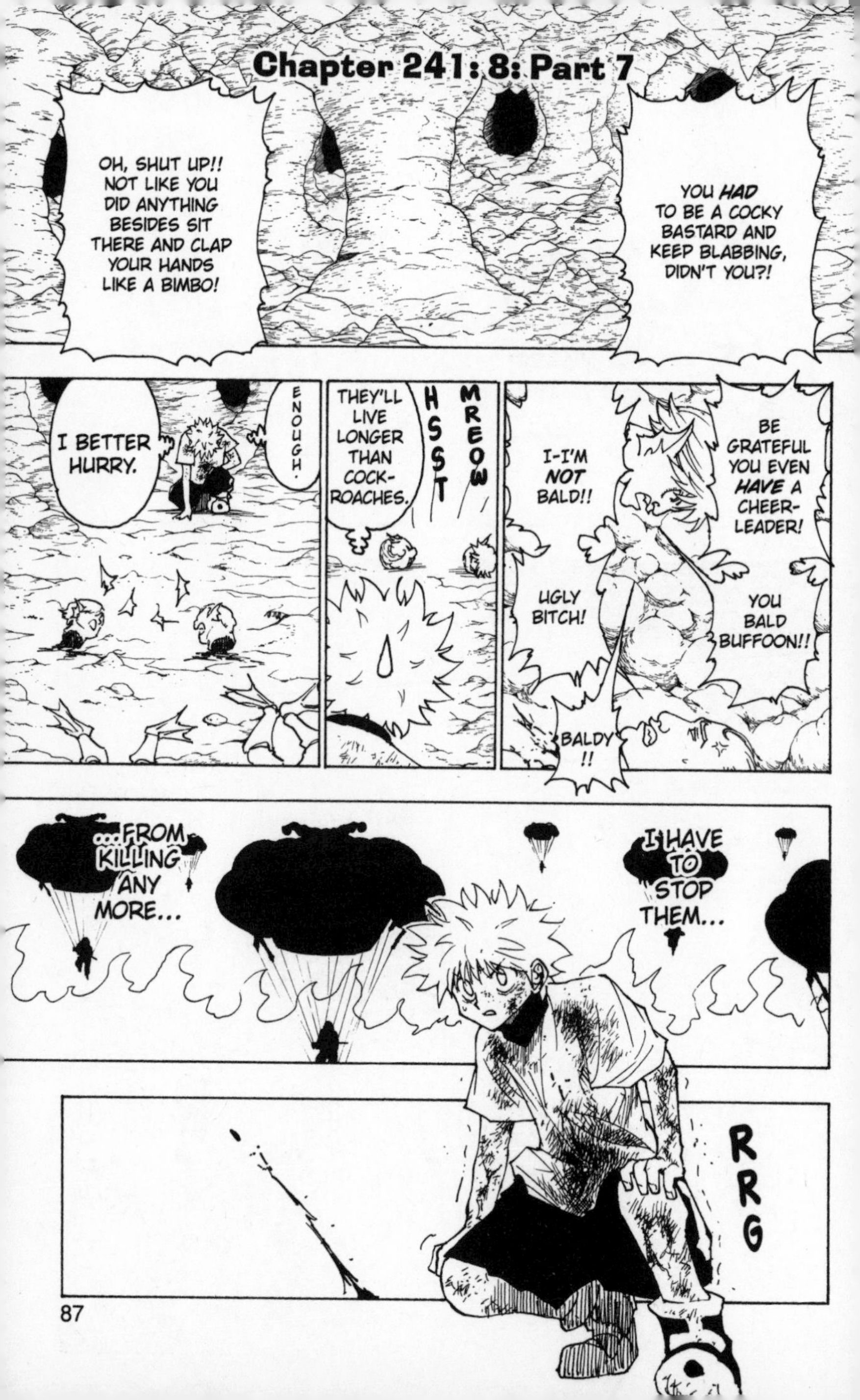
Chapter 241: 8: Part 7
YOU HAD TO BE A COCKY BASTARD AND KEEP BLABBING, DIDN'T YOU?!
OH, SHUT UP!! NOT LIKE YOU DID ANYTHING BESIDES SIT THERE AND CLAP YOUR HANDS LIKE A BIMBO!
BE GRATEFUL YOU EVEN HAVE A CHEER-LEADER!
I-I'M NOT BALD!!
YOU BALD BUFFOON!!
UGLY BITCH!
BALDY!!
MREOW
HSST
THEY'LL LIVE LONGER THAN COCK-ROACHES.
ENOUGH.
I BETTER HURRY.
I HAVE TO STOP THEM...
...FROM KILLING ANY MORE...
RRG

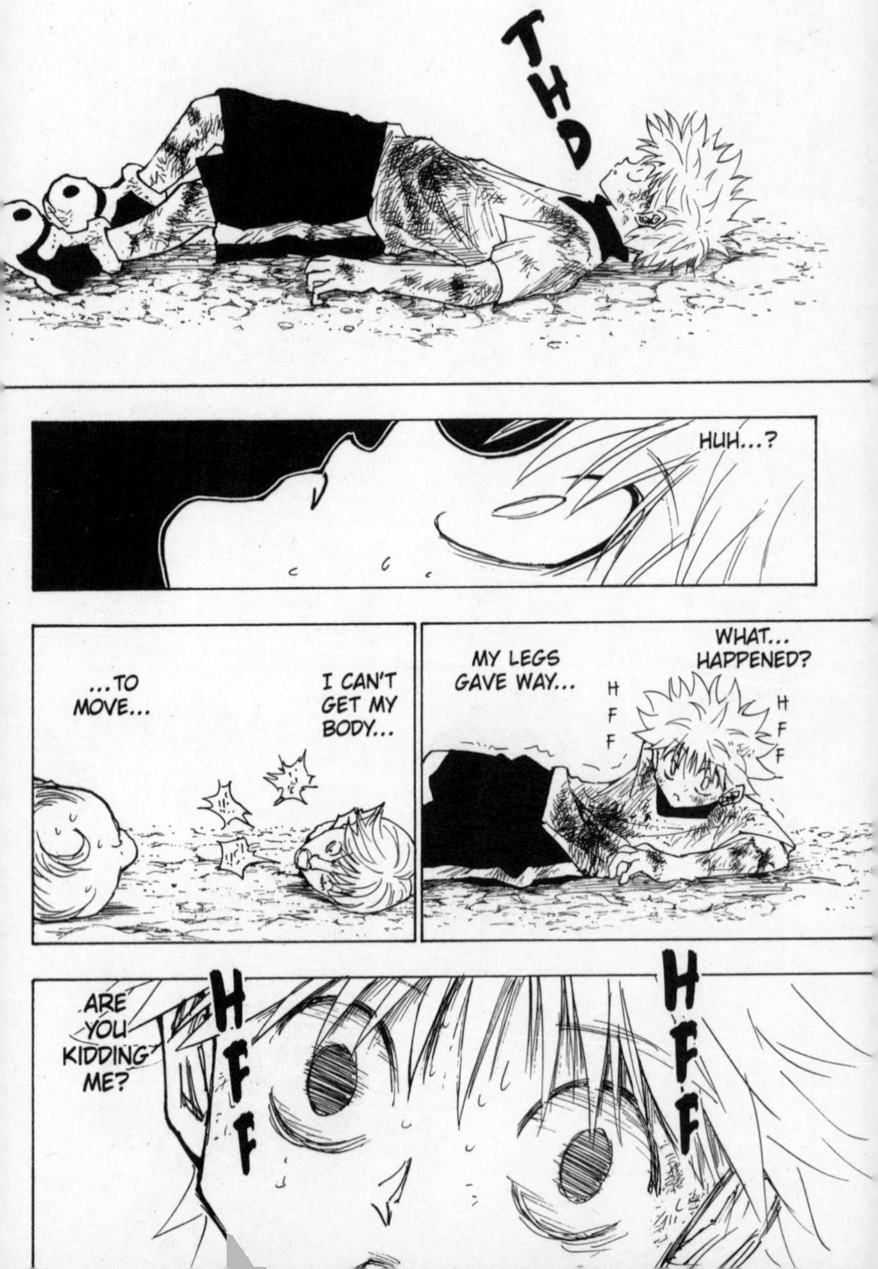
THD
HUH...?
WHAT... HAPPENED?
MY LEGS GAVE WAY...
HFF
HFF
I CAN'T GET MY BODY...
...TO MOVE...
HFF
HFF
ARE YOU KIDDING ME?

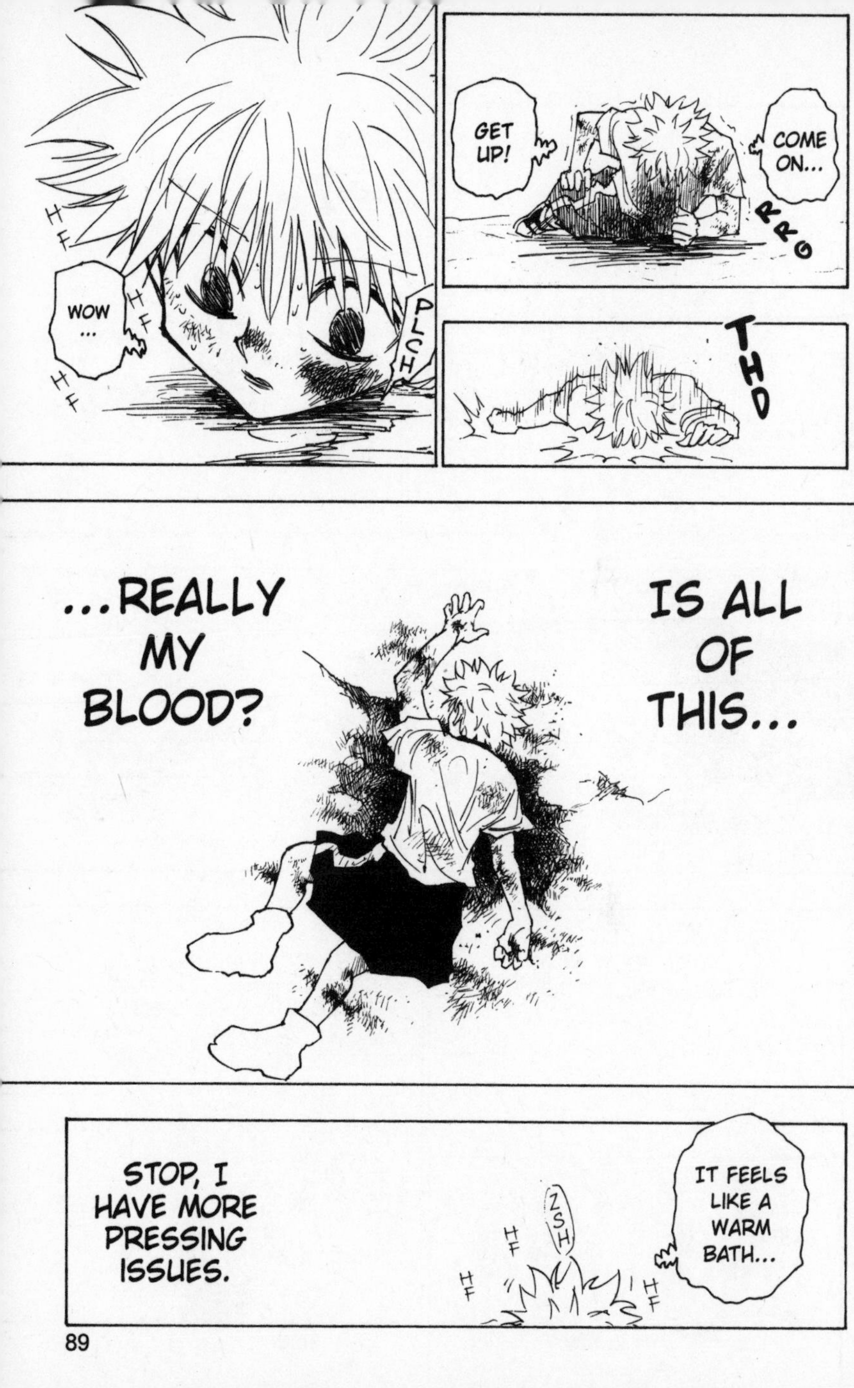
COME ON...
RRG
GET UP!
THD
PLCH
HF HF HF
WOW ...
IS ALL OF THIS...
...REALLY MY BLOOD?
IT FEELS LIKE A WARM BATH...
ZSH
HF HF HF
STOP, I HAVE MORE PRESSING ISSUES.

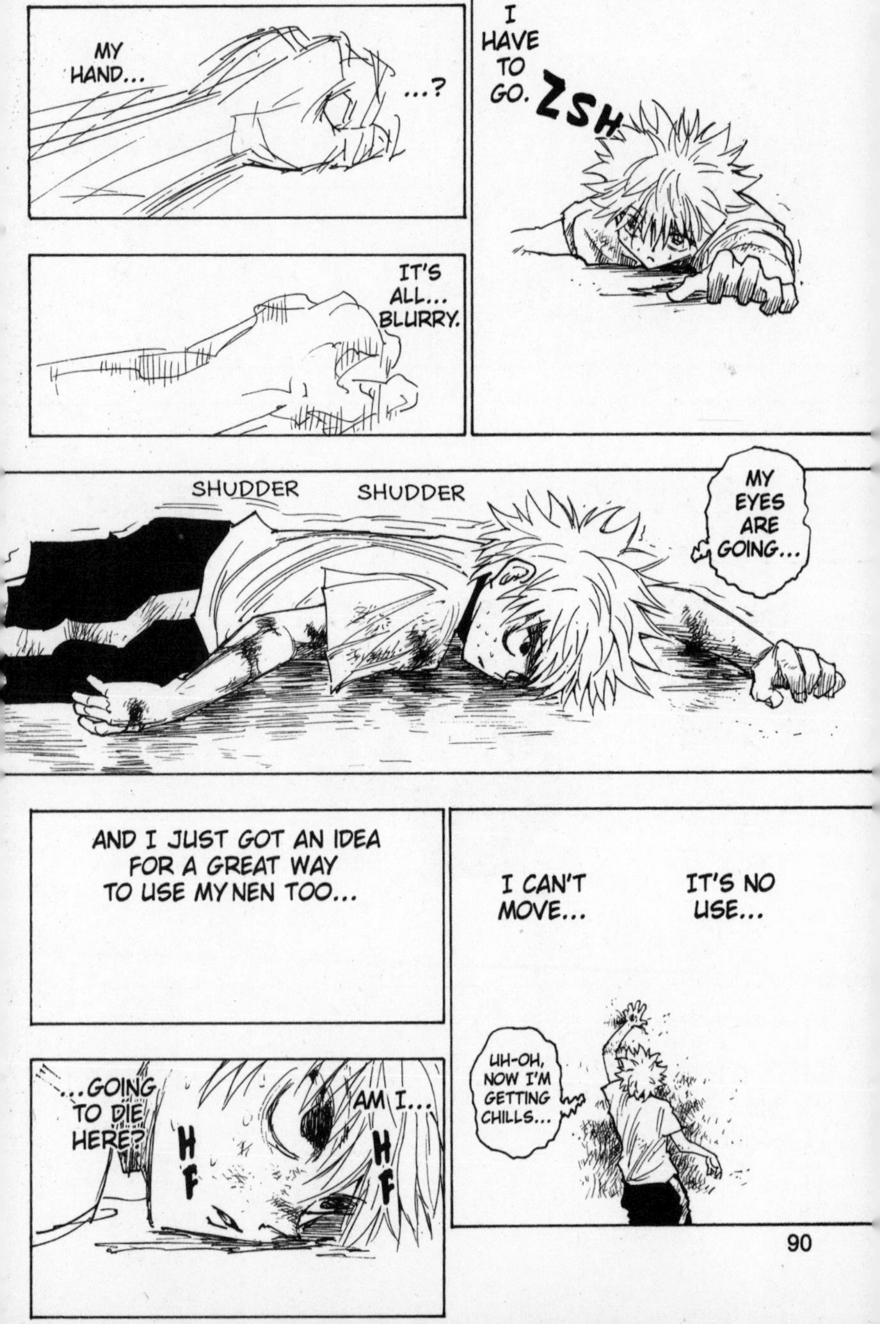
I HAVE TO GO.
ZSH
MY HAND...
...?
IT'S ALL... BLURRY.
MY EYES ARE GOING...
SHUDDER
SHUDDER
IT'S NO USE...
I CAN'T MOVE...
UH-OH, NOW I'M GETTING CHILLS...
AND I JUST GOT AN IDEA FOR A GREAT WAY TO USE MY NEN TOO...
AM I...
HF
HF
...GOING TO DIE HERE?

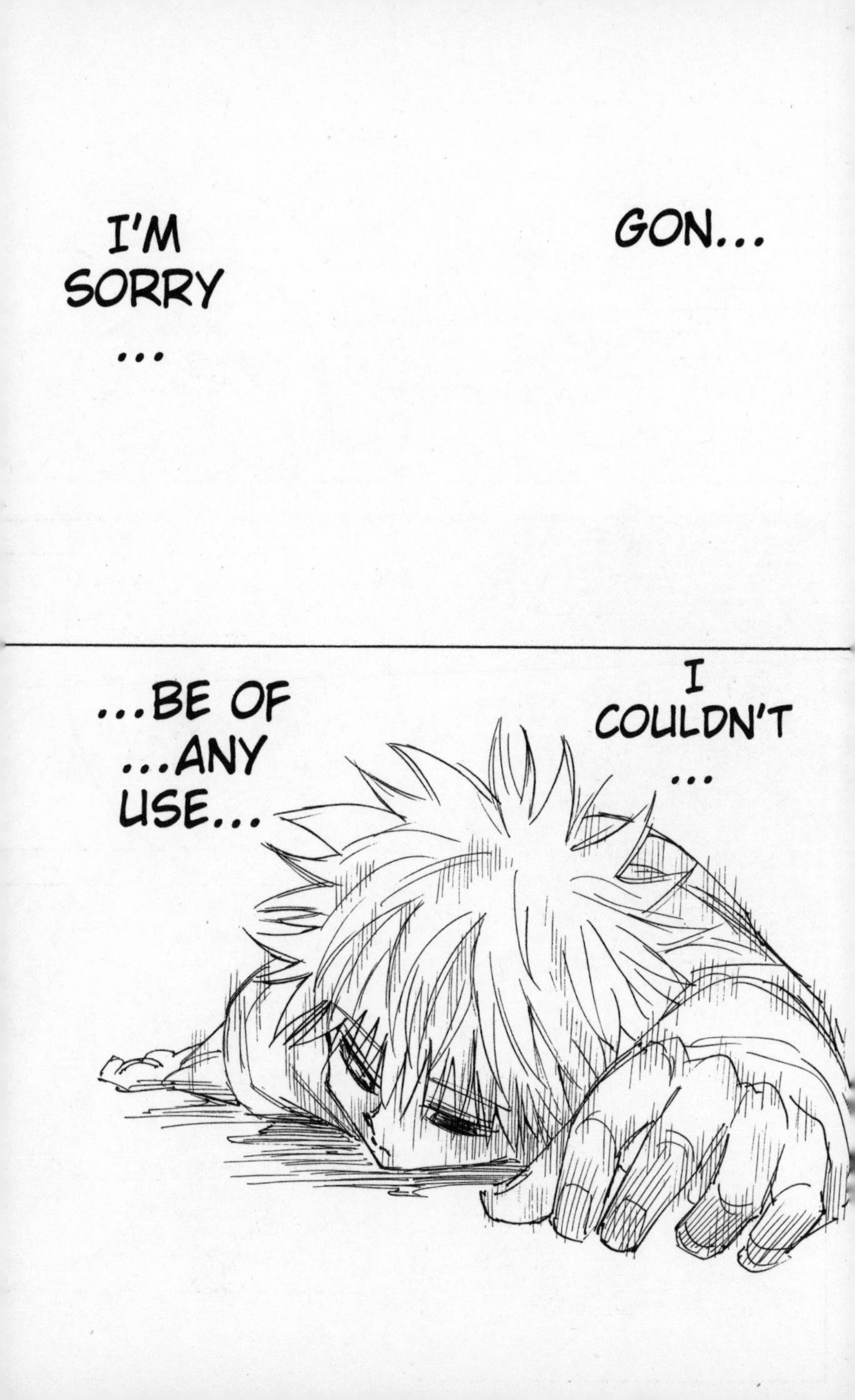
GON...
I'M SORRY ...
I COULDN'T ...
...BE OF ...ANY USE...

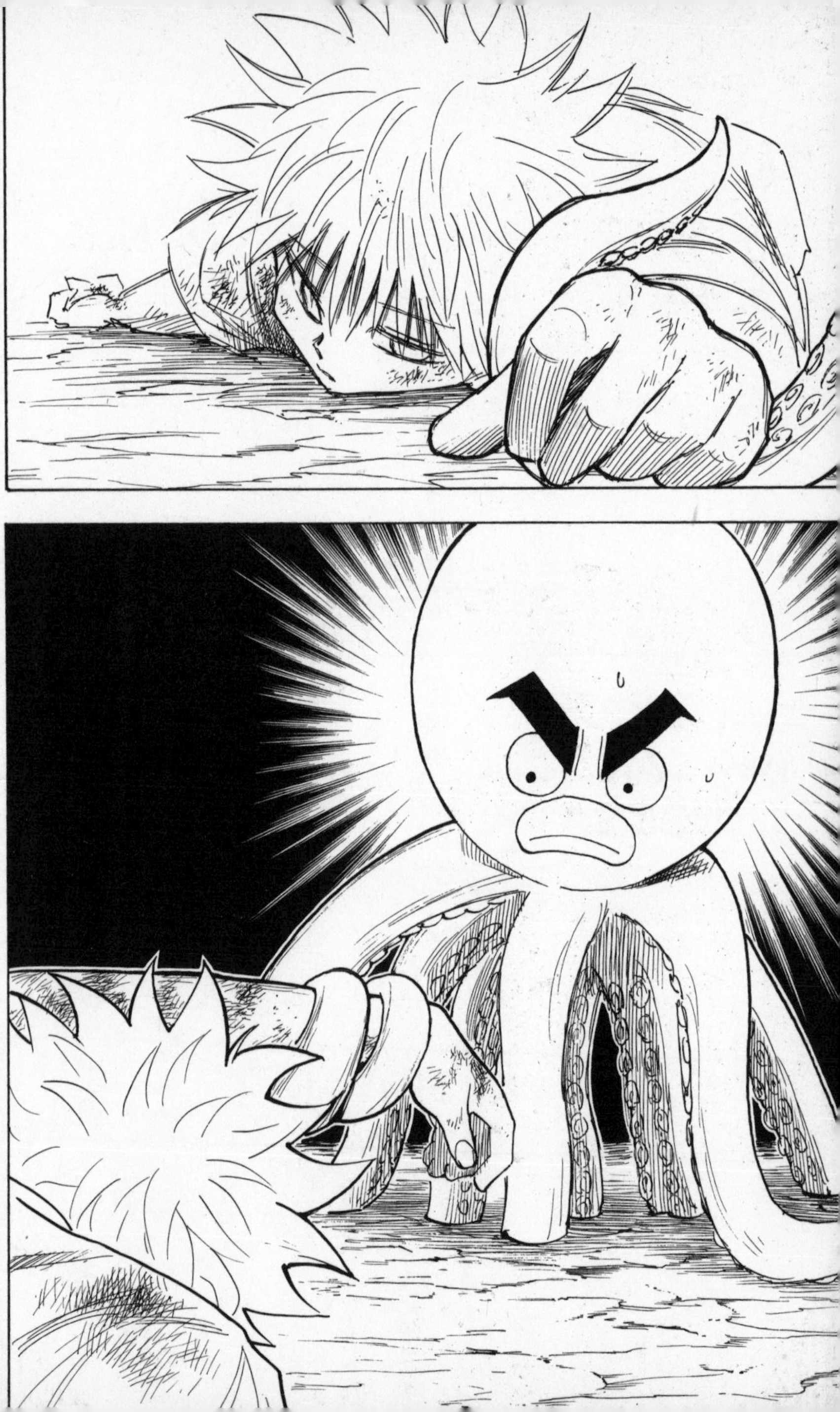

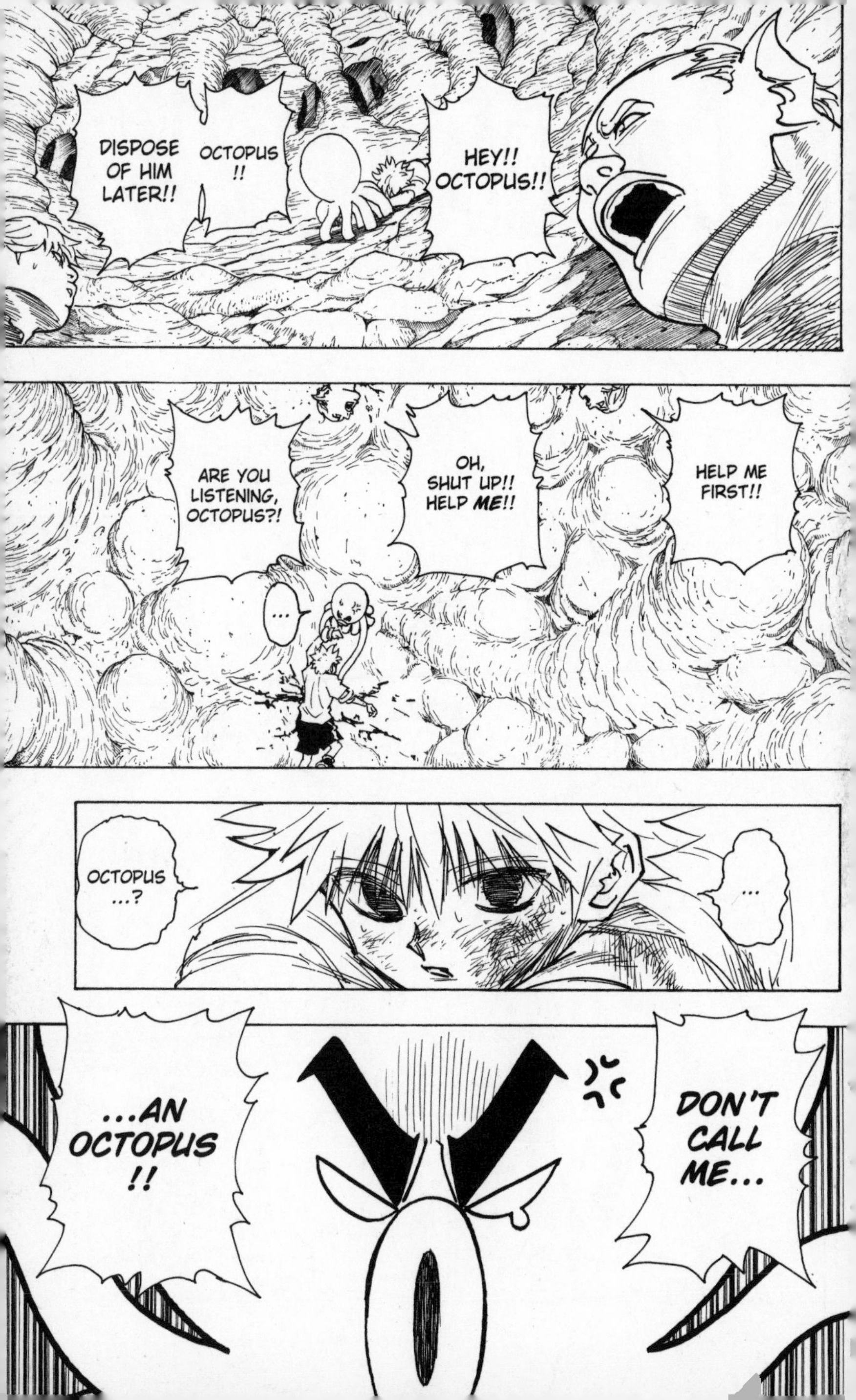
HEY!! OCTOPUS!!
OCTOPUS !!
DISPOSE OF HIM LATER!!
HELP ME FIRST!!
OH, SHUT UP!! HELP *ME*!!
ARE YOU LISTENING, OCTOPUS?!
...
...
OCTOPUS ...?
DON'T CALL ME...
...AN OCTOPUS !!

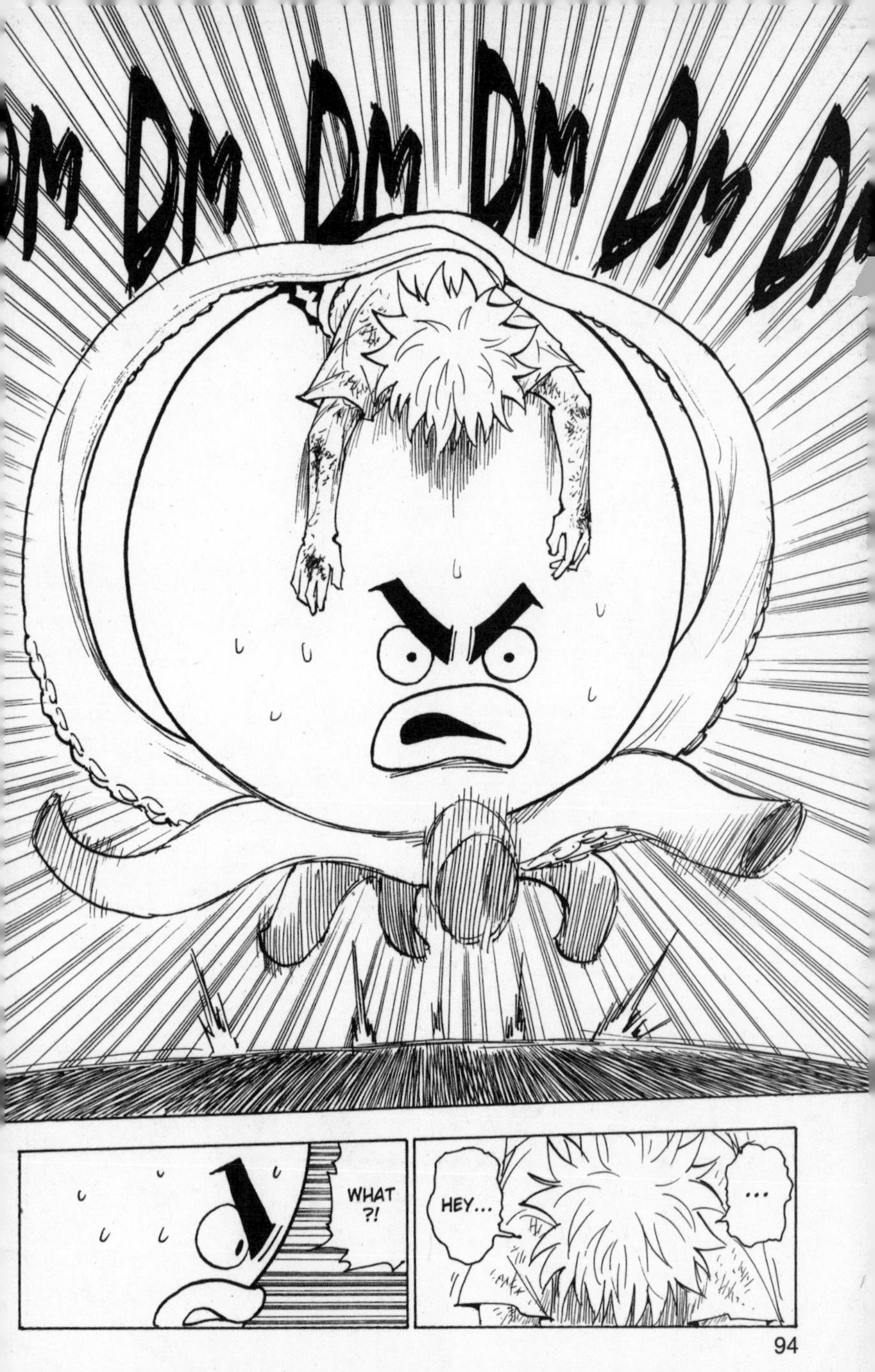
DM DM DM DM
...
HEY...
WHAT ?!

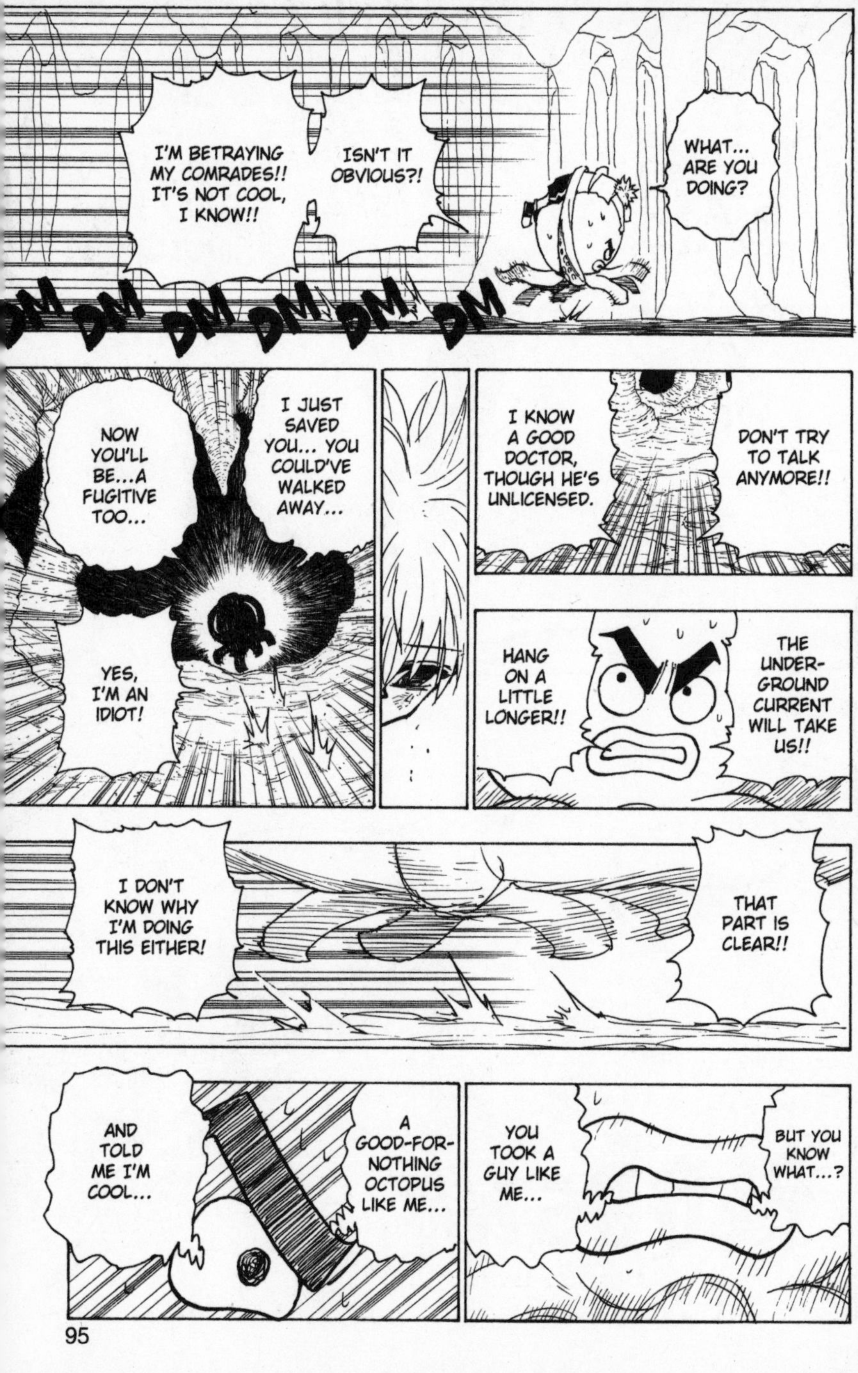
WHAT... ARE YOU DOING?
ISN'T IT OBVIOUS?!
I'M BETRAYING MY COMRADES!! IT'S NOT COOL, I KNOW!!
DM DM DM DM DM DM
DON'T TRY TO TALK ANYMORE!!
I KNOW A GOOD DOCTOR, THOUGH HE'S UNLICENSED.
THE UNDER-GROUND CURRENT WILL TAKE US!!
HANG ON A LITTLE LONGER!!
I JUST SAVED YOU... YOU COULD'VE WALKED AWAY...
NOW YOU'LL BE...A FUGITIVE TOO...
YES, I'M AN IDIOT!
THAT PART IS CLEAR!!
I DON'T KNOW WHY I'M DOING THIS EITHER!
BUT YOU KNOW WHAT...?
YOU TOOK A GUY LIKE ME...
A GOOD-FOR-NOTHING OCTOPUS LIKE ME...
AND TOLD ME I'M COOL...

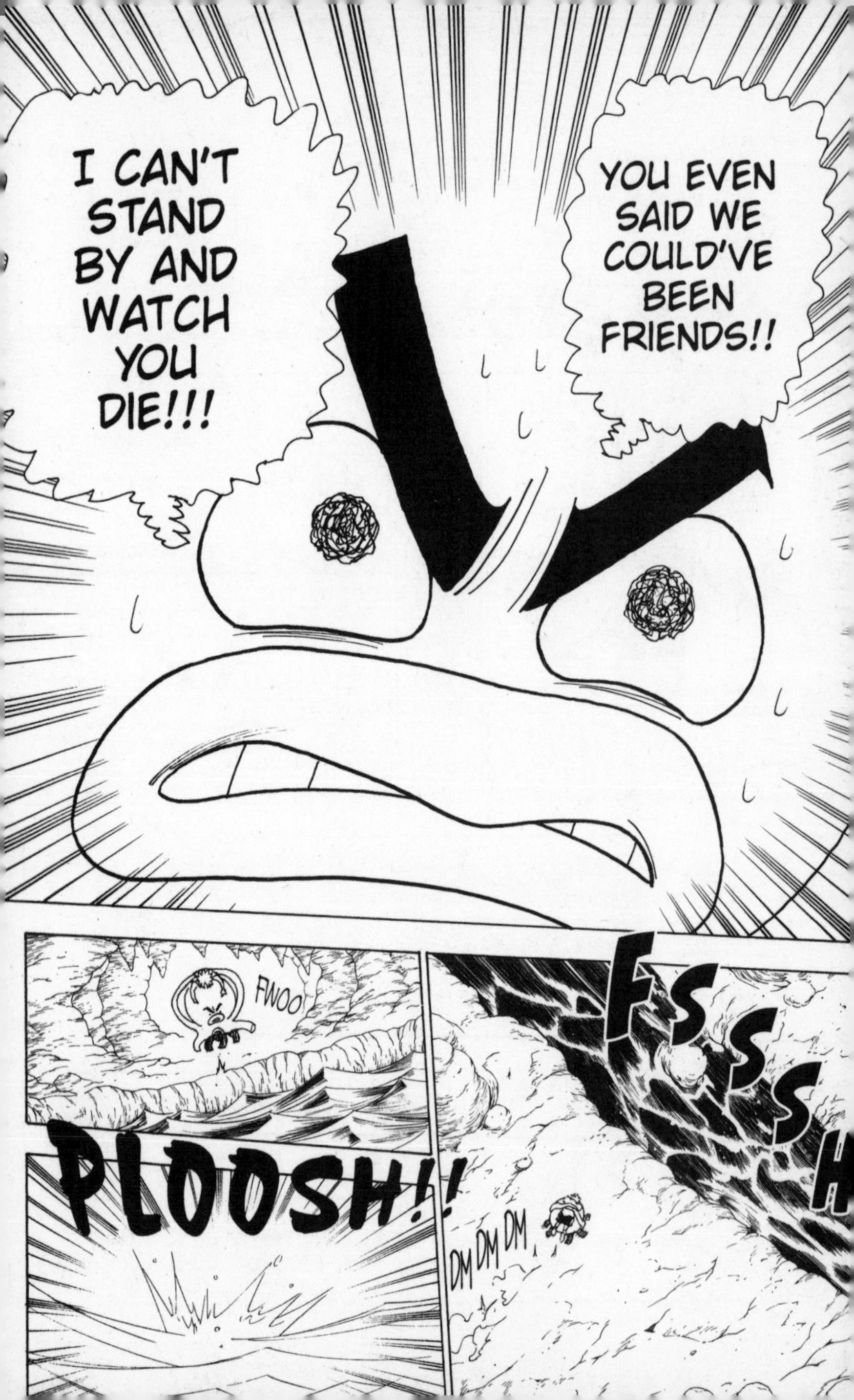
YOU EVEN SAID WE COULD'VE BEEN FRIENDS!!
I CAN'T STAND BY AND WATCH YOU DIE!!!
FSSSH
DM DM DM
FWOO
PLOOSH!!

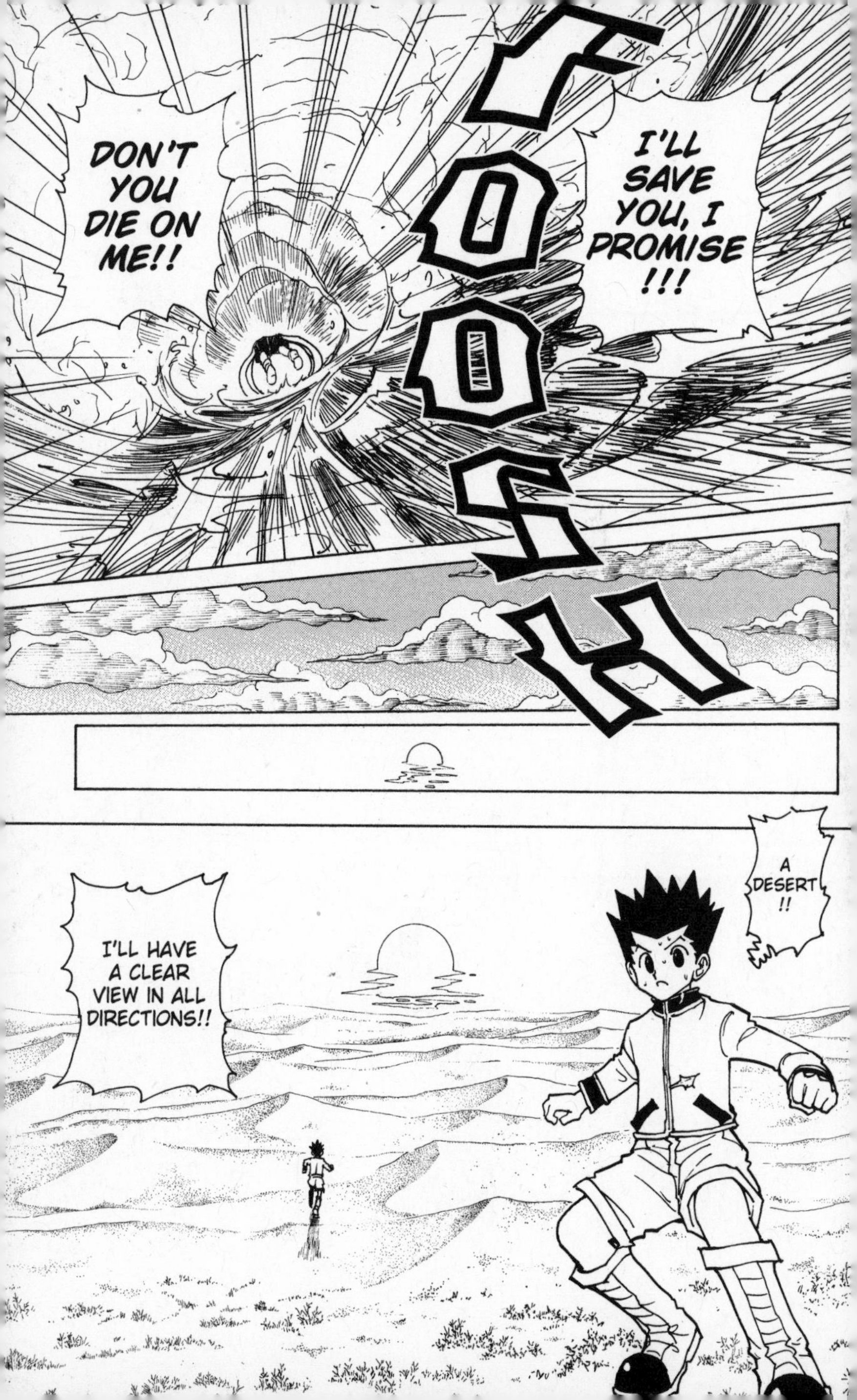
I'LL SAVE YOU, I PROMISE!!!
DON'T YOU DIE ON ME!!
FOOSH
A DESERT!!
I'LL HAVE A CLEAR VIEW IN ALL DIRECTIONS!!

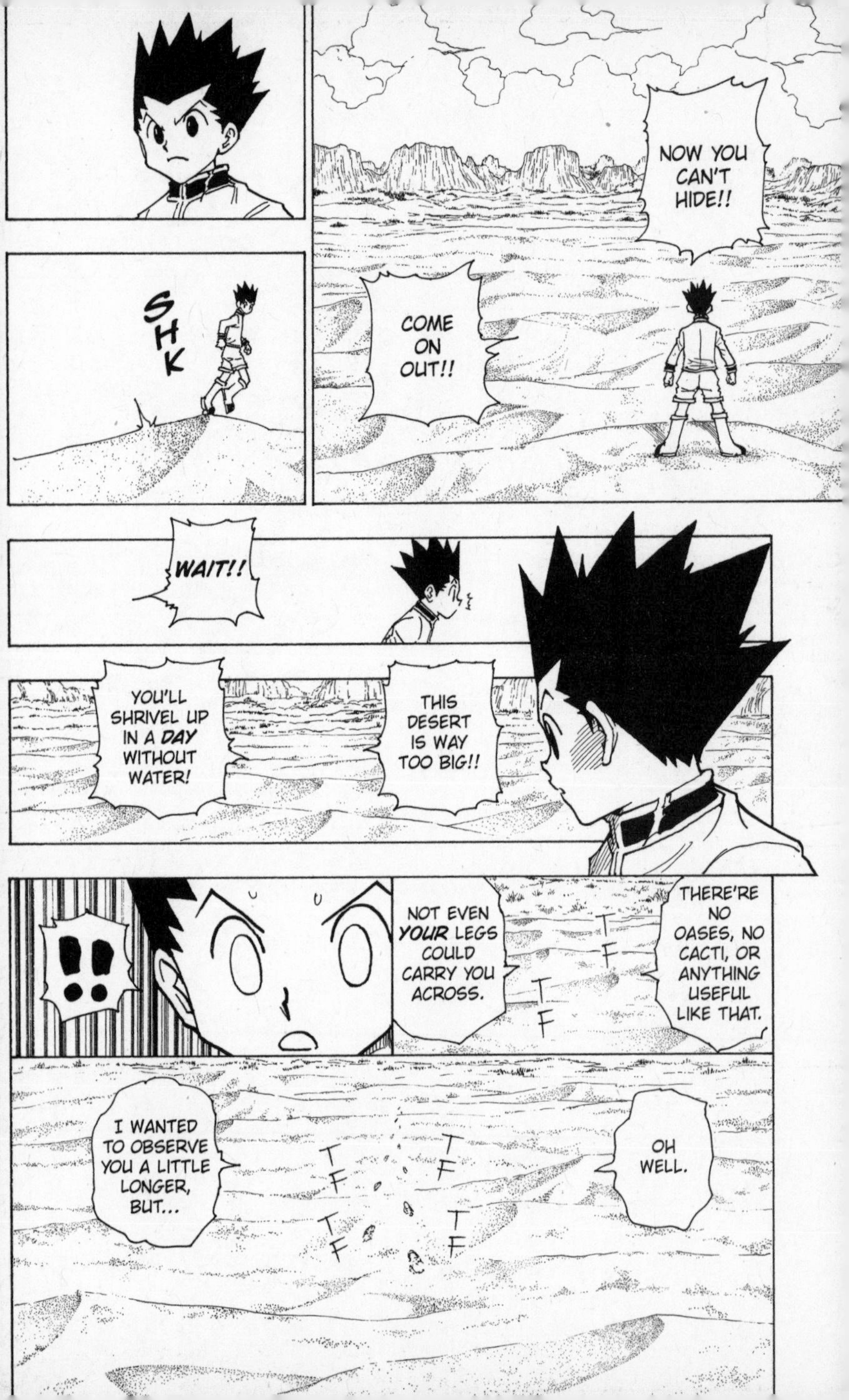
NOW YOU CAN'T HIDE!!
COME ON OUT!!
SHK
WAIT!!
THIS DESERT IS WAY TOO BIG!!
YOU'LL SHRIVEL UP IN A *DAY* WITHOUT WATER!
THERE'RE NO OASES, NO CACTI, OR ANYTHING USEFUL LIKE THAT.
TF TF
NOT EVEN *YOUR* LEGS COULD CARRY YOU ACROSS.
!!
OH WELL.
TF TF TF TF
I WANTED TO OBSERVE YOU A LITTLE LONGER, BUT...

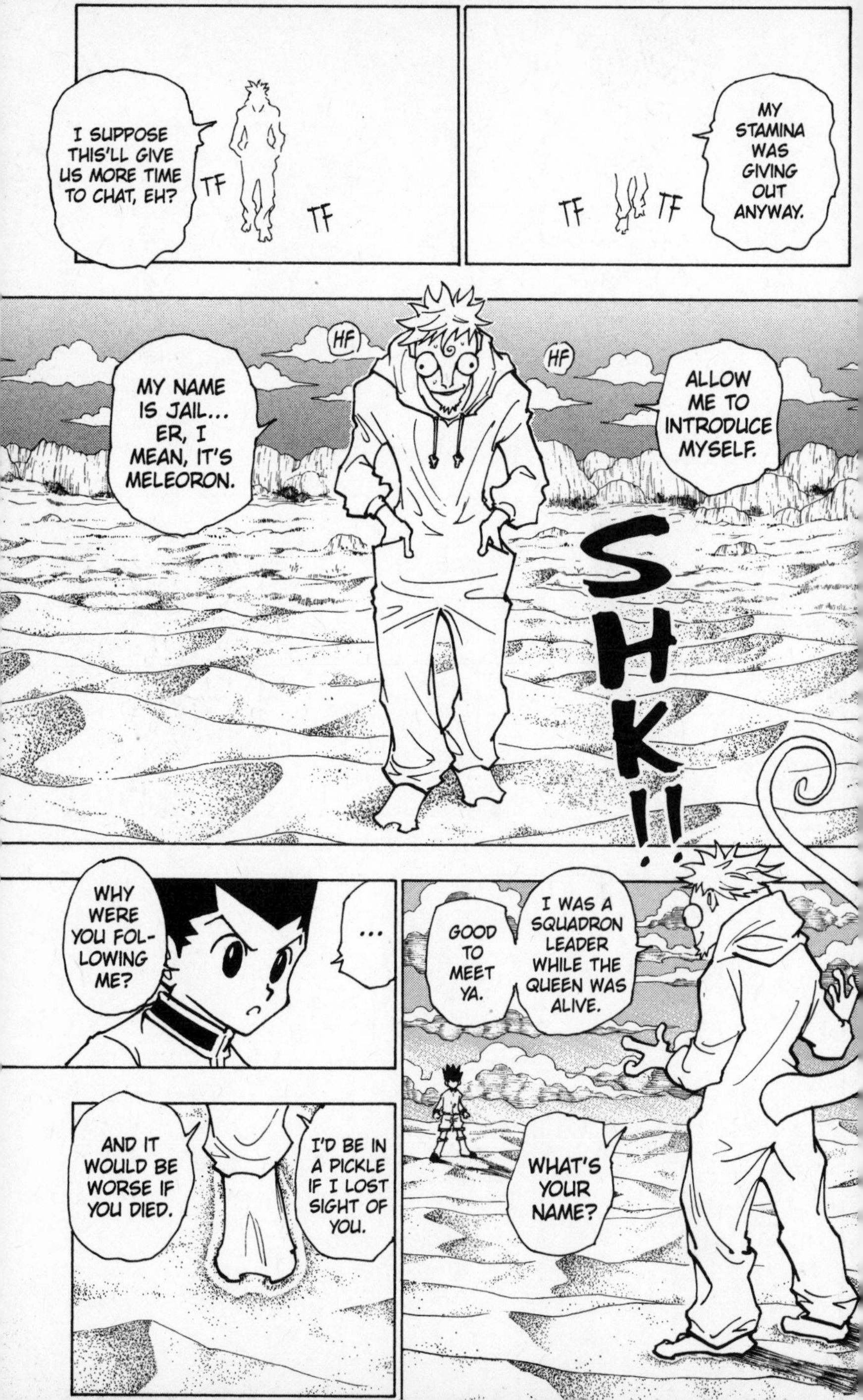
MY STAMINA WAS GIVING OUT ANYWAY.
TF TF
I SUPPOSE THIS'LL GIVE US MORE TIME TO CHAT, EH?
TF TF
ALLOW ME TO INTRODUCE MYSELF.
HF HF
MY NAME IS JAIL... ER, I MEAN, IT'S MELEORON.
SHK!!
I WAS A SQUADRON LEADER WHILE THE QUEEN WAS ALIVE.
GOOD TO MEET YA.
WHAT'S YOUR NAME?
...
WHY WERE YOU FOLLOWING ME?
I'D BE IN A PICKLE IF I LOST SIGHT OF YOU.
AND IT WOULD BE WORSE IF YOU DIED.

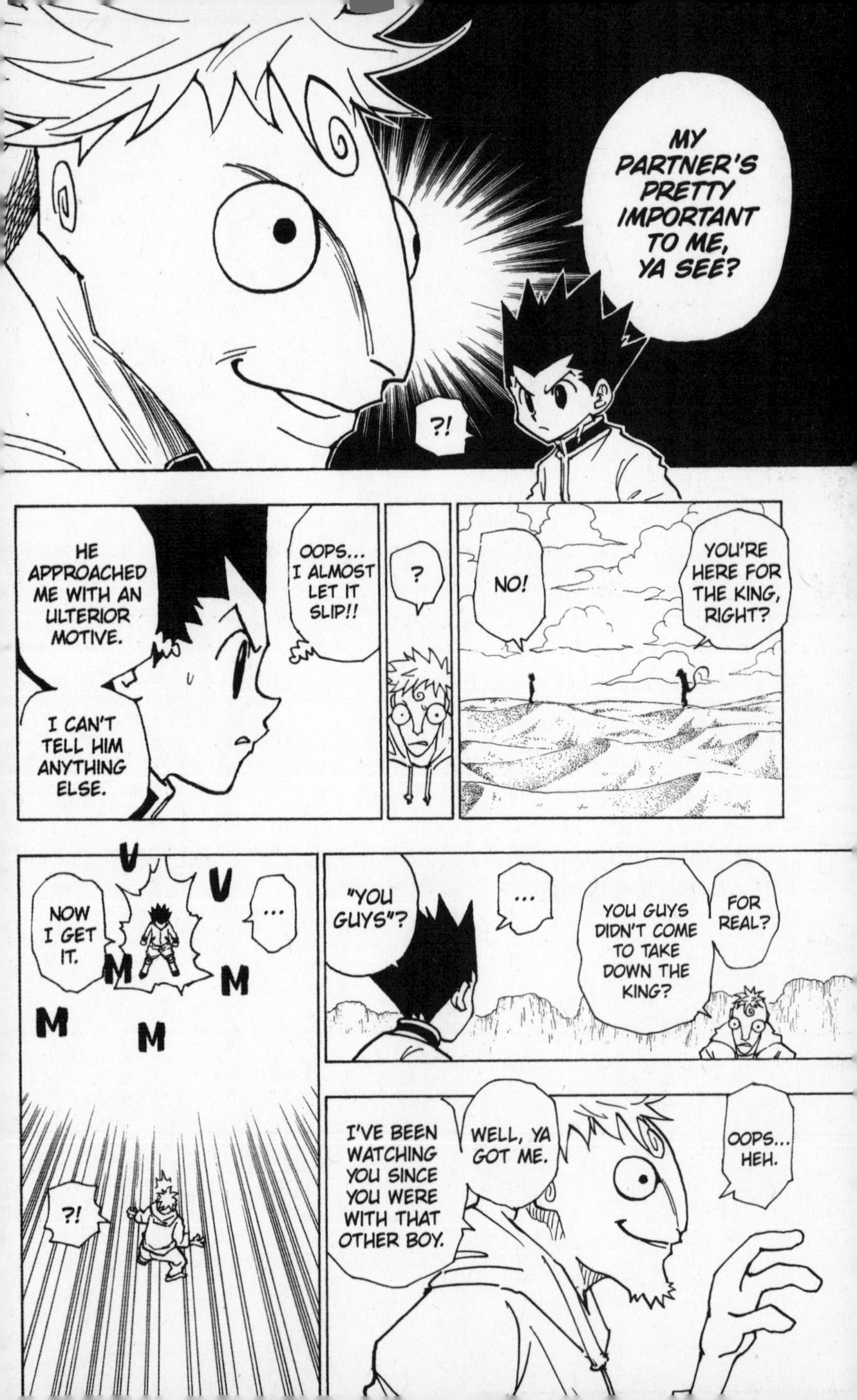
MY PARTNER'S PRETTY IMPORTANT TO ME, YA SEE?
?!
YOU'RE HERE FOR THE KING, RIGHT?
NO!
?
OOPS... I ALMOST LET IT SLIP!!
HE APPROACHED ME WITH AN ULTERIOR MOTIVE.
I CAN'T TELL HIM ANYTHING ELSE.
FOR REAL?
YOU GUYS DIDN'T COME TO TAKE DOWN THE KING?
...
"YOU GUYS"?
OOPS... HEH.
WELL, YA GOT ME.
I'VE BEEN WATCHING YOU SINCE YOU WERE WITH THAT OTHER BOY.
...
NOW I GET IT.
V V M M M M M
?!

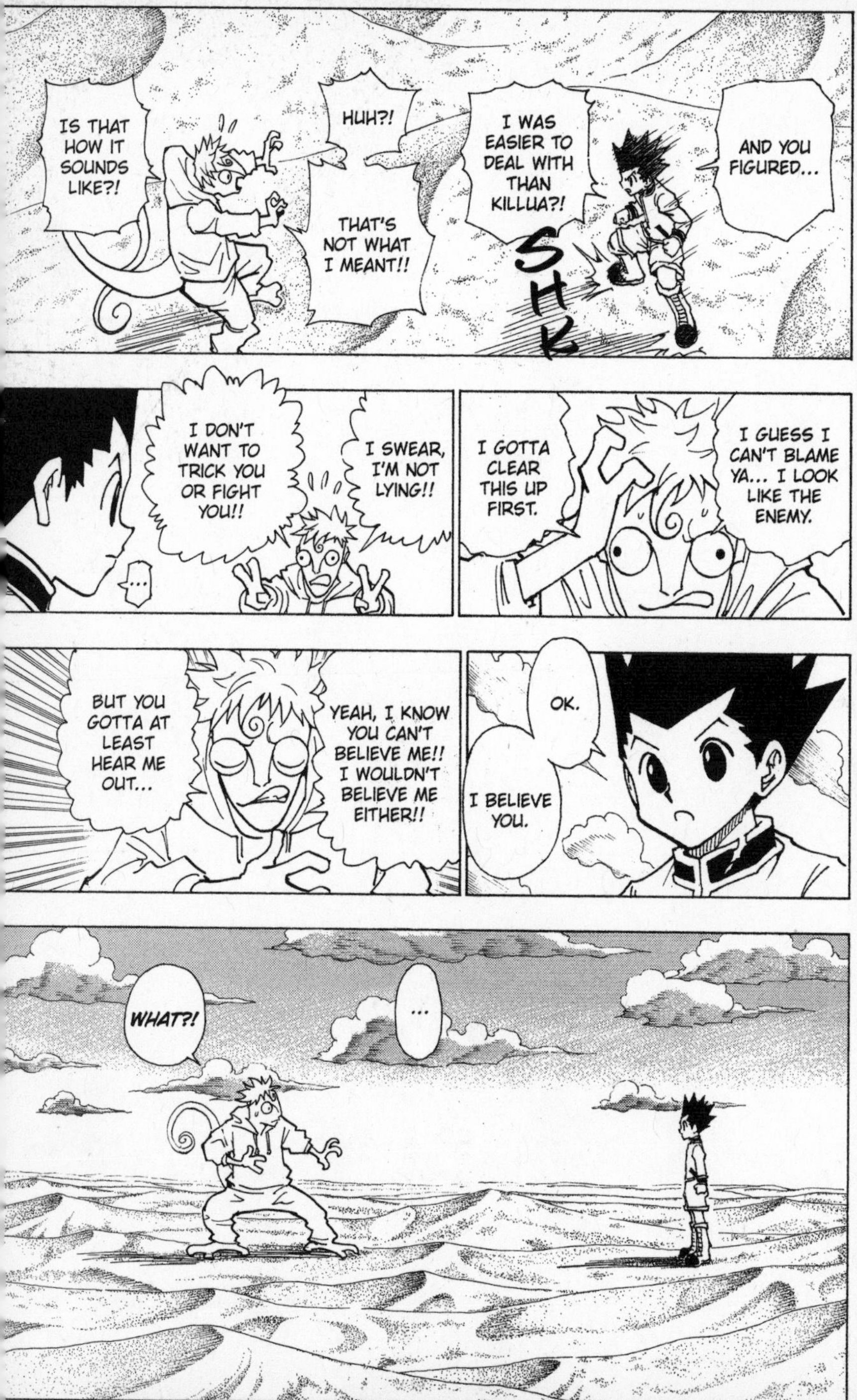
AND YOU FIGURED...
I WAS EASIER TO DEAL WITH THAN KILLUA?!
SHK
HUH?!
THAT'S NOT WHAT I MEANT!!
IS THAT HOW IT SOUNDS LIKE?!
I GUESS I CAN'T BLAME YA... I LOOK LIKE THE ENEMY.
I GOTTA CLEAR THIS UP FIRST.
I SWEAR, I'M NOT LYING!!
I DON'T WANT TO TRICK YOU OR FIGHT YOU!!
...
OK.
I BELIEVE YOU.
YEAH, I KNOW YOU CAN'T BELIEVE ME!! I WOULDN'T BELIEVE ME EITHER!!
BUT YOU GOTTA AT LEAST HEAR ME OUT...
...
WHAT?!

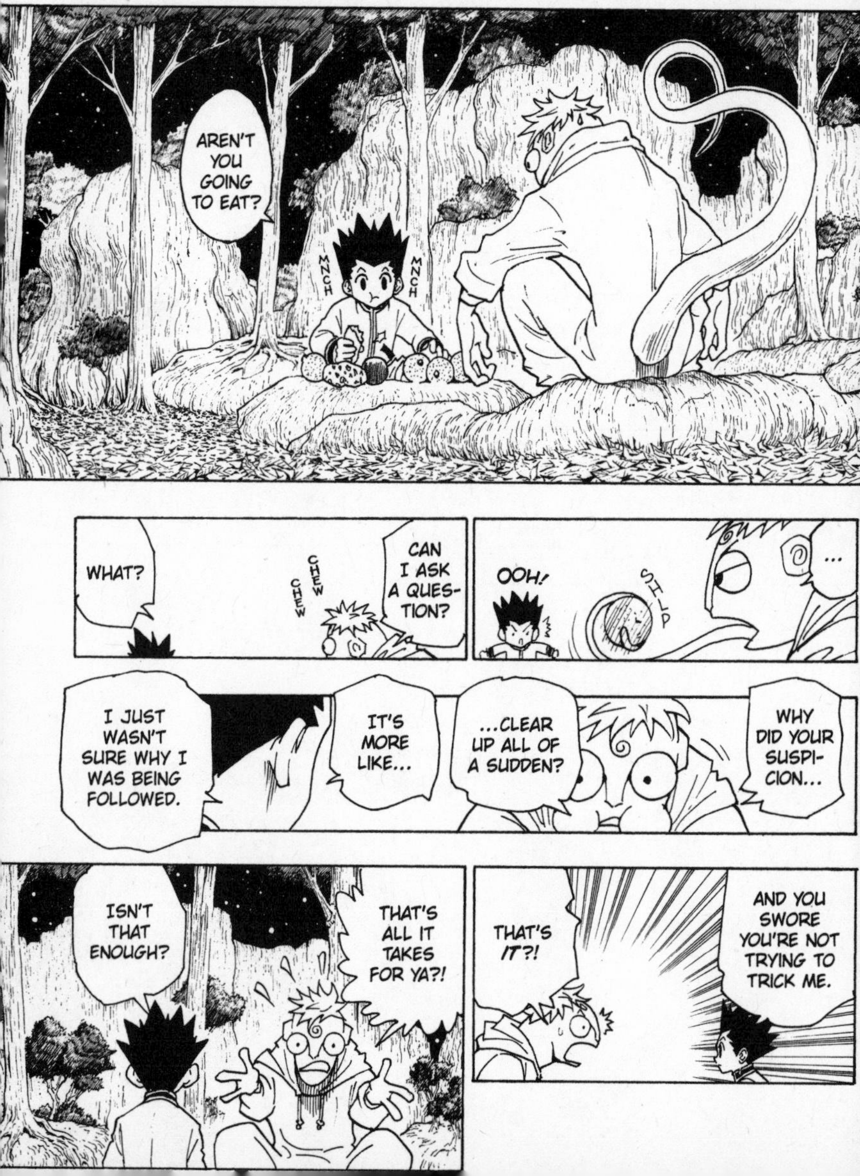
MNCH
MNCH
AREN'T YOU GOING TO EAT?
...
SHLP
OOH!
CAN I ASK A QUESTION?
CHEW
CHEW
WHAT?
WHY DID YOUR SUSPICION...
...CLEAR UP ALL OF A SUDDEN?
IT'S MORE LIKE...
I JUST WASN'T SURE WHY I WAS BEING FOLLOWED.
AND YOU SWORE YOU'RE NOT TRYING TO TRICK ME.
THAT'S *IT*?!
THAT'S ALL IT TAKES FOR YA?!
ISN'T THAT ENOUGH?

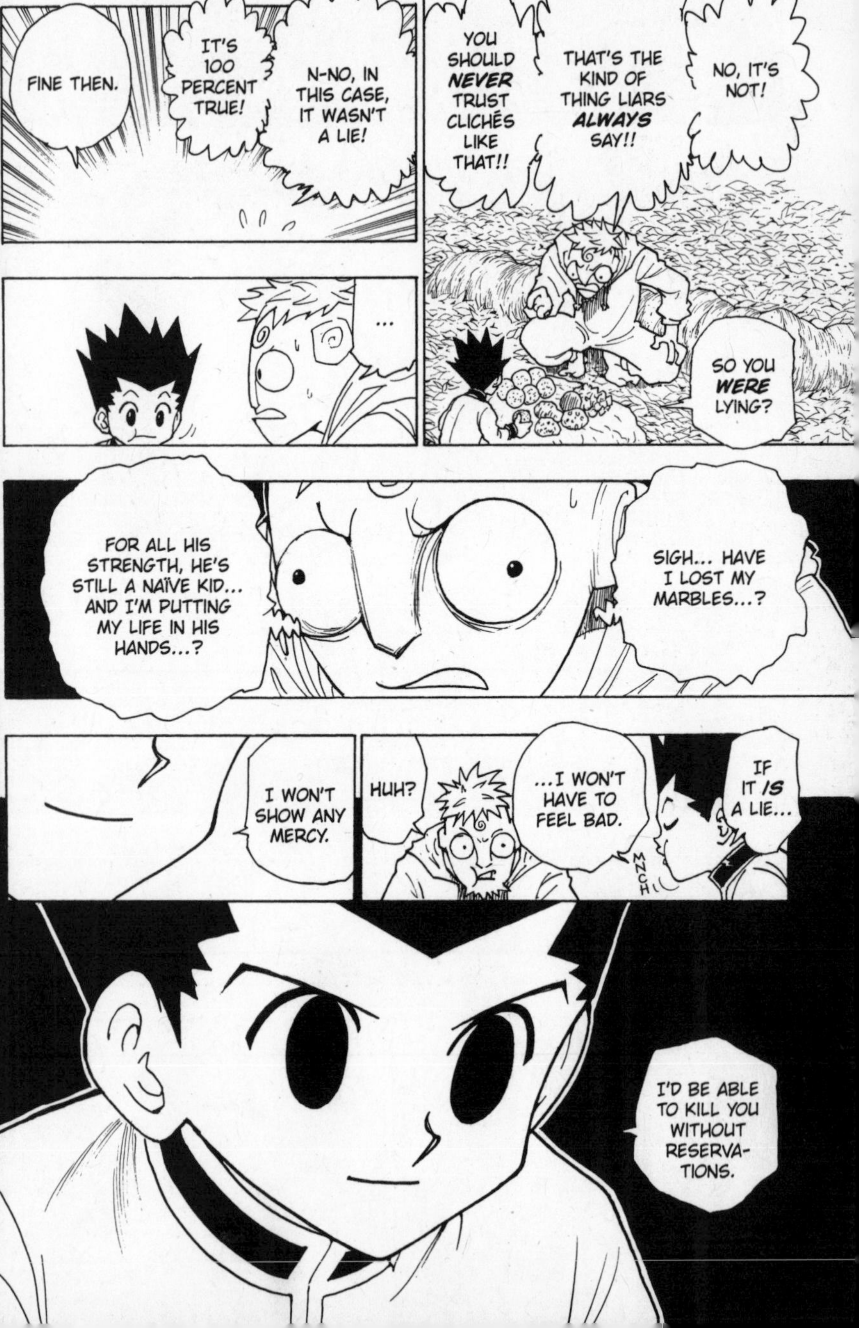
NO, IT'S NOT!
THAT'S THE KIND OF THING LIARS **ALWAYS** SAY!!
YOU SHOULD **NEVER** TRUST CLICHÉS LIKE THAT!!
SO YOU **WERE** LYING?
N-NO, IN THIS CASE, IT WASN'T A LIE!
IT'S 100 PERCENT TRUE!
FINE THEN.
...
SIGH... HAVE I LOST MY MARBLES...?
FOR ALL HIS STRENGTH, HE'S STILL A NAÏVE KID... AND I'M PUTTING MY LIFE IN HIS HANDS...?
IF IT ***IS*** A LIE...
...I WON'T HAVE TO FEEL BAD.
MNCH
HUH?
I WON'T SHOW ANY MERCY.
I'D BE ABLE TO KILL YOU WITHOUT RESERVATIONS.

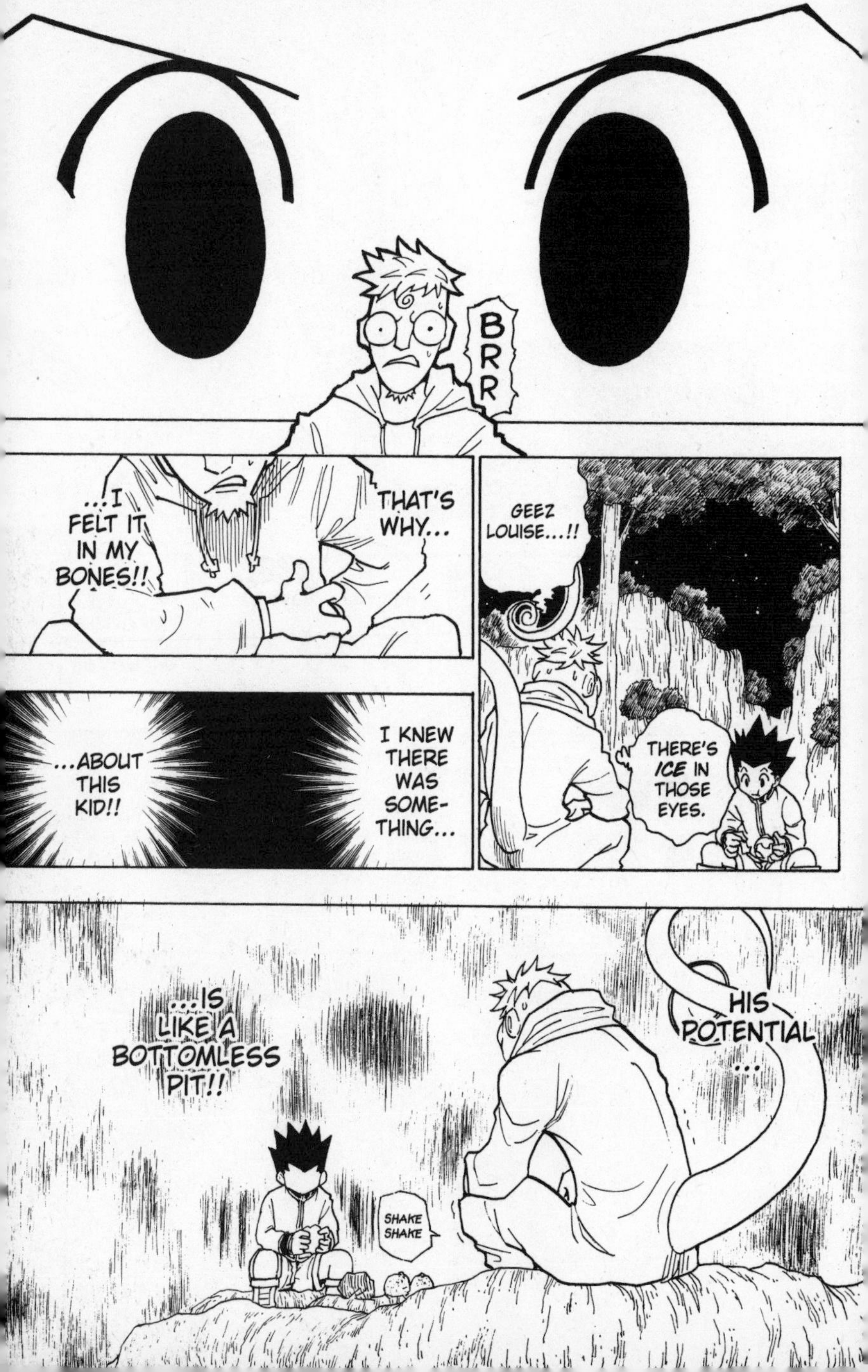
BRR
GEEZ LOUISE...!!
THERE'S *ICE* IN THOSE EYES.
THAT'S WHY...
...I FELT IT IN MY BONES!!
I KNEW THERE WAS SOME-THING...
...ABOUT THIS KID!!
HIS POTENTIAL...
...IS LIKE A BOTTOMLESS PIT!!
SHAKE SHAKE

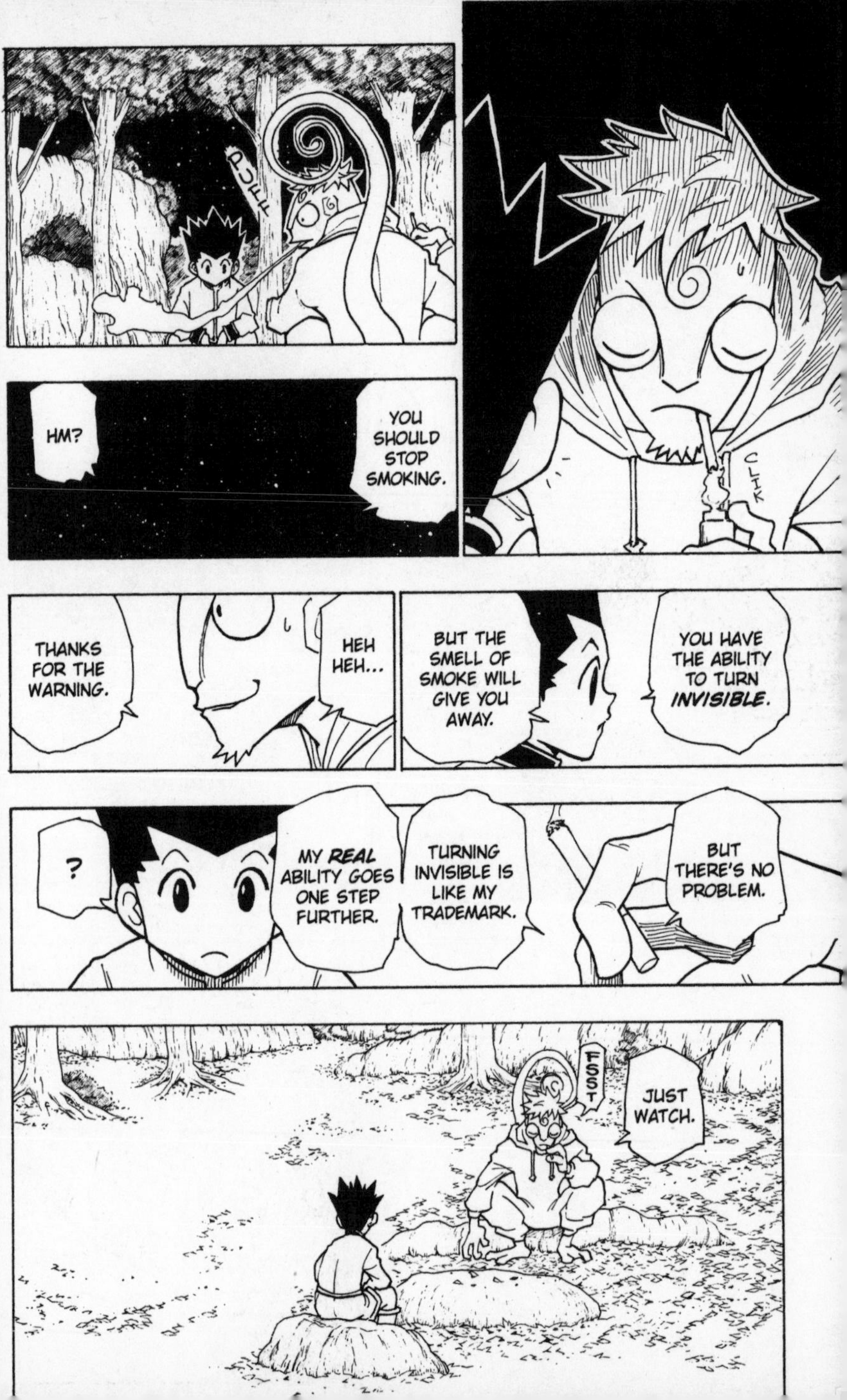
CLIK
PUFF
YOU SHOULD STOP SMOKING.
HM?
YOU HAVE THE ABILITY TO TURN INVISIBLE.
BUT THE SMELL OF SMOKE WILL GIVE YOU AWAY.
HEH HEH...
THANKS FOR THE WARNING.
BUT THERE'S NO PROBLEM.
TURNING INVISIBLE IS LIKE MY TRADEMARK.
MY REAL ABILITY GOES ONE STEP FURTHER.
?
FSST
JUST WATCH.

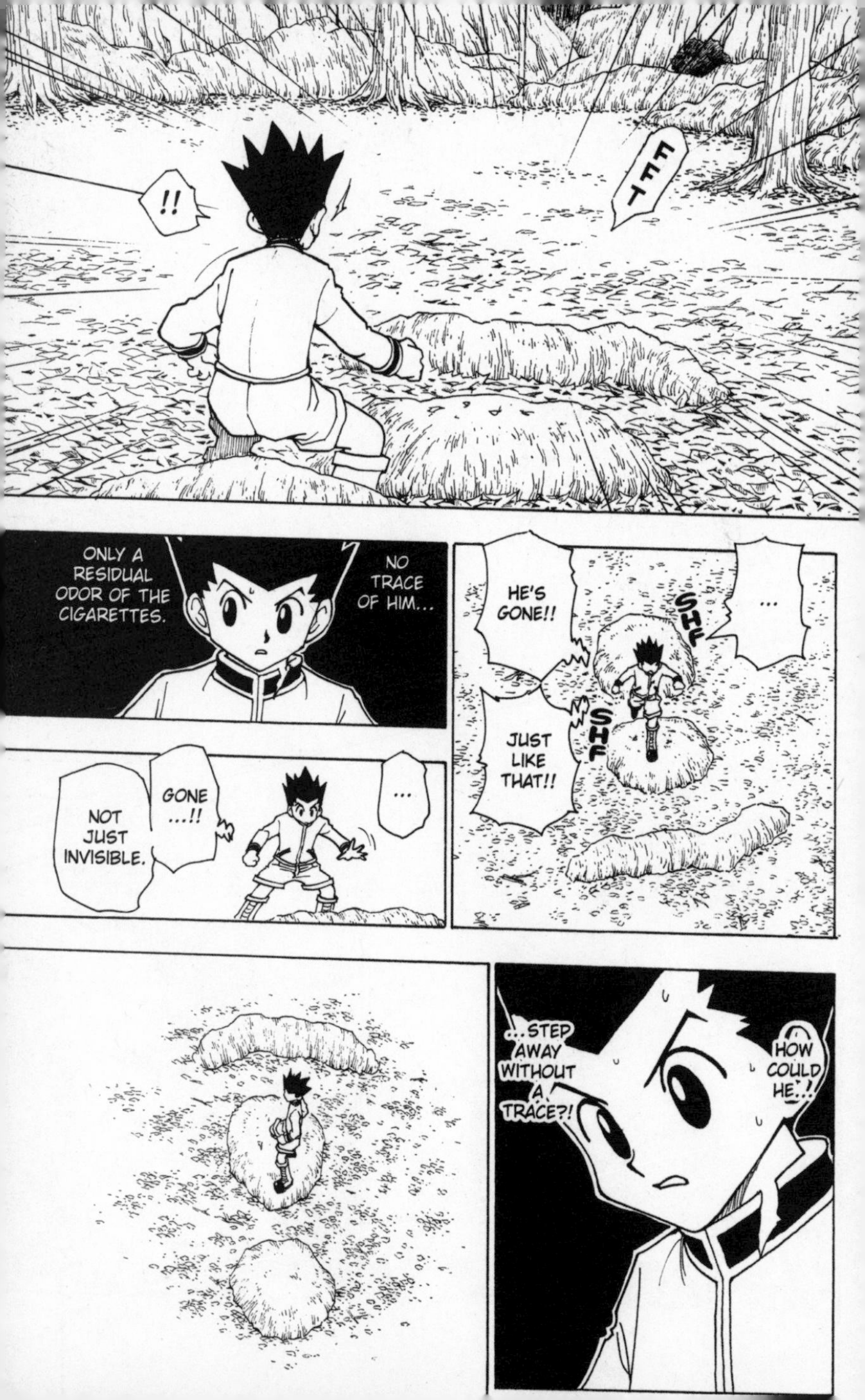
FFT
!!
...
SHF
HE'S GONE!!
SHF
JUST LIKE THAT!!
NO TRACE OF HIM...
ONLY A RESIDUAL ODOR OF THE CIGARETTES.
...
GONE ...!!
NOT JUST INVISIBLE.
HOW COULD HE..!
...STEP AWAY WITHOUT A TRACE?!

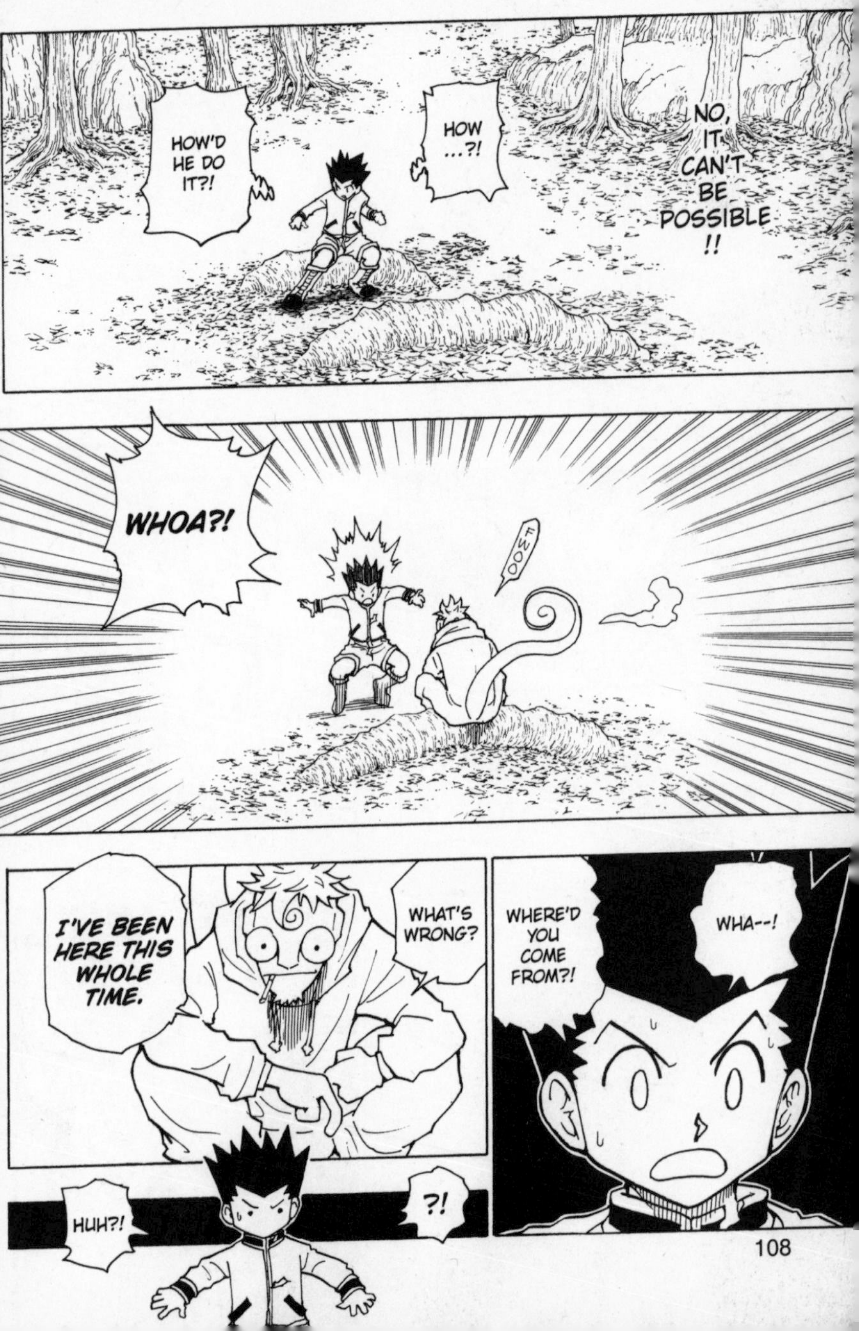
NO, IT CAN'T BE POSSIBLE!!
HOW ...?!
HOW'D HE DO IT?!
WHOA?!
FWOO
WHA--!
WHERE'D YOU COME FROM?!
WHAT'S WRONG?
I'VE BEEN HERE THIS WHOLE TIME.
?!
HUH?!

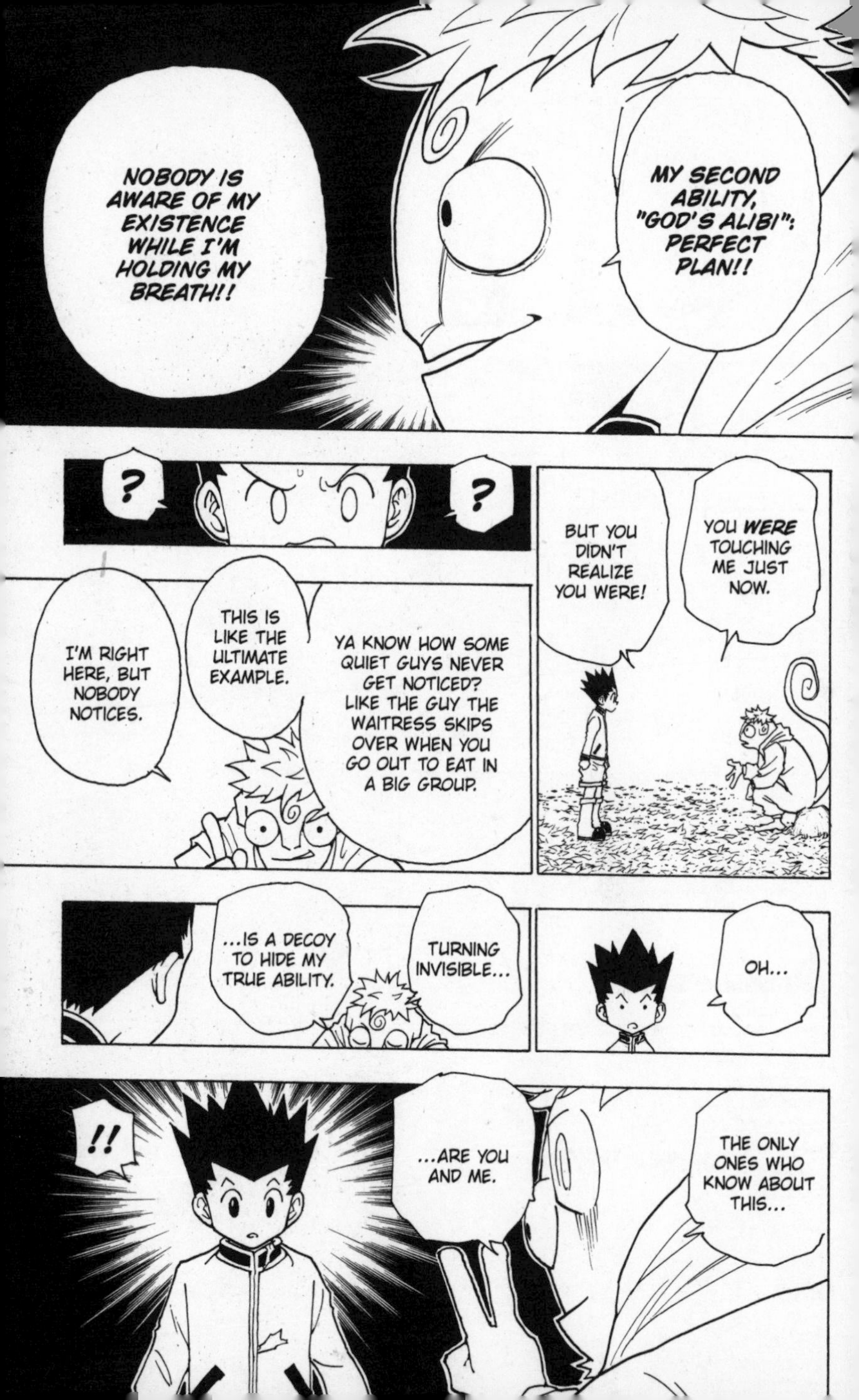
MY SECOND ABILITY, "GOD'S ALIBI": PERFECT PLAN!!
NOBODY IS AWARE OF MY EXISTENCE WHILE I'M HOLDING MY BREATH!!
YOU *WERE* TOUCHING ME JUST NOW.
BUT YOU DIDN'T REALIZE YOU WERE!
?
?
YA KNOW HOW SOME QUIET GUYS NEVER GET NOTICED? LIKE THE GUY THE WAITRESS SKIPS OVER WHEN YOU GO OUT TO EAT IN A BIG GROUP.
THIS IS LIKE THE ULTIMATE EXAMPLE.
I'M RIGHT HERE, BUT NOBODY NOTICES.
OH...
TURNING INVISIBLE...
...IS A DECOY TO HIDE MY TRUE ABILITY.
THE ONLY ONES WHO KNOW ABOUT THIS...
...ARE YOU AND ME.
!!

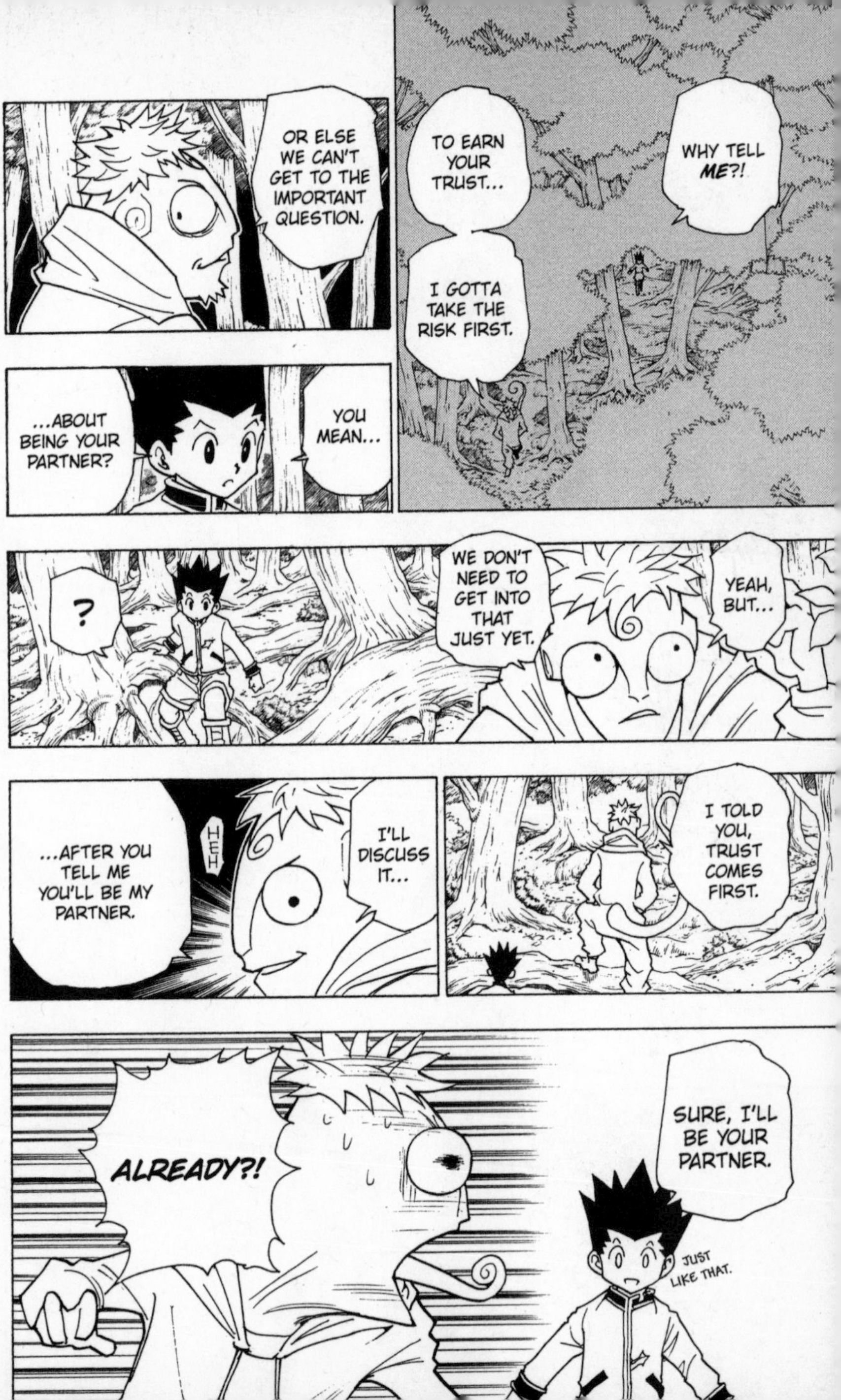
WHY TELL *ME*?!
TO EARN YOUR TRUST...
I GOTTA TAKE THE RISK FIRST.
OR ELSE WE CAN'T GET TO THE IMPORTANT QUESTION.
YOU MEAN...
...ABOUT BEING YOUR PARTNER?
YEAH, BUT...
WE DON'T NEED TO GET INTO THAT JUST YET.
?
I TOLD YOU, TRUST COMES FIRST.
HEH
I'LL DISCUSS IT...
...AFTER YOU TELL ME YOU'LL BE MY PARTNER.
SURE, I'LL BE YOUR PARTNER.
JUST LIKE THAT.
ALREADY?!

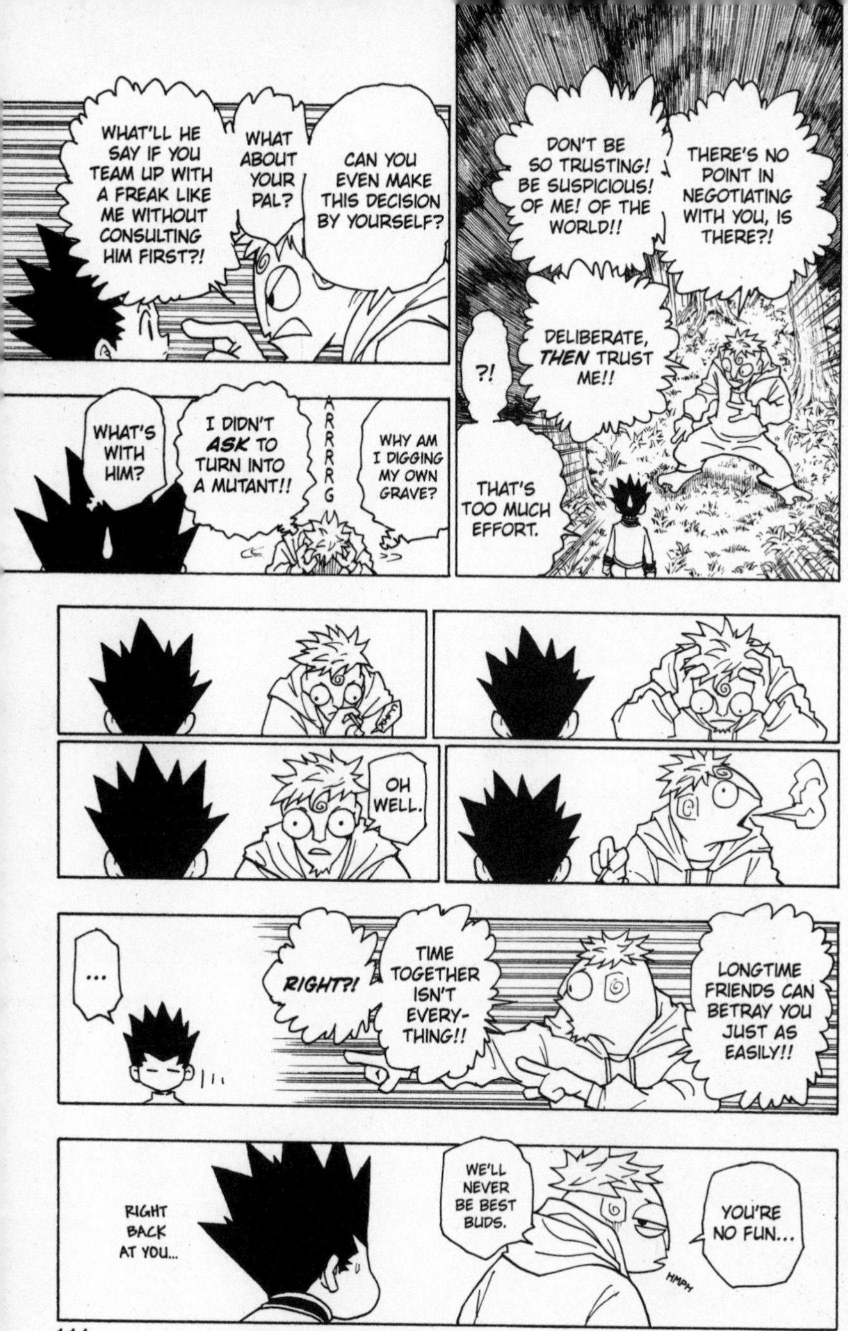
THERE'S NO POINT IN NEGOTIATING WITH YOU, IS THERE?!
DON'T BE SO TRUSTING! BE SUSPICIOUS! OF ME! OF THE WORLD!!
DELIBERATE, *THEN* TRUST ME!!
?!
THAT'S TOO MUCH EFFORT.
CAN YOU EVEN MAKE THIS DECISION BY YOURSELF?
WHAT ABOUT YOUR PAL?
WHAT'LL HE SAY IF YOU TEAM UP WITH A FREAK LIKE ME WITHOUT CONSULTING HIM FIRST?!
WHY AM I DIGGING MY OWN GRAVE?
ARRRRG
I DIDN'T *ASK* TO TURN INTO A MUTANT!!
WHAT'S WITH HIM?
OH WELL.
LONGTIME FRIENDS CAN BETRAY YOU JUST AS EASILY!!
TIME TOGETHER ISN'T EVERY-THING!!
RIGHT?!
...
YOU'RE NO FUN...
HMPH
WE'LL NEVER BE BEST BUDS.
RIGHT BACK AT YOU...

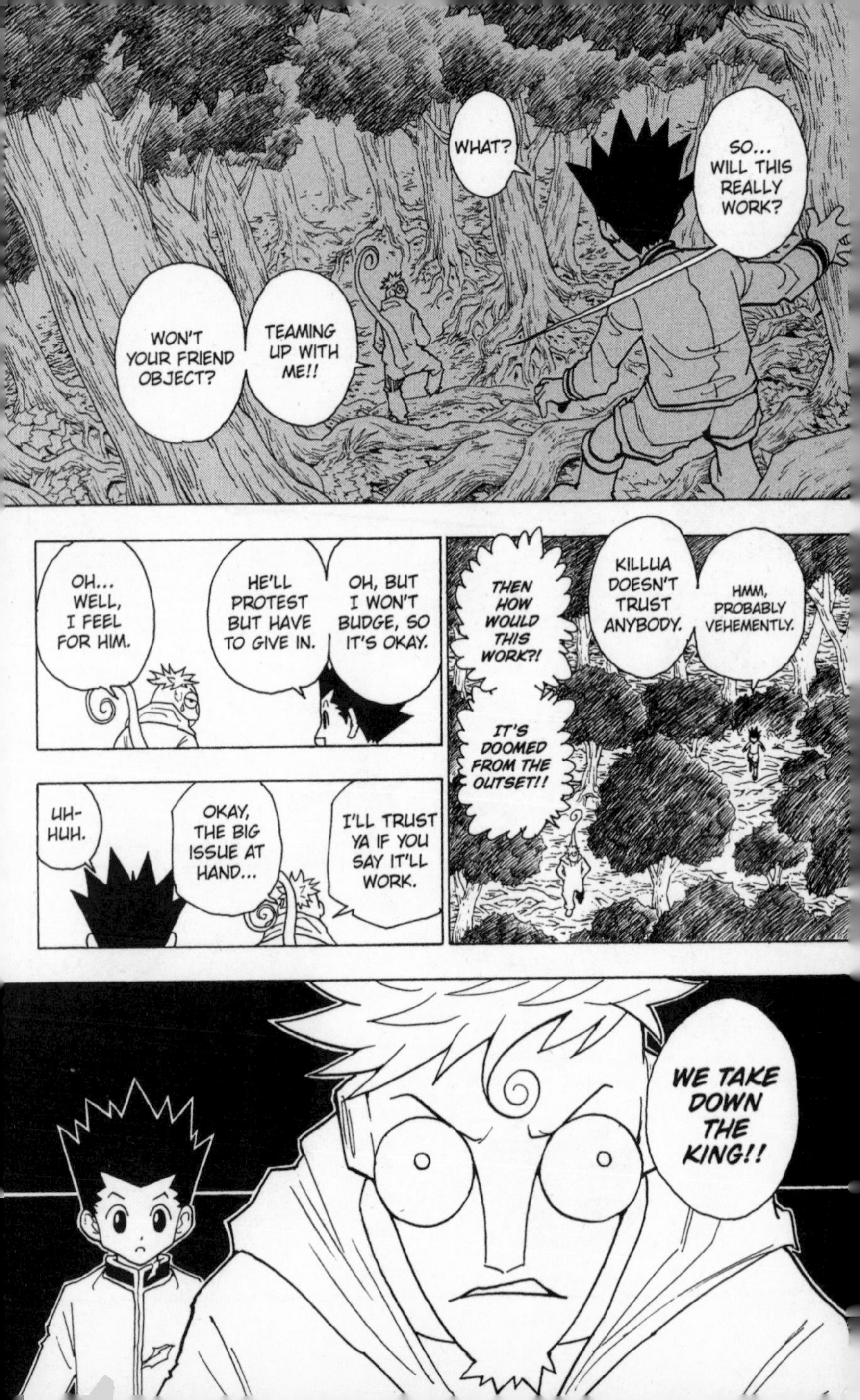
SO... WILL THIS REALLY WORK?
WHAT?
TEAMING UP WITH ME!!
WON'T YOUR FRIEND OBJECT?
HMM, PROBABLY VEHEMENTLY.
KILLUA DOESN'T TRUST ANYBODY.
THEN HOW WOULD THIS WORK?!
IT'S DOOMED FROM THE OUTSET!!
OH, BUT I WON'T BUDGE, SO IT'S OKAY.
HE'LL PROTEST BUT HAVE TO GIVE IN.
OH... WELL, I FEEL FOR HIM.
I'LL TRUST YA IF YOU SAY IT'LL WORK.
OKAY, THE BIG ISSUE AT HAND...
UH-HUH.
WE TAKE DOWN THE KING!!

READ THIS WAY

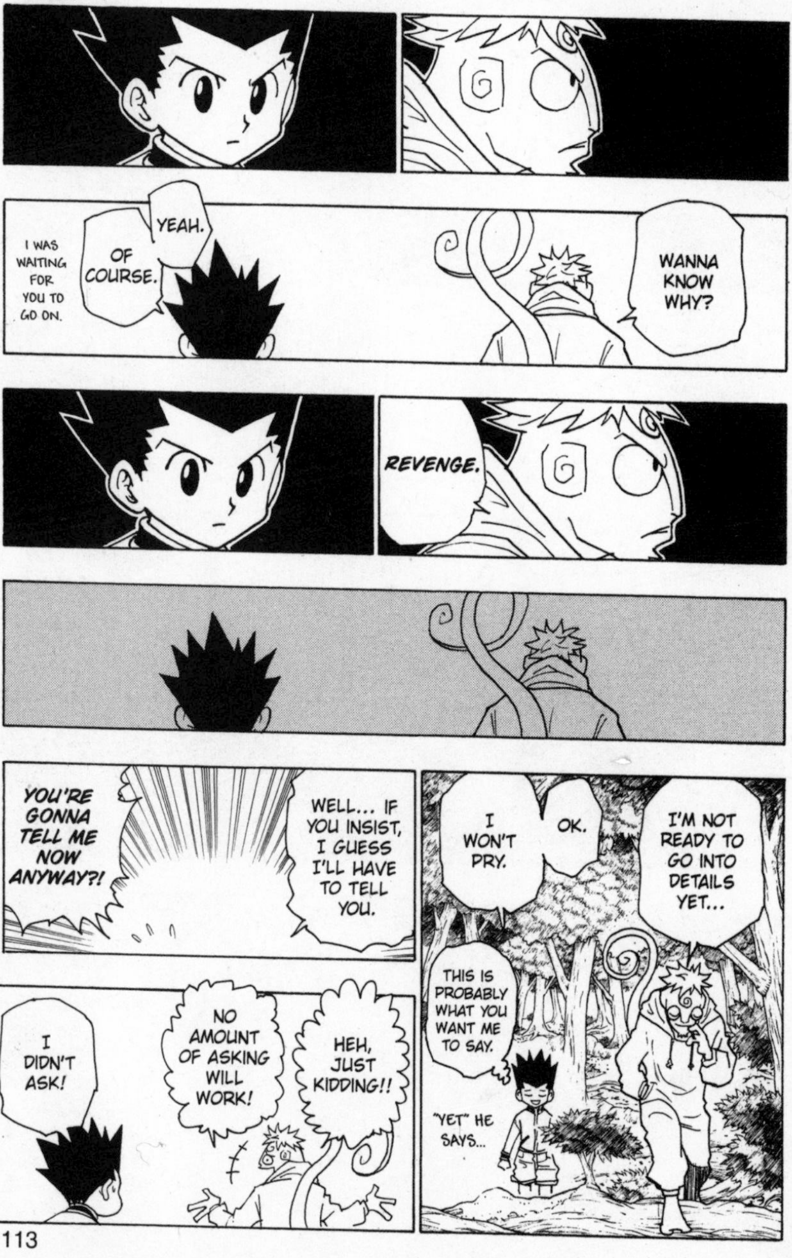
WANNA KNOW WHY?
YEAH.
OF COURSE.
I WAS WAITING FOR YOU TO GO ON.
REVENGE.
I'M NOT READY TO GO INTO DETAILS YET...
OK.
I WON'T PRY.
THIS IS PROBABLY WHAT YOU WANT ME TO SAY.
"YET" HE SAYS...
WELL... IF YOU INSIST, I GUESS I'LL HAVE TO TELL YOU.
YOU'RE GONNA TELL ME NOW ANYWAY?!
HEH, JUST KIDDING!!
NO AMOUNT OF ASKING WILL WORK!
I DIDN'T ASK!

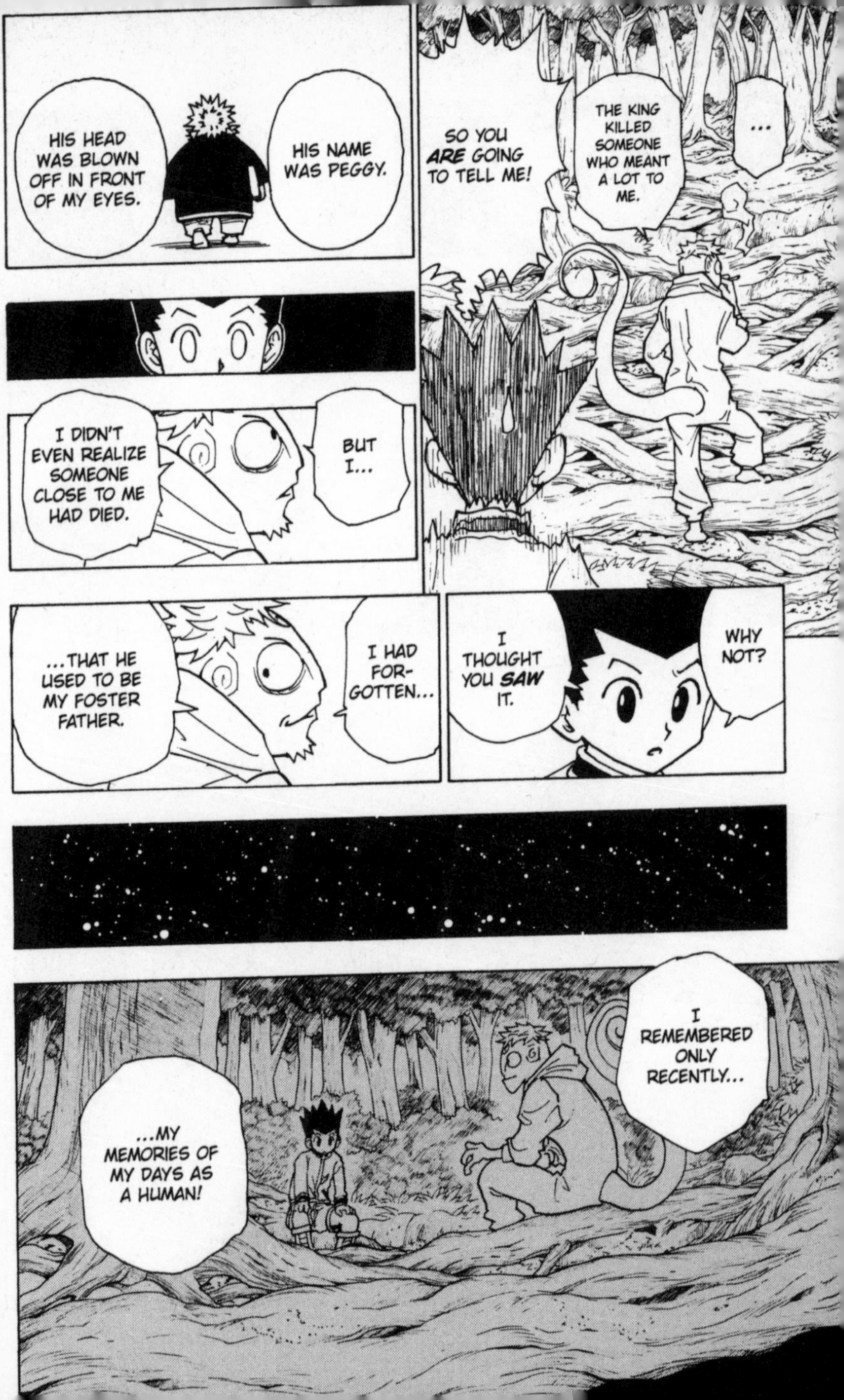
...
THE KING KILLED SOMEONE WHO MEANT A LOT TO ME.
SO YOU *ARE* GOING TO TELL ME!
HIS NAME WAS PEGGY.
HIS HEAD WAS BLOWN OFF IN FRONT OF MY EYES.
BUT I...
I DIDN'T EVEN REALIZE SOMEONE CLOSE TO ME HAD DIED.
WHY NOT?
I THOUGHT YOU *SAW* IT.
I HAD FOR-GOTTEN...
...THAT HE USED TO BE MY FOSTER FATHER.
I REMEMBERED ONLY RECENTLY...
...MY MEMORIES OF MY DAYS AS A HUMAN!

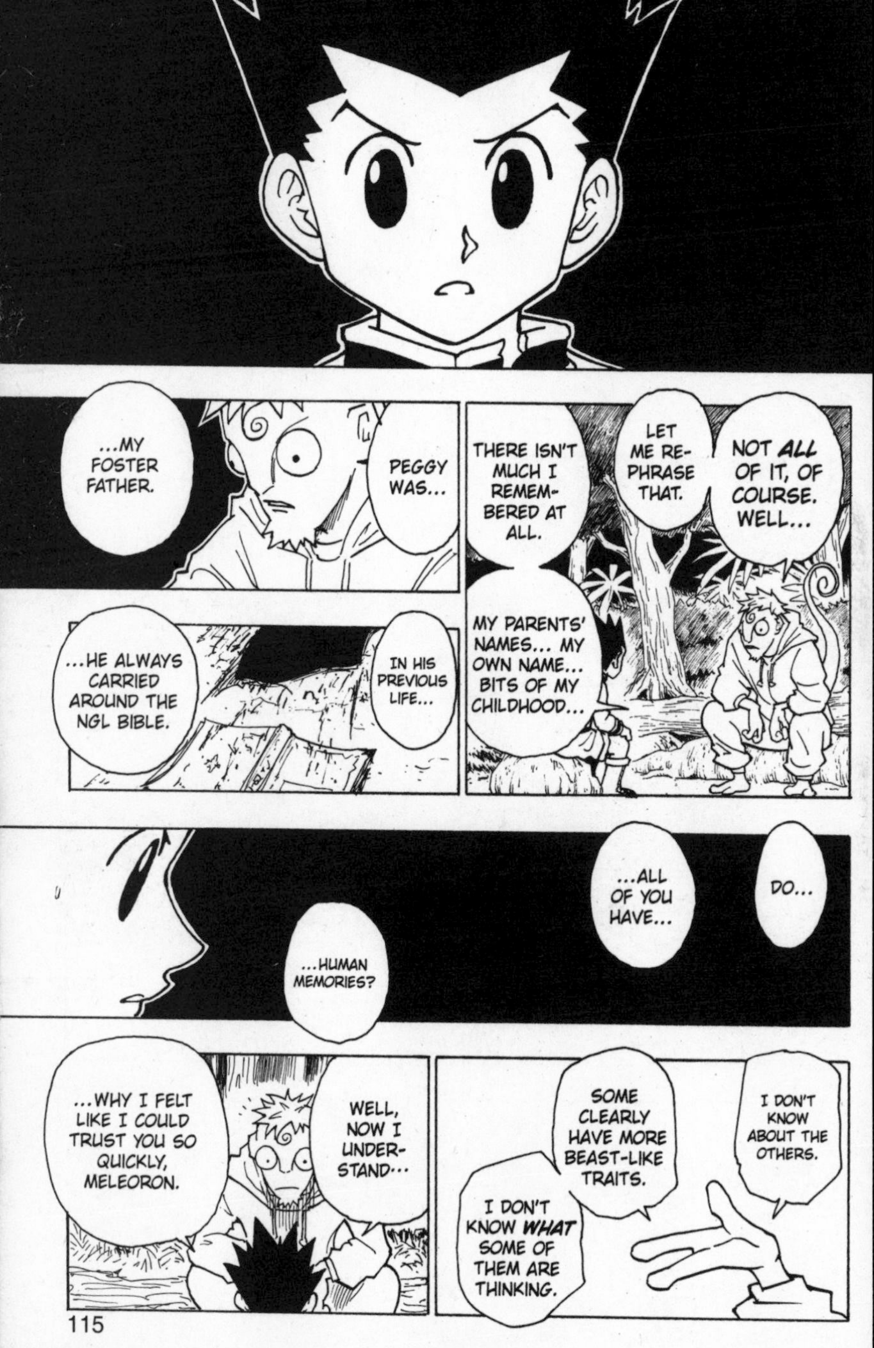
NOT **ALL** OF IT, OF COURSE. WELL...
LET ME RE-PHRASE THAT.
THERE ISN'T MUCH I REMEMBERED AT ALL.
MY PARENTS' NAMES... MY OWN NAME... BITS OF MY CHILDHOOD...
PEGGY WAS...
...MY FOSTER FATHER.
IN HIS PREVIOUS LIFE...
...HE ALWAYS CARRIED AROUND THE NGL BIBLE.
DO...
...ALL OF YOU HAVE...
...HUMAN MEMORIES?
I DON'T KNOW ABOUT THE OTHERS.
SOME CLEARLY HAVE MORE BEAST-LIKE TRAITS.
I DON'T KNOW **WHAT** SOME OF THEM ARE THINKING.
WELL, NOW I UNDER-STAND...
...WHY I FELT LIKE I COULD TRUST YOU SO QUICKLY, MELEORON.

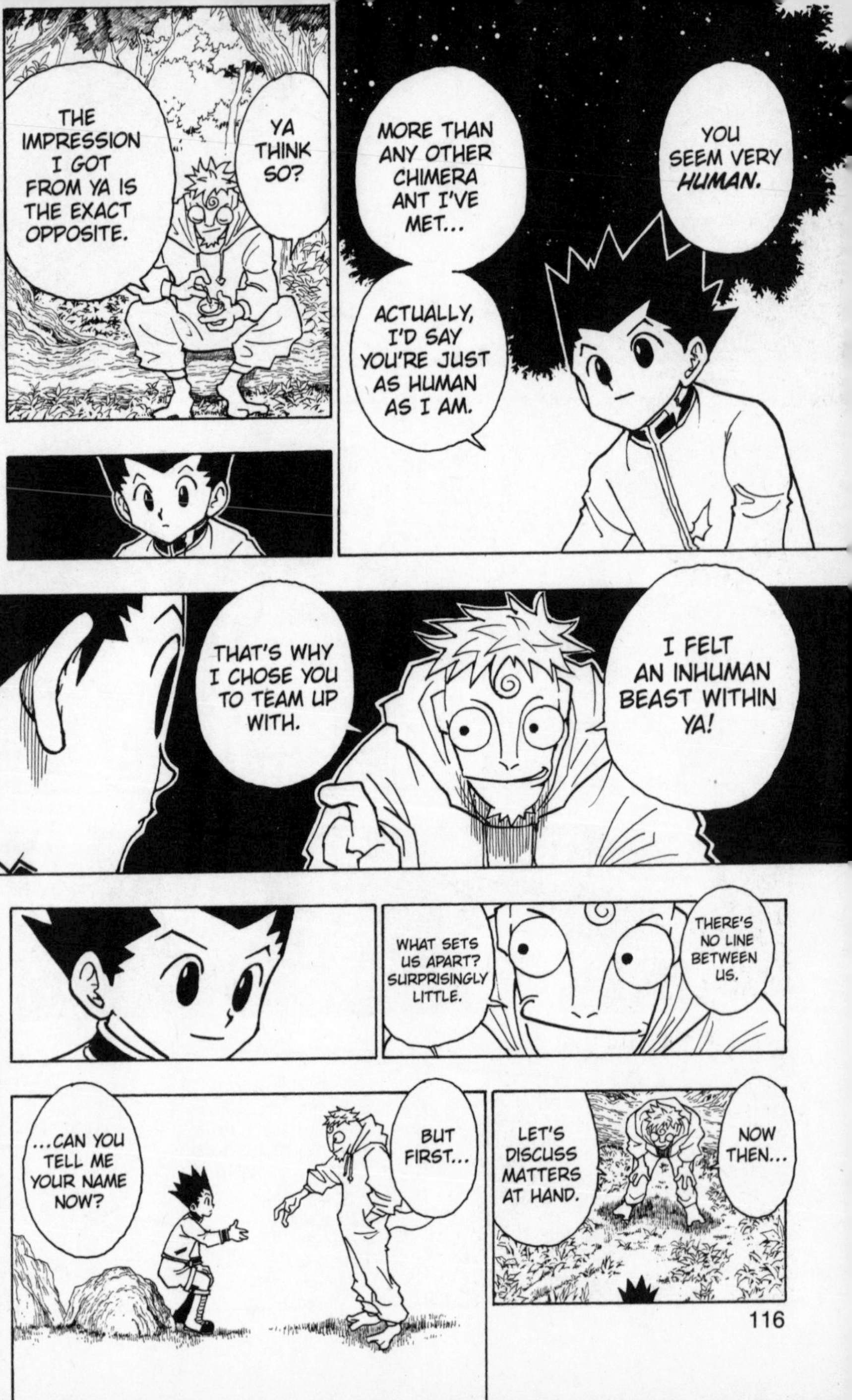
YOU SEEM VERY *HUMAN.*
MORE THAN ANY OTHER CHIMERA ANT I'VE MET...
ACTUALLY, I'D SAY YOU'RE JUST AS HUMAN AS I AM.
YA THINK SO?
THE IMPRESSION I GOT FROM YA IS THE EXACT OPPOSITE.
I FELT AN INHUMAN BEAST WITHIN YA!
THAT'S WHY I CHOSE YOU TO TEAM UP WITH.
THERE'S NO LINE BETWEEN US.
WHAT SETS US APART? SURPRISINGLY LITTLE.
NOW THEN...
LET'S DISCUSS MATTERS AT HAND.
BUT FIRST...
...CAN YOU TELL ME YOUR NAME NOW?

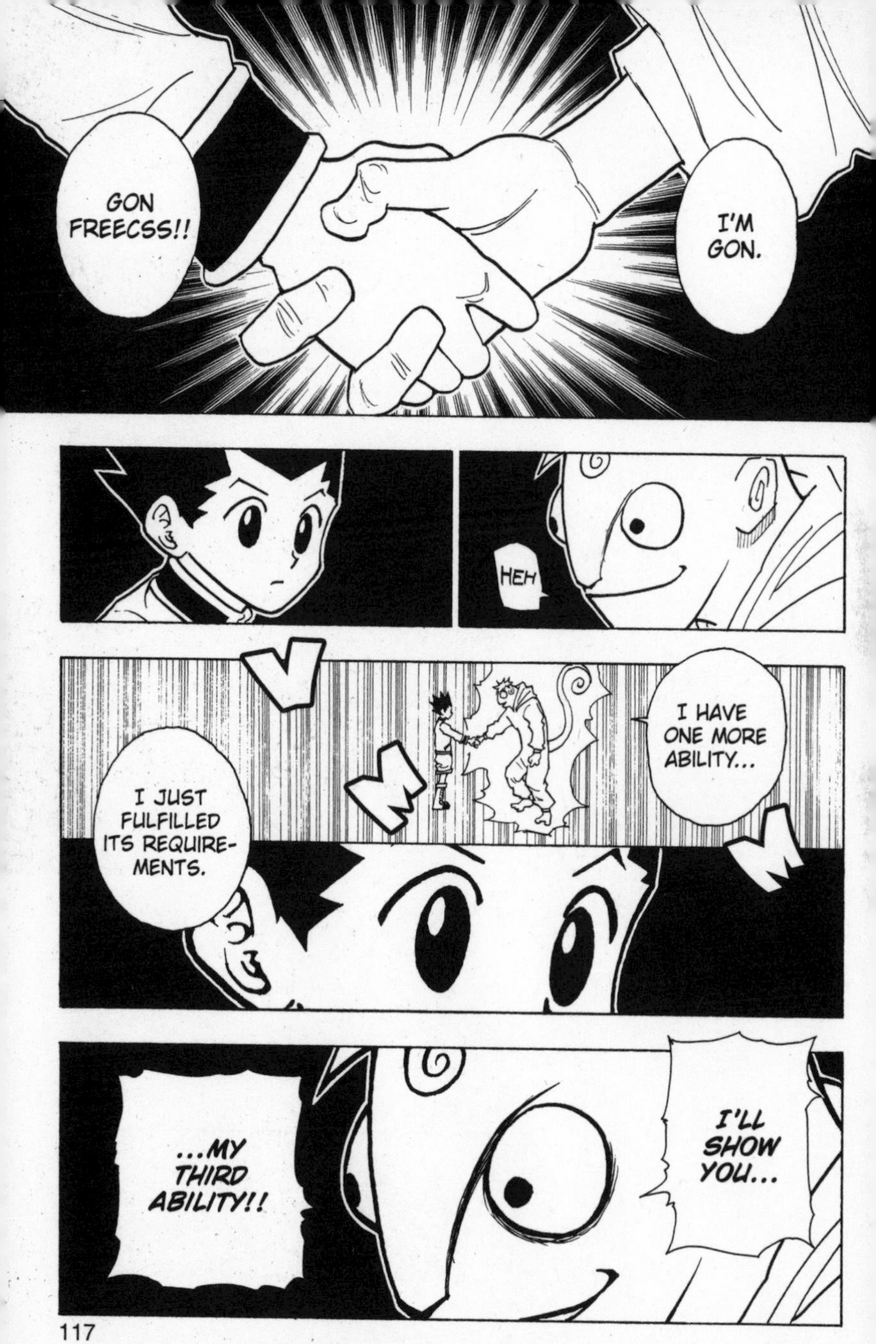
I'M GON.
GON FREECSS!!
HEH
I HAVE ONE MORE ABILITY...
I JUST FULFILLED ITS REQUIREMENTS.
I'LL SHOW YOU...
...MY THIRD ABILITY!!

Chapter 243: 7: Part 2

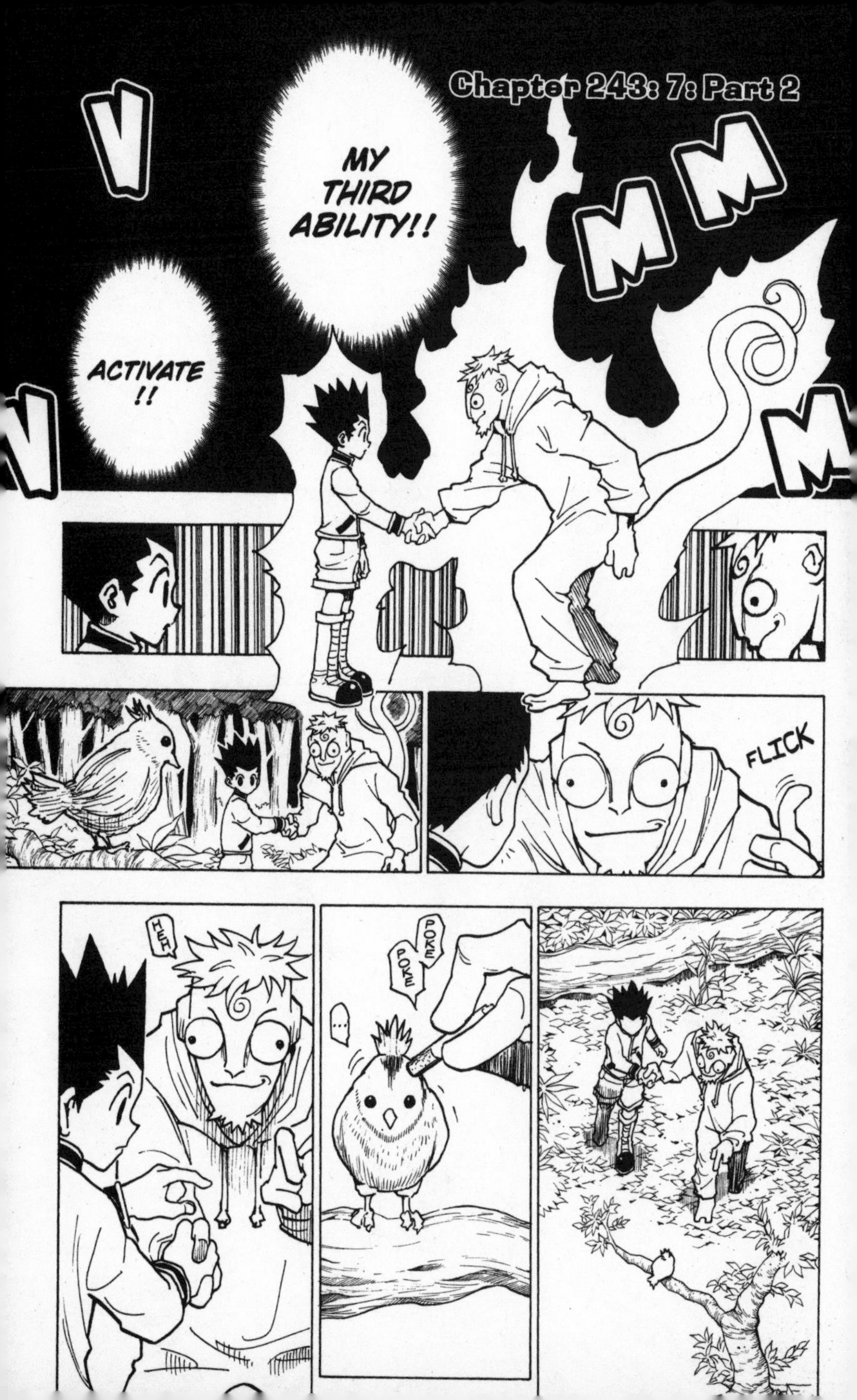
MMM
MY THIRD ABILITY!!
ACTIVATE !!
VVV
FLICK
POKE POKE
...
HEH

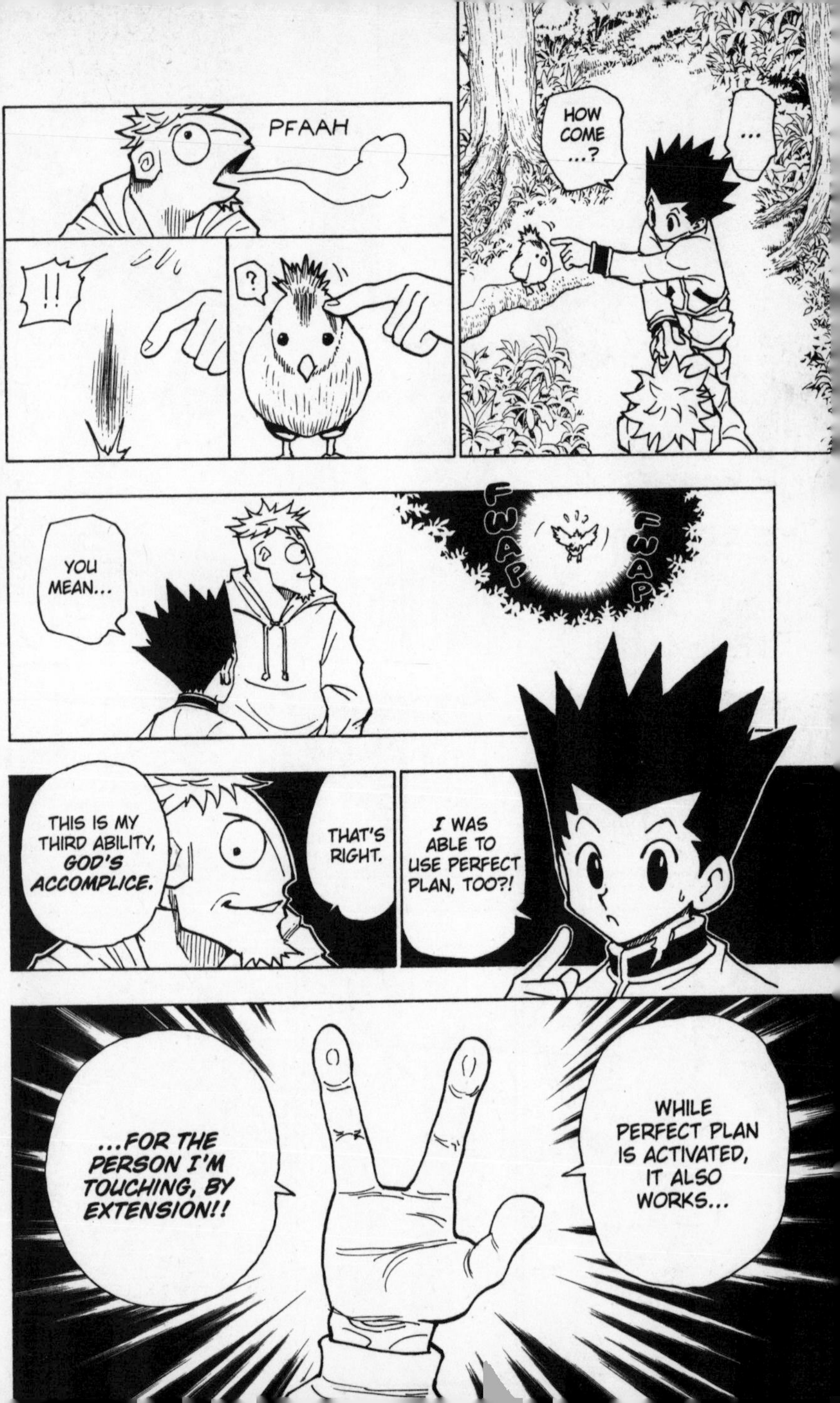
...
HOW COME ...?
PFAAH
?
!!
FWAP
FWAP
YOU MEAN...
I WAS ABLE TO USE PERFECT PLAN, TOO?!
THAT'S RIGHT.
THIS IS MY THIRD ABILITY, GOD'S ACCOMPLICE.
WHILE PERFECT PLAN IS ACTIVATED, IT ALSO WORKS...
...FOR THE PERSON I'M TOUCHING, BY EXTENSION!!

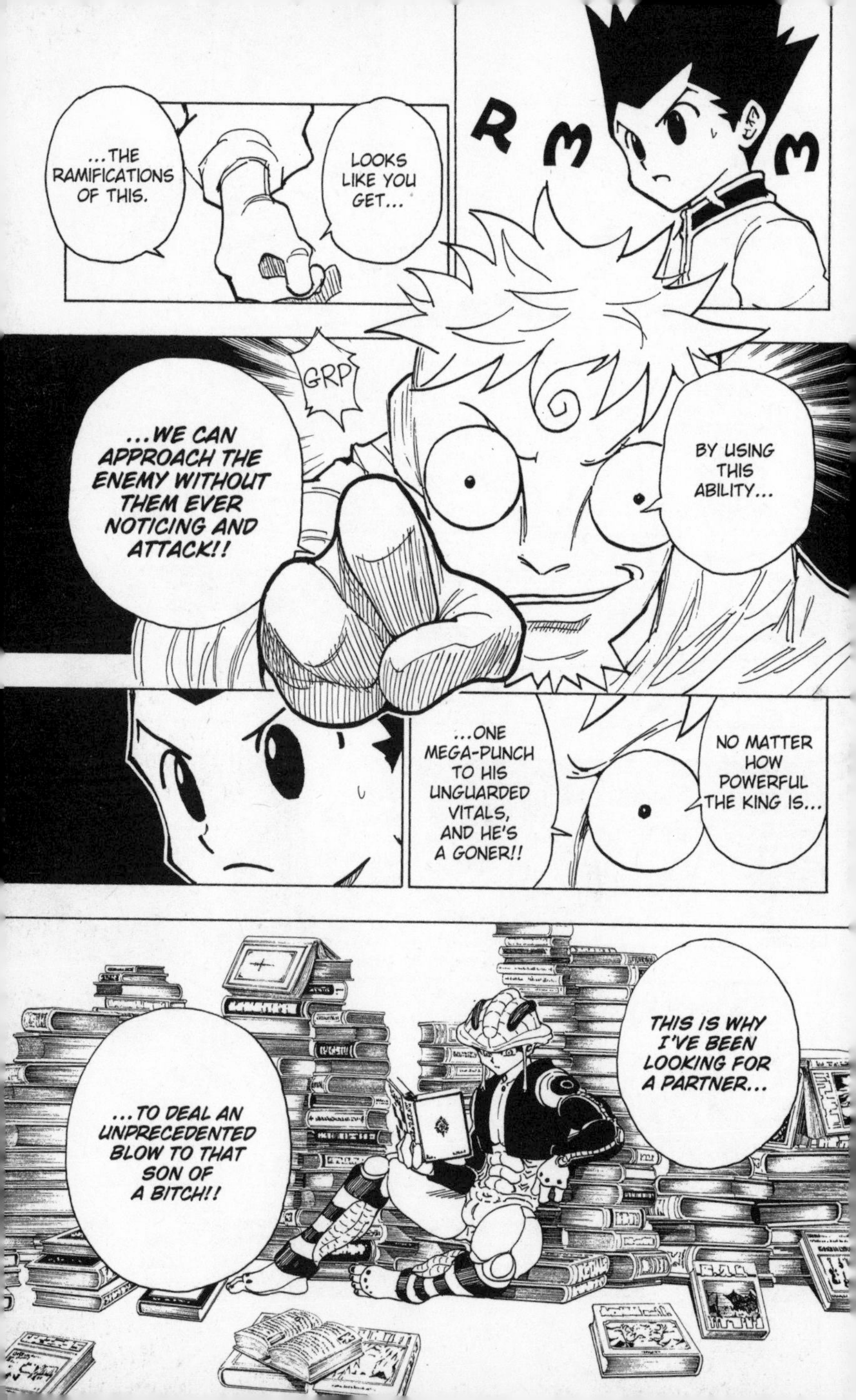
RMM
LOOKS LIKE YOU GET...
...THE RAMIFICATIONS OF THIS.
BY USING THIS ABILITY...
GRP
...WE CAN APPROACH THE ENEMY WITHOUT THEM EVER NOTICING AND ATTACK!!
NO MATTER HOW POWERFUL THE KING IS...
...ONE MEGA-PUNCH TO HIS UNGUARDED VITALS, AND HE'S A GONER!!
THIS IS WHY I'VE BEEN LOOKING FOR A PARTNER...
...TO DEAL AN UNPRECEDENTED BLOW TO THAT SON OF A BITCH!!

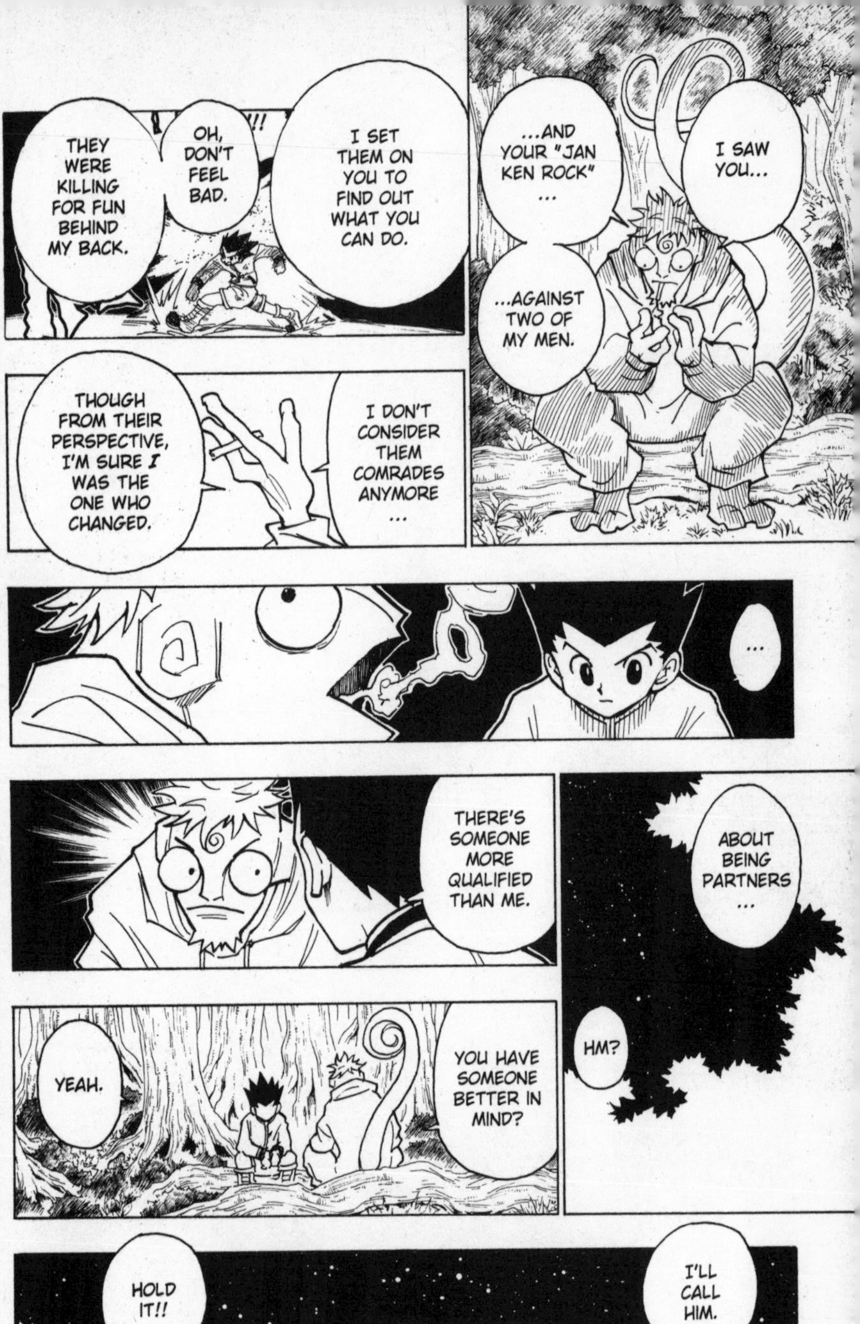
I SAW YOU...
...AND YOUR "JAN KEN ROCK" ...
...AGAINST TWO OF MY MEN.
I SET THEM ON YOU TO FIND OUT WHAT YOU CAN DO.
OH, DON'T FEEL BAD.
THEY WERE KILLING FOR FUN BEHIND MY BACK.
I DON'T CONSIDER THEM COMRADES ANYMORE ...
THOUGH FROM THEIR PERSPECTIVE, I'M SURE *I* WAS THE ONE WHO CHANGED.
...
ABOUT BEING PARTNERS ...
HM?
THERE'S SOMEONE MORE QUALIFIED THAN ME.
YOU HAVE SOMEONE BETTER IN MIND?
YEAH.
I'LL CALL HIM.
HOLD IT!!

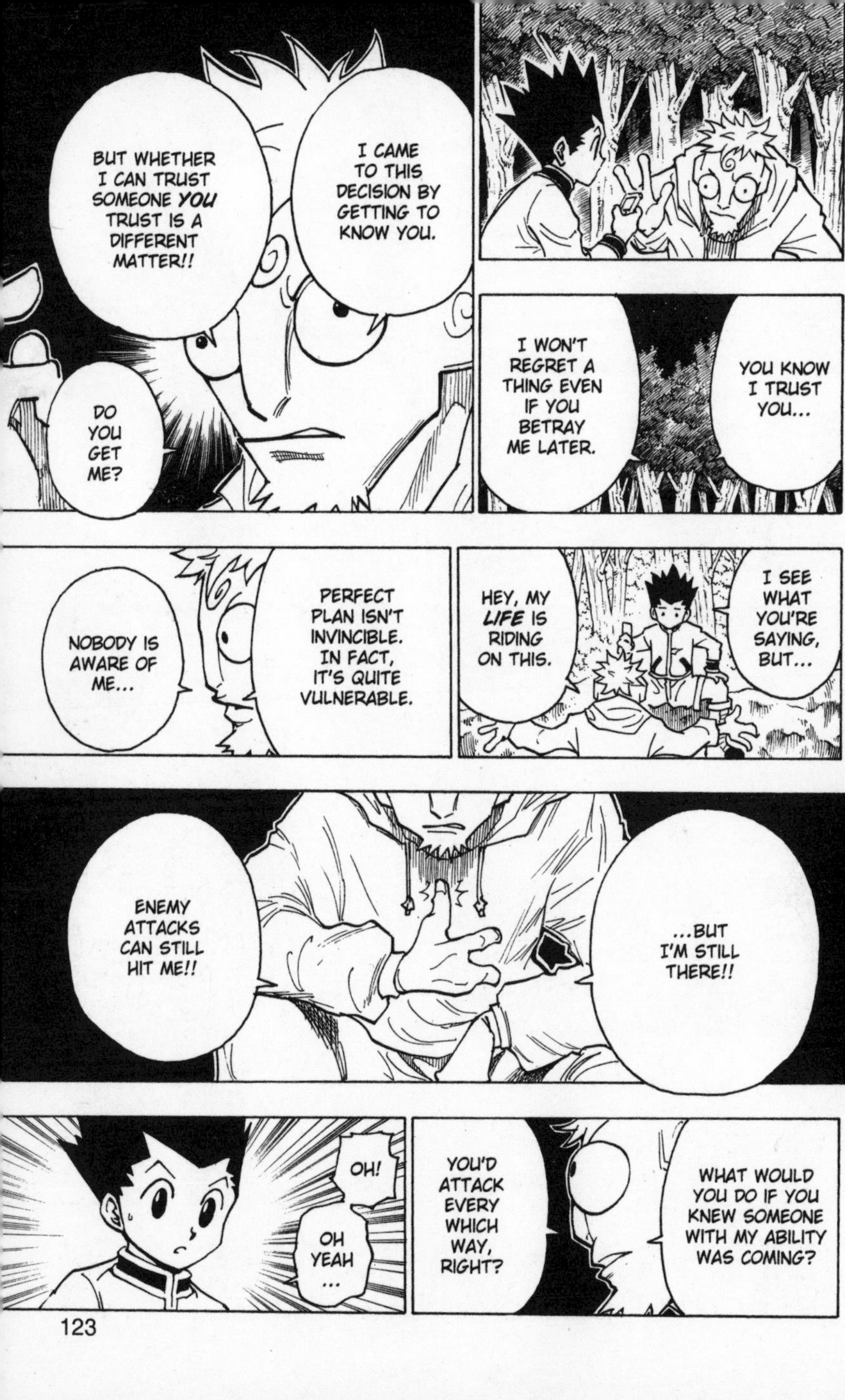
YOU KNOW I TRUST YOU...
I WON'T REGRET A THING EVEN IF YOU BETRAY ME LATER.
I CAME TO THIS DECISION BY GETTING TO KNOW YOU.
BUT WHETHER I CAN TRUST SOMEONE *YOU* TRUST IS A DIFFERENT MATTER!!
DO YOU GET ME?
I SEE WHAT YOU'RE SAYING, BUT...
HEY, MY *LIFE* IS RIDING ON THIS.
PERFECT PLAN ISN'T INVINCIBLE. IN FACT, IT'S QUITE VULNERABLE.
NOBODY IS AWARE OF ME...
...BUT I'M STILL THERE!!
ENEMY ATTACKS CAN STILL HIT ME!!
WHAT WOULD YOU DO IF YOU KNEW SOMEONE WITH MY ABILITY WAS COMING?
YOU'D ATTACK EVERY WHICH WAY, RIGHT?
OH!
OH YEAH ...

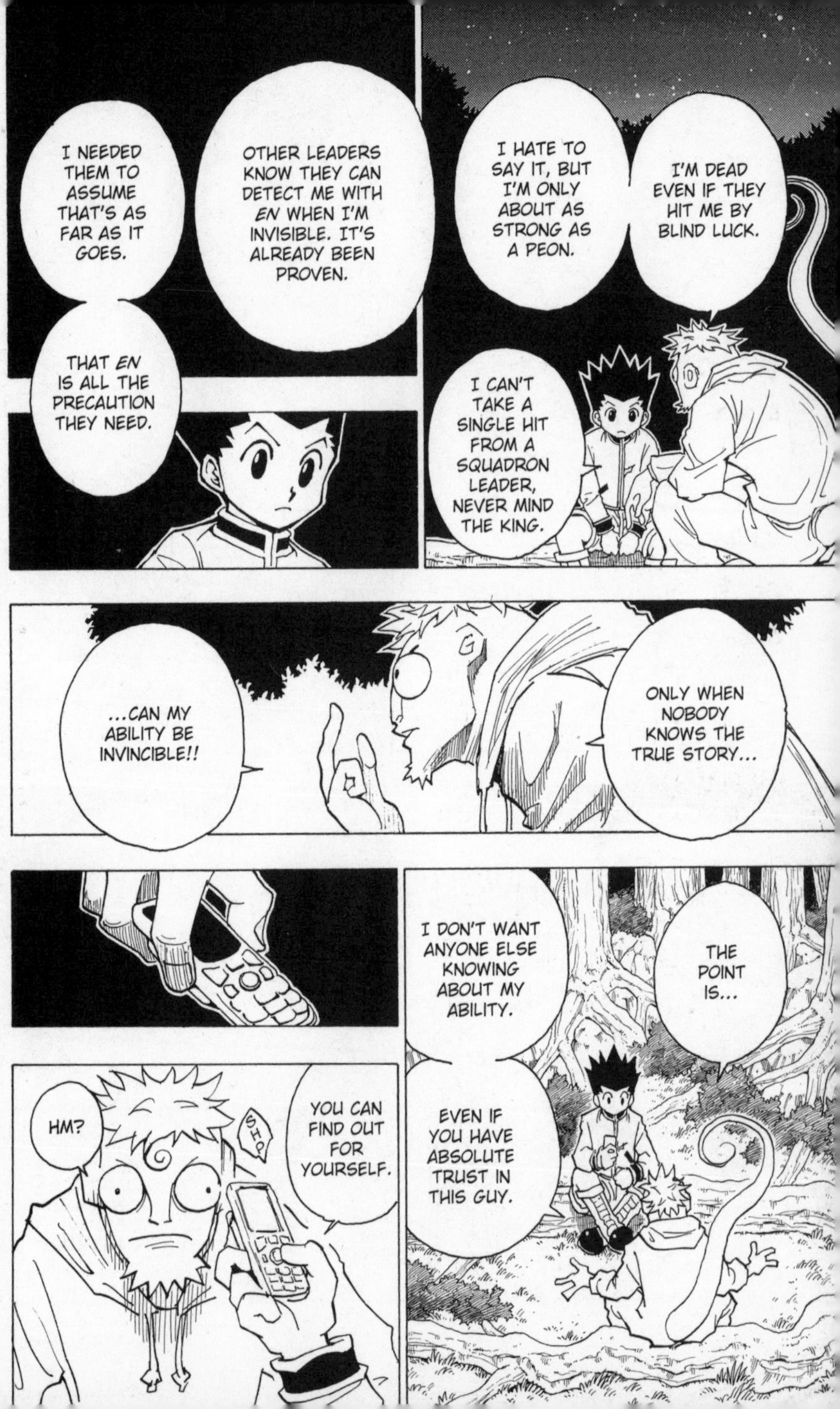
I'M DEAD EVEN IF THEY HIT ME BY BLIND LUCK.
I HATE TO SAY IT, BUT I'M ONLY ABOUT AS STRONG AS A PEON.
I CAN'T TAKE A SINGLE HIT FROM A SQUADRON LEADER, NEVER MIND THE KING.
OTHER LEADERS KNOW THEY CAN DETECT ME WITH *EN* WHEN I'M INVISIBLE. IT'S ALREADY BEEN PROVEN.
I NEEDED THEM TO ASSUME THAT'S AS FAR AS IT GOES.
THAT *EN* IS ALL THE PRECAUTION THEY NEED.
ONLY WHEN NOBODY KNOWS THE TRUE STORY...
...CAN MY ABILITY BE INVINCIBLE!!
THE POINT IS...
I DON'T WANT ANYONE ELSE KNOWING ABOUT MY ABILITY.
EVEN IF YOU HAVE ABSOLUTE TRUST IN THIS GUY.
YOU CAN FIND OUT FOR YOURSELF.
SHP
HM?

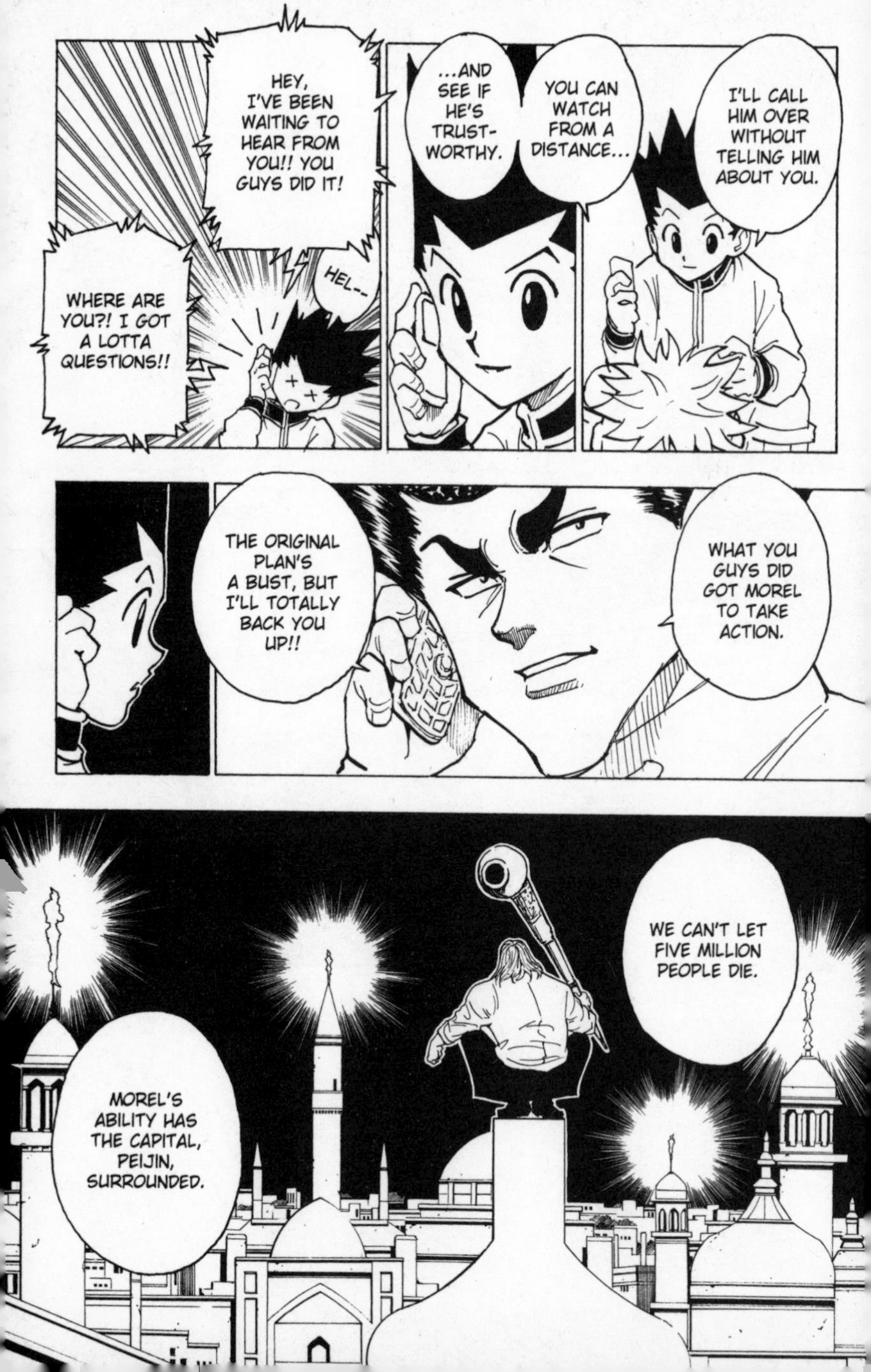
I'LL CALL HIM OVER WITHOUT TELLING HIM ABOUT YOU.
YOU CAN WATCH FROM A DISTANCE...
...AND SEE IF HE'S TRUST-WORTHY.
HEL--
HEY, I'VE BEEN WAITING TO HEAR FROM YOU!! YOU GUYS DID IT!
WHERE ARE YOU?! I GOT A LOTTA QUESTIONS!!
WHAT YOU GUYS DID GOT MOREL TO TAKE ACTION.
THE ORIGINAL PLAN'S A BUST, BUT I'LL TOTALLY BACK YOU UP!!
WE CAN'T LET FIVE MILLION PEOPLE DIE.
MOREL'S ABILITY HAS THE CAPITAL, PEIJIN, SURROUNDED.

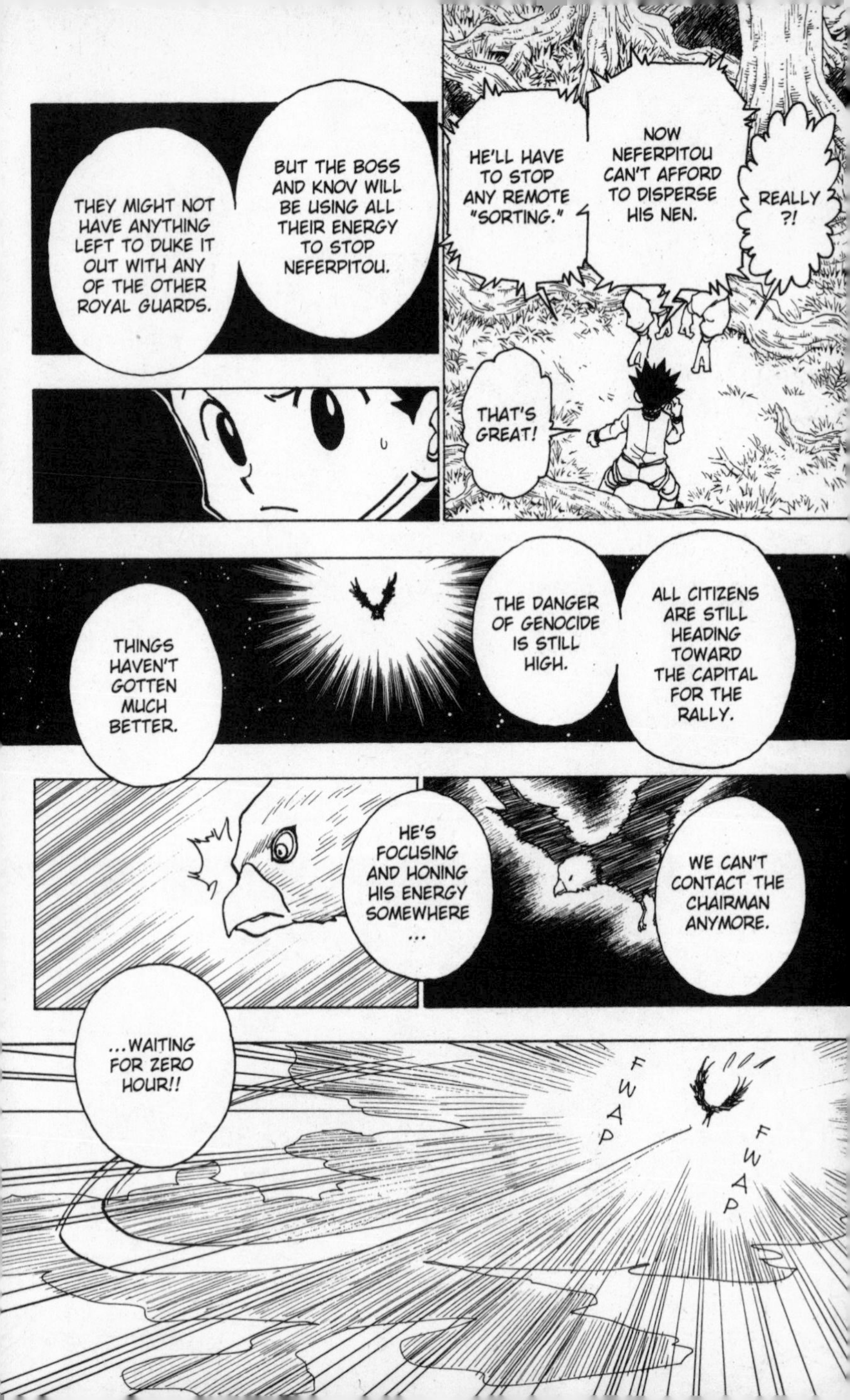
REALLY ?!
NOW NEFERPITOU CAN'T AFFORD TO DISPERSE HIS NEN.
HE'LL HAVE TO STOP ANY REMOTE "SORTING."
THAT'S GREAT!
BUT THE BOSS AND KNOV WILL BE USING ALL THEIR ENERGY TO STOP NEFERPITOU.
THEY MIGHT NOT HAVE ANYTHING LEFT TO DUKE IT OUT WITH ANY OF THE OTHER ROYAL GUARDS.
ALL CITIZENS ARE STILL HEADING TOWARD THE CAPITAL FOR THE RALLY.
THE DANGER OF GENOCIDE IS STILL HIGH.
THINGS HAVEN'T GOTTEN MUCH BETTER.
WE CAN'T CONTACT THE CHAIRMAN ANYMORE.
HE'S FOCUSING AND HONING HIS ENERGY SOMEWHERE ...
FWAP
FWAP
...WAITING FOR ZERO HOUR!!

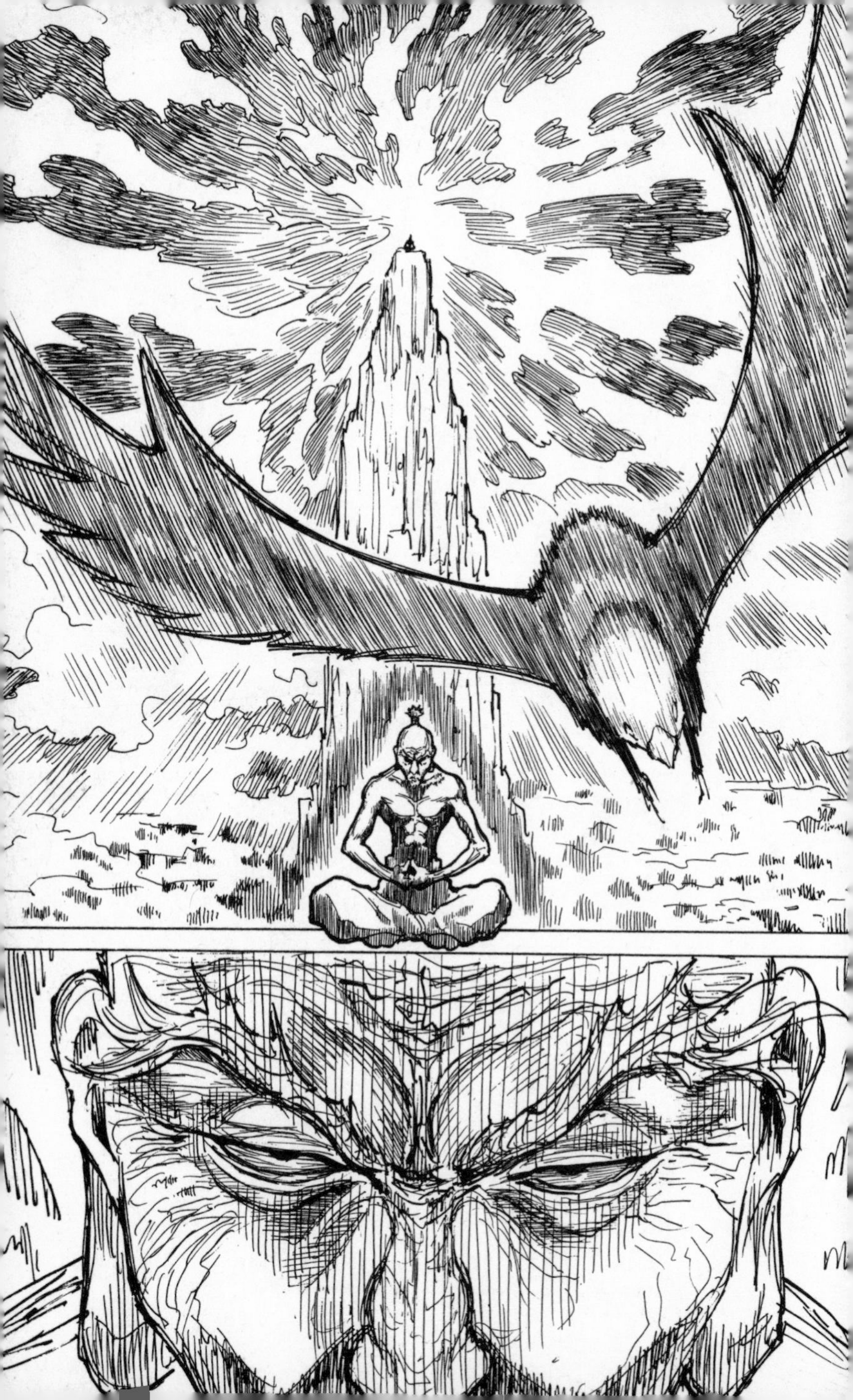

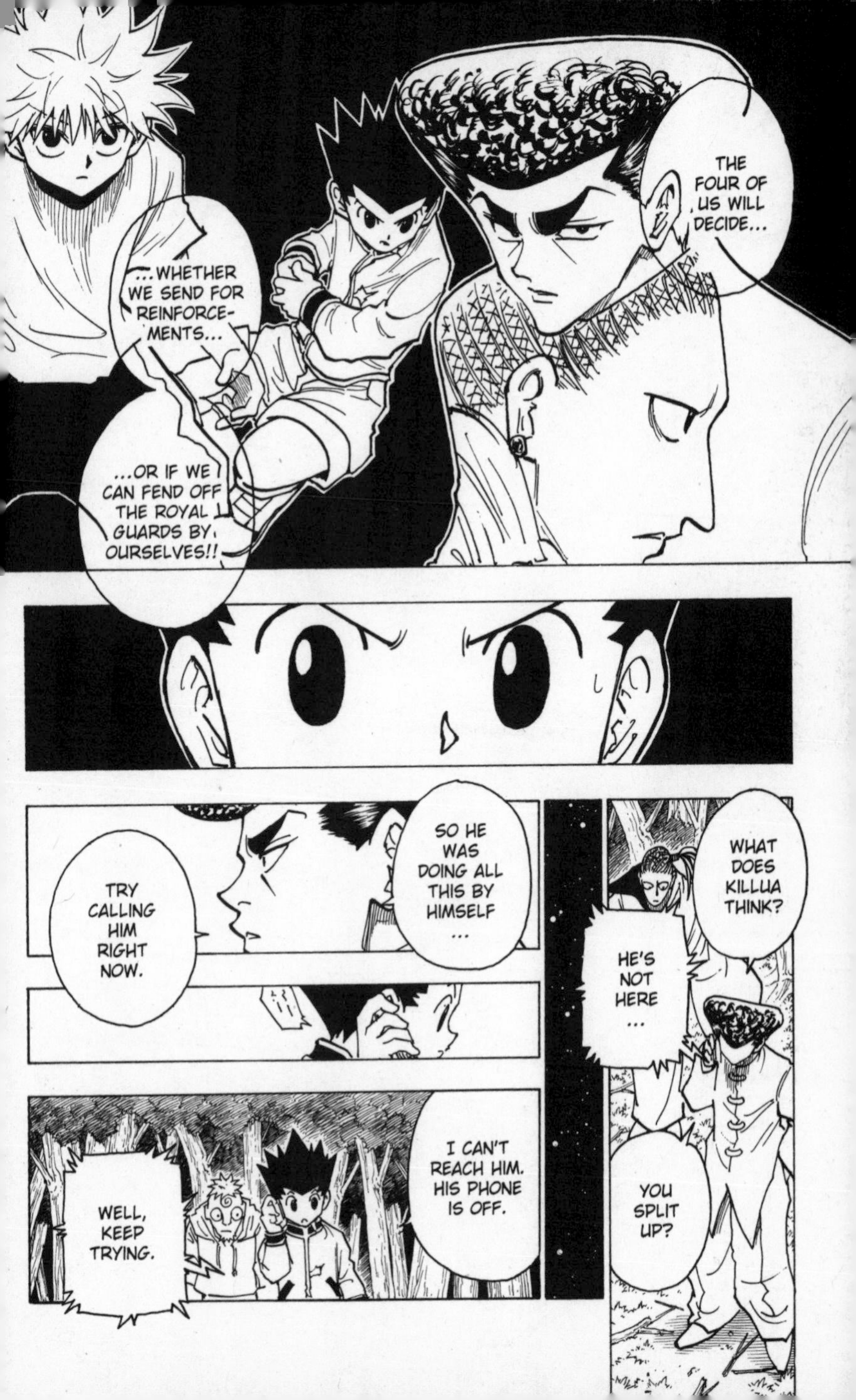
THE FOUR OF US WILL DECIDE...
...WHETHER WE SEND FOR REINFORCE-MENTS...
...OR IF WE CAN FEND OFF THE ROYAL GUARDS BY OURSELVES!!
WHAT DOES KILLUA THINK?
HE'S NOT HERE ...
YOU SPLIT UP?
SO HE WAS DOING ALL THIS BY HIMSELF ...
TRY CALLING HIM RIGHT NOW.
I CAN'T REACH HIM. HIS PHONE IS OFF.
WELL, KEEP TRYING.

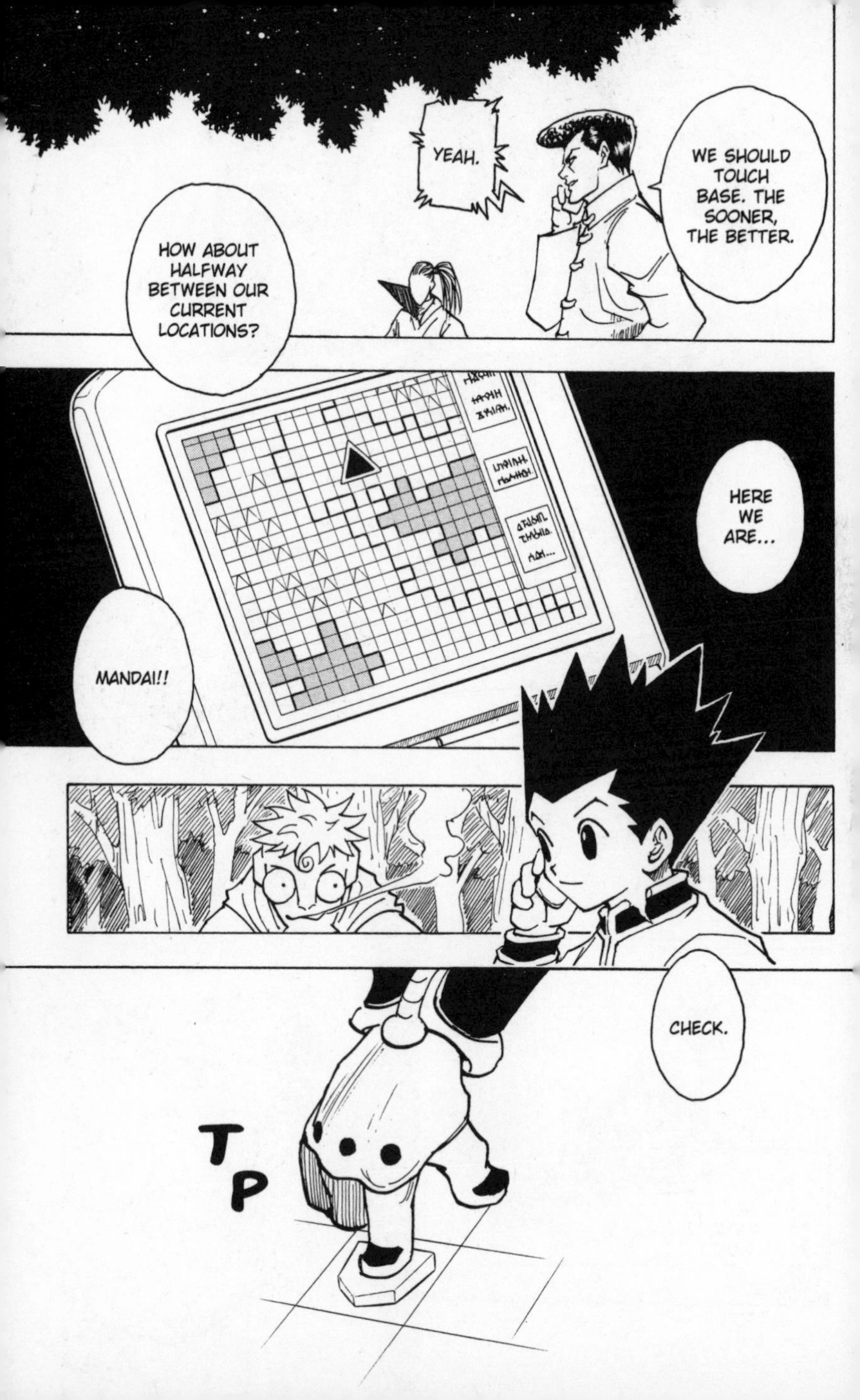
WE SHOULD TOUCH BASE. THE SOONER, THE BETTER.
YEAH.
HOW ABOUT HALFWAY BETWEEN OUR CURRENT LOCATIONS?
HERE WE ARE...
MANDAI!!
CHECK.
TP

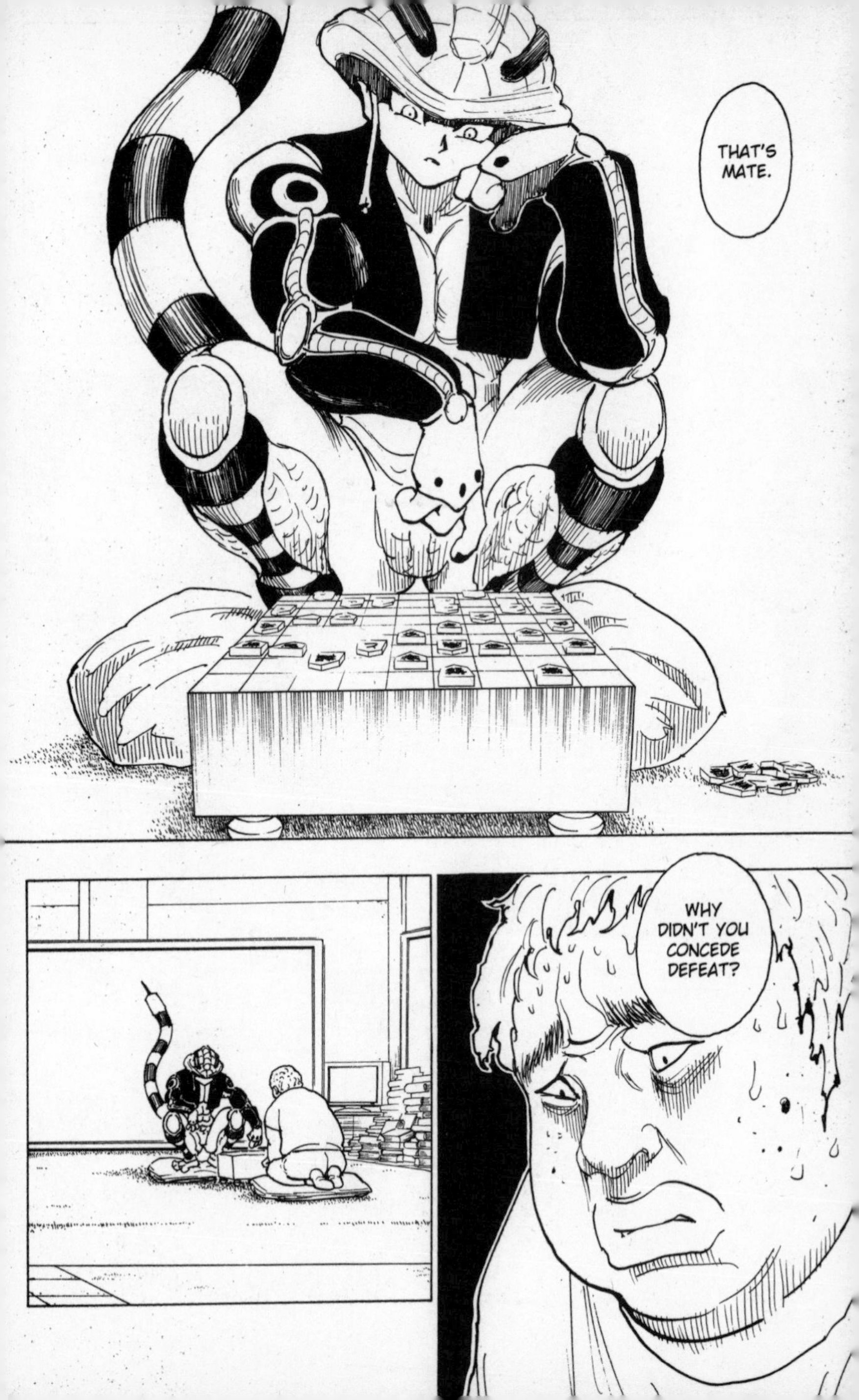
THAT'S MATE.
WHY DIDN'T YOU CONCEDE DEFEAT?

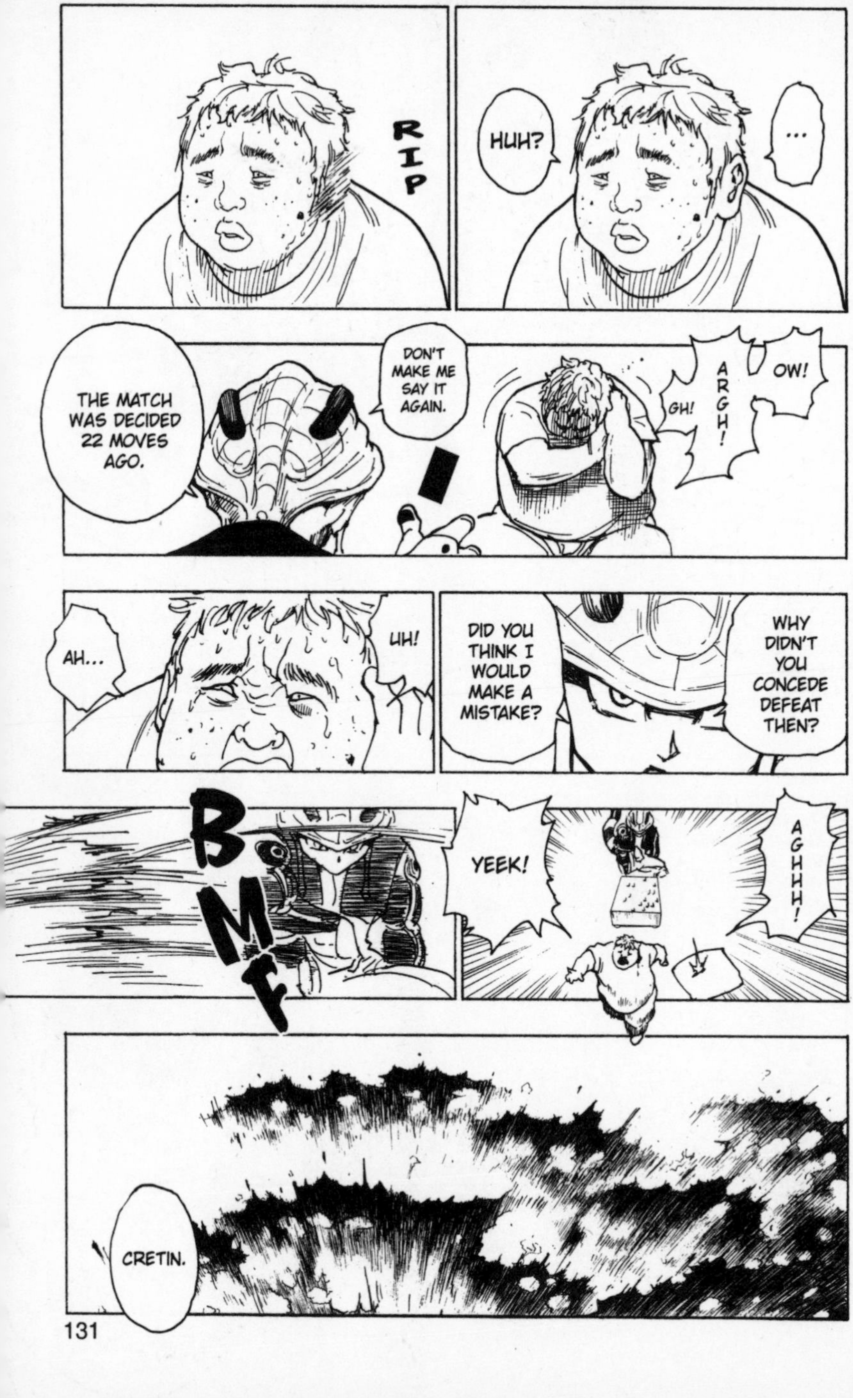
...
HUH?
RIP
OW!
ARGH!
GH!
DON'T MAKE ME SAY IT AGAIN.
THE MATCH WAS DECIDED 22 MOVES AGO.
WHY DIDN'T YOU CONCEDE DEFEAT THEN?
DID YOU THINK I WOULD MAKE A MISTAKE?
UH!
AH...
AGHHH!
YEEK!
BMF
CRETIN.

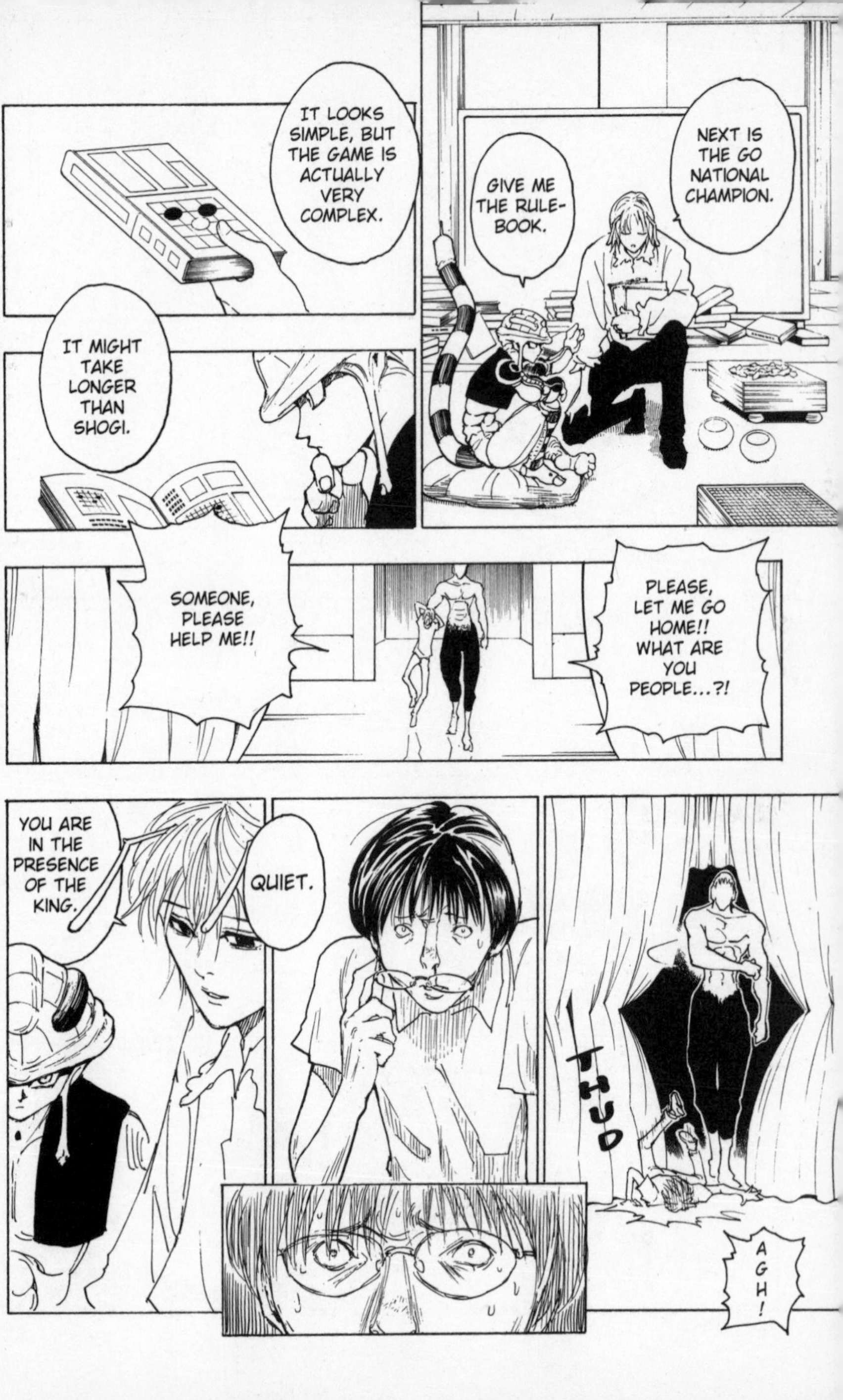
NEXT IS THE GO NATIONAL CHAMPION.
GIVE ME THE RULE-BOOK.
IT LOOKS SIMPLE, BUT THE GAME IS ACTUALLY VERY COMPLEX.
IT MIGHT TAKE LONGER THAN SHOGI.
PLEASE, LET ME GO HOME!! WHAT ARE YOU PEOPLE...?!
SOMEONE, PLEASE HELP ME!!
THUD
AGH!
QUIET.
YOU ARE IN THE PRESENCE OF THE KING.

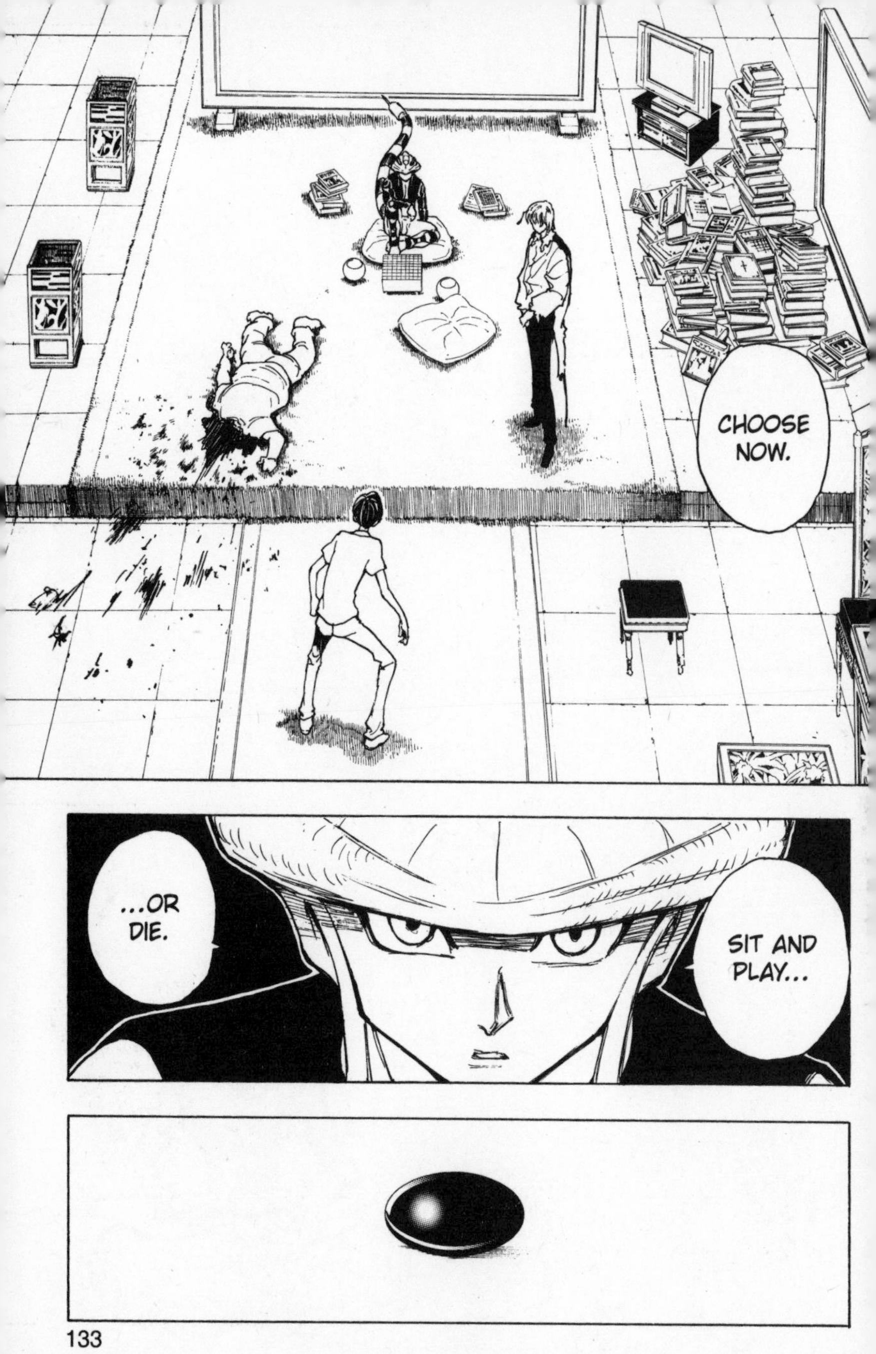
CHOOSE NOW.
SIT AND PLAY...
...OR DIE.

Chapter 244: 6: Part 1

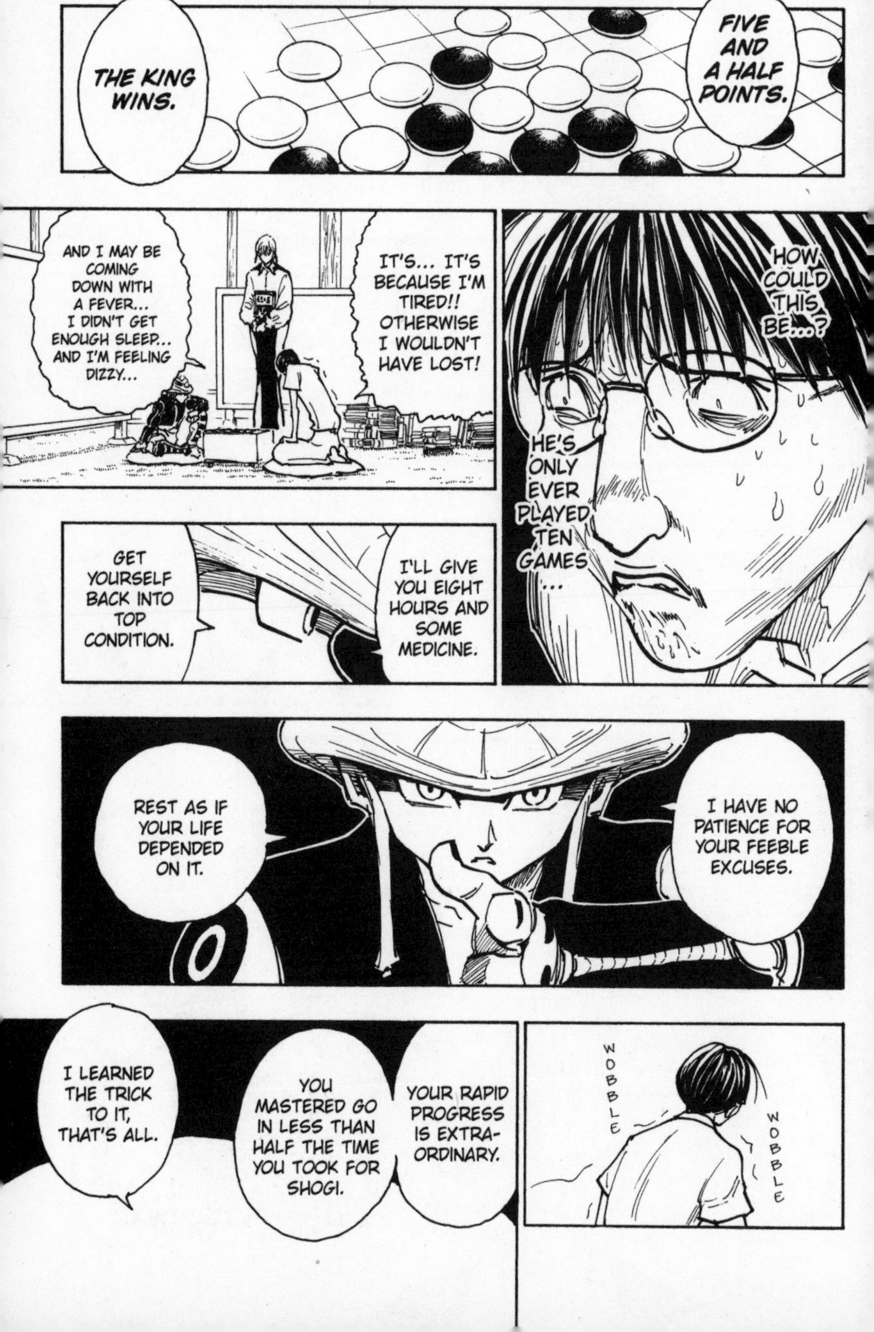
FIVE AND A HALF POINTS.
THE KING WINS.
HOW COULD THIS BE...?
HE'S ONLY EVER PLAYED TEN GAMES...
IT'S... IT'S BECAUSE I'M TIRED!! OTHERWISE I WOULDN'T HAVE LOST!
AND I MAY BE COMING DOWN WITH A FEVER... I DIDN'T GET ENOUGH SLEEP... AND I'M FEELING DIZZY...
I'LL GIVE YOU EIGHT HOURS AND SOME MEDICINE.
GET YOURSELF BACK INTO TOP CONDITION.
I HAVE NO PATIENCE FOR YOUR FEEBLE EXCUSES.
REST AS IF YOUR LIFE DEPENDED ON IT.
WOBBLE
WOBBLE
YOUR RAPID PROGRESS IS EXTRA-ORDINARY.
YOU MASTERED GO IN LESS THAN HALF THE TIME YOU TOOK FOR SHOGI.
I LEARNED THE TRICK TO IT, THAT'S ALL.

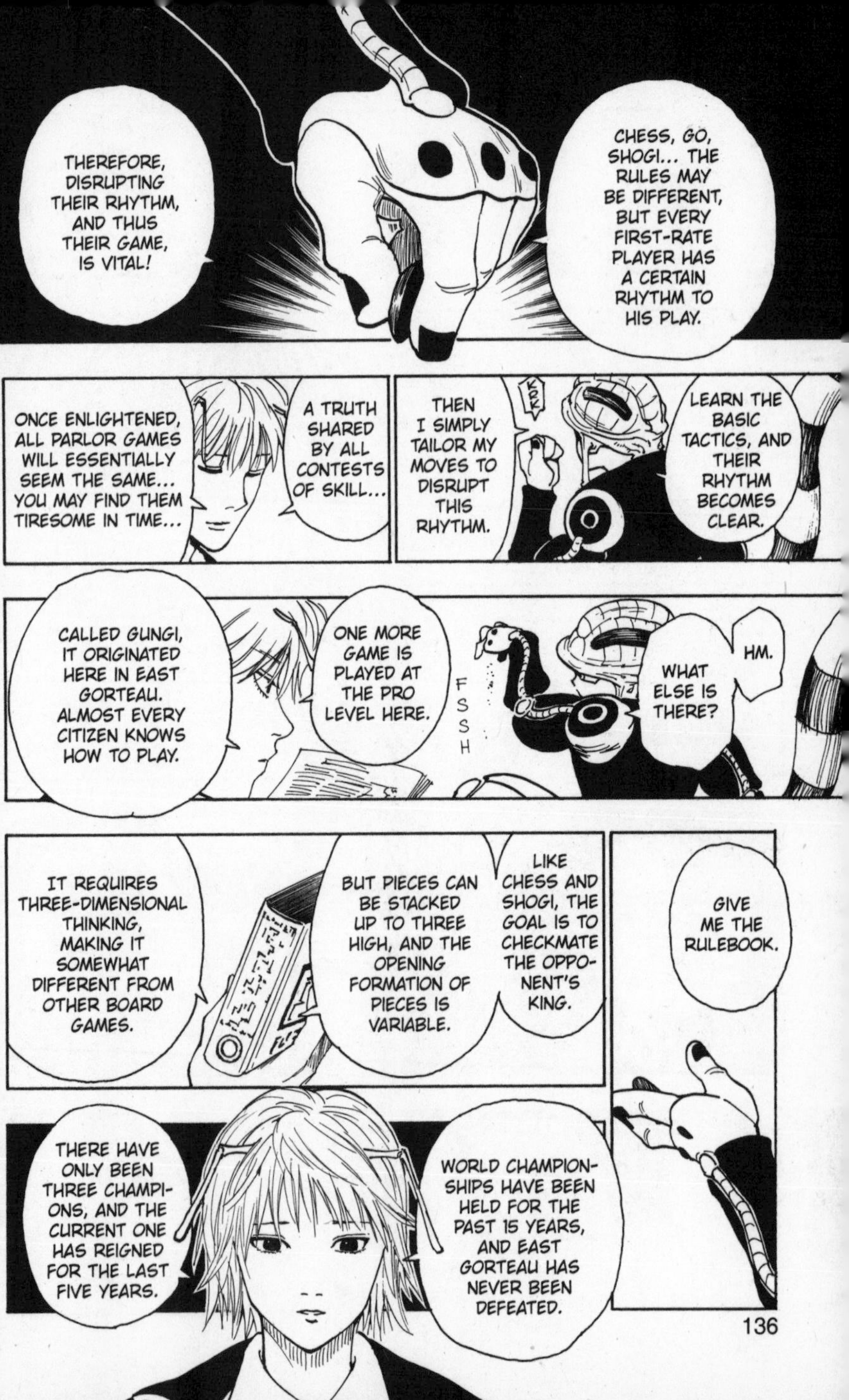
CHESS, GO, SHOGI... THE RULES MAY BE DIFFERENT, BUT EVERY FIRST-RATE PLAYER HAS A CERTAIN RHYTHM TO HIS PLAY.
THEREFORE, DISRUPTING THEIR RHYTHM, AND THUS THEIR GAME, IS VITAL!
LEARN THE BASIC TACTICS, AND THEIR RHYTHM BECOMES CLEAR.
KRK
THEN I SIMPLY TAILOR MY MOVES TO DISRUPT THIS RHYTHM.
A TRUTH SHARED BY ALL CONTESTS OF SKILL...
ONCE ENLIGHTENED, ALL PARLOR GAMES WILL ESSENTIALLY SEEM THE SAME... YOU MAY FIND THEM TIRESOME IN TIME...
HM.
WHAT ELSE IS THERE?
FSSH
ONE MORE GAME IS PLAYED AT THE PRO LEVEL HERE.
CALLED GUNGI, IT ORIGINATED HERE IN EAST GORTEAU. ALMOST EVERY CITIZEN KNOWS HOW TO PLAY.
GIVE ME THE RULEBOOK.
LIKE CHESS AND SHOGI, THE GOAL IS TO CHECKMATE THE OPPONENT'S KING.
BUT PIECES CAN BE STACKED UP TO THREE HIGH, AND THE OPENING FORMATION OF PIECES IS VARIABLE.
IT REQUIRES THREE-DIMENSIONAL THINKING, MAKING IT SOMEWHAT DIFFERENT FROM OTHER BOARD GAMES.
WORLD CHAMPIONSHIPS HAVE BEEN HELD FOR THE PAST 15 YEARS, AND EAST GORTEAU HAS NEVER BEEN DEFEATED.
THERE HAVE ONLY BEEN THREE CHAMPIONS, AND THE CURRENT ONE HAS REIGNED FOR THE LAST FIVE YEARS.

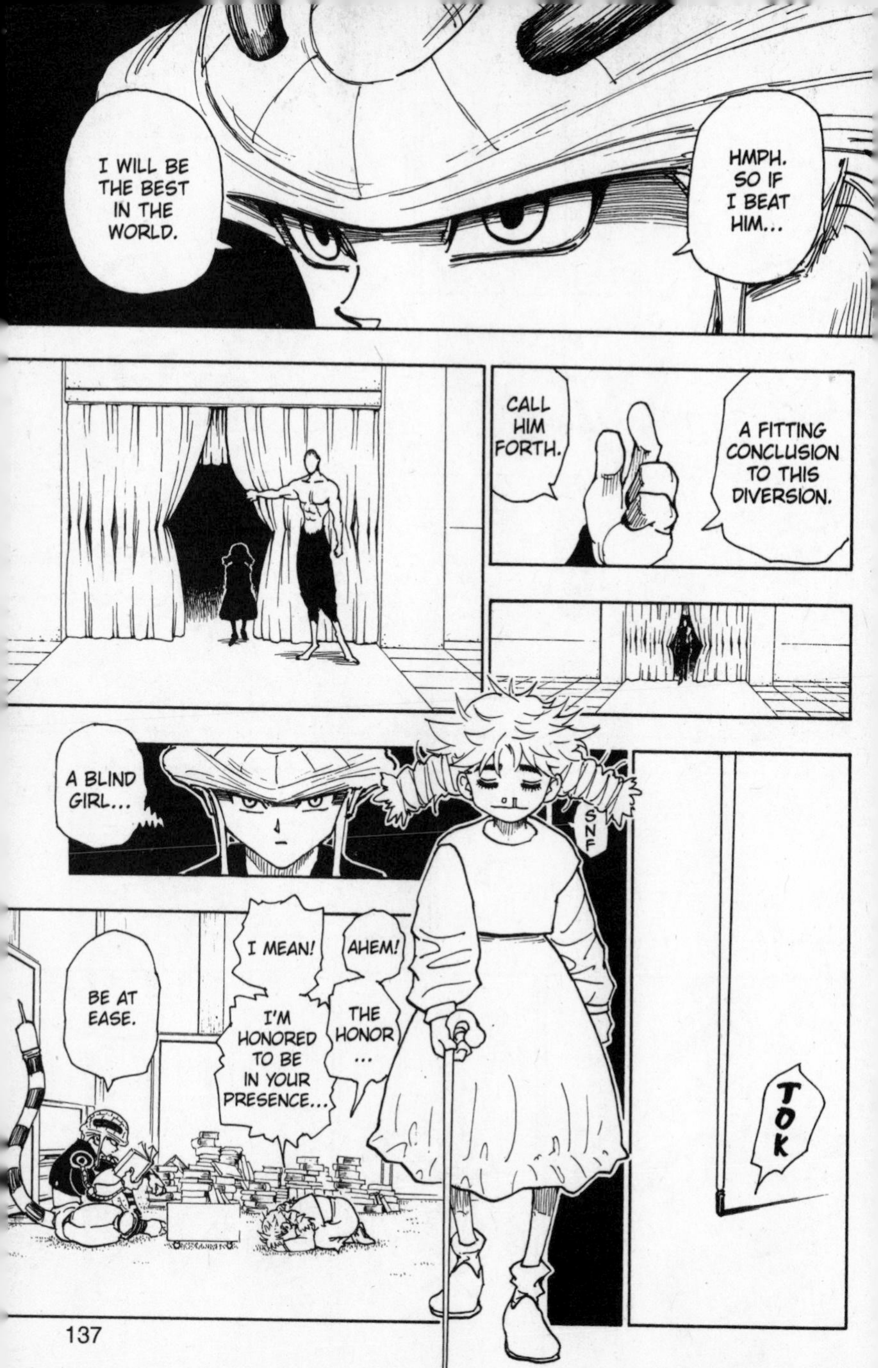
HMPH. SO IF I BEAT HIM...
I WILL BE THE BEST IN THE WORLD.
A FITTING CONCLUSION TO THIS DIVERSION.
CALL HIM FORTH.
TOK
A BLIND GIRL...
SNF
AHEM!
THE HONOR...
I MEAN!
I'M HONORED TO BE IN YOUR PRESENCE...
BE AT EASE.

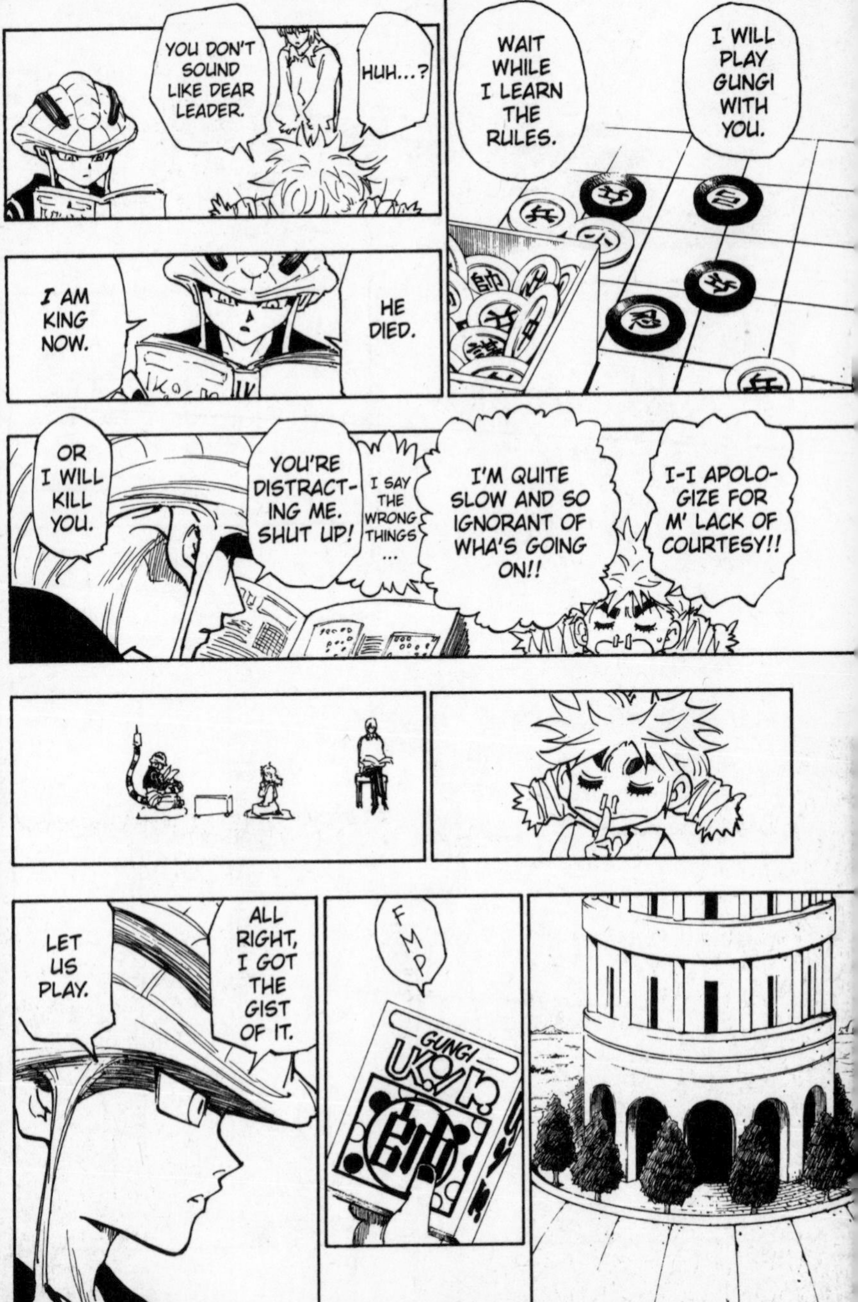
I WILL PLAY GUNGI WITH YOU.
WAIT WHILE I LEARN THE RULES.
HUH...?
YOU DON'T SOUND LIKE DEAR LEADER.
HE DIED.
I AM KING NOW.
I-I APOLOGIZE FOR M' LACK OF COURTESY!!
I'M QUITE SLOW AND SO IGNORANT OF WHA'S GOING ON!!
I SAY THE WRONG THINGS ...
YOU'RE DISTRACTING ME. SHUT UP!
OR I WILL KILL YOU.
FMP
GUNGI
ALL RIGHT, I GOT THE GIST OF IT.
LET US PLAY.

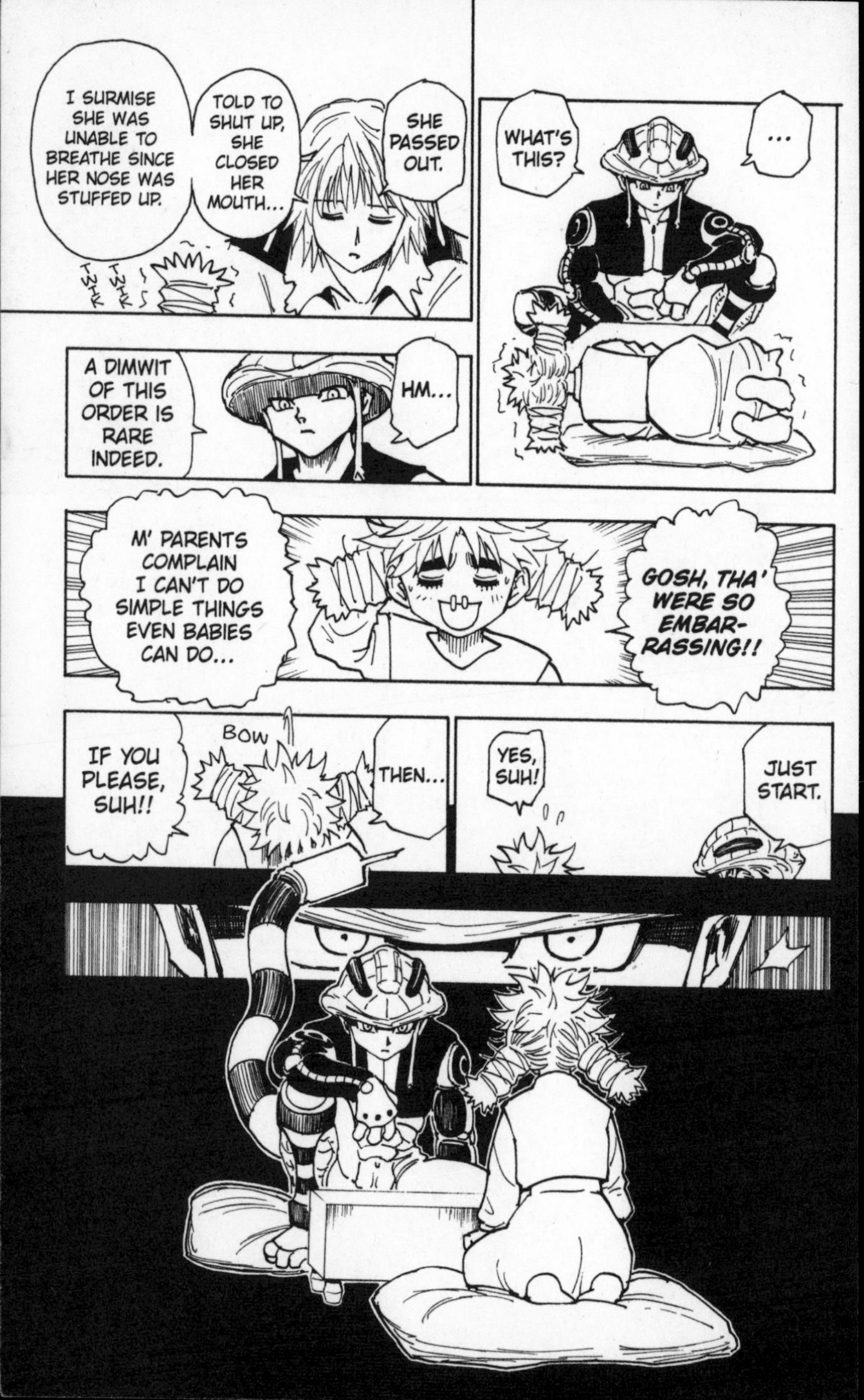
...
WHAT'S THIS?
SHE PASSED OUT.
TOLD TO SHUT UP, SHE CLOSED HER MOUTH...
I SURMISE SHE WAS UNABLE TO BREATHE SINCE HER NOSE WAS STUFFED UP.
TWIK TWIK
HM...
A DIMWIT OF THIS ORDER IS RARE INDEED.
GOSH, THA' WERE SO EMBAR-RASSING!!
M' PARENTS COMPLAIN I CAN'T DO SIMPLE THINGS EVEN BABIES CAN DO...
JUST START.
YES, SUH!
THEN...
BOW
IF YOU PLEASE, SUH!!

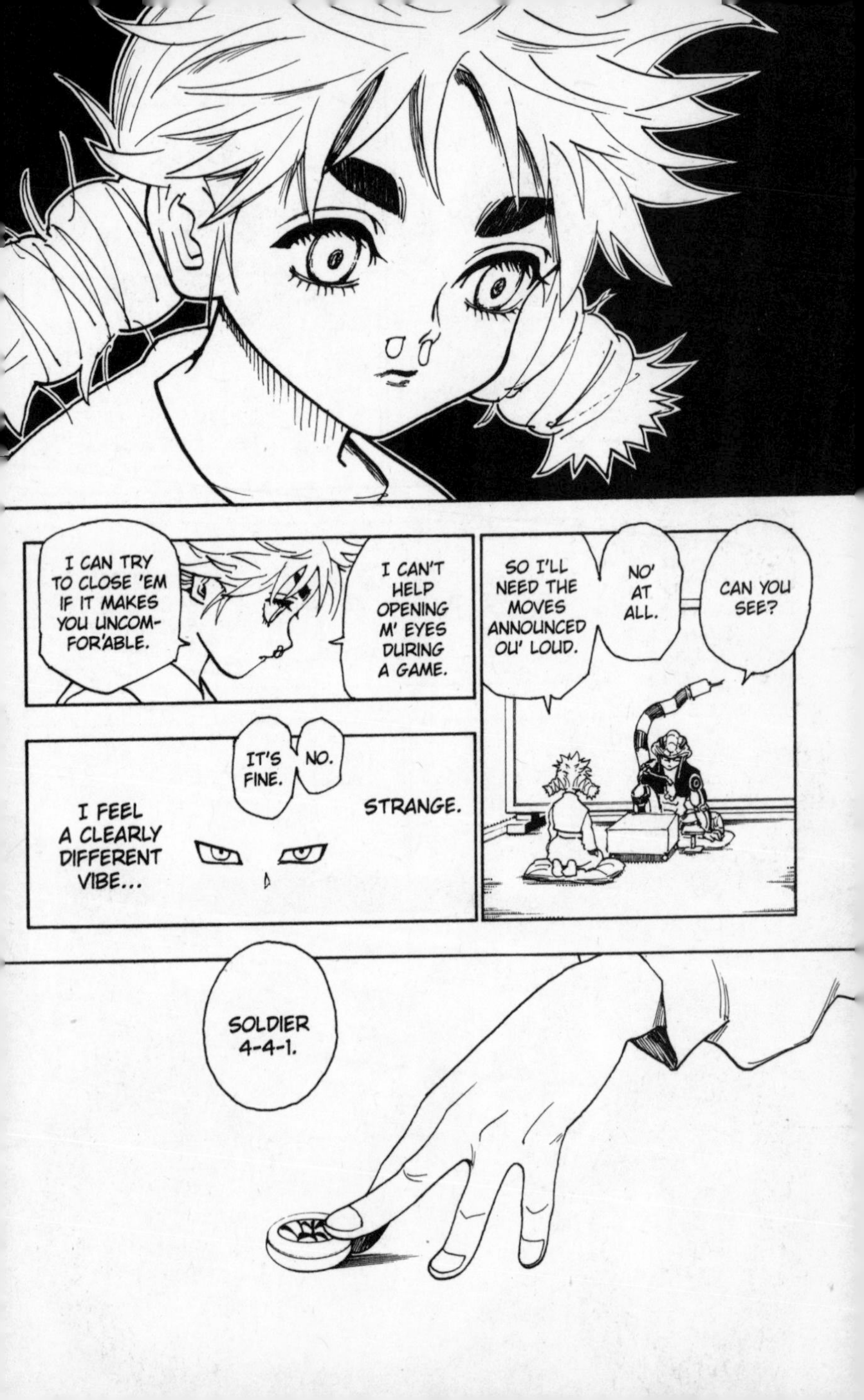
CAN YOU SEE?
NO' AT ALL.
SO I'LL NEED THE MOVES ANNOUNCED OU' LOUD.
I CAN'T HELP OPENING M' EYES DURING A GAME.
I CAN TRY TO CLOSE 'EM IF IT MAKES YOU UNCOM-FOR'ABLE.
NO.
IT'S FINE.
STRANGE.
I FEEL A CLEARLY DIFFERENT VIBE...
SOLDIER 4-4-1.

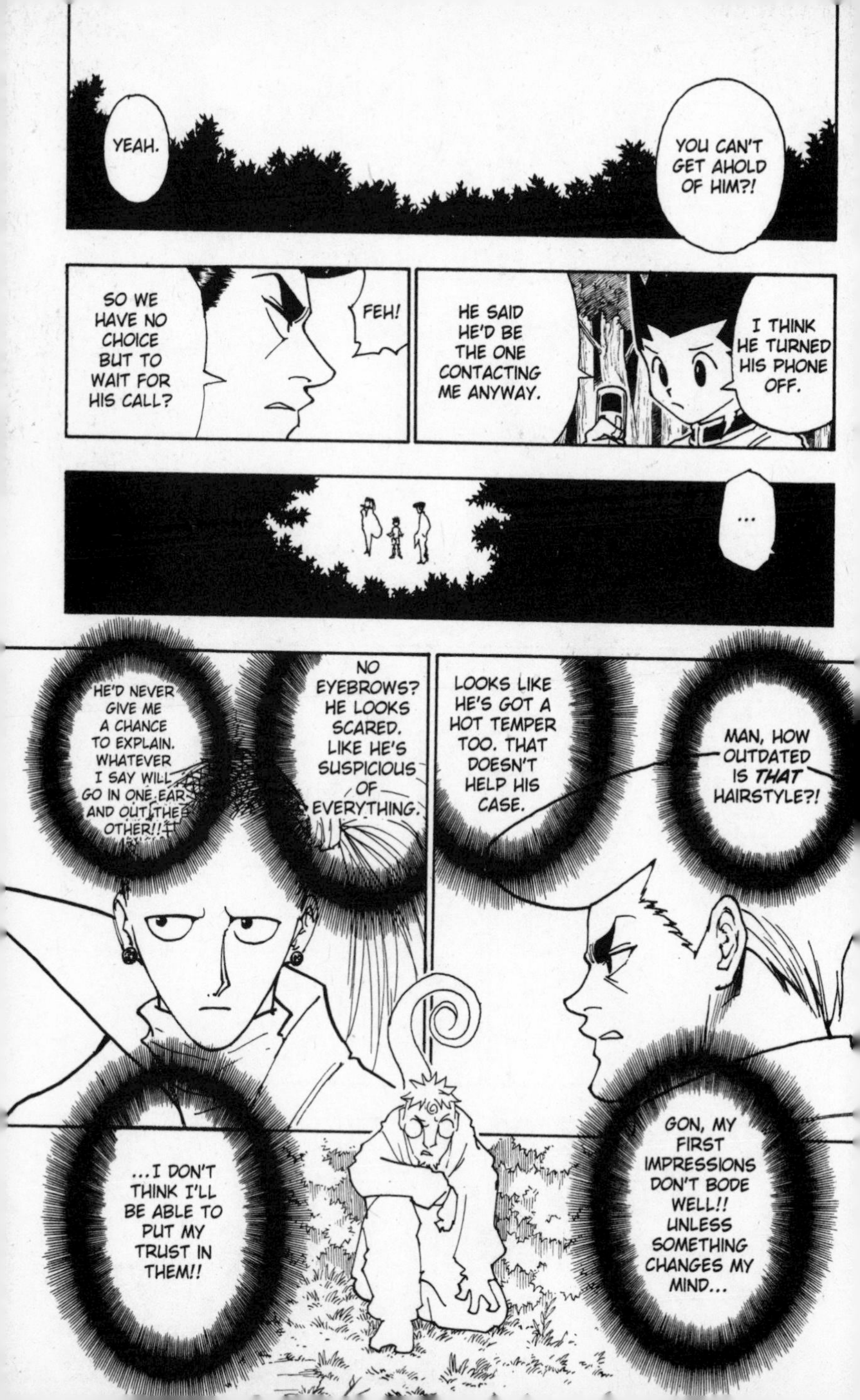
YOU CAN'T GET AHOLD OF HIM?!
YEAH.
I THINK HE TURNED HIS PHONE OFF.
HE SAID HE'D BE THE ONE CONTACTING ME ANYWAY.
FEH!
SO WE HAVE NO CHOICE BUT TO WAIT FOR HIS CALL?
...
MAN, HOW OUTDATED IS *THAT* HAIRSTYLE?!
LOOKS LIKE HE'S GOT A HOT TEMPER TOO. THAT DOESN'T HELP HIS CASE.
NO EYEBROWS? HE LOOKS SCARED. LIKE HE'S SUSPICIOUS OF EVERYTHING.
HE'D NEVER GIVE ME A CHANCE TO EXPLAIN. WHATEVER I SAY WILL GO IN ONE EAR AND OUT THE OTHER!!
GON, MY FIRST IMPRESSIONS DON'T BODE WELL!! UNLESS SOMETHING CHANGES MY MIND...
...I DON'T THINK I'LL BE ABLE TO PUT MY TRUST IN THEM!!

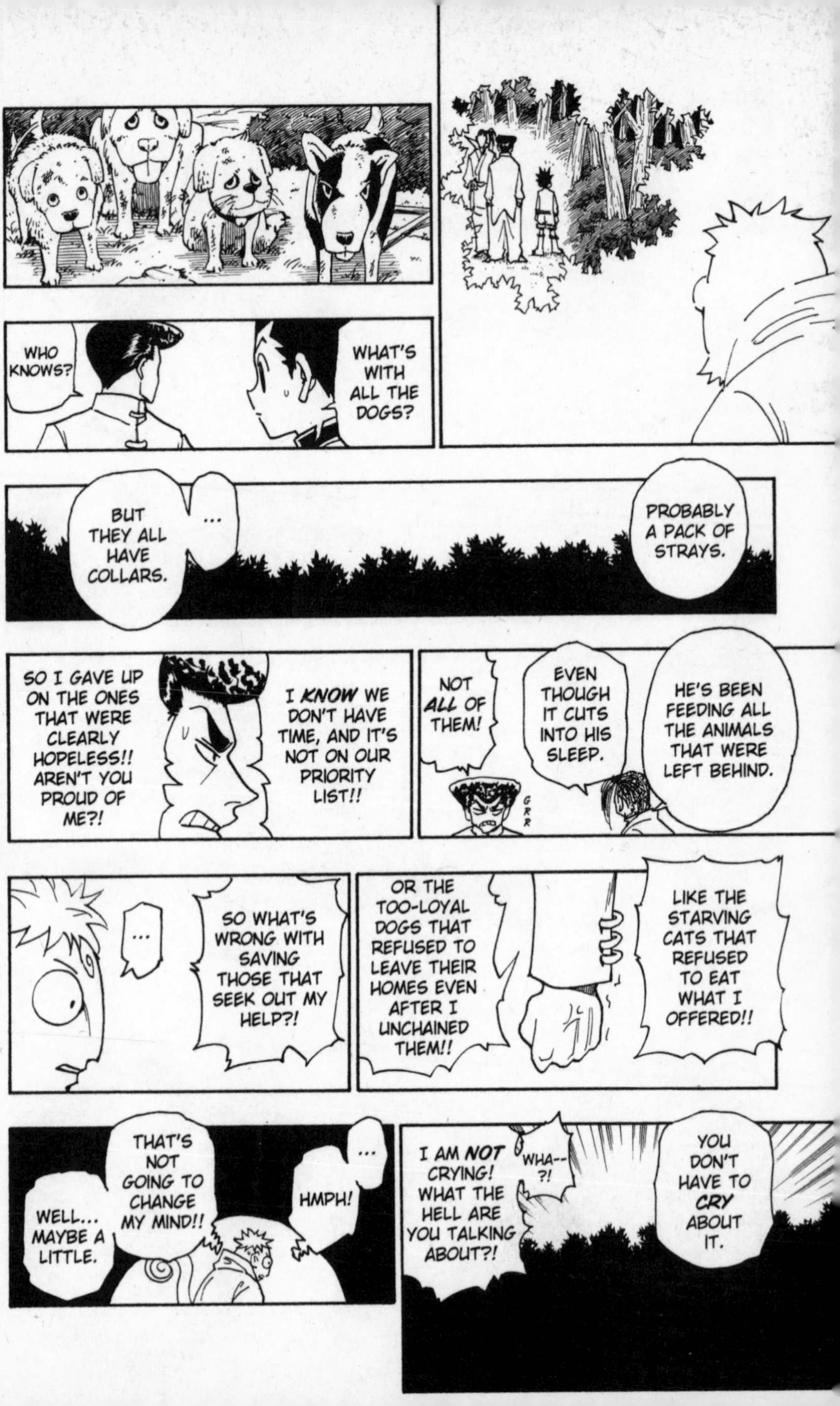
WHAT'S WITH ALL THE DOGS?
WHO KNOWS?
PROBABLY A PACK OF STRAYS.
...
BUT THEY ALL HAVE COLLARS.
HE'S BEEN FEEDING ALL THE ANIMALS THAT WERE LEFT BEHIND.
EVEN THOUGH IT CUTS INTO HIS SLEEP.
NOT ALL OF THEM!
GRR
I KNOW WE DON'T HAVE TIME, AND IT'S NOT ON OUR PRIORITY LIST!!
SO I GAVE UP ON THE ONES THAT WERE CLEARLY HOPELESS!! AREN'T YOU PROUD OF ME?!
LIKE THE STARVING CATS THAT REFUSED TO EAT WHAT I OFFERED!!
OR THE TOO-LOYAL DOGS THAT REFUSED TO LEAVE THEIR HOMES EVEN AFTER I UNCHAINED THEM!!
SO WHAT'S WRONG WITH SAVING THOSE THAT SEEK OUT MY HELP?!
...
YOU DON'T HAVE TO CRY ABOUT IT.
WHA--?!
I AM NOT CRYING! WHAT THE HELL ARE YOU TALKING ABOUT?!
...
HMPH!
THAT'S NOT GOING TO CHANGE MY MIND!!
WELL... MAYBE A LITTLE.

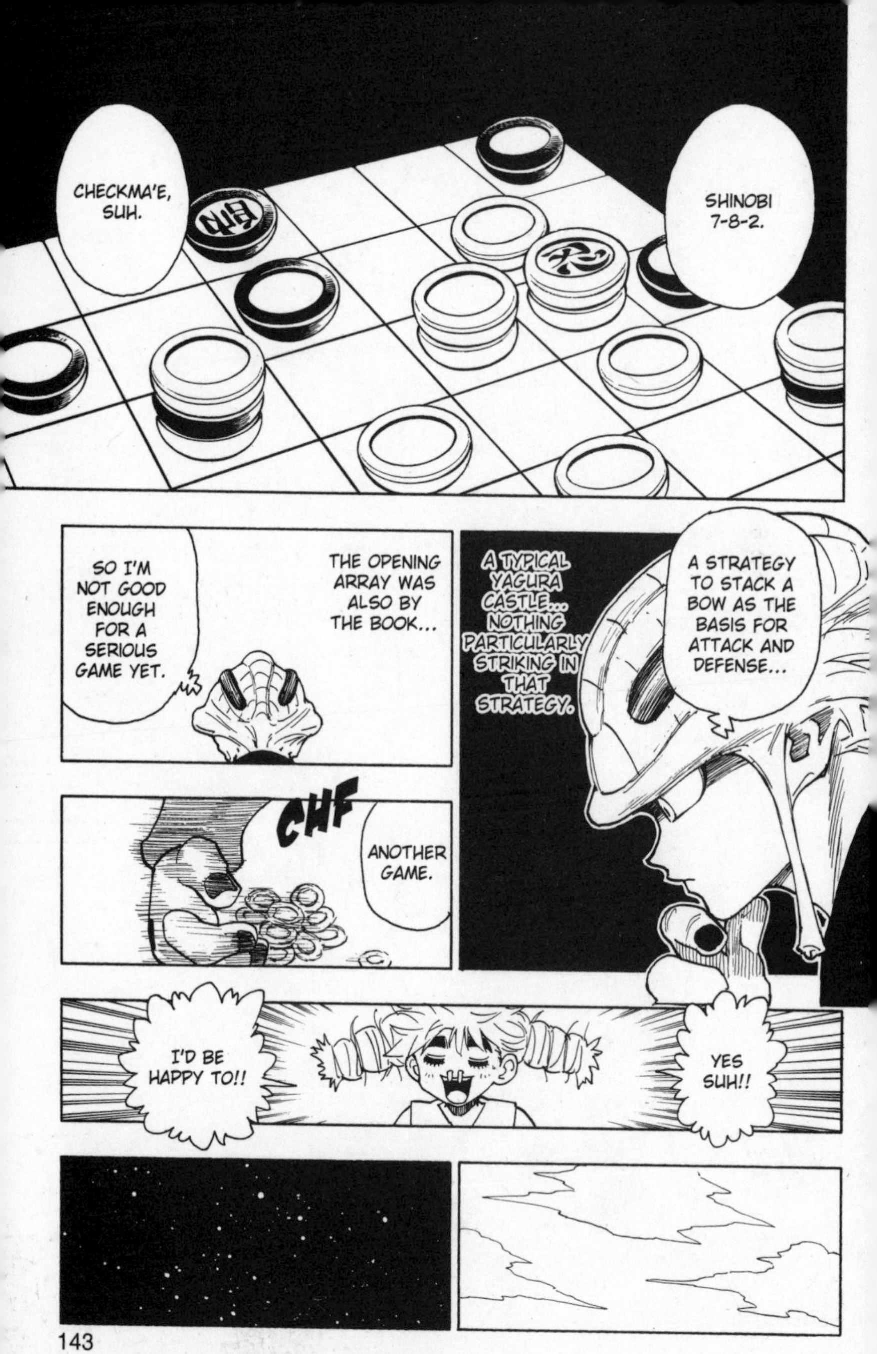
SHINOBI 7-8-2.
CHECKMA'E, SUH.
A STRATEGY TO STACK A BOW AS THE BASIS FOR ATTACK AND DEFENSE...
A TYPICAL YAGURA CASTLE... NOTHING PARTICULARLY STRIKING IN THAT STRATEGY.
THE OPENING ARRAY WAS ALSO BY THE BOOK...
SO I'M NOT GOOD ENOUGH FOR A SERIOUS GAME YET.
ANOTHER GAME.
CHF
YES SUH!!
I'D BE HAPPY TO!!

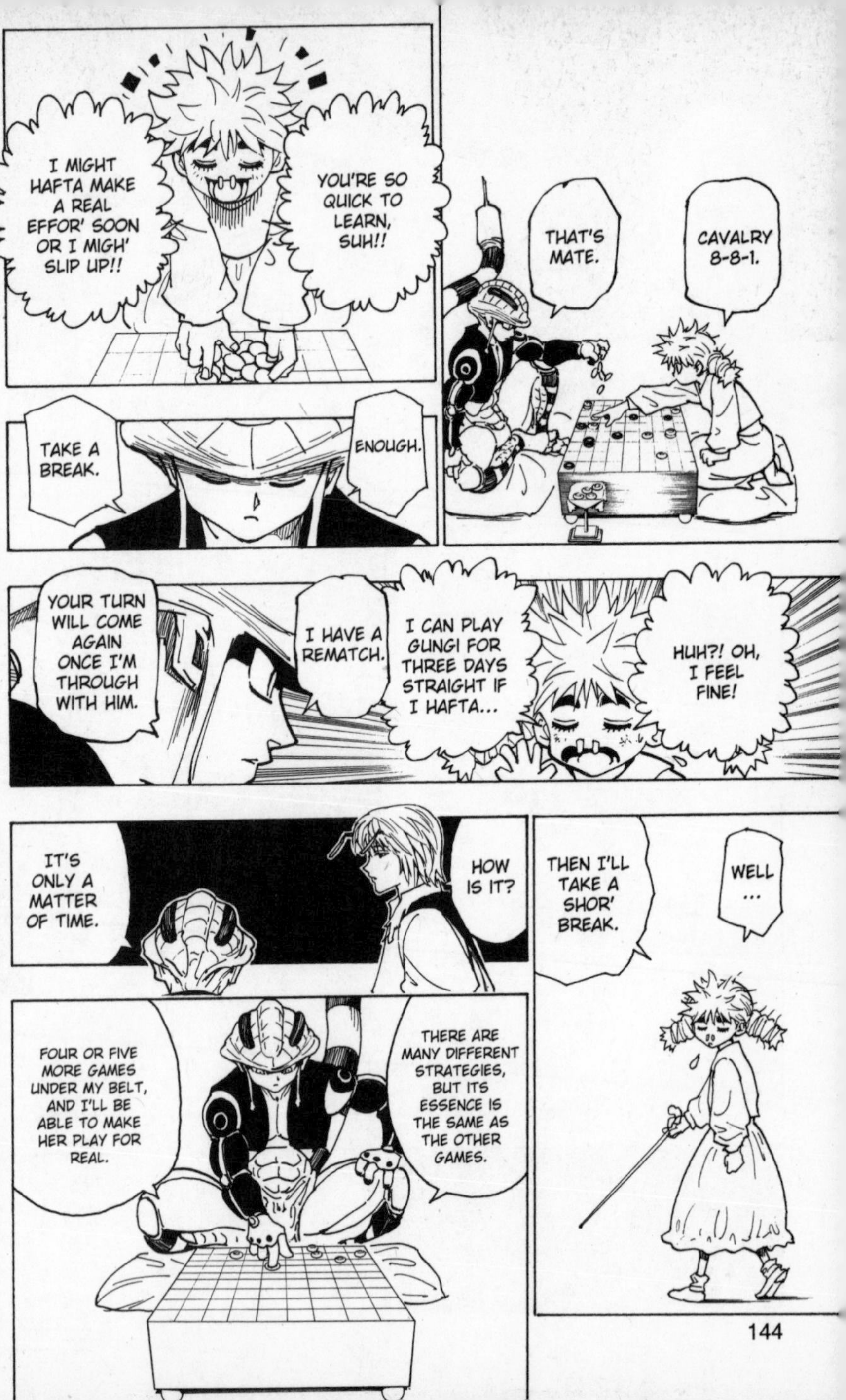
CAVALRY 8-8-1.
THAT'S MATE.
YOU'RE SO QUICK TO LEARN, SUH!!
I MIGHT HAFTA MAKE A REAL EFFOR' SOON OR I MIGH' SLIP UP!!
ENOUGH.
TAKE A BREAK.
HUH?! OH, I FEEL FINE!
I CAN PLAY GUNGI FOR THREE DAYS STRAIGHT IF I HAFTA...
I HAVE A REMATCH.
YOUR TURN WILL COME AGAIN ONCE I'M THROUGH WITH HIM.
WELL ...
THEN I'LL TAKE A SHOR' BREAK.
HOW IS IT?
IT'S ONLY A MATTER OF TIME.
THERE ARE MANY DIFFERENT STRATEGIES, BUT ITS ESSENCE IS THE SAME AS THE OTHER GAMES.
FOUR OR FIVE MORE GAMES UNDER MY BELT, AND I'LL BE ABLE TO MAKE HER PLAY FOR REAL.

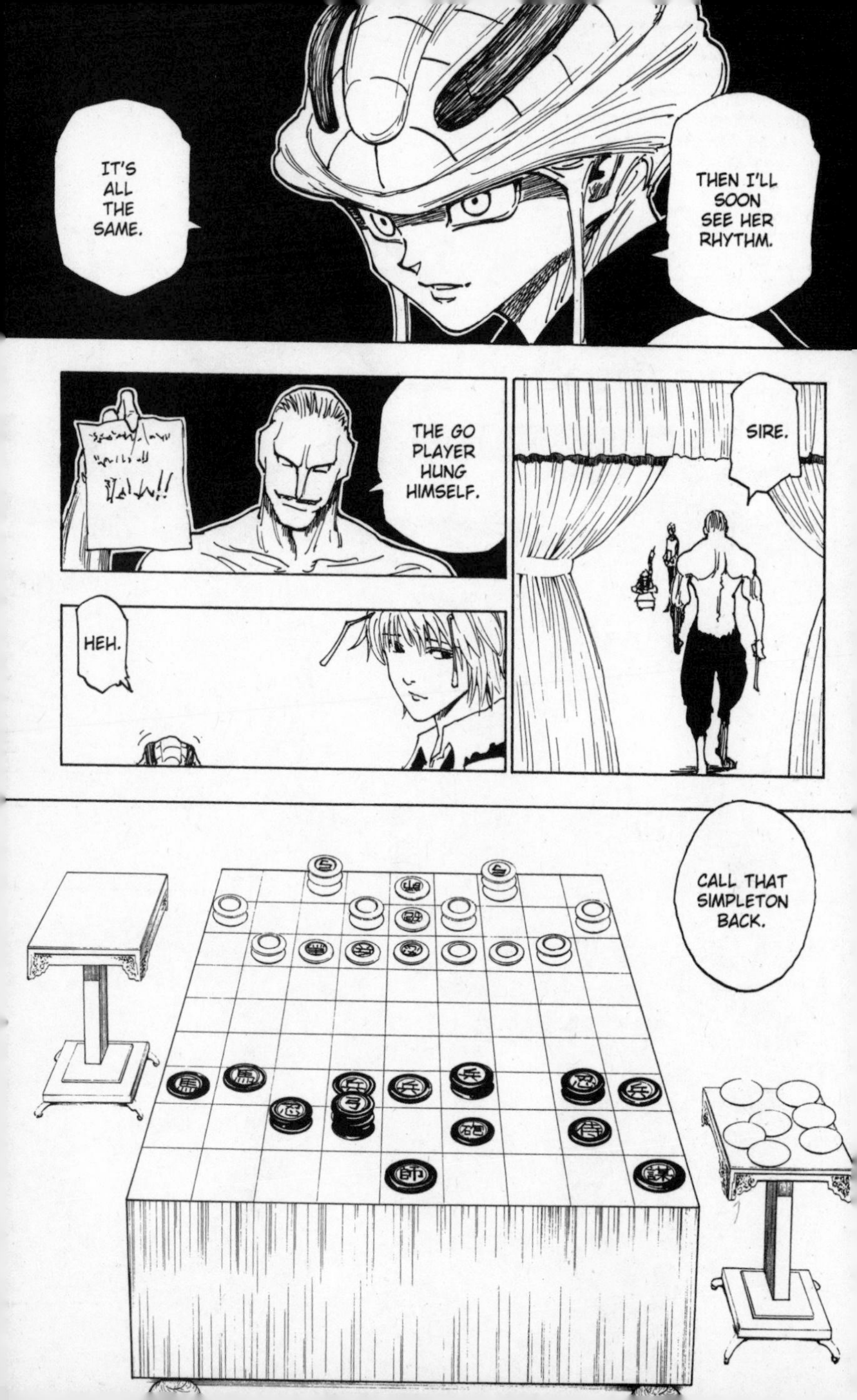
THEN I'LL SOON SEE HER RHYTHM.
IT'S ALL THE SAME.
SIRE.
THE GO PLAYER HUNG HIMSELF.
HEH.
CALL THAT SIMPLETON BACK.

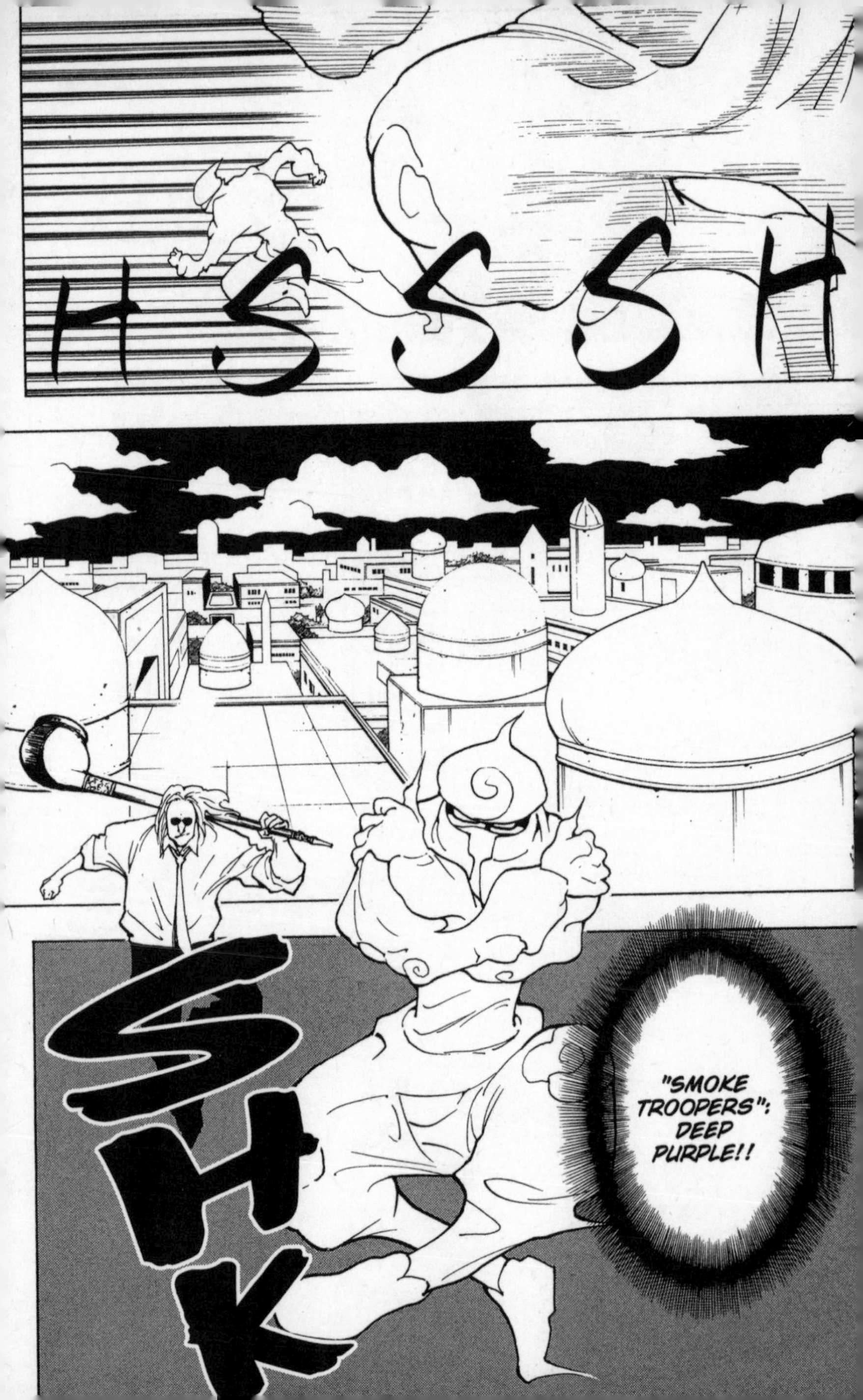
HSSSH
"SMOKE TROOPERS": DEEP PURPLE!!
SHK

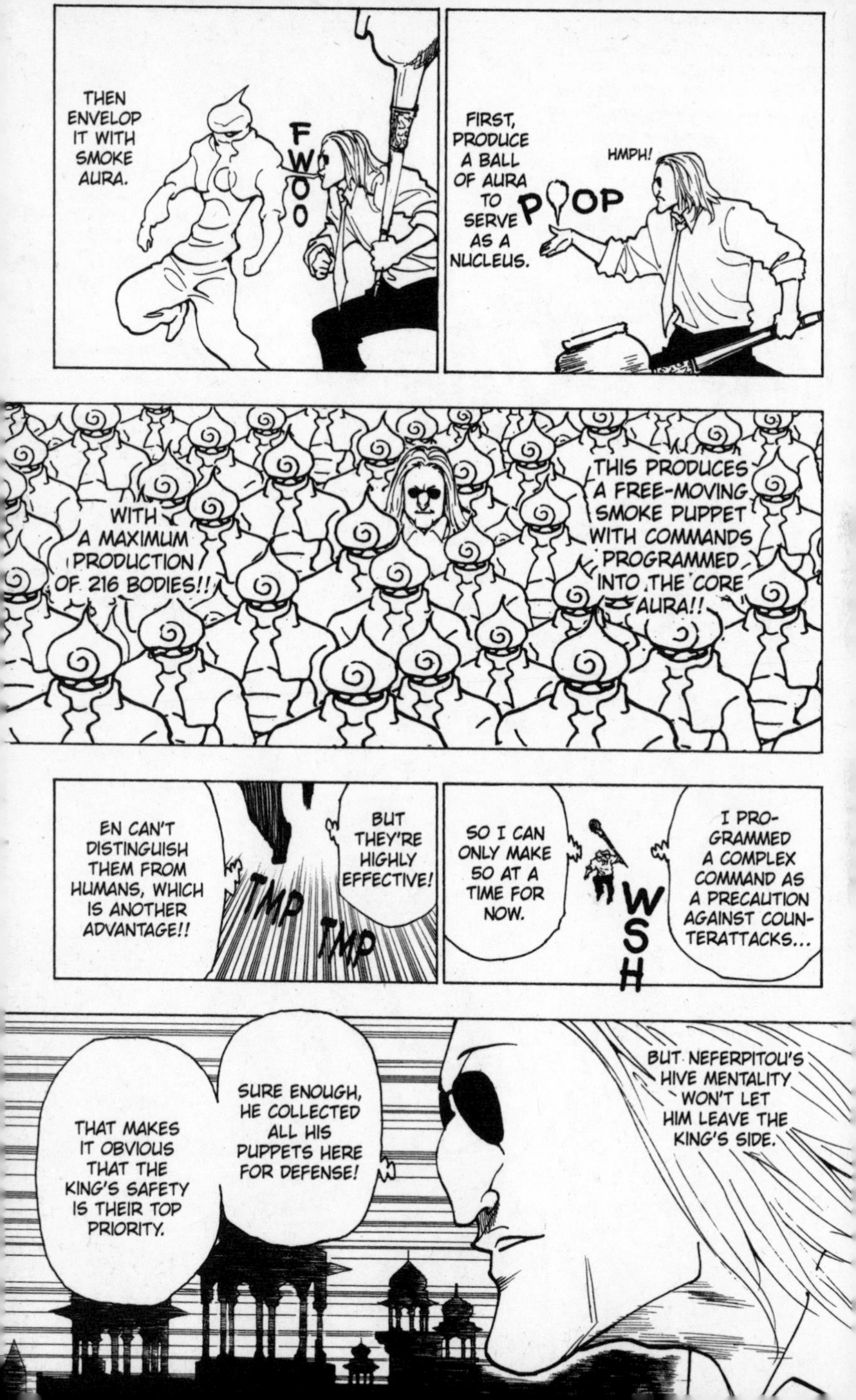
HMPH!
FIRST, PRODUCE A BALL OF AURA TO SERVE AS A NUCLEUS.
POP
FWOO
THEN ENVELOP IT WITH SMOKE AURA.
THIS PRODUCES A FREE-MOVING SMOKE PUPPET WITH COMMANDS PROGRAMMED INTO THE CORE AURA!!
WITH A MAXIMUM PRODUCTION OF 216 BODIES!!
I PRO-GRAMMED A COMPLEX COMMAND AS A PRECAUTION AGAINST COUN-TERATTACKS...
WSH
SO I CAN ONLY MAKE 50 AT A TIME FOR NOW.
BUT THEY'RE HIGHLY EFFECTIVE!
TMP TMP
EN CAN'T DISTINGUISH THEM FROM HUMANS, WHICH IS ANOTHER ADVANTAGE!!
BUT NEFERPITOU'S HIVE MENTALITY WON'T LET HIM LEAVE THE KING'S SIDE.
SURE ENOUGH, HE COLLECTED ALL HIS PUPPETS HERE FOR DEFENSE!
THAT MAKES IT OBVIOUS THAT THE KING'S SAFETY IS THEIR TOP PRIORITY.

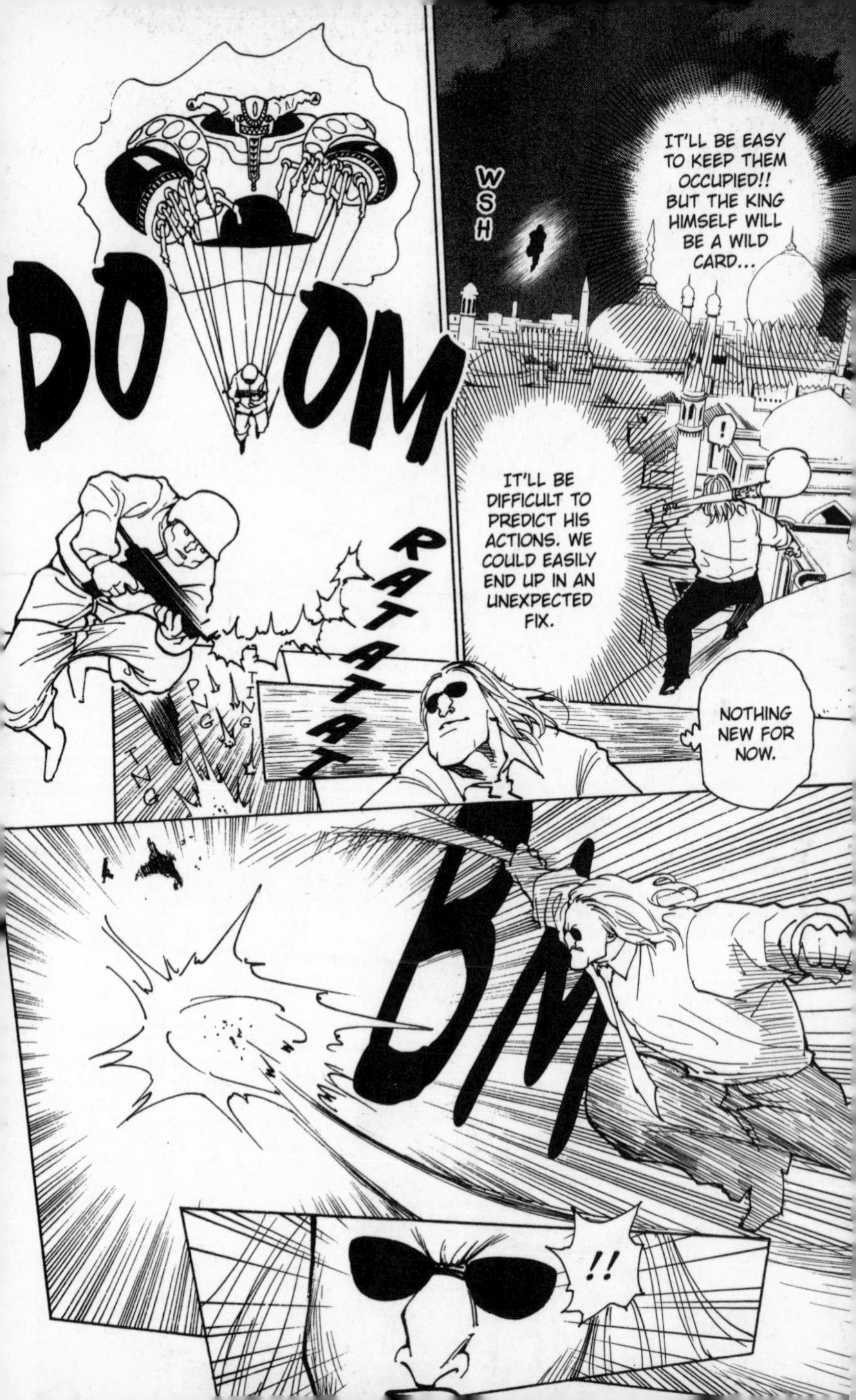
WSH
IT'LL BE EASY TO KEEP THEM OCCUPIED!! BUT THE KING HIMSELF WILL BE A WILD CARD...
DOOM
!
IT'LL BE DIFFICULT TO PREDICT HIS ACTIONS. WE COULD EASILY END UP IN AN UNEXPECTED FIX.
RATATATAT
PING
TING
NOTHING NEW FOR NOW.
BM
!!

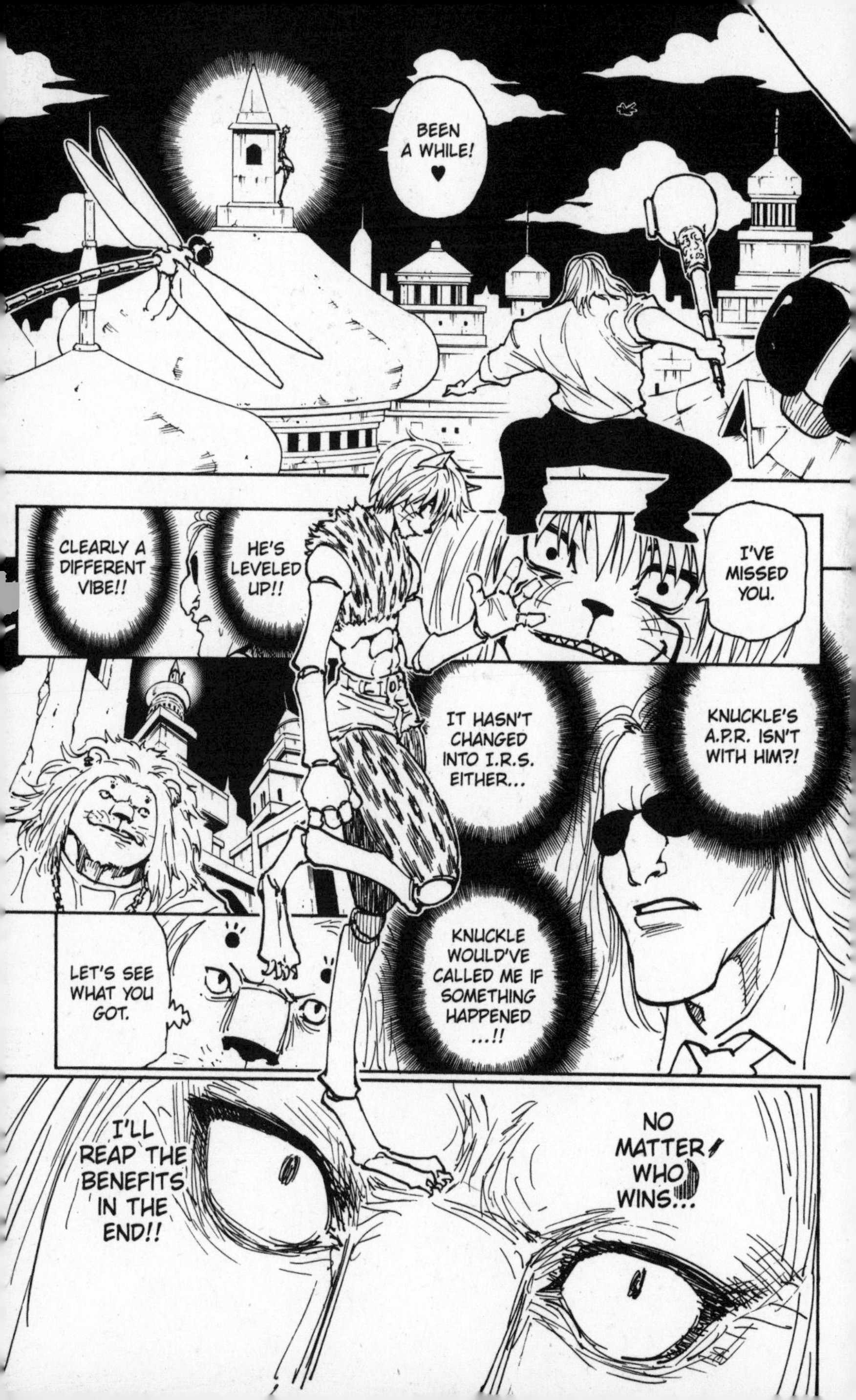
BEEN A WHILE! ♥
I'VE MISSED YOU.
HE'S LEVELED UP!!
CLEARLY A DIFFERENT VIBE!!
KNUCKLE'S A.P.R. ISN'T WITH HIM?!
IT HASN'T CHANGED INTO I.R.S. EITHER...
KNUCKLE WOULD'VE CALLED ME IF SOMETHING HAPPENED ...!!
LET'S SEE WHAT YOU GOT.
NO MATTER WHO WINS...
I'LL REAP THE BENEFITS IN THE END!!

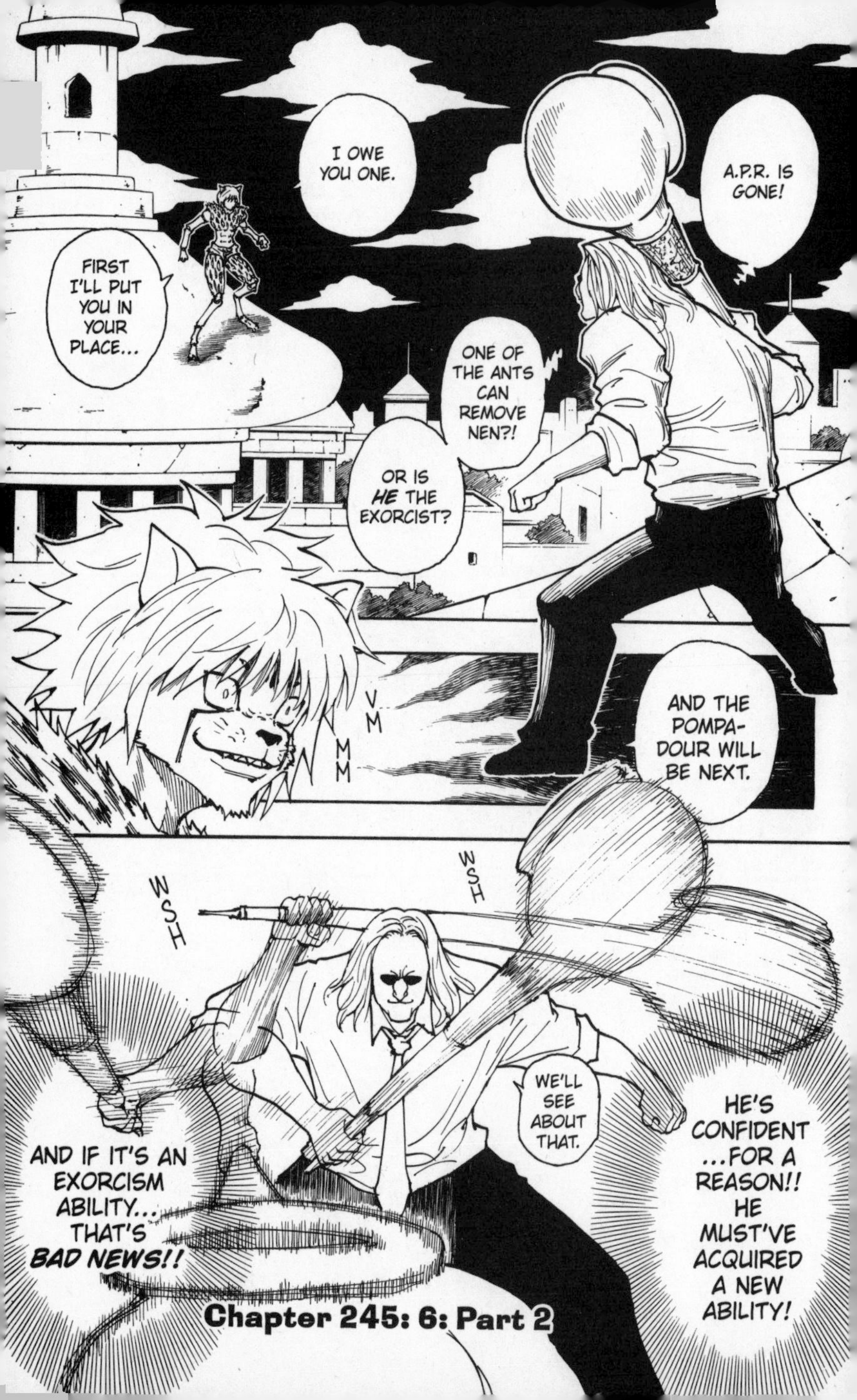
A.P.R. IS GONE!
I OWE YOU ONE.
FIRST I'LL PUT YOU IN YOUR PLACE...
ONE OF THE ANTS CAN REMOVE NEN?!
OR IS *HE* THE EXORCIST?
VMMM
AND THE POMPADOUR WILL BE NEXT.
WSH
WSH
HE'S CONFIDENT ...FOR A REASON!! HE MUST'VE ACQUIRED A NEW ABILITY!
WE'LL SEE ABOUT THAT.
AND IF IT'S AN EXORCISM ABILITY... THAT'S *BAD NEWS!!*
Chapter 245: 6: Part 2

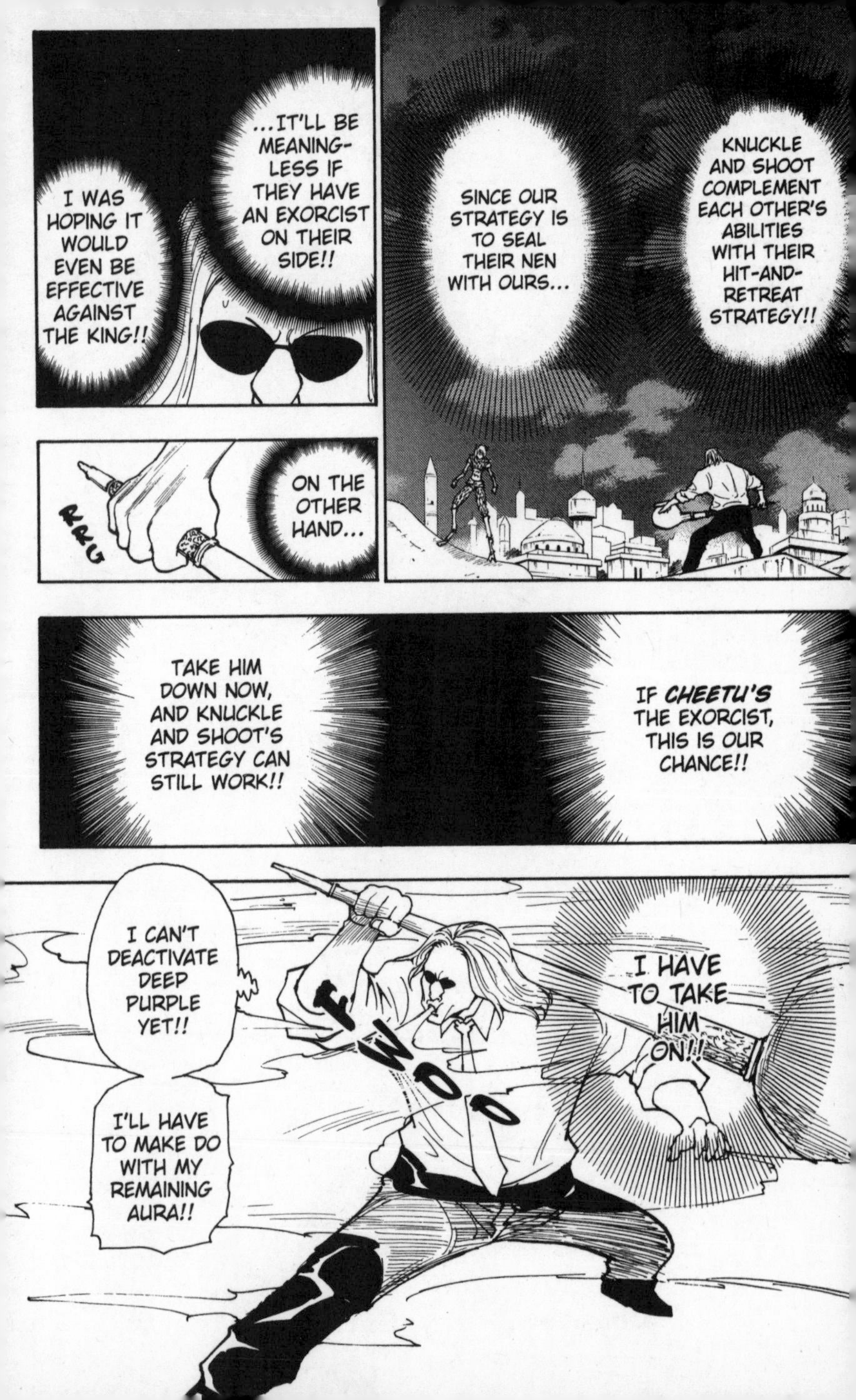
KNUCKLE AND SHOOT COMPLEMENT EACH OTHER'S ABILITIES WITH THEIR HIT-AND-RETREAT STRATEGY!!
SINCE OUR STRATEGY IS TO SEAL THEIR NEN WITH OURS...
...IT'LL BE MEANING-LESS IF THEY HAVE AN EXORCIST ON THEIR SIDE!!
I WAS HOPING IT WOULD EVEN BE EFFECTIVE AGAINST THE KING!!
ON THE OTHER HAND...
RRG
IF *CHEETU'S* THE EXORCIST, THIS IS OUR CHANCE!!
TAKE HIM DOWN NOW, AND KNUCKLE AND SHOOT'S STRATEGY CAN STILL WORK!!
I HAVE TO TAKE HIM ON!!
I CAN'T DEACTIVATE DEEP PURPLE YET!!
FWOOP
I'LL HAVE TO MAKE DO WITH MY REMAINING AURA!!

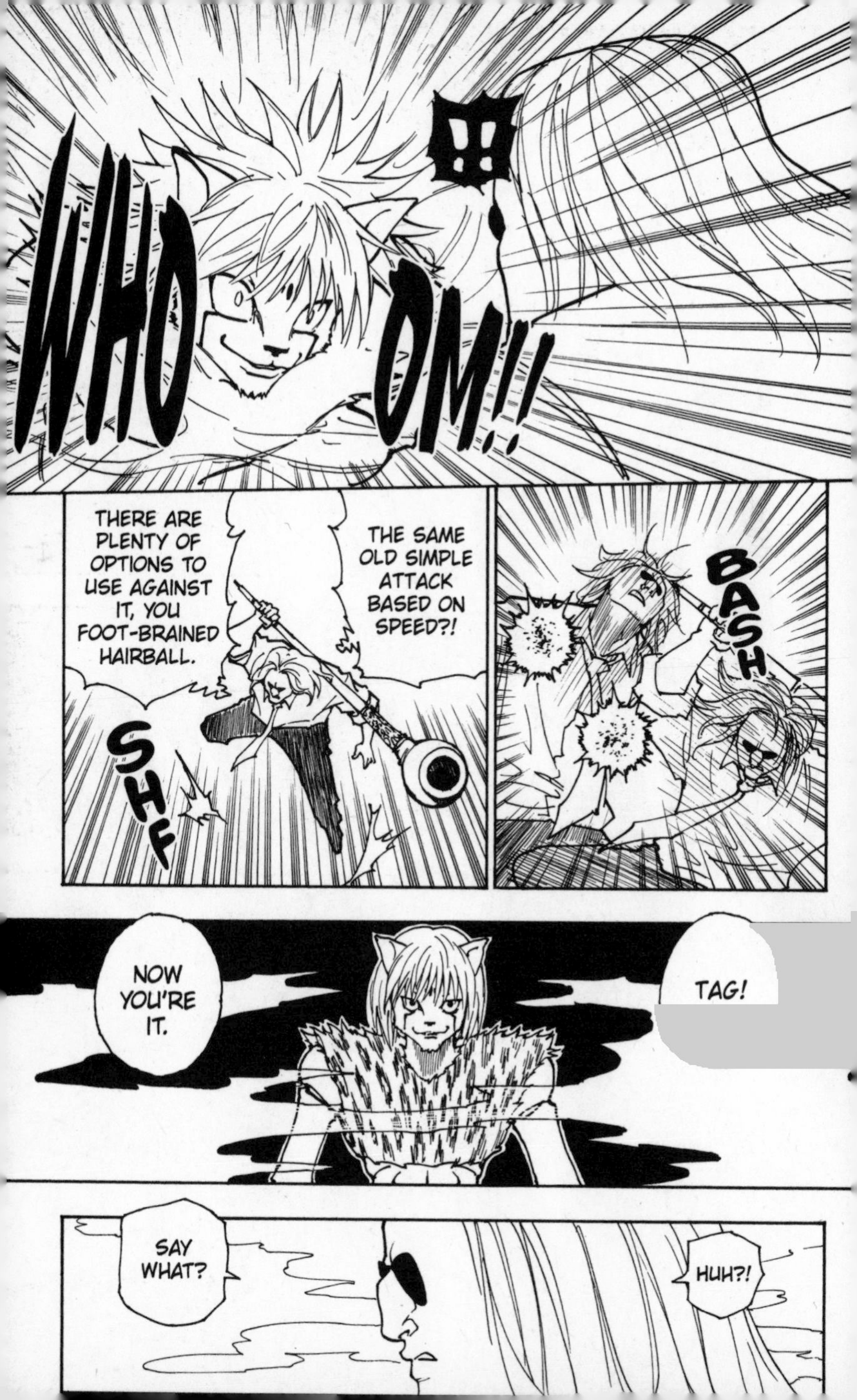
!!
WHOOM!!
BASH
THE SAME OLD SIMPLE ATTACK BASED ON SPEED?!
THERE ARE PLENTY OF OPTIONS TO USE AGAINST IT, YOU FOOT-BRAINED HAIRBALL.
SHF
TAG!
NOW YOU'RE IT.
HUH?!
SAY WHAT?

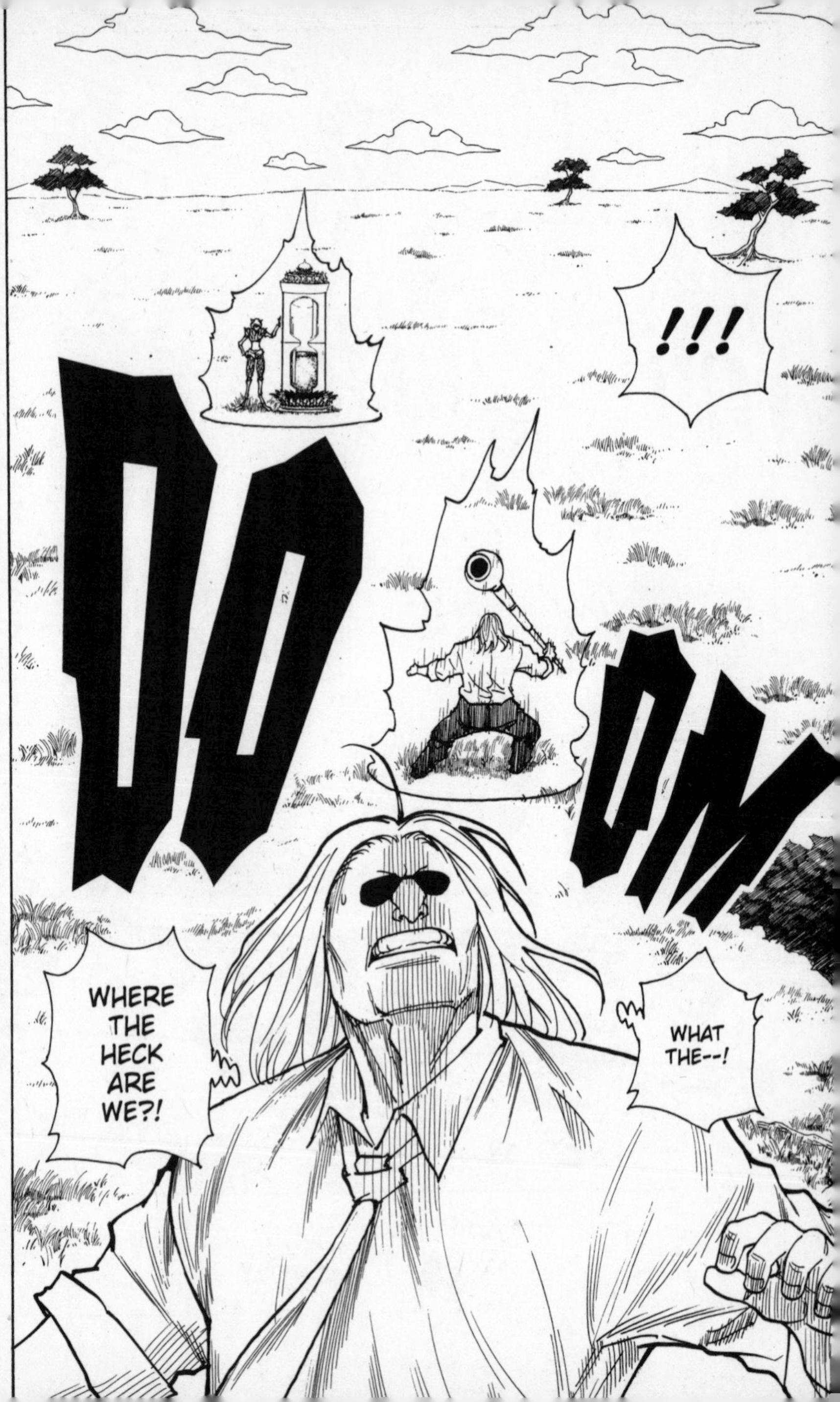
!!!
DOOM
WHAT THE--!
WHERE THE HECK ARE WE?!

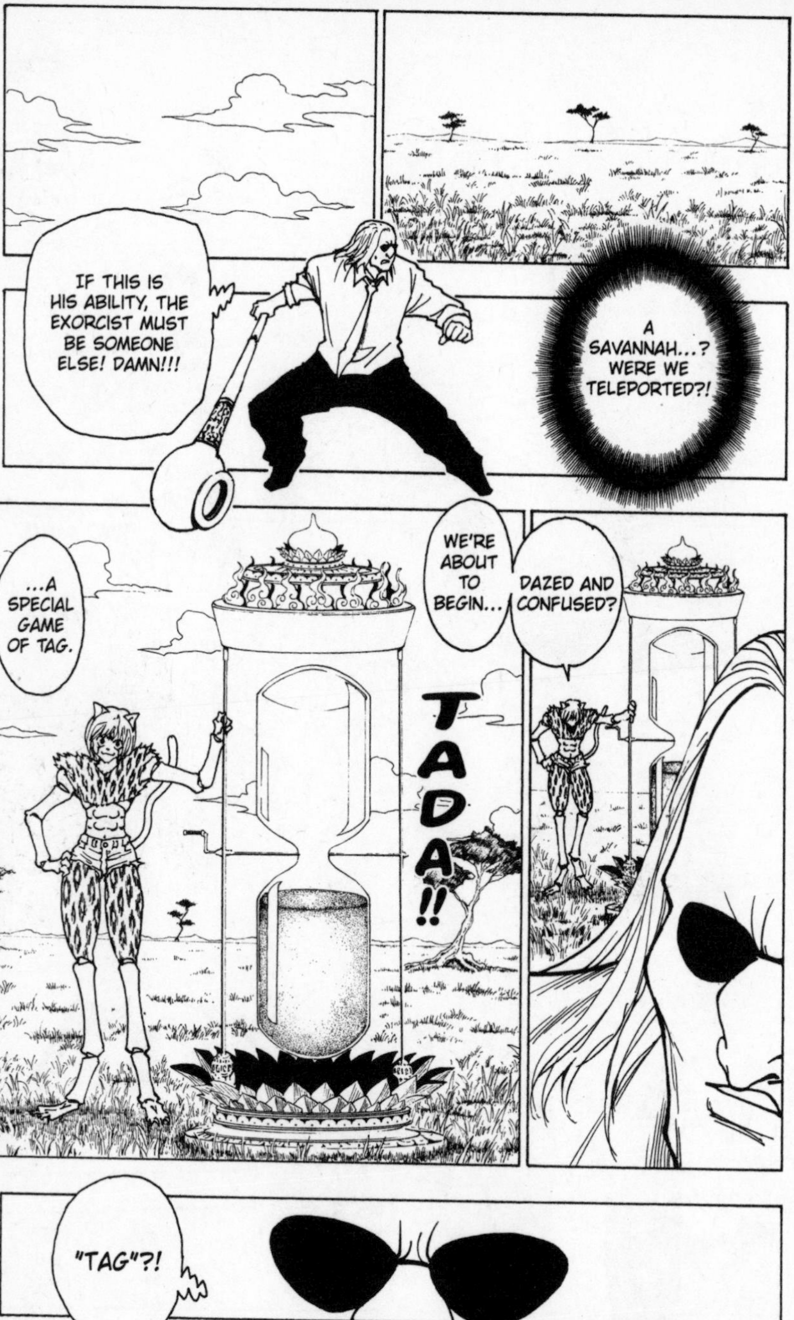
A SAVANNAH...? WERE WE TELEPORTED?!
IF THIS IS HIS ABILITY, THE EXORCIST MUST BE SOMEONE ELSE! DAMN!!!
DAZED AND CONFUSED?
WE'RE ABOUT TO BEGIN...
TADA!!
...A SPECIAL GAME OF TAG.
"TAG"?!

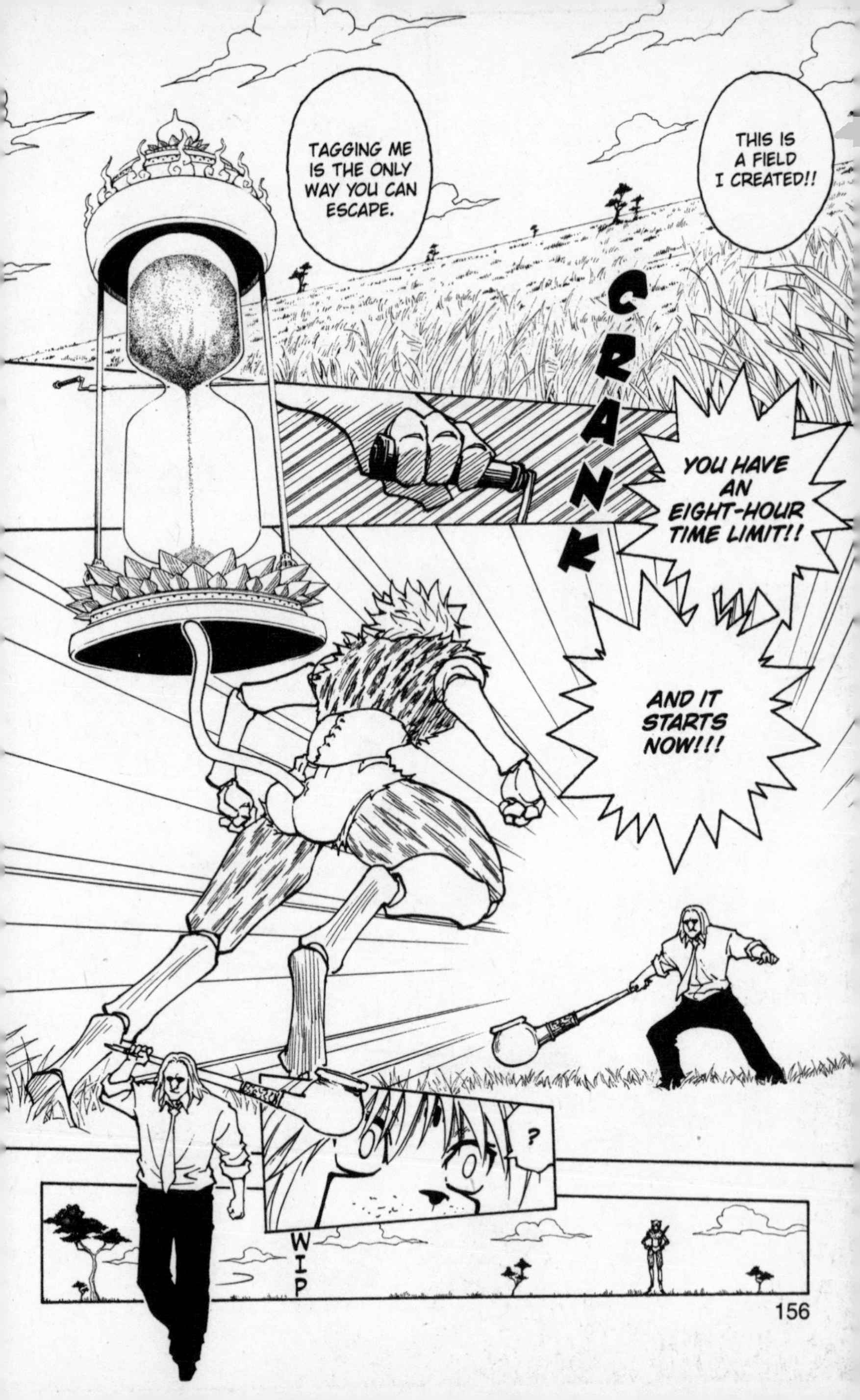
THIS IS A FIELD I CREATED!!
TAGGING ME IS THE ONLY WAY YOU CAN ESCAPE.
CRANK
YOU HAVE AN EIGHT-HOUR TIME LIMIT!!
AND IT STARTS NOW!!!
?
WIP

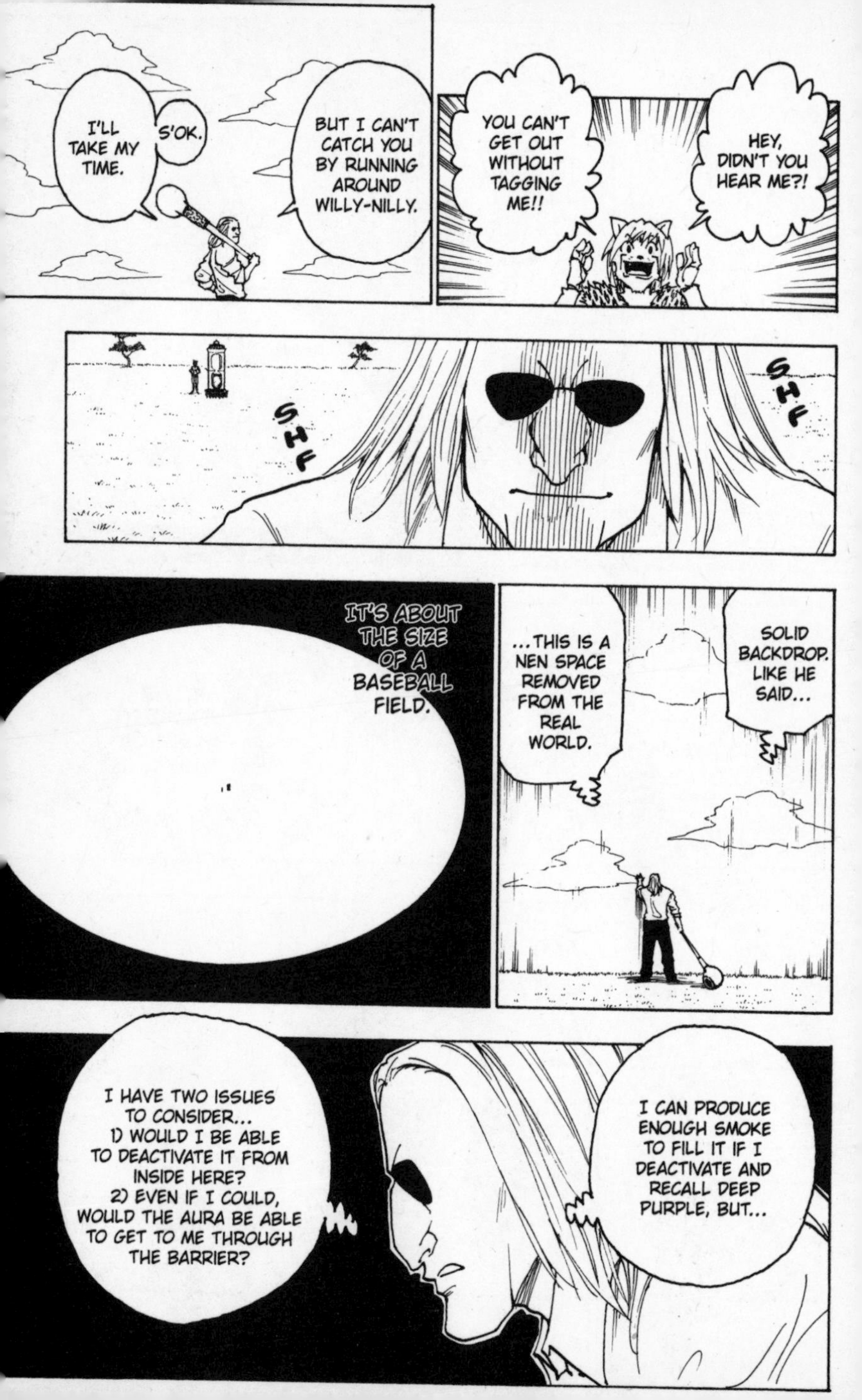
HEY, DIDN'T YOU HEAR ME?!
YOU CAN'T GET OUT WITHOUT TAGGING ME!!
BUT I CAN'T CATCH YOU BY RUNNING AROUND WILLY-NILLY.
S'OK.
I'LL TAKE MY TIME.
SHF
SHF
SOLID BACKDROP. LIKE HE SAID...
...THIS IS A NEN SPACE REMOVED FROM THE REAL WORLD.
IT'S ABOUT THE SIZE OF A BASEBALL FIELD.
I CAN PRODUCE ENOUGH SMOKE TO FILL IT IF I DEACTIVATE AND RECALL DEEP PURPLE, BUT...
I HAVE TWO ISSUES TO CONSIDER... 1) WOULD I BE ABLE TO DEACTIVATE IT FROM INSIDE HERE? 2) EVEN IF I COULD, WOULD THE AURA BE ABLE TO GET TO ME THROUGH THE BARRIER?

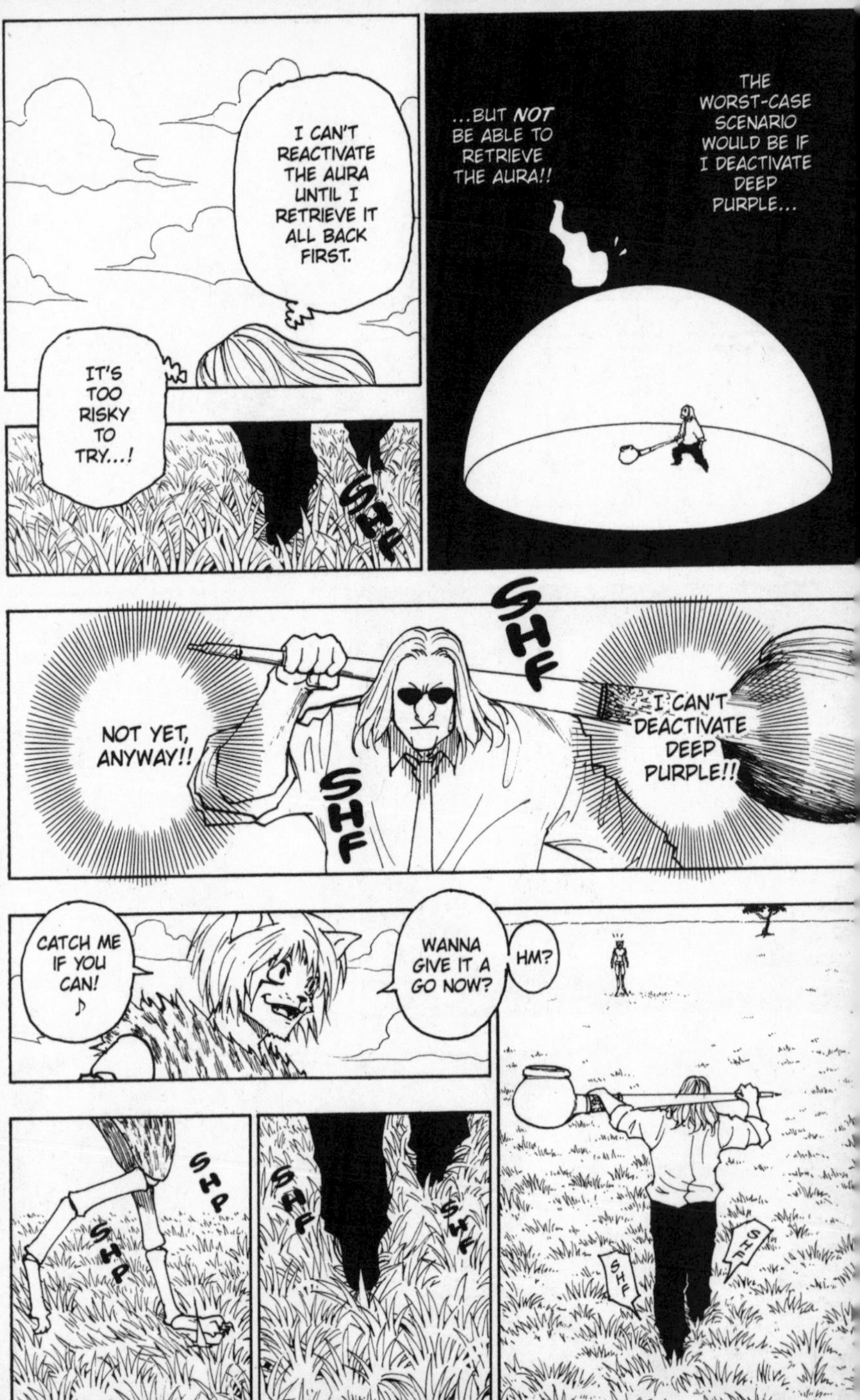
THE WORST-CASE SCENARIO WOULD BE IF I DEACTIVATE DEEP PURPLE...
...BUT NOT BE ABLE TO RETRIEVE THE AURA!!
I CAN'T REACTIVATE THE AURA UNTIL I RETRIEVE IT ALL BACK FIRST.
IT'S TOO RISKY TO TRY...!
SHF
SHF
I CAN'T DEACTIVATE DEEP PURPLE!!
NOT YET, ANYWAY!!
SHF
HM?
SHF
SHF
WANNA GIVE IT A GO NOW?
CATCH ME IF YOU CAN! ♪
SHF
SHF
SHP
SHP

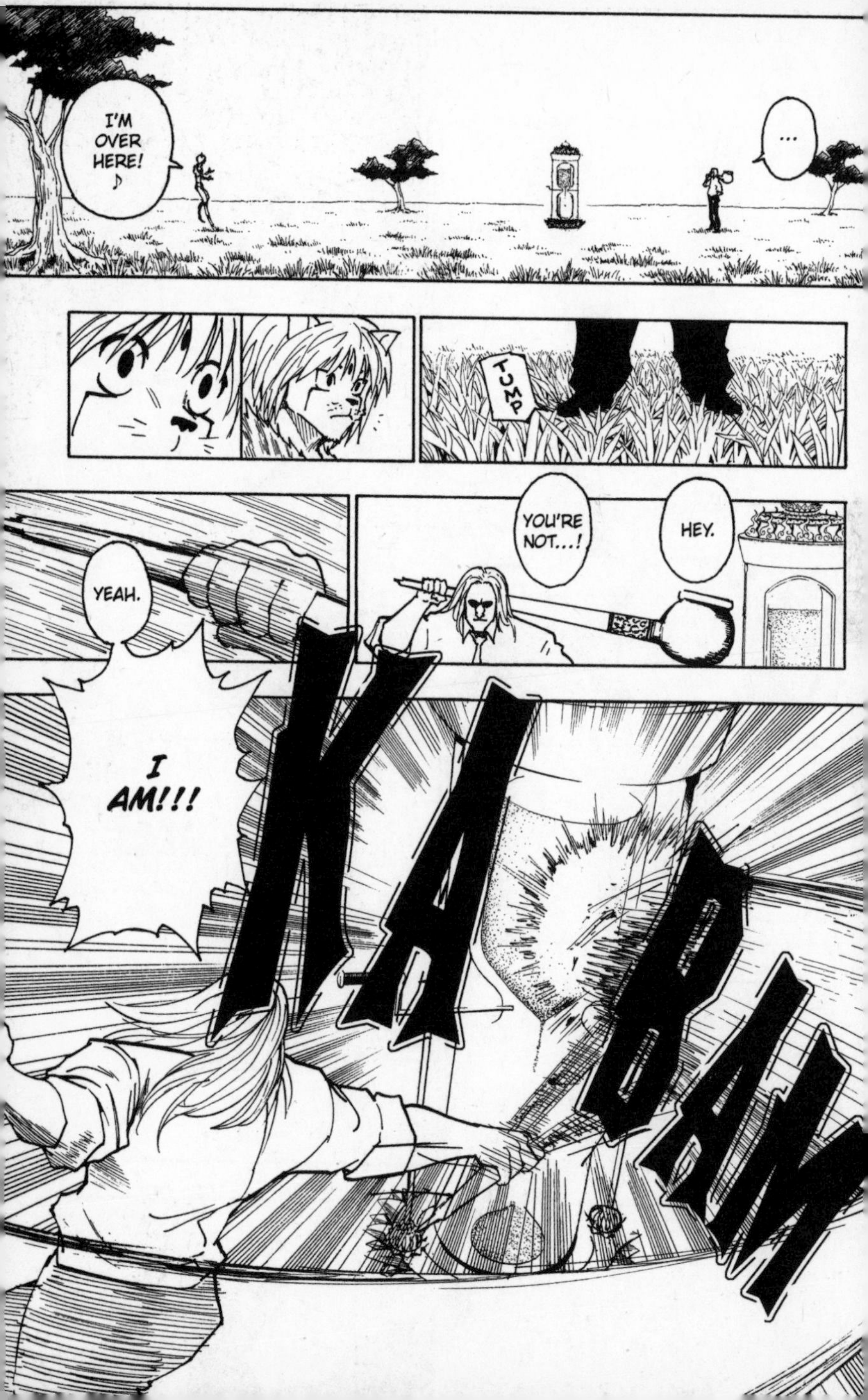
...
I'M OVER HERE! ♪
TUMP
HEY.
YOU'RE NOT...!
YEAH.
I AM!!!
KABAM

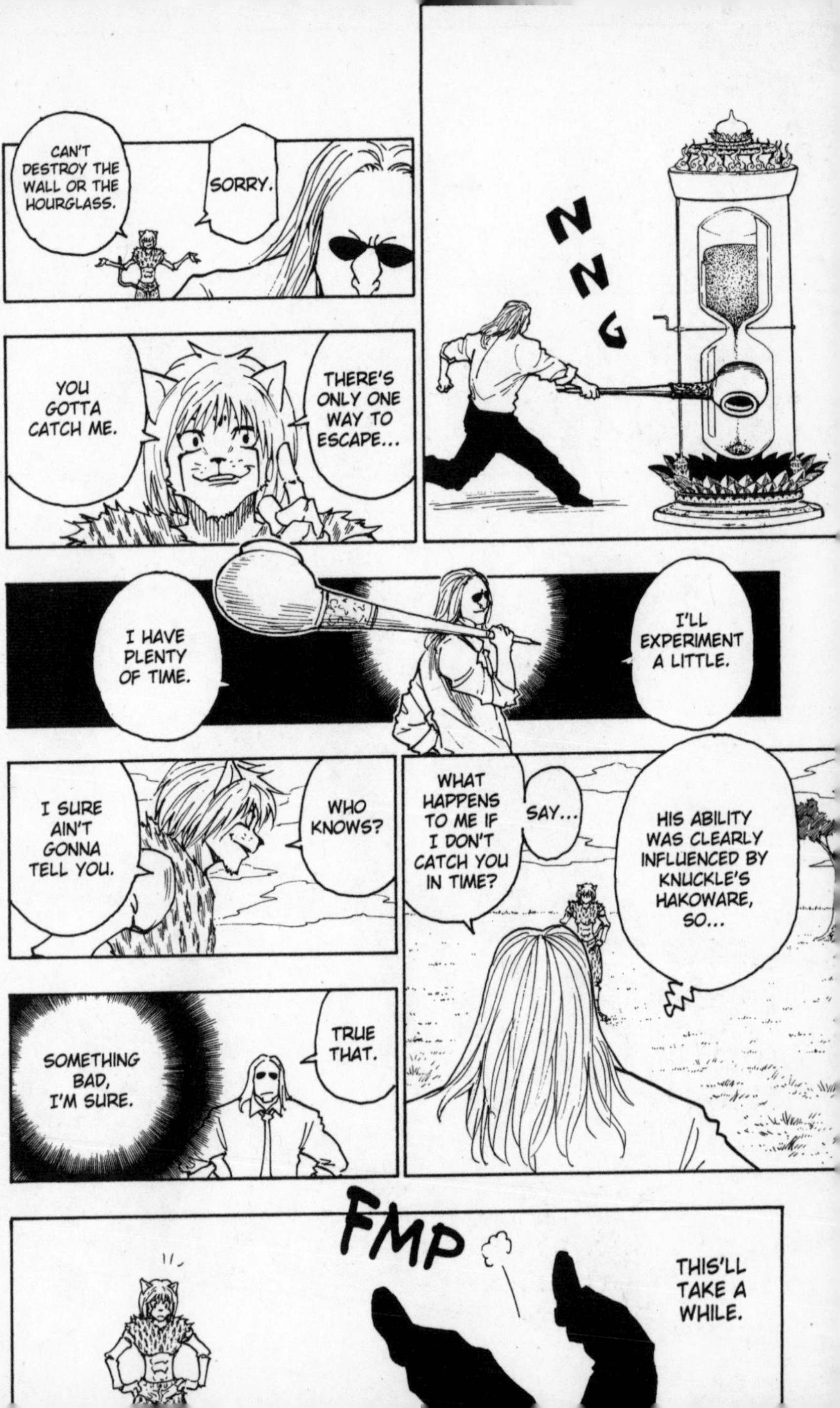
NNG
SORRY.
CAN'T DESTROY THE WALL OR THE HOURGLASS.
THERE'S ONLY ONE WAY TO ESCAPE...
YOU GOTTA CATCH ME.
I'LL EXPERIMENT A LITTLE.
I HAVE PLENTY OF TIME.
HIS ABILITY WAS CLEARLY INFLUENCED BY KNUCKLE'S HAKOWARE, SO...
SAY...
WHAT HAPPENS TO ME IF I DON'T CATCH YOU IN TIME?
WHO KNOWS?
I SURE AIN'T GONNA TELL YOU.
TRUE THAT.
SOMETHING BAD, I'M SURE.
FMP
THIS'LL TAKE A WHILE.

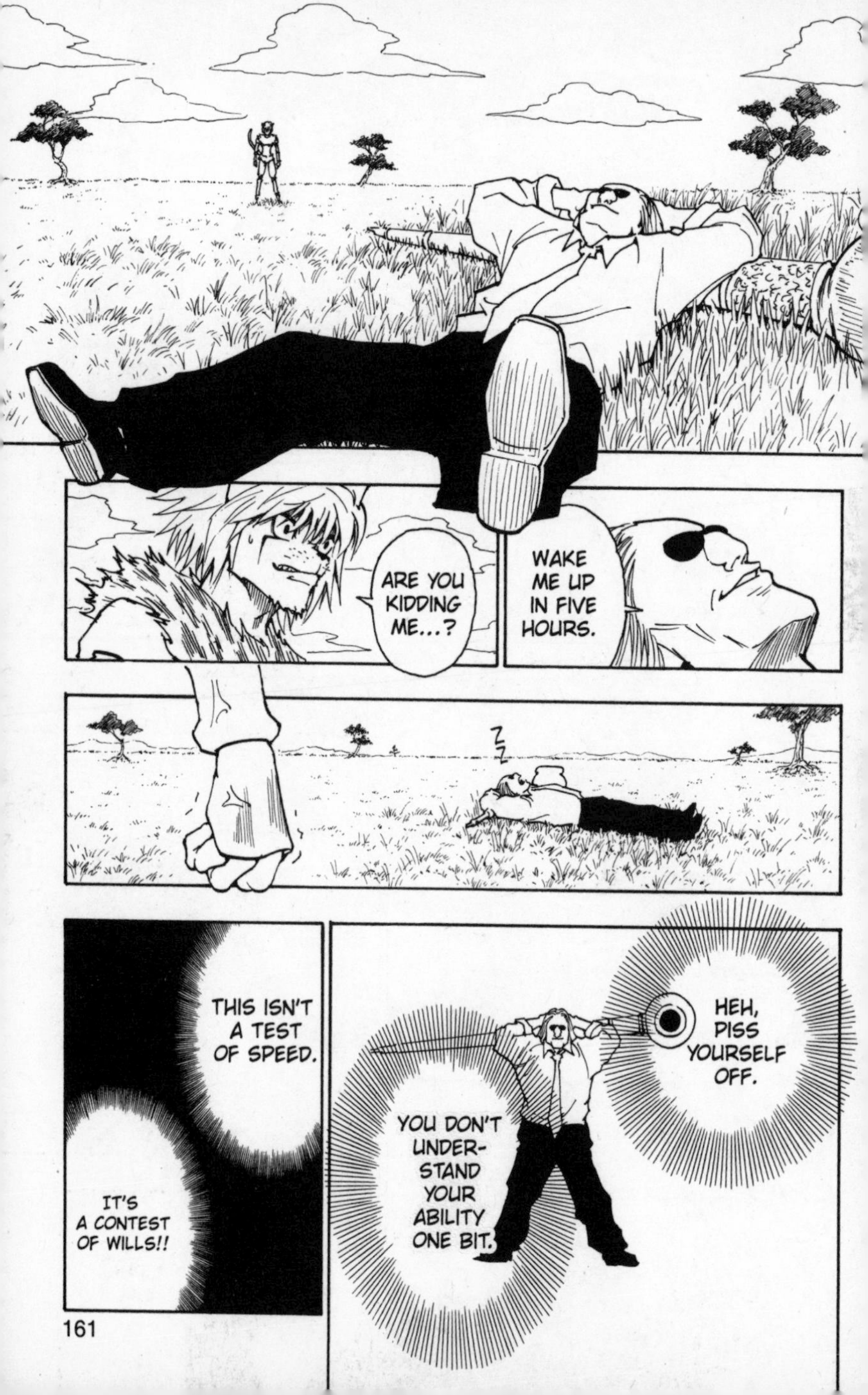
WAKE ME UP IN FIVE HOURS.
ARE YOU KIDDING ME...?
HEH, PISS YOURSELF OFF.
YOU DON'T UNDER-STAND YOUR ABILITY ONE BIT.
THIS ISN'T A TEST OF SPEED.
IT'S A CONTEST OF WILLS!!

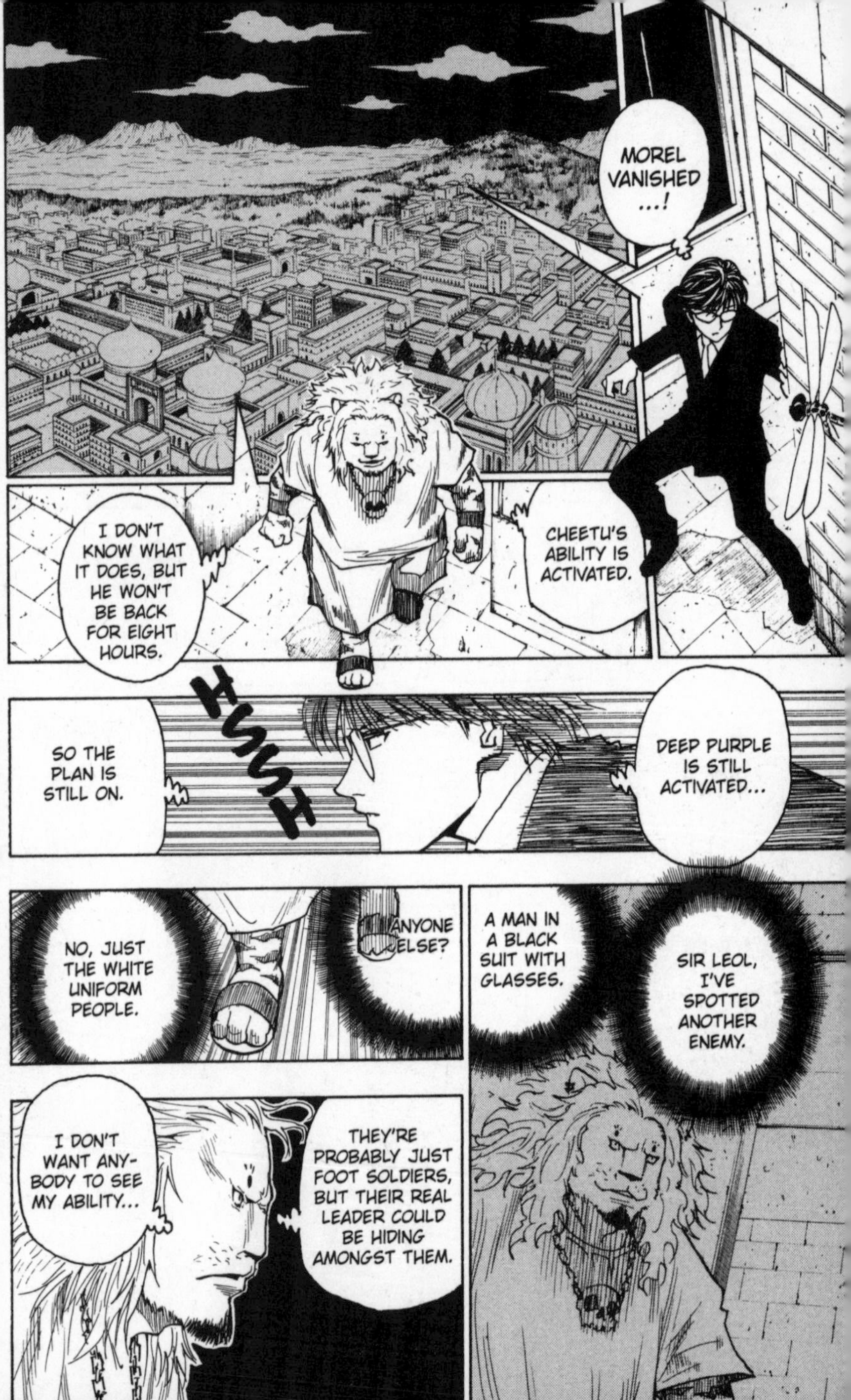
MOREL VANISHED ...!
CHEETU'S ABILITY IS ACTIVATED.
I DON'T KNOW WHAT IT DOES, BUT HE WON'T BE BACK FOR EIGHT HOURS.
DEEP PURPLE IS STILL ACTIVATED...
HSSSH
SO THE PLAN IS STILL ON.
SIR LEOL, I'VE SPOTTED ANOTHER ENEMY.
A MAN IN A BLACK SUIT WITH GLASSES.
ANYONE ELSE?
NO, JUST THE WHITE UNIFORM PEOPLE.
THEY'RE PROBABLY JUST FOOT SOLDIERS, BUT THEIR REAL LEADER COULD BE HIDING AMONGST THEM.
I DON'T WANT ANY-BODY TO SEE MY ABILITY...

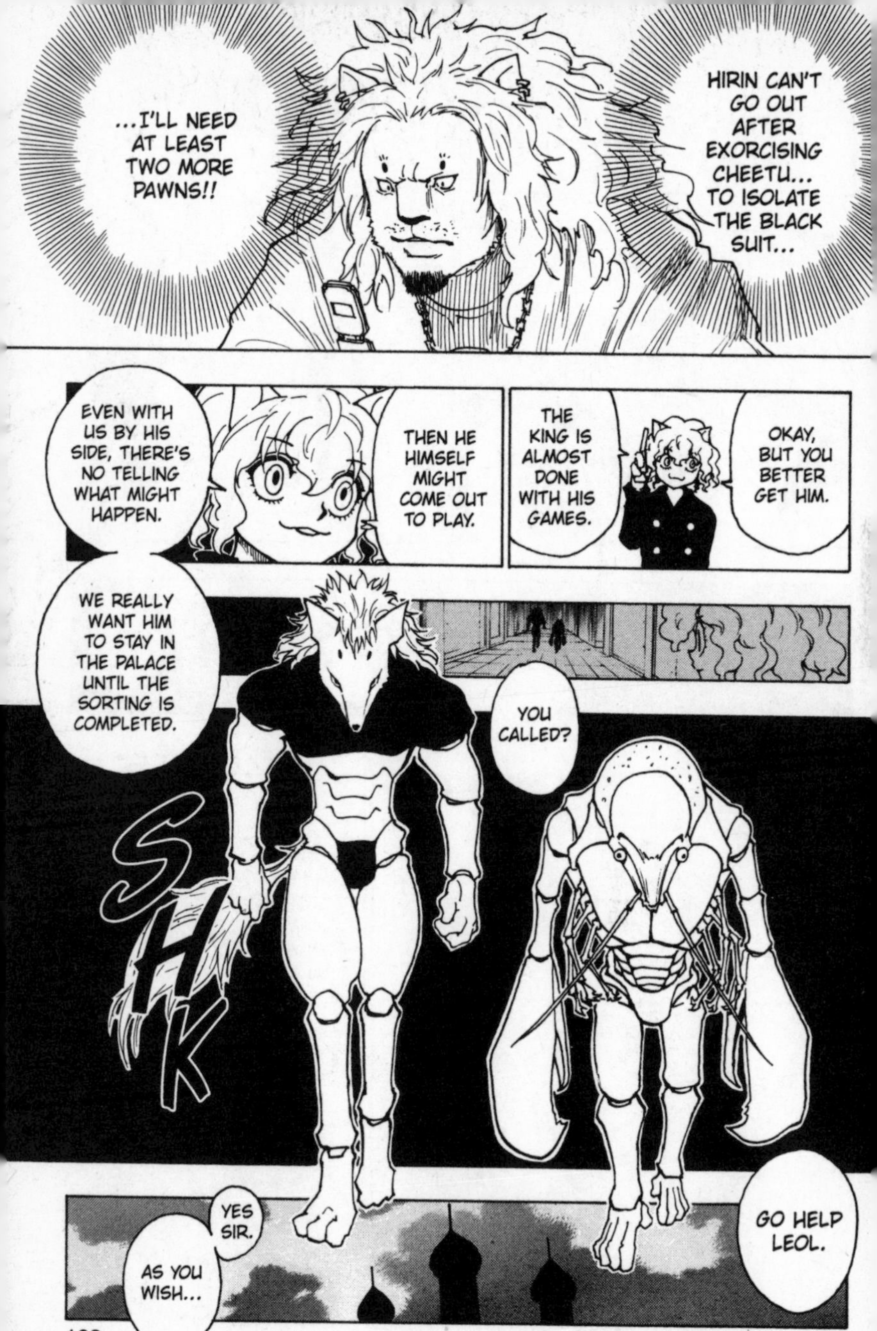
HIRIN CAN'T GO OUT AFTER EXORCISING CHEETU... TO ISOLATE THE BLACK SUIT...
...I'LL NEED AT LEAST TWO MORE PAWNS!!
OKAY, BUT YOU BETTER GET HIM.
THE KING IS ALMOST DONE WITH HIS GAMES.
THEN HE HIMSELF MIGHT COME OUT TO PLAY.
EVEN WITH US BY HIS SIDE, THERE'S NO TELLING WHAT MIGHT HAPPEN.
WE REALLY WANT HIM TO STAY IN THE PALACE UNTIL THE SORTING IS COMPLETED.
YOU CALLED?
SHK
GO HELP LEOL.
YES SIR.
AS YOU WISH...

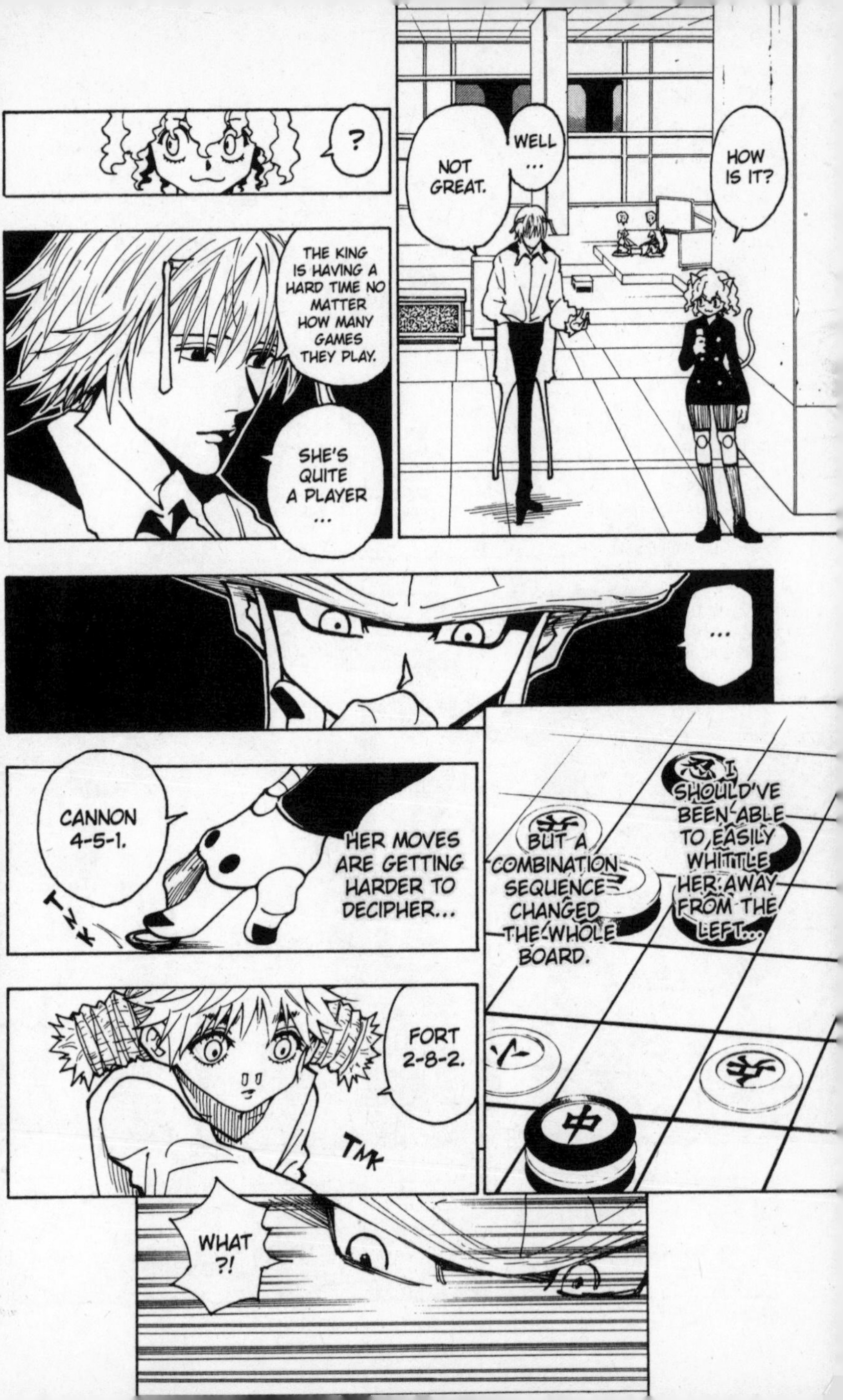
HOW IS IT?
WELL ...
NOT GREAT.
?
THE KING IS HAVING A HARD TIME NO MATTER HOW MANY GAMES THEY PLAY.
SHE'S QUITE A PLAYER ...
...
I SHOULD'VE BEEN ABLE TO EASILY WHITTLE HER AWAY FROM THE LEFT...
BUT A COMBINATION SEQUENCE CHANGED THE WHOLE BOARD.
CANNON 4-5-1.
TZK
HER MOVES ARE GETTING HARDER TO DECIPHER...
FORT 2-8-2.
TMK
WHAT ?!

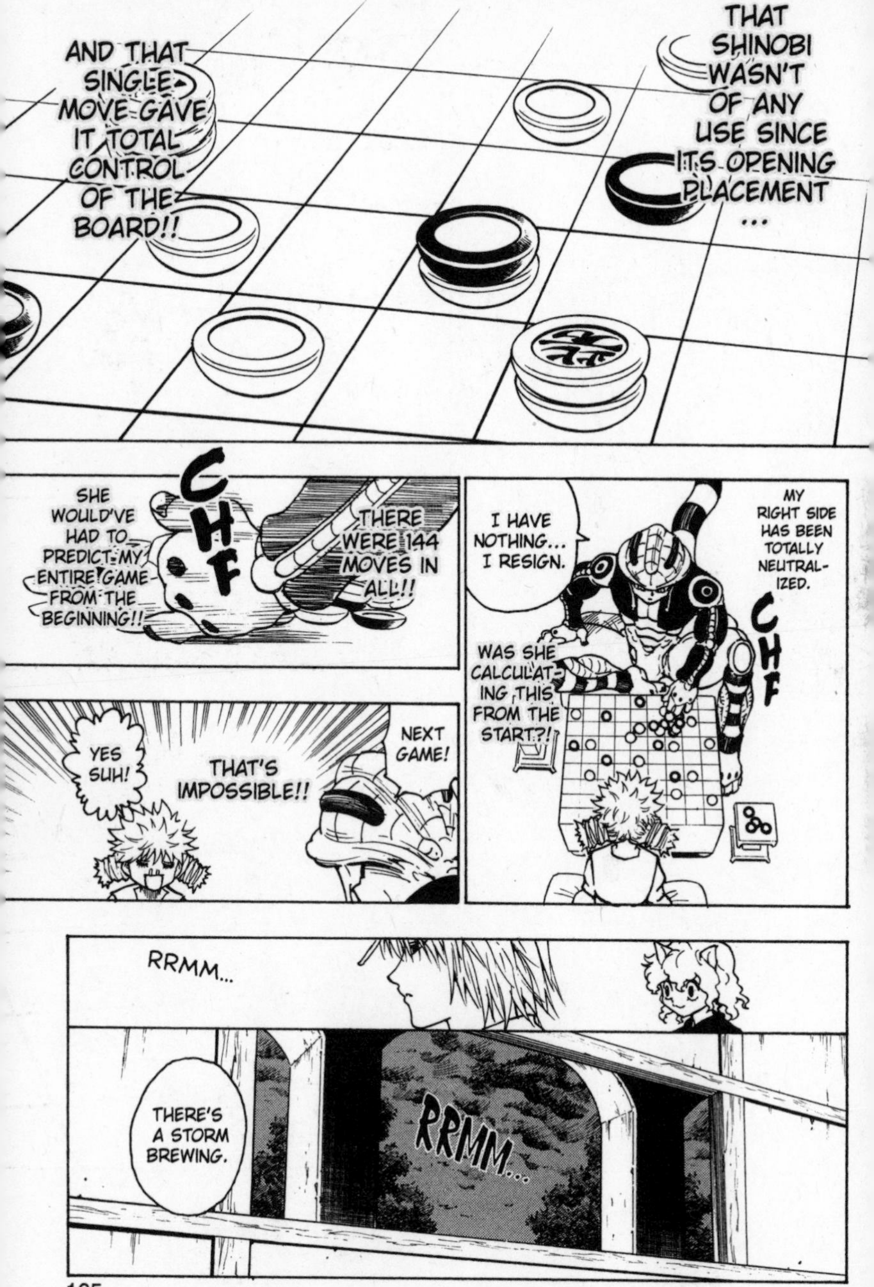
THAT SHINOBI WASN'T OF ANY USE SINCE ITS OPENING PLACEMENT...
AND THAT SINGLE MOVE GAVE IT TOTAL CONTROL OF THE BOARD!!
MY RIGHT SIDE HAS BEEN TOTALLY NEUTRALIZED.
I HAVE NOTHING... I RESIGN.
CHF
WAS SHE CALCULATING THIS FROM THE START?!
THERE WERE 144 MOVES IN ALL!!
CHF
SHE WOULD'VE HAD TO PREDICT MY ENTIRE GAME FROM THE BEGINNING!!
NEXT GAME!
THAT'S IMPOSSIBLE!!
YES SUH!
RRMM...
RRMM...
THERE'S A STORM BREWING.

Chapter 246: 6: Part 3

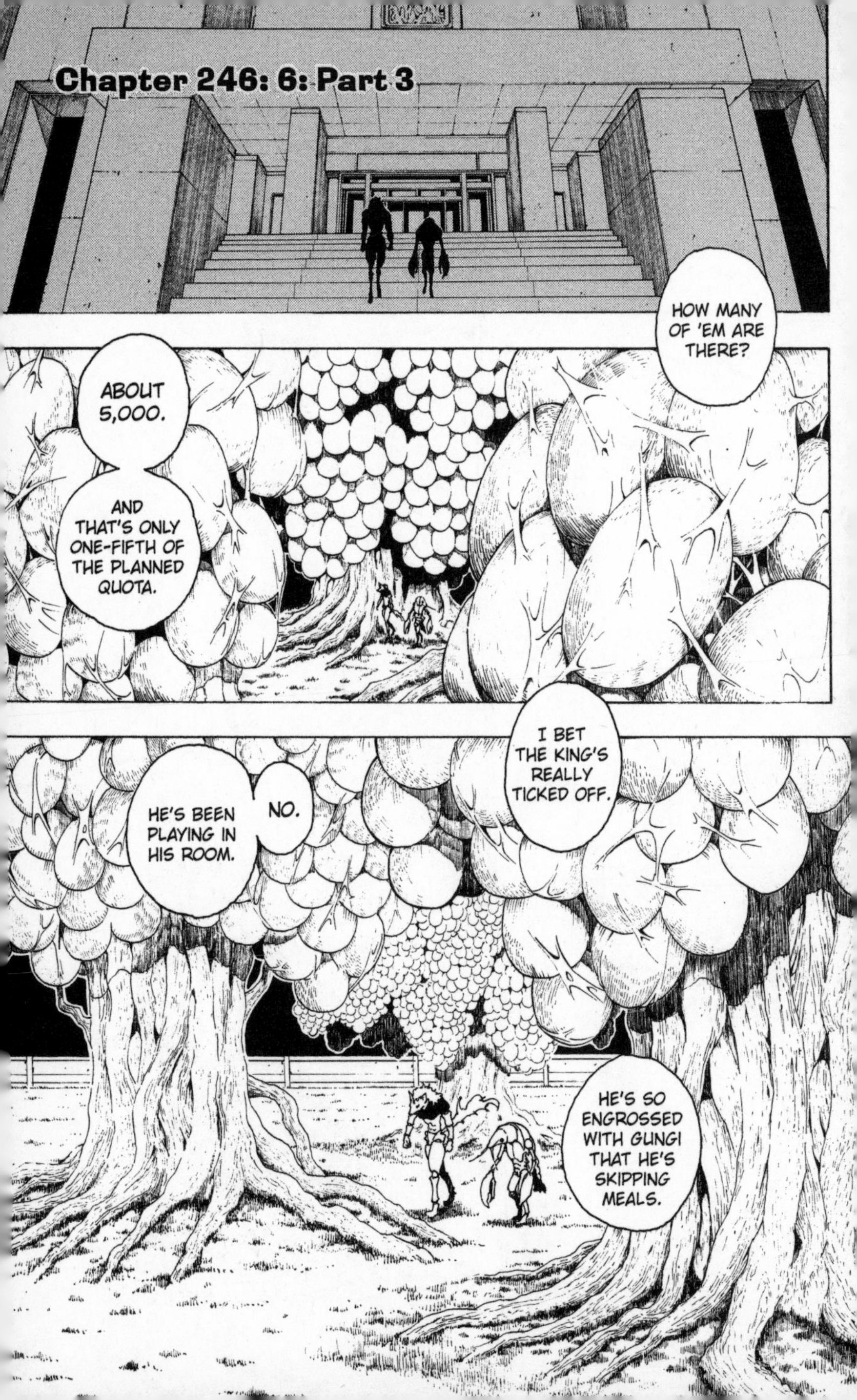
HOW MANY OF 'EM ARE THERE?
ABOUT 5,000.
AND THAT'S ONLY ONE-FIFTH OF THE PLANNED QUOTA.
I BET THE KING'S REALLY TICKED OFF.
NO.
HE'S BEEN PLAYING IN HIS ROOM.
HE'S SO ENGROSSED WITH GUNGI THAT HE'S SKIPPING MEALS.

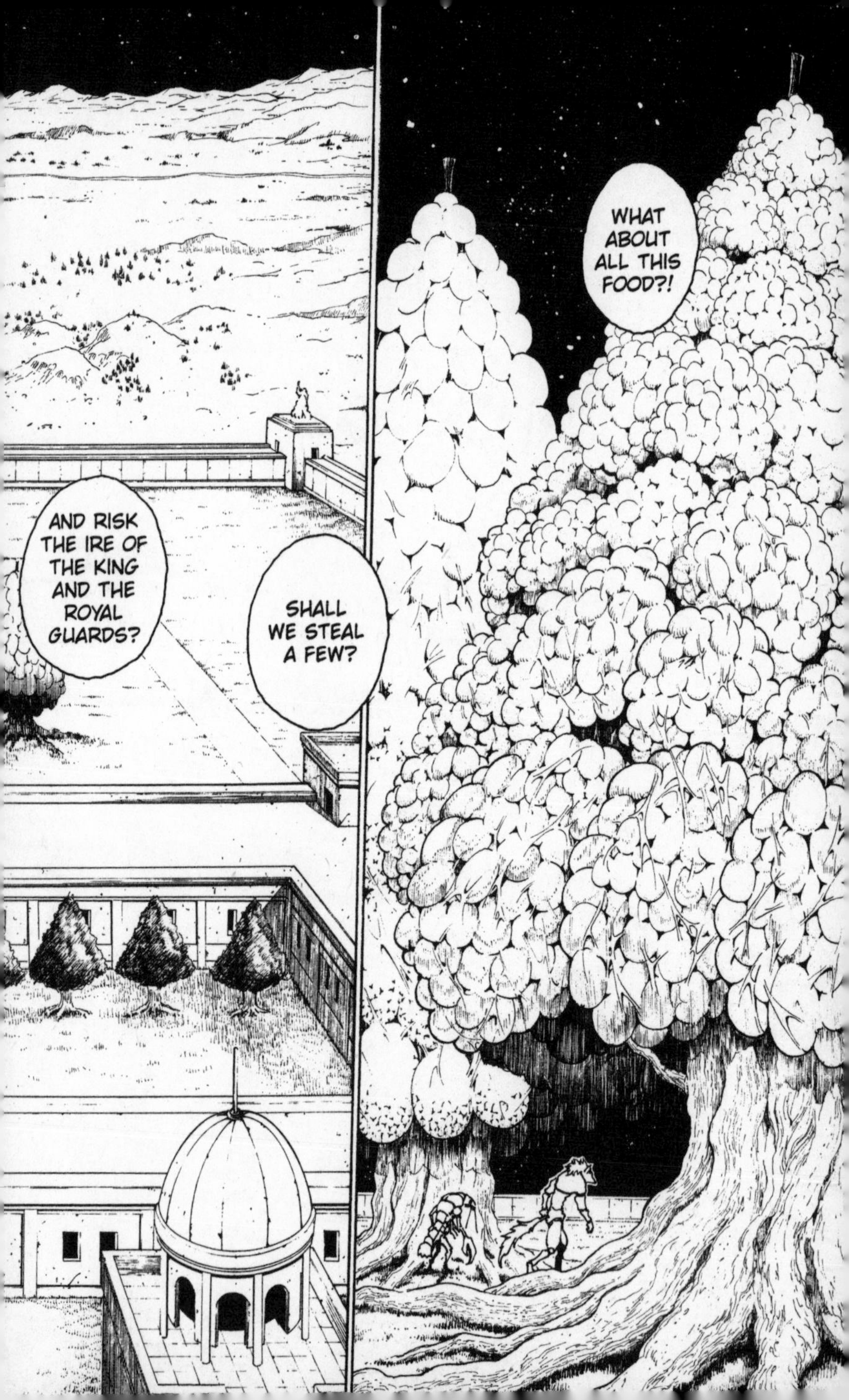
WHAT ABOUT ALL THIS FOOD?!
SHALL WE STEAL A FEW?
AND RISK THE IRE OF THE KING AND THE ROYAL GUARDS?

Chapter 246: 6: Part 3

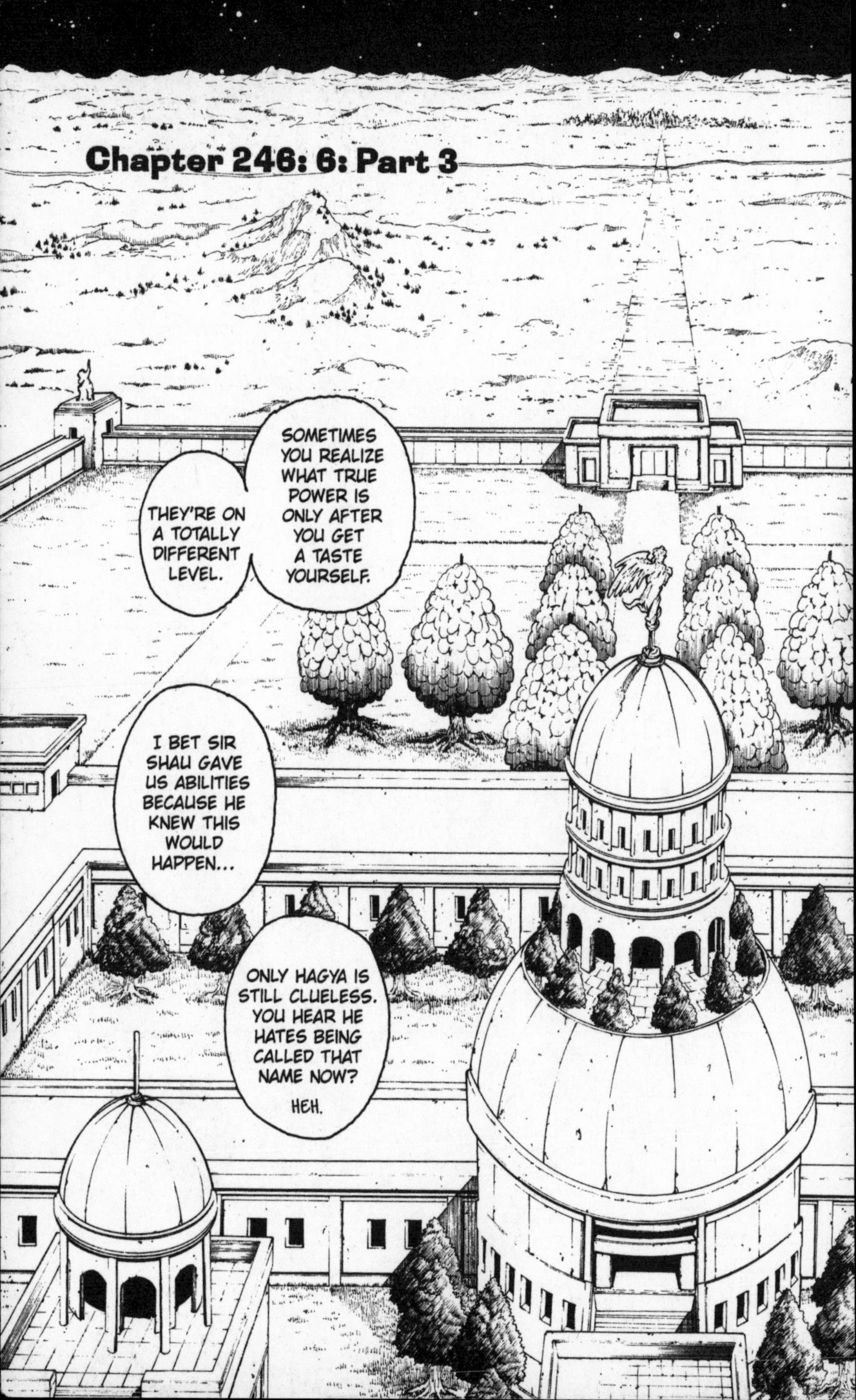
SOMETIMES YOU REALIZE WHAT TRUE POWER IS ONLY AFTER YOU GET A TASTE YOURSELF.
THEY'RE ON A TOTALLY DIFFERENT LEVEL.
I BET SIR SHAU GAVE US ABILITIES BECAUSE HE KNEW THIS WOULD HAPPEN...
ONLY HAGYA IS STILL CLUELESS. YOU HEAR HE HATES BEING CALLED THAT NAME NOW?
HEH.

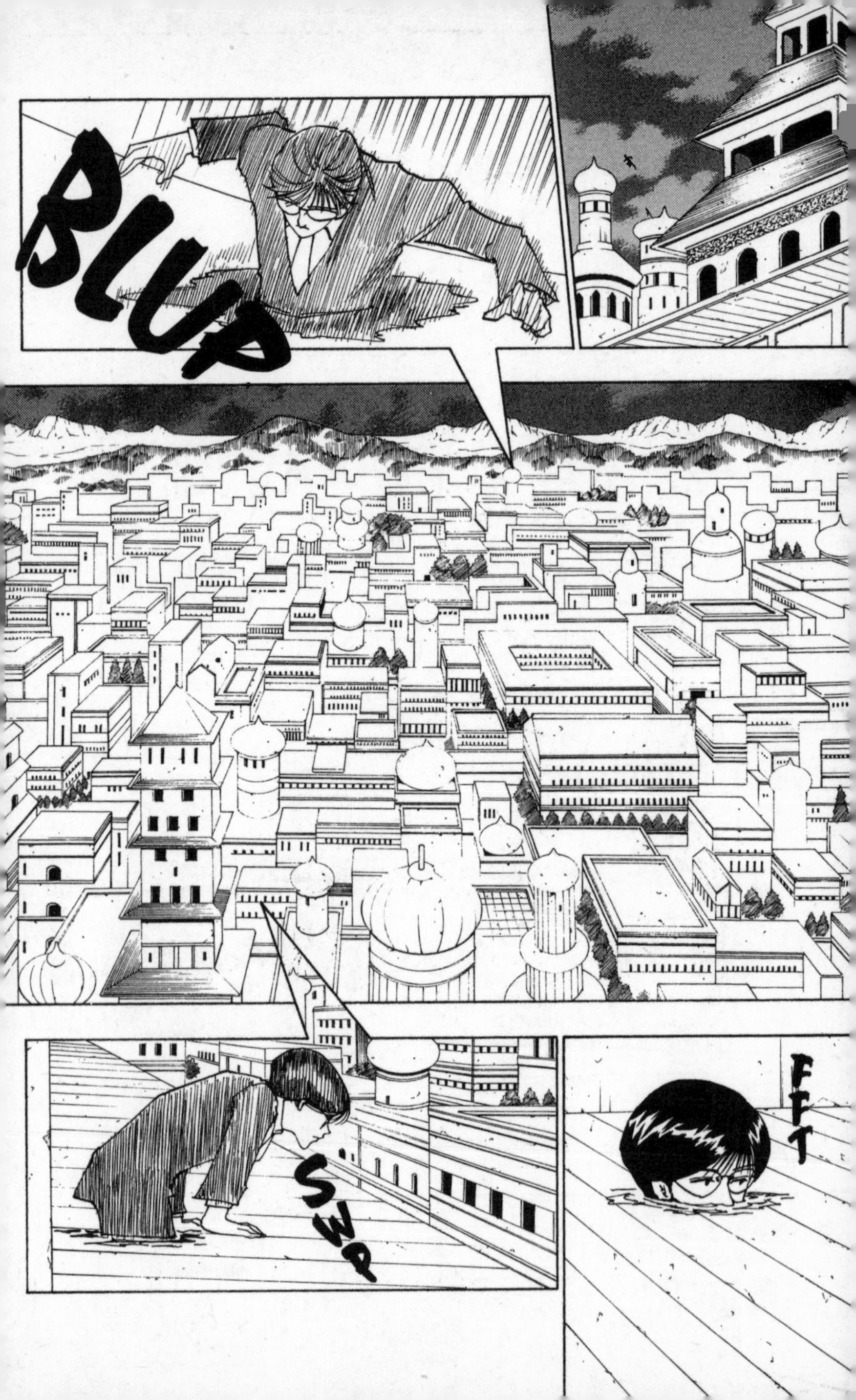
BLUP
FFT
SWP

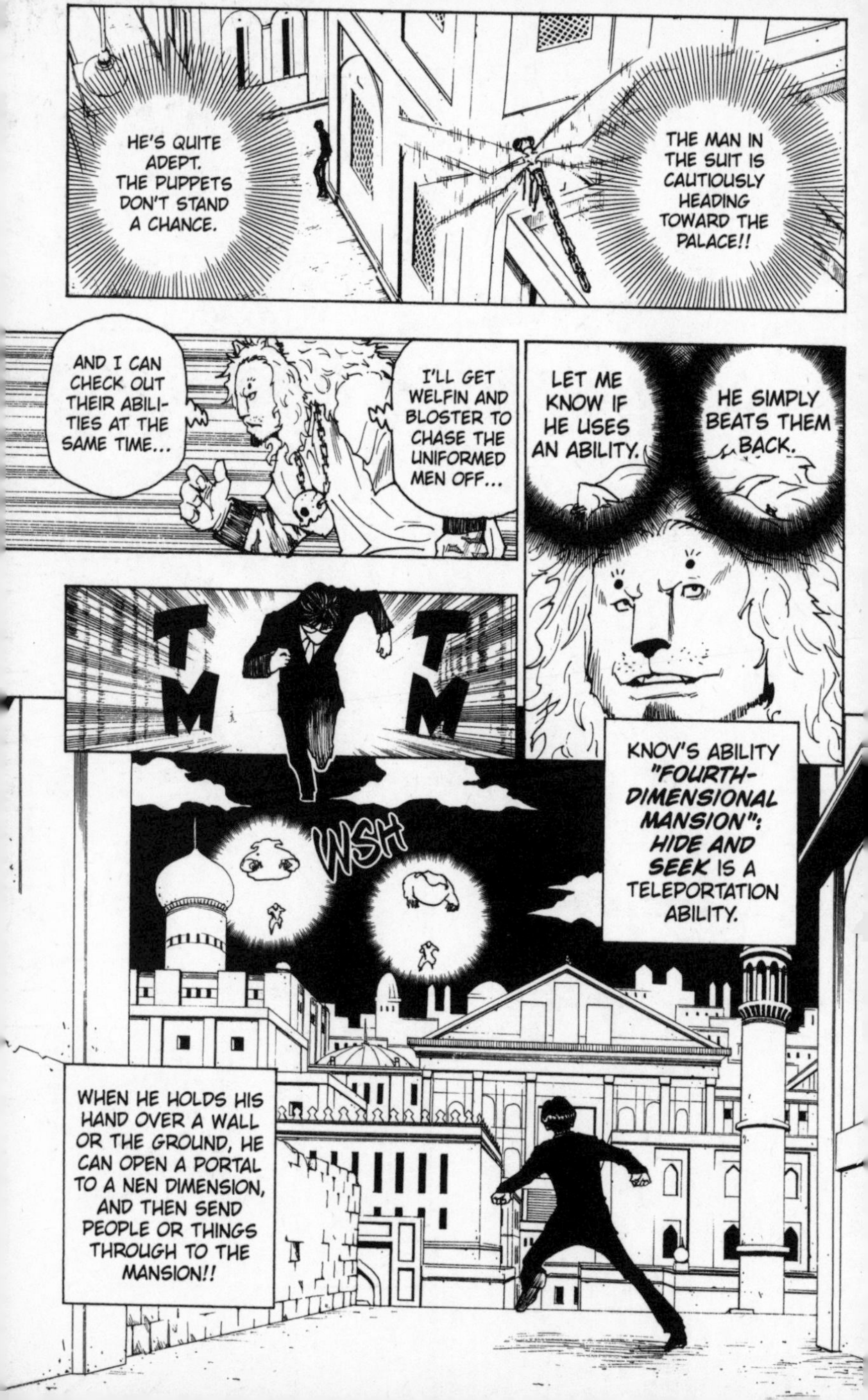
THE MAN IN THE SUIT IS CAUTIOUSLY HEADING TOWARD THE PALACE!!
HE'S QUITE ADEPT. THE PUPPETS DON'T STAND A CHANCE.
HE SIMPLY BEATS THEM BACK.
LET ME KNOW IF HE USES AN ABILITY.
I'LL GET WELFIN AND BLOSTER TO CHASE THE UNIFORMED MEN OFF...
AND I CAN CHECK OUT THEIR ABILITIES AT THE SAME TIME...
TMTM
WSH
KNOV'S ABILITY "FOURTH-DIMENSIONAL MANSION": HIDE AND SEEK IS A TELEPORTATION ABILITY.
WHEN HE HOLDS HIS HAND OVER A WALL OR THE GROUND, HE CAN OPEN A PORTAL TO A NEN DIMENSION, AND THEN SEND PEOPLE OR THINGS THROUGH TO THE MANSION!!

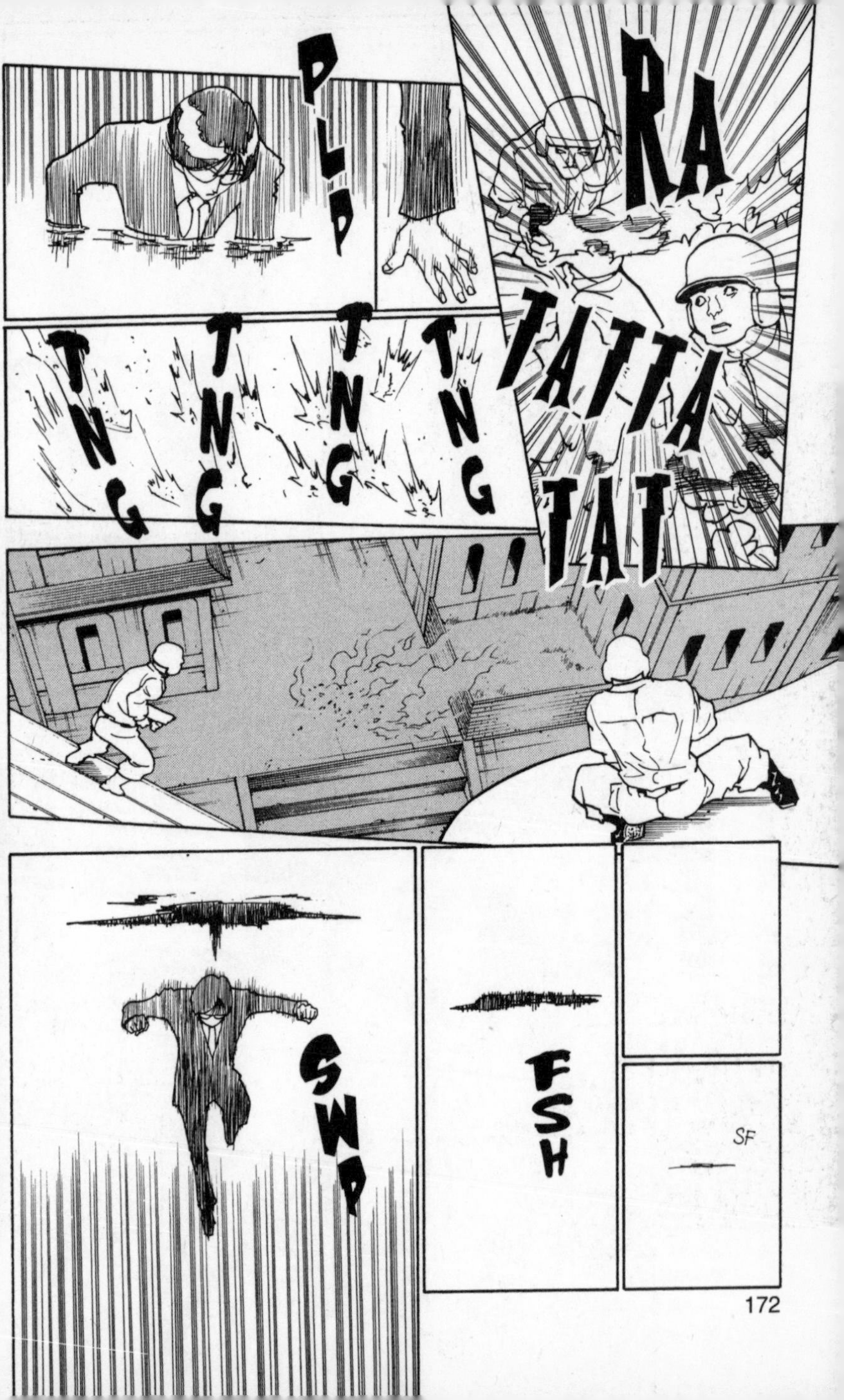
RA
TATTA
TAT
PLP
TNG
TNG
TNG
TNG
SF
FSH
SWP

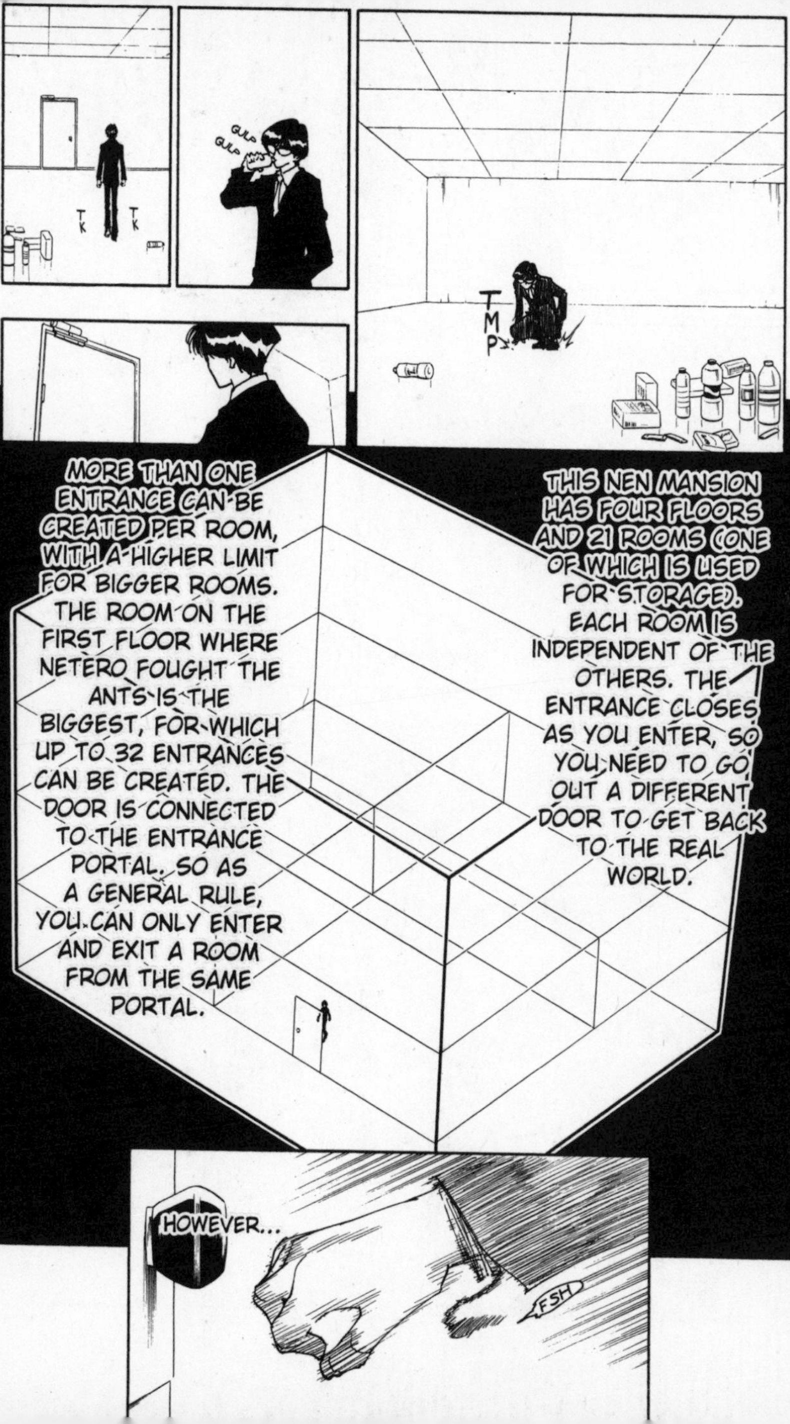
TMP
GULP GULP
TK TK
THIS NEN MANSION HAS FOUR FLOORS AND 21 ROOMS (ONE OF WHICH IS USED FOR STORAGE). EACH ROOM IS INDEPENDENT OF THE OTHERS. THE ENTRANCE CLOSES AS YOU ENTER, SO YOU NEED TO GO OUT A DIFFERENT DOOR TO GET BACK TO THE REAL WORLD.
MORE THAN ONE ENTRANCE CAN BE CREATED PER ROOM, WITH A HIGHER LIMIT FOR BIGGER ROOMS. THE ROOM ON THE FIRST FLOOR WHERE NETERO FOUGHT THE ANTS IS THE BIGGEST, FOR WHICH UP TO 32 ENTRANCES CAN BE CREATED. THE DOOR IS CONNECTED TO THE ENTRANCE PORTAL, SO AS A GENERAL RULE, YOU CAN ONLY ENTER AND EXIT A ROOM FROM THE SAME PORTAL.
HOWEVER...
FSH

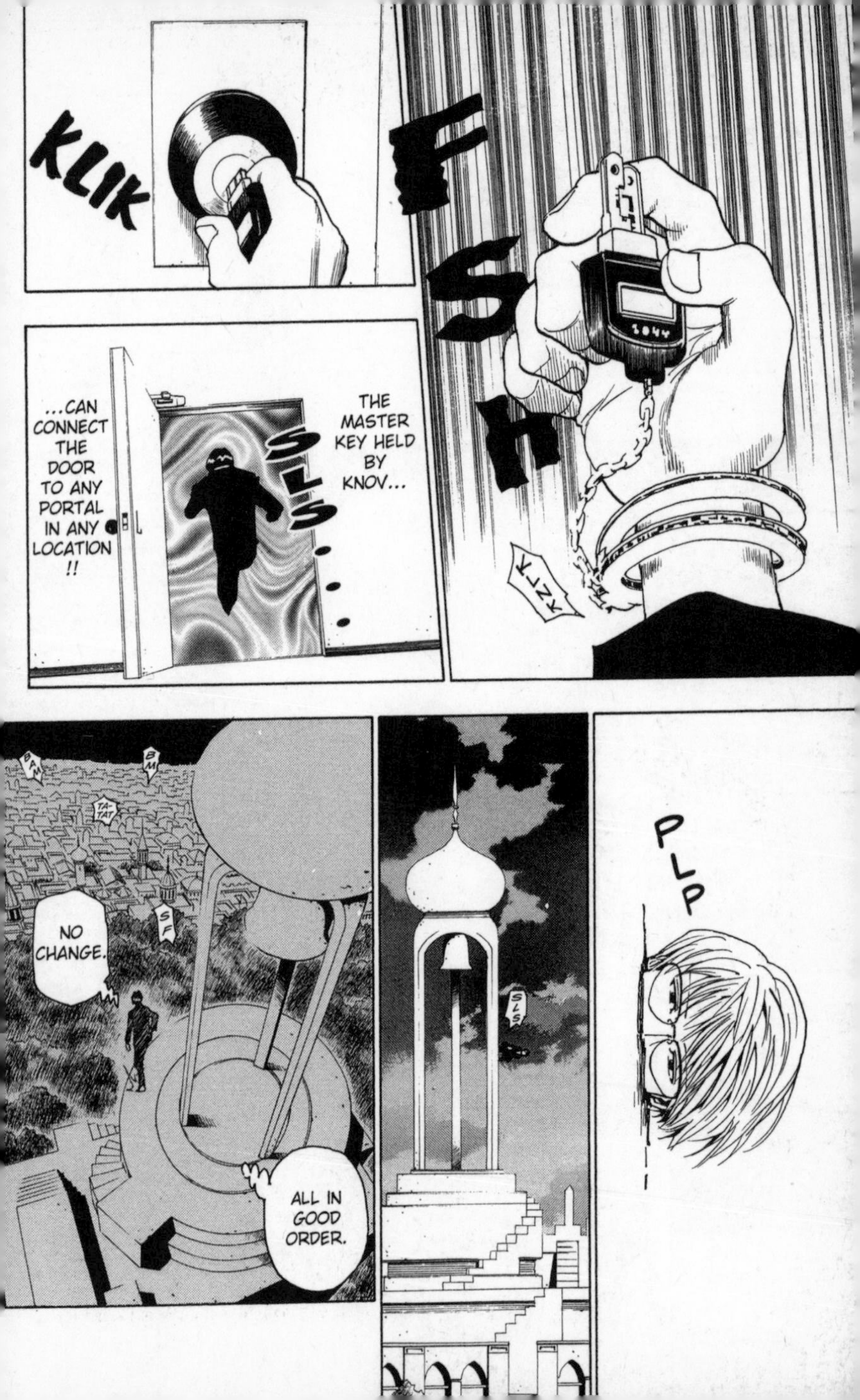
FSSH
KLZK
KLIK
THE MASTER KEY HELD BY KNOV...
SLS...
...CAN CONNECT THE DOOR TO ANY PORTAL IN ANY LOCATION !!
PLP
SLS
BAM
BM
TA-TAT
SF
NO CHANGE.
ALL IN GOOD ORDER.

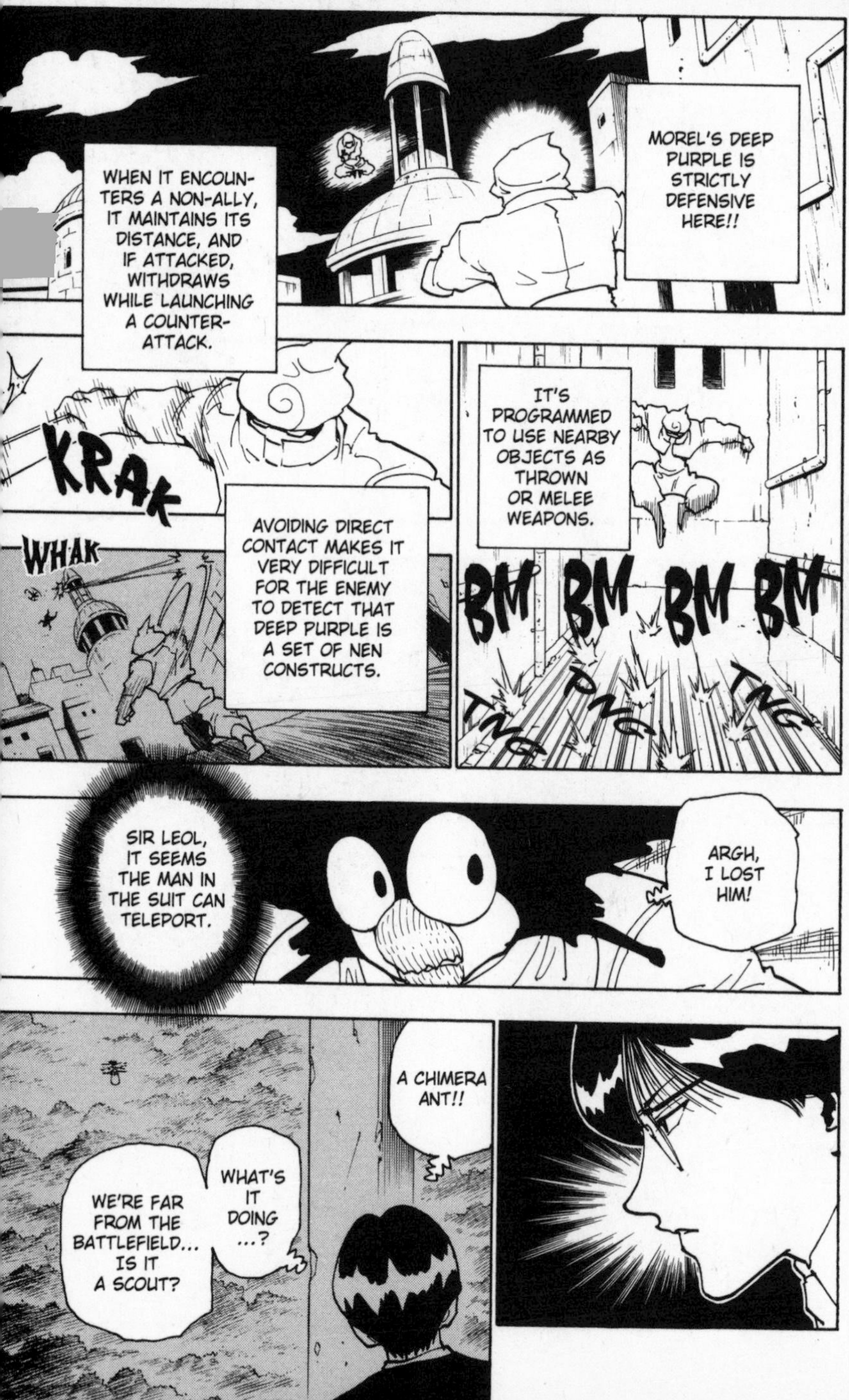
MOREL'S DEEP PURPLE IS STRICTLY DEFENSIVE HERE!!
WHEN IT ENCOUNTERS A NON-ALLY, IT MAINTAINS ITS DISTANCE, AND IF ATTACKED, WITHDRAWS WHILE LAUNCHING A COUNTER-ATTACK.
IT'S PROGRAMMED TO USE NEARBY OBJECTS AS THROWN OR MELEE WEAPONS.
BM BM BM BM
TNG
PNG
TNG
KRAK
AVOIDING DIRECT CONTACT MAKES IT VERY DIFFICULT FOR THE ENEMY TO DETECT THAT DEEP PURPLE IS A SET OF NEN CONSTRUCTS.
WHAK
ARGH, I LOST HIM!
SIR LEOL, IT SEEMS THE MAN IN THE SUIT CAN TELEPORT.
A CHIMERA ANT!!
WHAT'S IT DOING ...?
WE'RE FAR FROM THE BATTLEFIELD... IS IT A SCOUT?

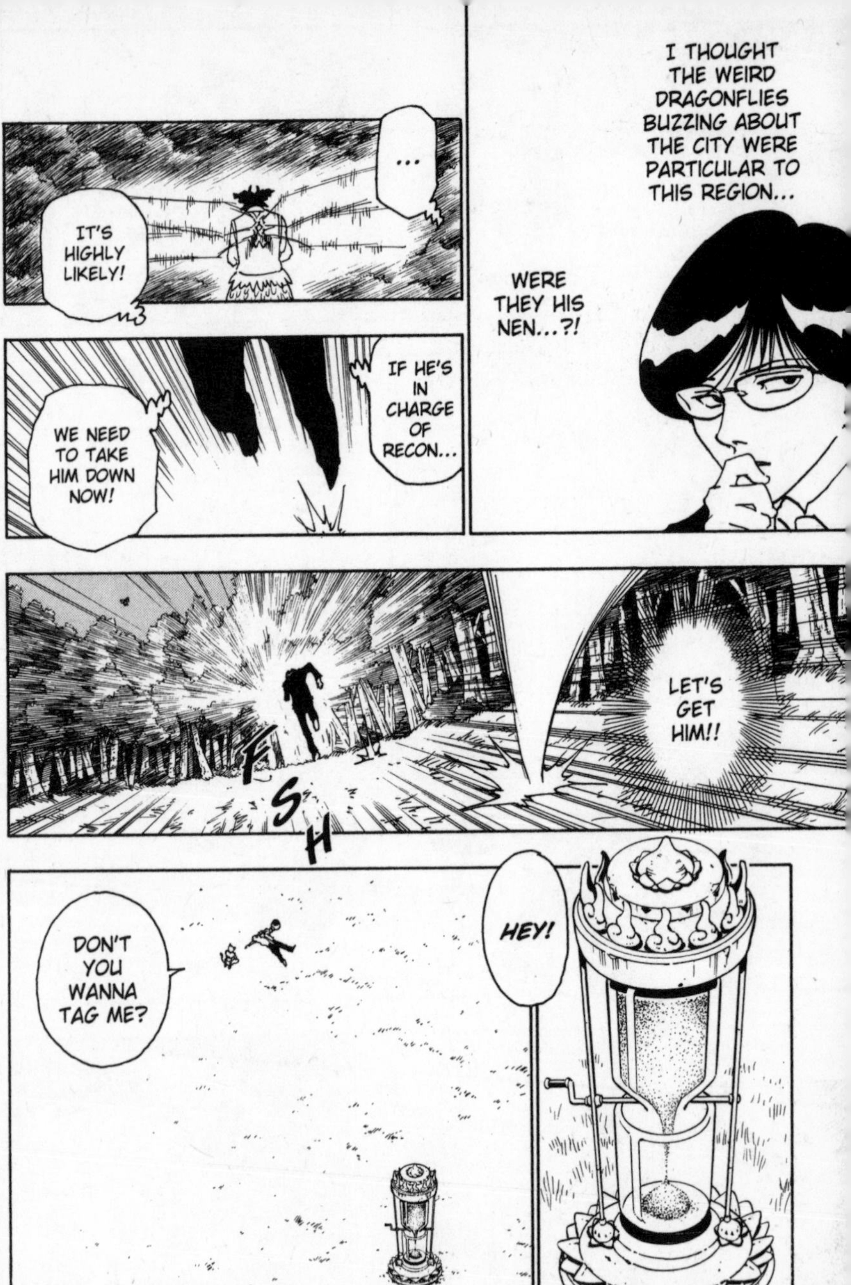

I THOUGHT THE WEIRD DRAGONFLIES BUZZING ABOUT THE CITY WERE PARTICULAR TO THIS REGION...
WERE THEY HIS NEN...?!
...
IT'S HIGHLY LIKELY!
IF HE'S IN CHARGE OF RECON...
WE NEED TO TAKE HIM DOWN NOW!
LET'S GET HIM!!
FSH
HEY!
DON'T YOU WANNA TAG ME?

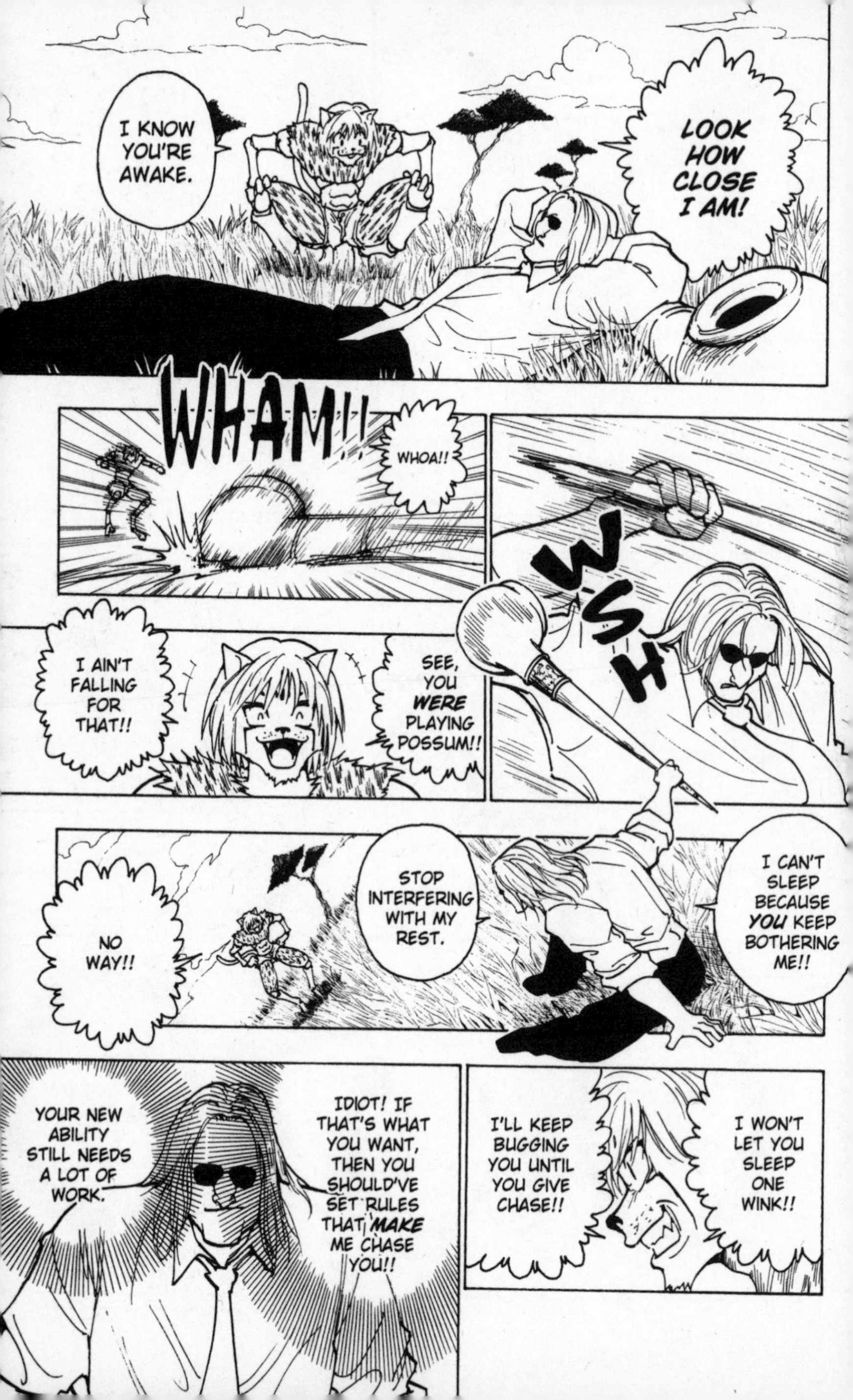
LOOK HOW CLOSE I AM!
I KNOW YOU'RE AWAKE.
WSH
WHAM!!
WHOA!!
SEE, YOU *WERE* PLAYING POSSUM!!
I AIN'T FALLING FOR THAT!!
I CAN'T SLEEP BECAUSE *YOU* KEEP BOTHERING ME!!
STOP INTERFERING WITH MY REST.
NO WAY!!
I WON'T LET YOU SLEEP ONE WINK!!
I'LL KEEP BUGGING YOU UNTIL YOU GIVE CHASE!!
IDIOT! IF THAT'S WHAT YOU WANT, THEN YOU SHOULD'VE SET RULES THAT *MAKE* ME CHASE YOU!!
YOUR NEW ABILITY STILL NEEDS A LOT OF WORK.

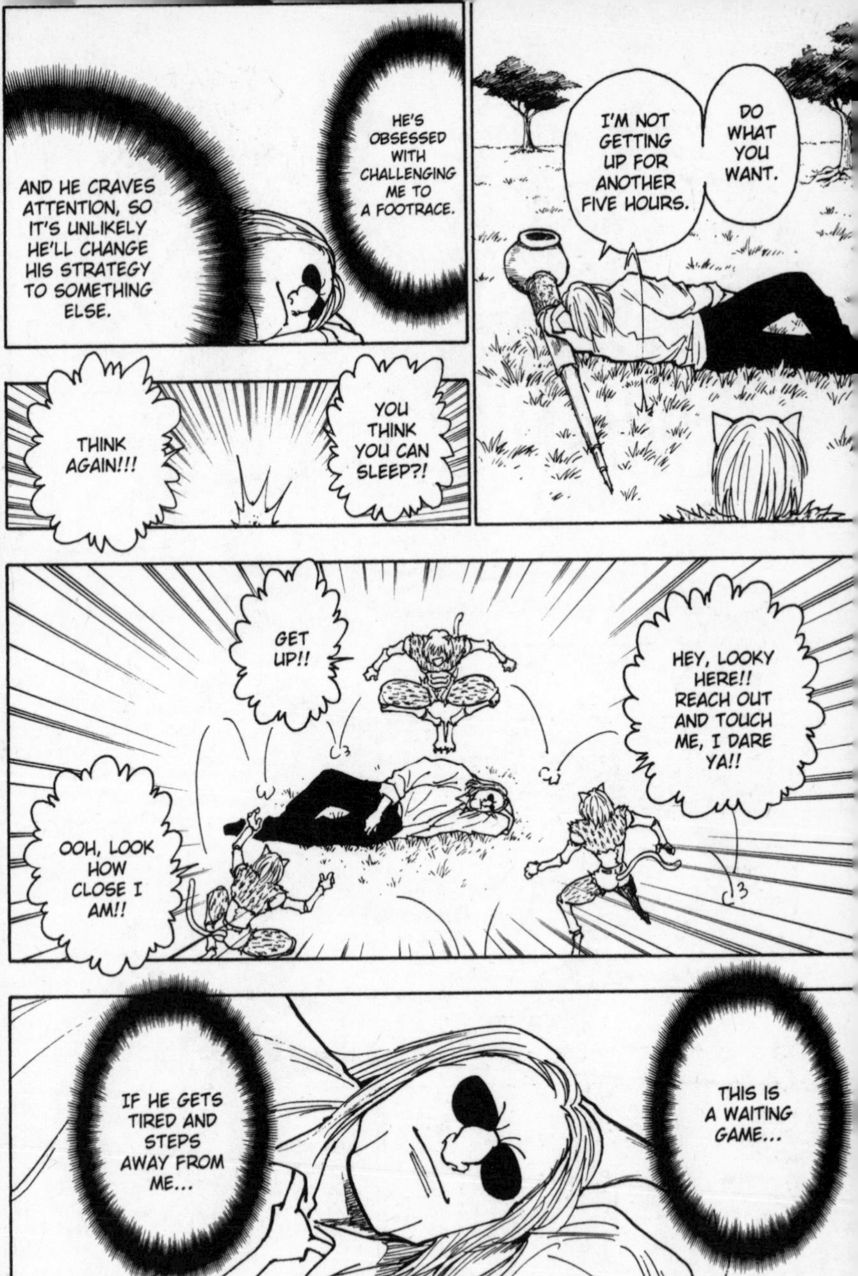
DO WHAT YOU WANT.
I'M NOT GETTING UP FOR ANOTHER FIVE HOURS.
HE'S OBSESSED WITH CHALLENGING ME TO A FOOTRACE.
AND HE CRAVES ATTENTION, SO IT'S UNLIKELY HE'LL CHANGE HIS STRATEGY TO SOMETHING ELSE.
YOU THINK YOU CAN SLEEP?!
THINK AGAIN!!!
HEY, LOOKY HERE!! REACH OUT AND TOUCH ME, I DARE YA!!
GET UP!!
OOH, LOOK HOW CLOSE I AM!!
THIS IS A WAITING GAME...
IF HE GETS TIRED AND STEPS AWAY FROM ME...

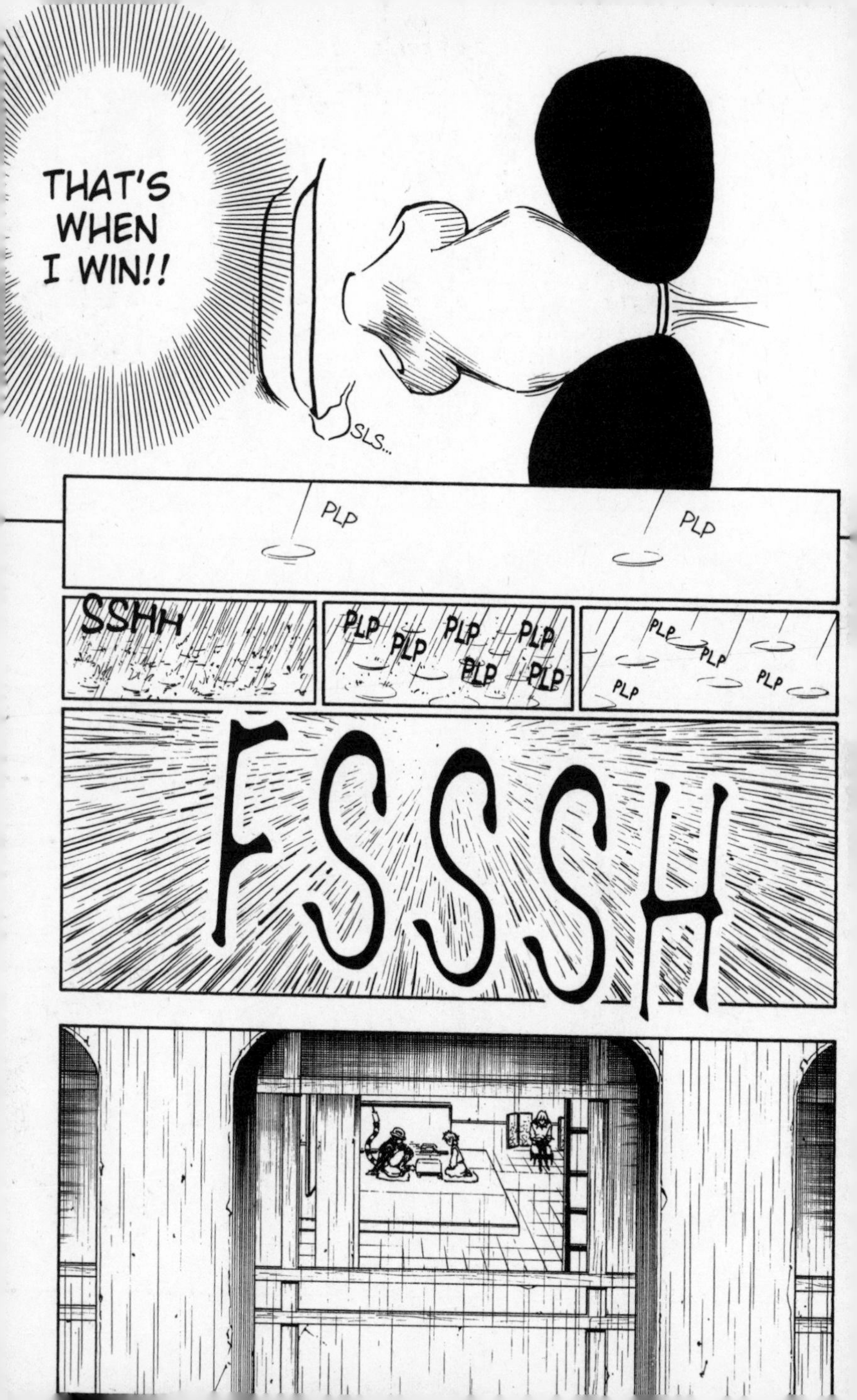
THAT'S WHEN I WIN!!
SLS...
PLP
PLP
PLP PLP PLP PLP
PLP PLP PLP PLP PLP PLP
SSHH
FSSSH

SHINOBI 8-1-1.

CANNON 2-3-1.

FORT 9-1-1.

SOLDIER 7-9-1.

SOLDIER 2-3-1.

KING 1-5-1.

KING 9-9-1.

TMK

TMK

TMK

TMK

TMK

TMK

TMK...

TMK

MORTAR 2-7-2.

THE KING IS ISOLATED...!

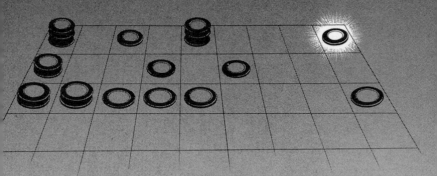

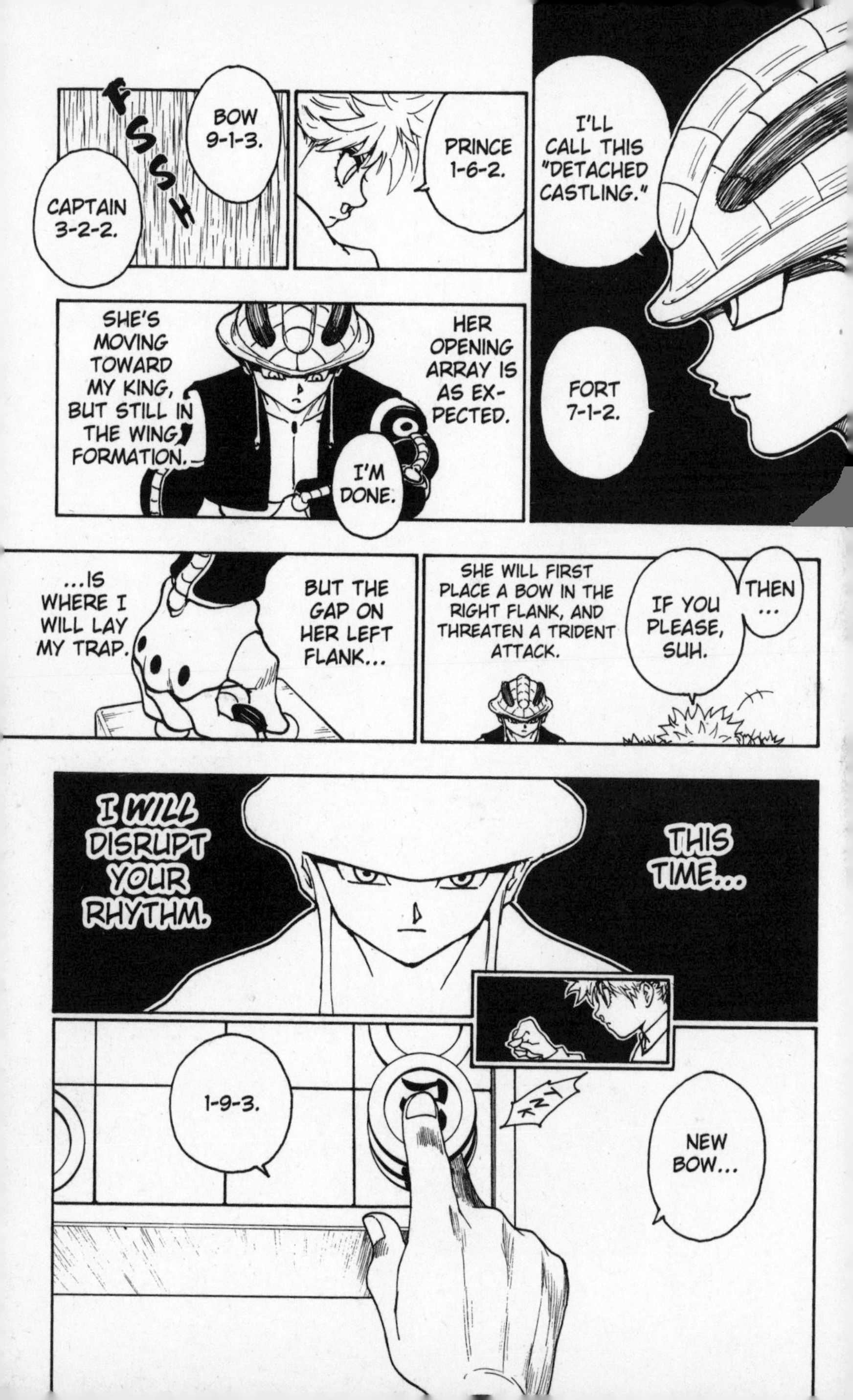
I'LL CALL THIS "DETACHED CASTLING."
FORT 7-1-2.
PRINCE 1-6-2.
BOW 9-1-3.
FSSH
CAPTAIN 3-2-2.
HER OPENING ARRAY IS AS EXPECTED.
SHE'S MOVING TOWARD MY KING, BUT STILL IN THE WING FORMATION.
I'M DONE.
THEN...
IF YOU PLEASE, SUH.
SHE WILL FIRST PLACE A BOW IN THE RIGHT FLANK, AND THREATEN A TRIDENT ATTACK.
BUT THE GAP ON HER LEFT FLANK...
...IS WHERE I WILL LAY MY TRAP.
THIS TIME...
I WILL DISRUPT YOUR RHYTHM.
NEW BOW...
TNK
1-9-3.

Chapter 247: 6: Part 4

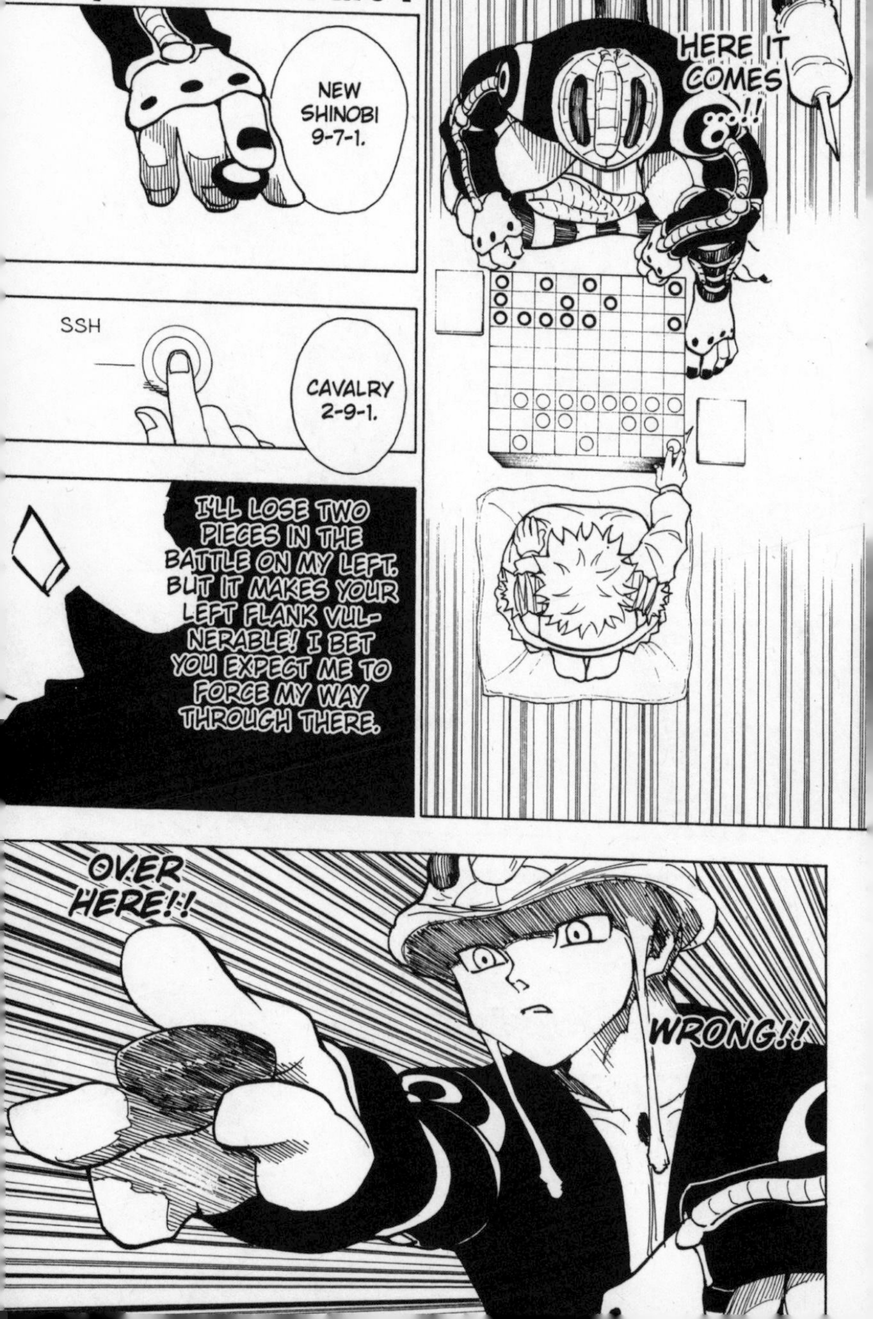
HERE IT COMES!!
NEW SHINOBI 9-7-1.
SSH
CAVALRY 2-9-1.
I'LL LOSE TWO PIECES IN THE BATTLE ON MY LEFT. BUT IT MAKES YOUR LEFT FLANK VULNERABLE! I BET YOU EXPECT ME TO FORCE MY WAY THROUGH THERE.
OVER HERE!!
WRONG!!

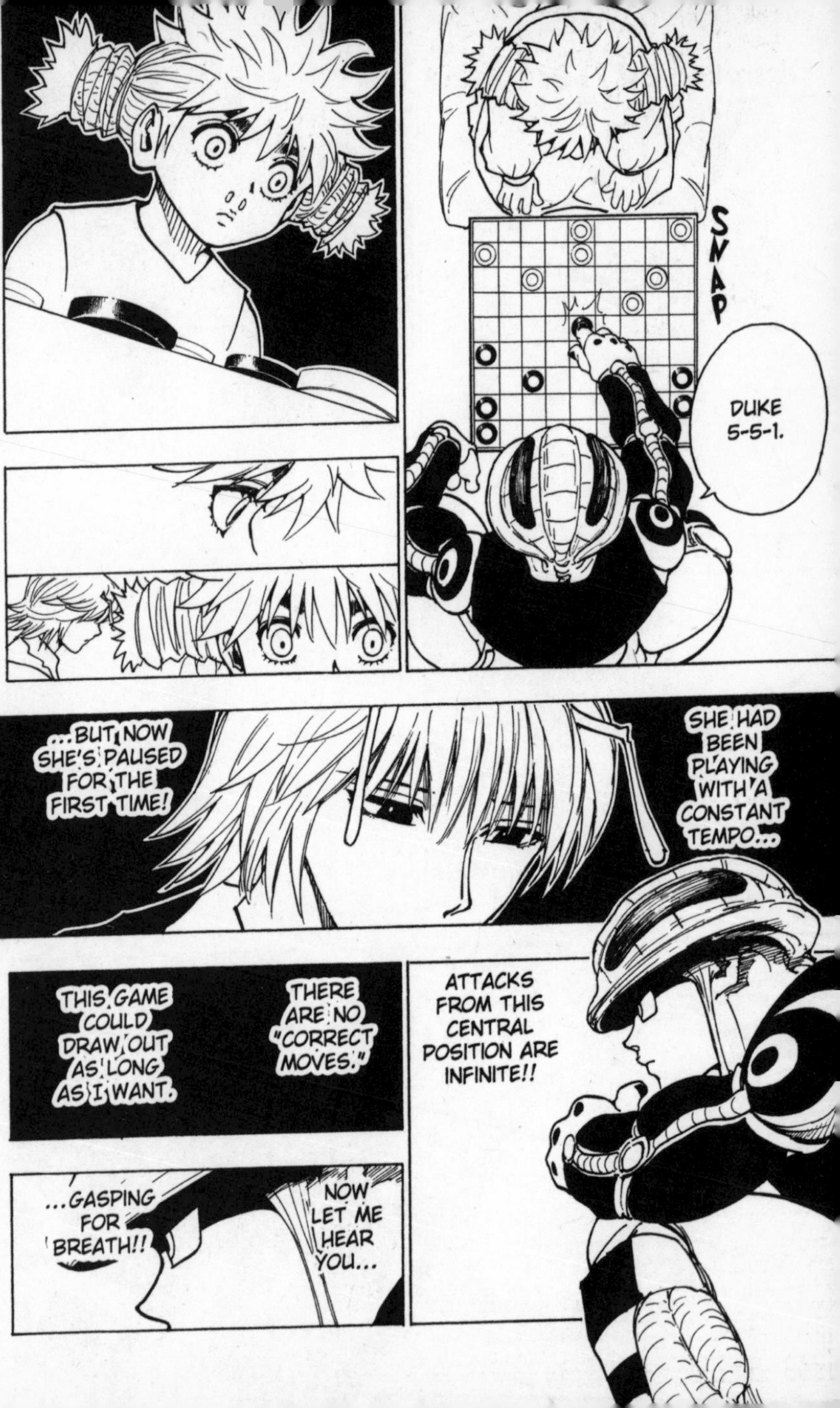
SNAP
DUKE 5-5-1.
SHE HAD BEEN PLAYING WITH A CONSTANT TEMPO...
...BUT NOW SHE'S PAUSED FOR THE FIRST TIME!
ATTACKS FROM THIS CENTRAL POSITION ARE INFINITE!!
THERE ARE NO "CORRECT MOVES."
THIS GAME COULD DRAW OUT AS LONG AS I WANT.
NOW LET ME HEAR YOU...
...GASPING FOR BREATH!!

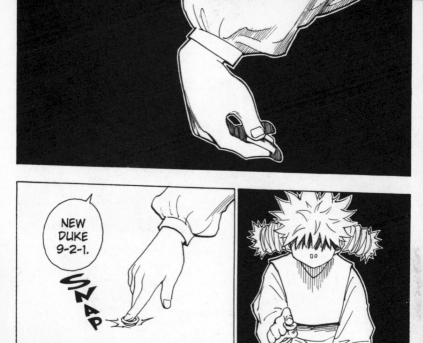

NEW
DUKE
9-2-1.

SNAP

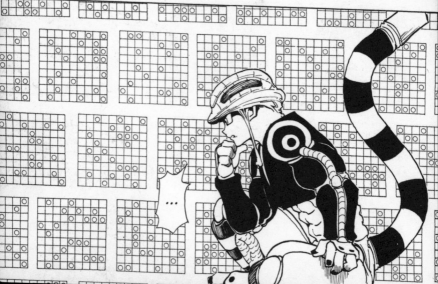

...

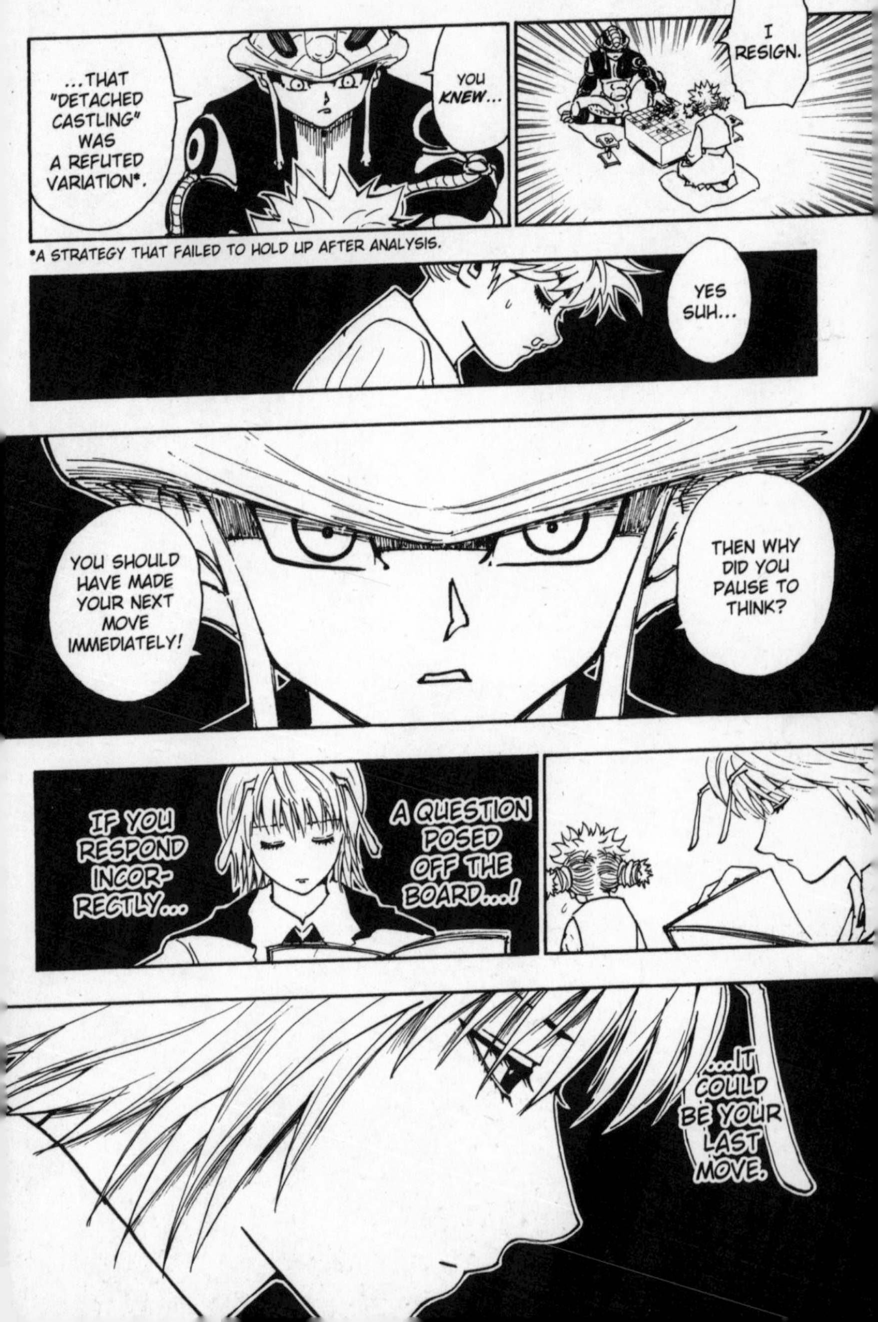
I RESIGN.
YOU KNEW...
...THAT "DETACHED CASTLING" WAS A REFUTED VARIATION*.
*A STRATEGY THAT FAILED TO HOLD UP AFTER ANALYSIS.
YES SUH...
THEN WHY DID YOU PAUSE TO THINK?
YOU SHOULD HAVE MADE YOUR NEXT MOVE IMMEDIATELY!
A QUESTION POSED OFF THE BOARD...!
IF YOU RESPOND INCOR-RECTLY...
...IT COULD BE YOUR LAST MOVE.

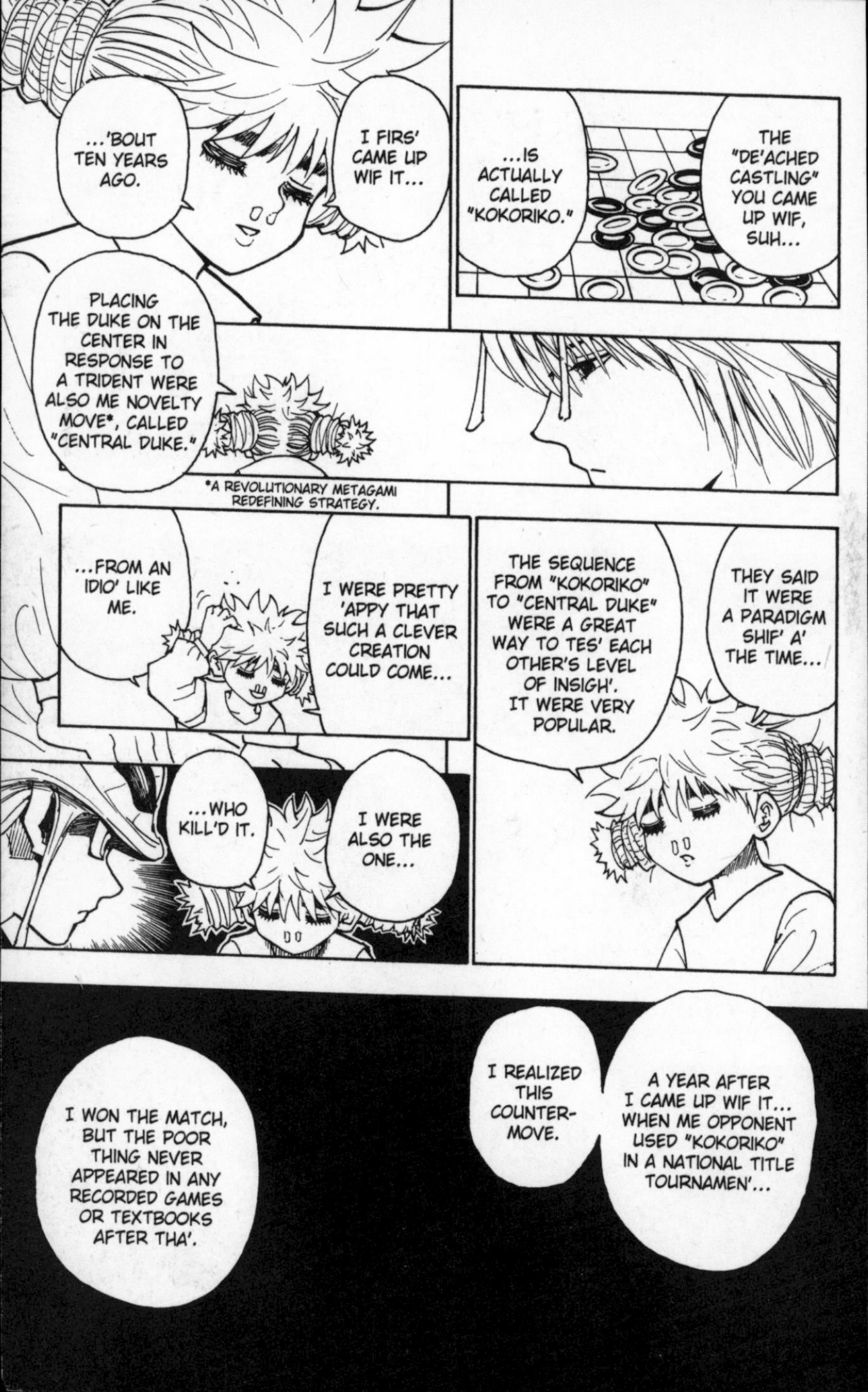
THE "DE'ACHED CASTLING" YOU CAME UP WIF, SUH...
...IS ACTUALLY CALLED "KOKORIKO."
I FIRS' CAME UP WIF IT...
...'BOUT TEN YEARS AGO.
PLACING THE DUKE ON THE CENTER IN RESPONSE TO A TRIDENT WERE ALSO ME NOVELTY MOVE*, CALLED "CENTRAL DUKE."
*A REVOLUTIONARY METAGAMI REDEFINING STRATEGY.
THEY SAID IT WERE A PARADIGM SHIF' A' THE TIME...
THE SEQUENCE FROM "KOKORIKO" TO "CENTRAL DUKE" WERE A GREAT WAY TO TES' EACH OTHER'S LEVEL OF INSIGH'. IT WERE VERY POPULAR.
I WERE PRETTY 'APPY THAT SUCH A CLEVER CREATION COULD COME...
...FROM AN IDIO' LIKE ME.
I WERE ALSO THE ONE...
...WHO KILL'D IT.
A YEAR AFTER I CAME UP WIF IT... WHEN ME OPPONENT USED "KOKORIKO" IN A NATIONAL TITLE TOURNAMEN'...
I REALIZED THIS COUNTER-MOVE.
I WON THE MATCH, BUT THE POOR THING NEVER APPEARED IN ANY RECORDED GAMES OR TEXTBOOKS AFTER THA'.

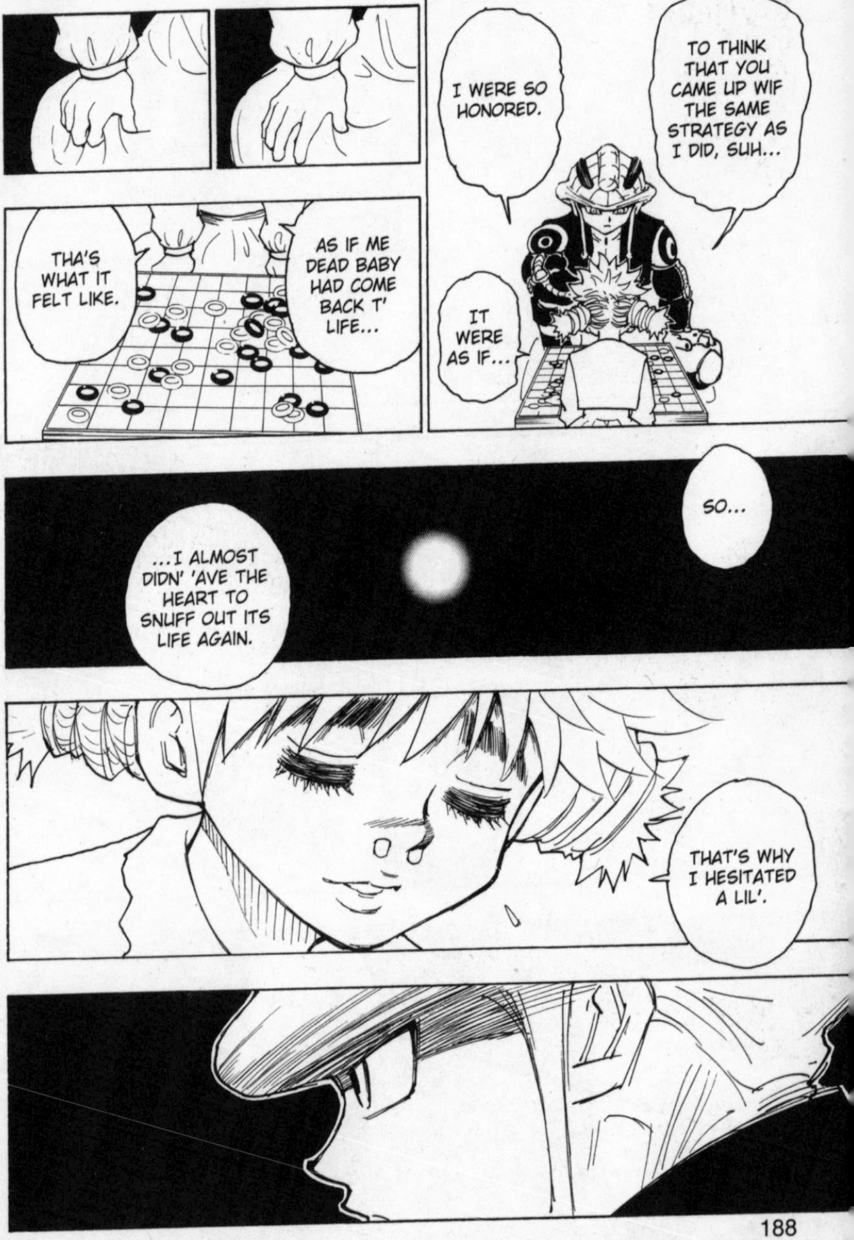
TO THINK THAT YOU CAME UP WIF THE SAME STRATEGY AS I DID, SUH...
I WERE SO HONORED.
IT WERE AS IF...
AS IF ME DEAD BABY HAD COME BACK T' LIFE...
THA'S WHAT IT FELT LIKE.
SO...
...I ALMOST DIDN' 'AVE THE HEART TO SNUFF OUT ITS LIFE AGAIN.
THAT'S WHY I HESITATED A LIL'.

READ THIS WAY

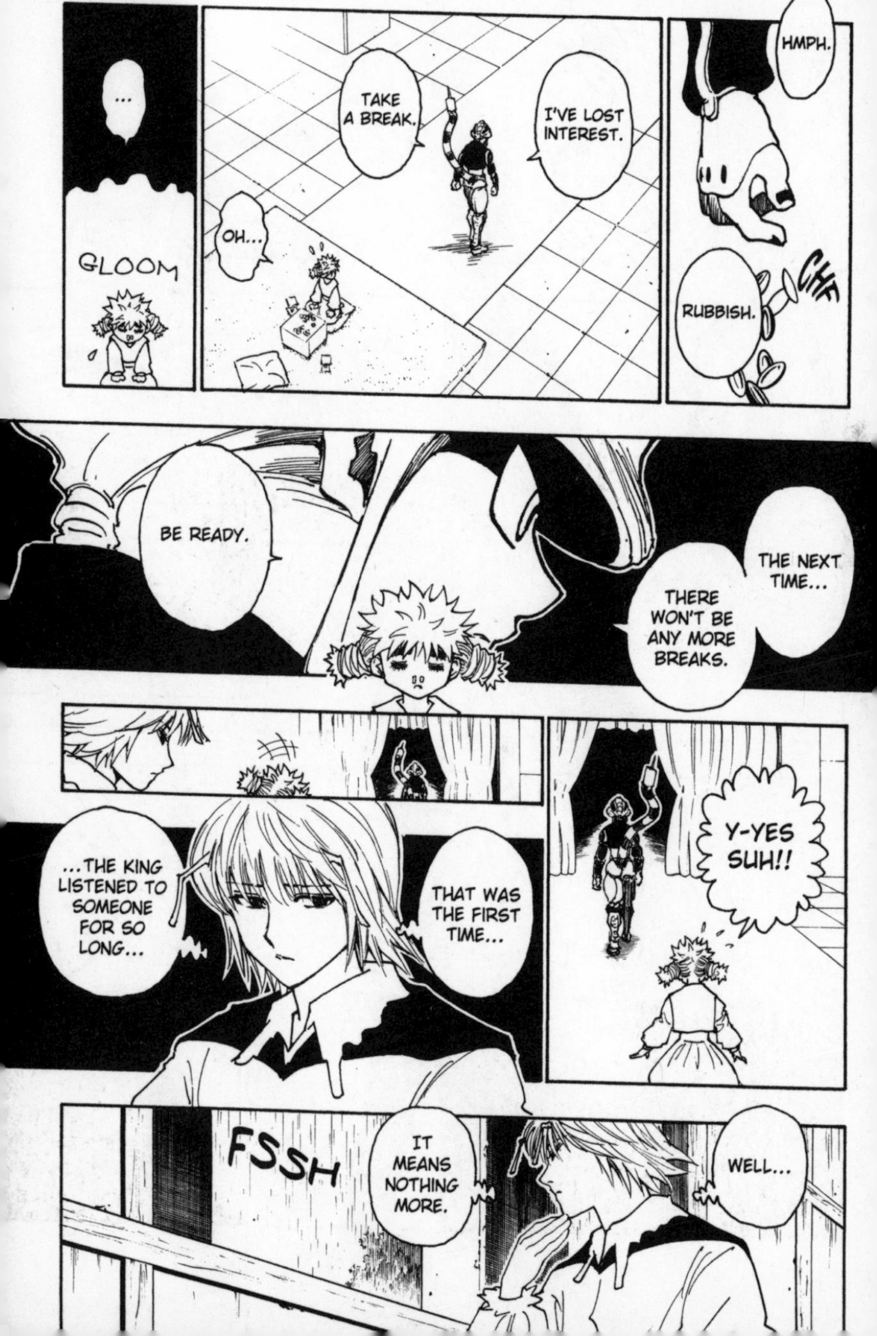
HMPH.
RUBBISH.
CHF
I'VE LOST INTEREST.
TAKE A BREAK.
OH...
...
GLOOM
THE NEXT TIME...
THERE WON'T BE ANY MORE BREAKS.
BE READY.
Y-YES SUH!!
THAT WAS THE FIRST TIME...
...THE KING LISTENED TO SOMEONE FOR SO LONG...
WELL...
IT MEANS NOTHING MORE.
FSSH

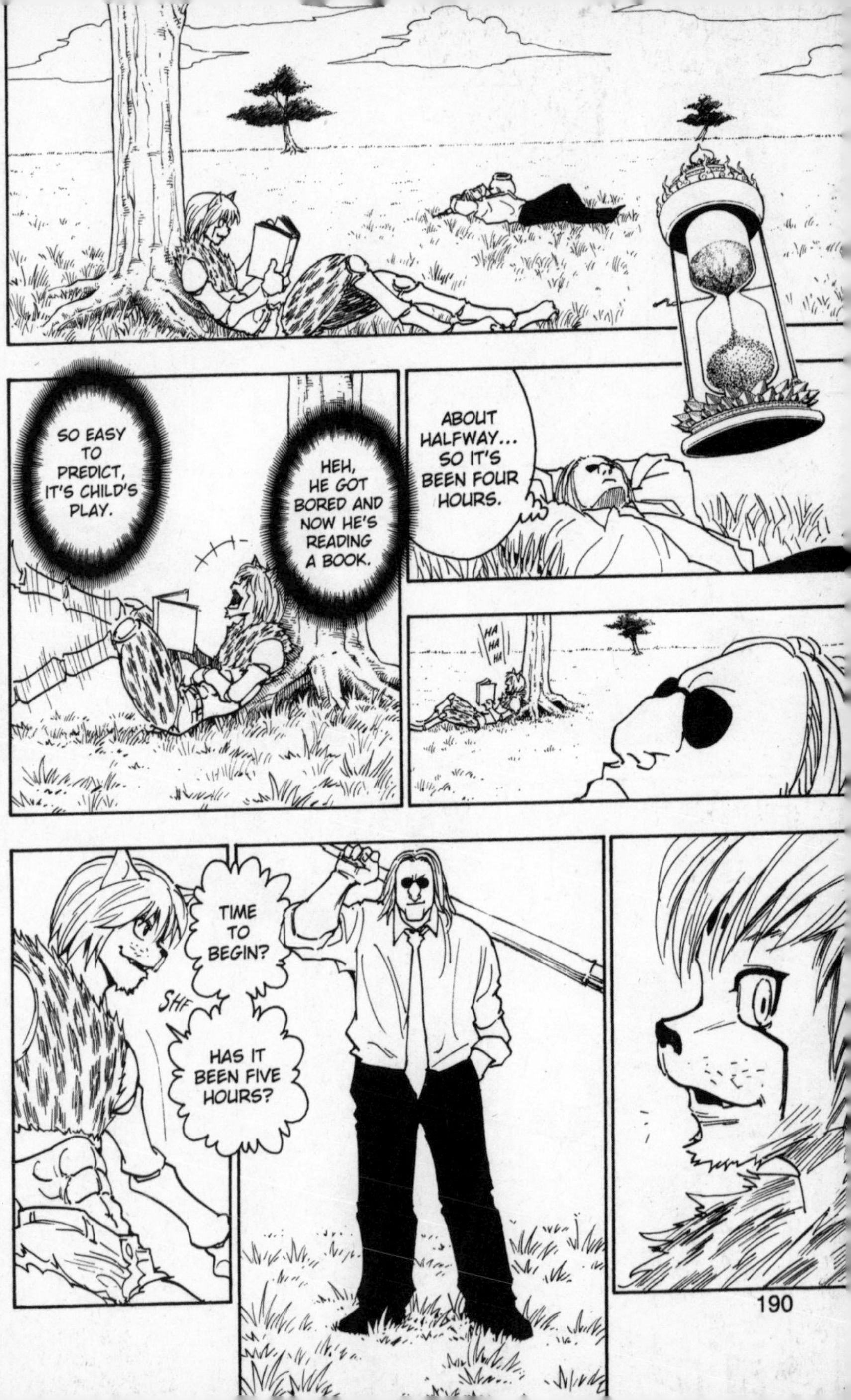
ABOUT HALFWAY... SO IT'S BEEN FOUR HOURS.
HA HA HA
HEH, HE GOT BORED AND NOW HE'S READING A BOOK.
SO EASY TO PREDICT, IT'S CHILD'S PLAY.
TIME TO BEGIN?
HAS IT BEEN FIVE HOURS?
SHF

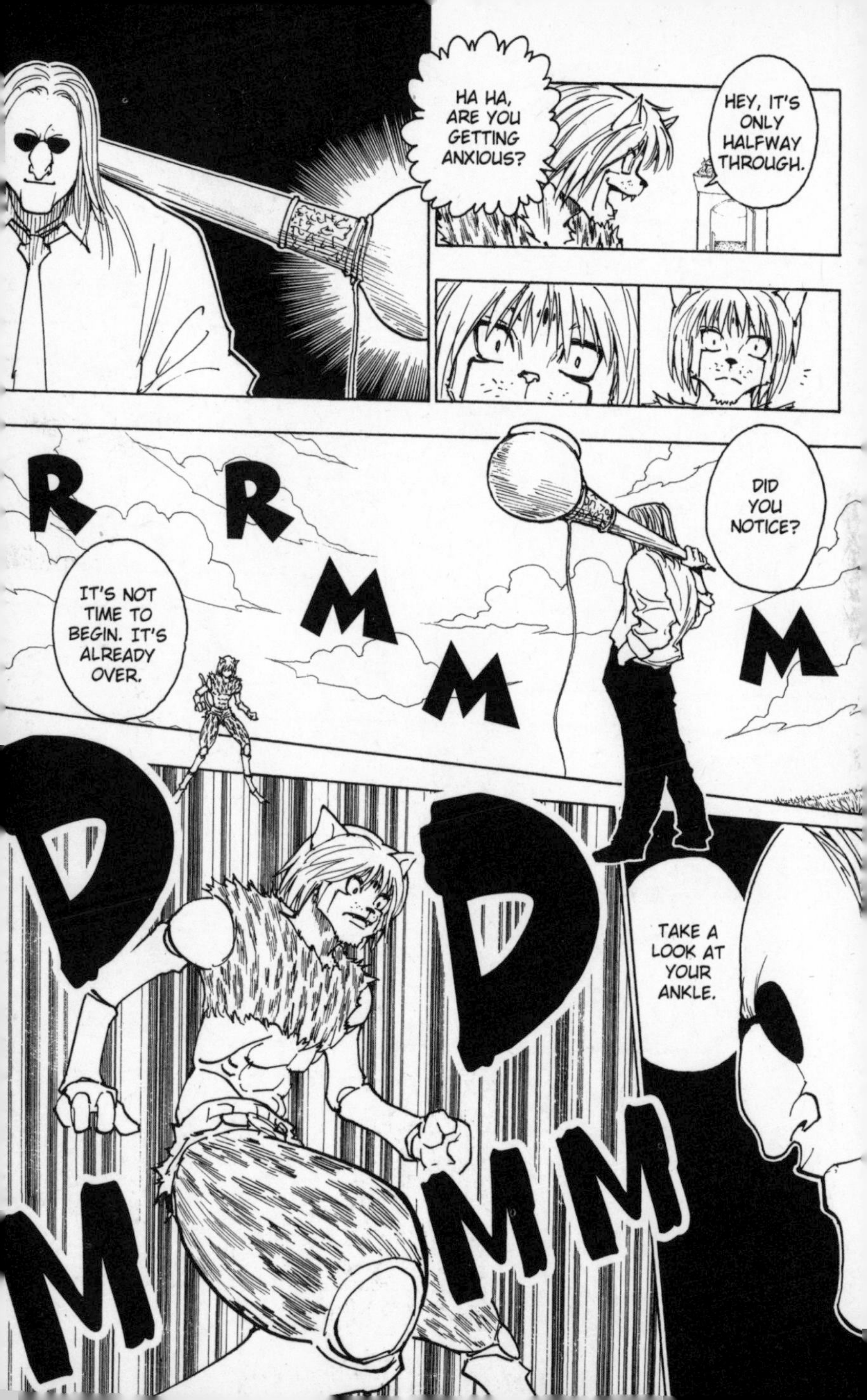
HEY, IT'S ONLY HALFWAY THROUGH.
HA HA, ARE YOU GETTING ANXIOUS?
DID YOU NOTICE?
IT'S NOT TIME TO BEGIN. IT'S ALREADY OVER.
RRMMMM
TAKE A LOOK AT YOUR ANKLE.
DDMMM

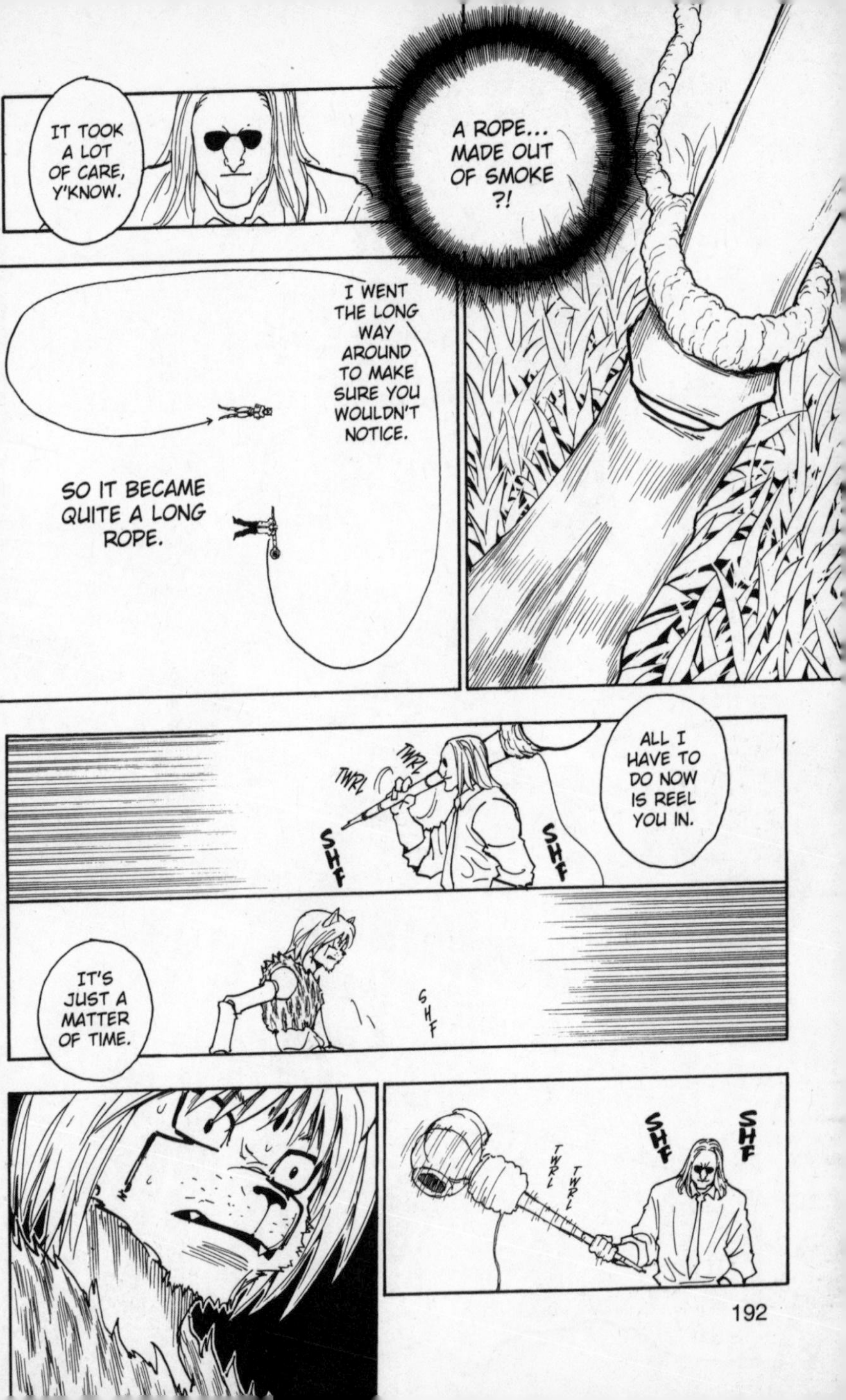
A ROPE... MADE OUT OF SMOKE ?!
IT TOOK A LOT OF CARE, Y'KNOW.
I WENT THE LONG WAY AROUND TO MAKE SURE YOU WOULDN'T NOTICE.
SO IT BECAME QUITE A LONG ROPE.
ALL I HAVE TO DO NOW IS REEL YOU IN.
SHF
TWRL
TWRL
SHF
IT'S JUST A MATTER OF TIME.
SHF
SHF
SHF
TWRL
TWRL

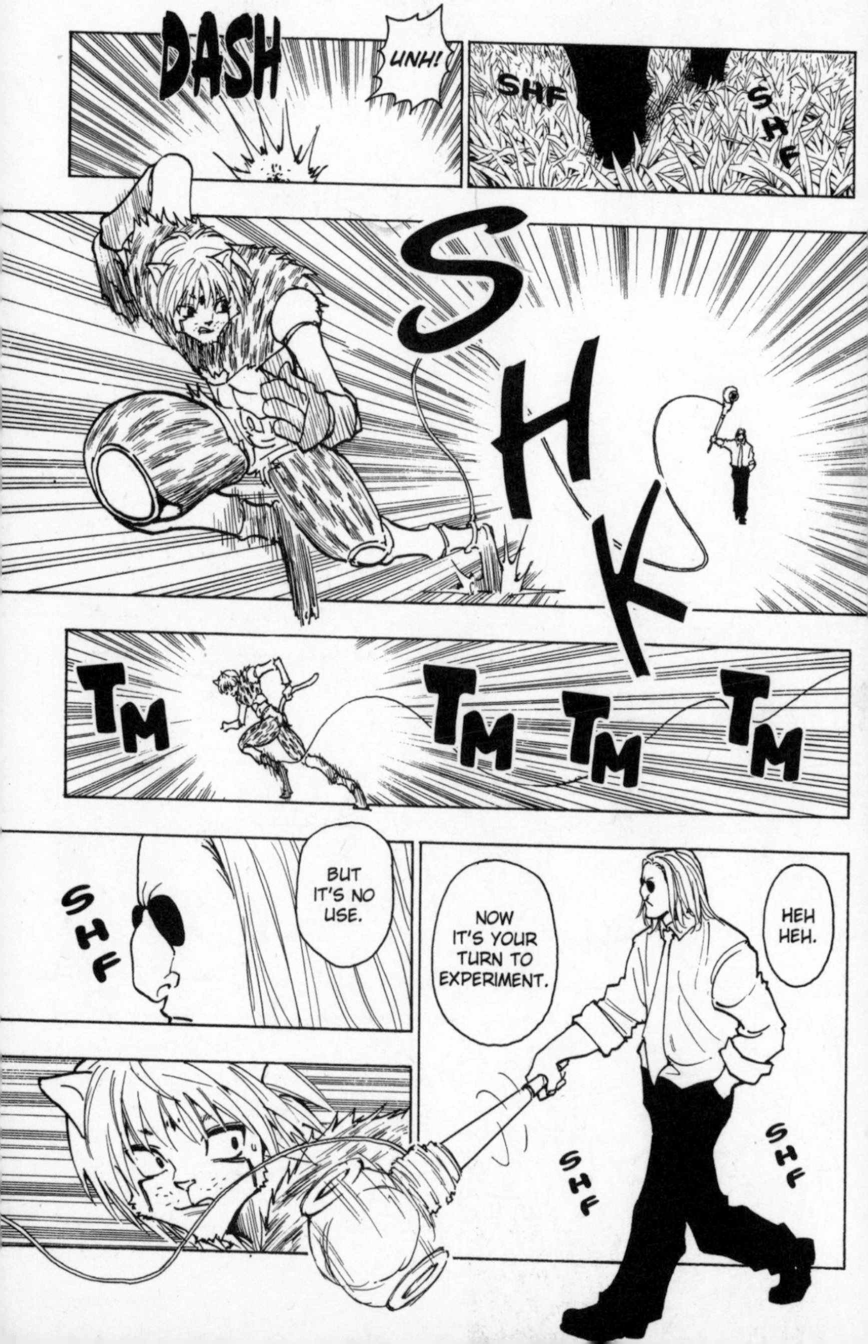
SHF
SHF
UNH!
DASH
SHK
TM
TM
TM
TM
HEH HEH.
NOW IT'S YOUR TURN TO EXPERIMENT.
SHF
SHF
BUT IT'S NO USE.
SHF

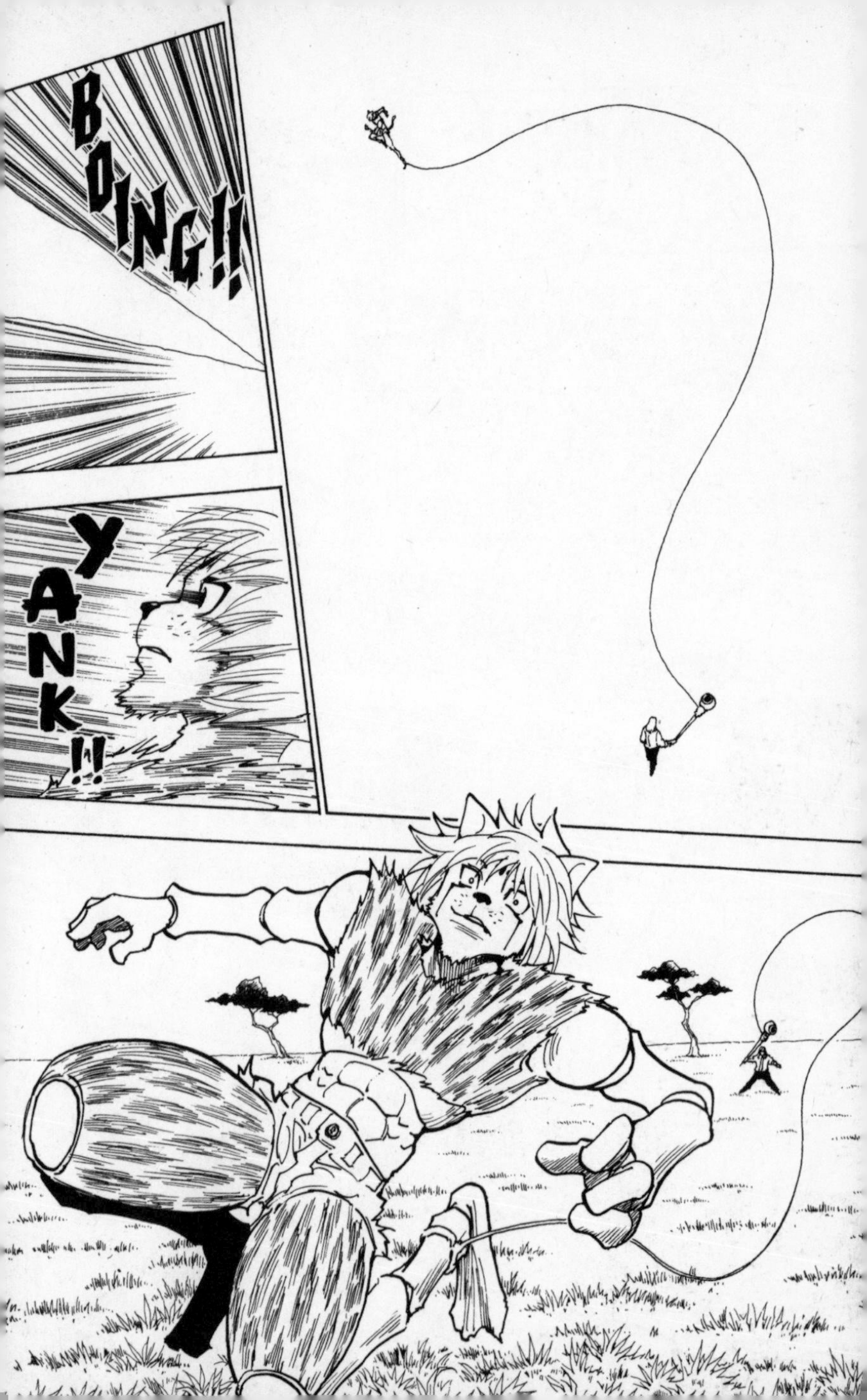
BOING!!
YANK!!

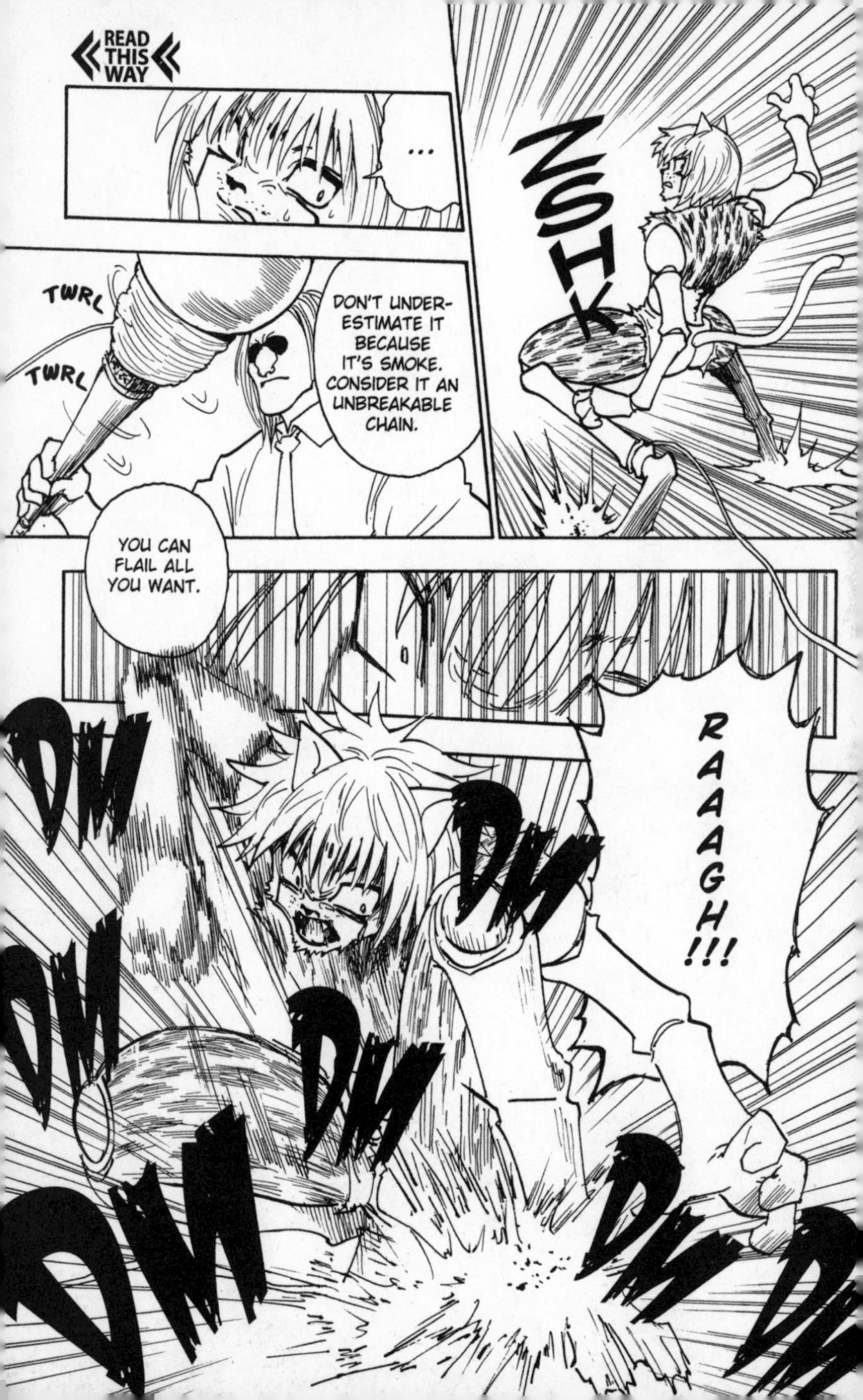
READ THIS WAY
ZSHK
...
DON'T UNDER-ESTIMATE IT BECAUSE IT'S SMOKE. CONSIDER IT AN UNBREAKABLE CHAIN.
TWRL
TWRL
YOU CAN FLAIL ALL YOU WANT.
RAAAGH!!!
DW
DW
DW
DW
DW
DW
DW
DW

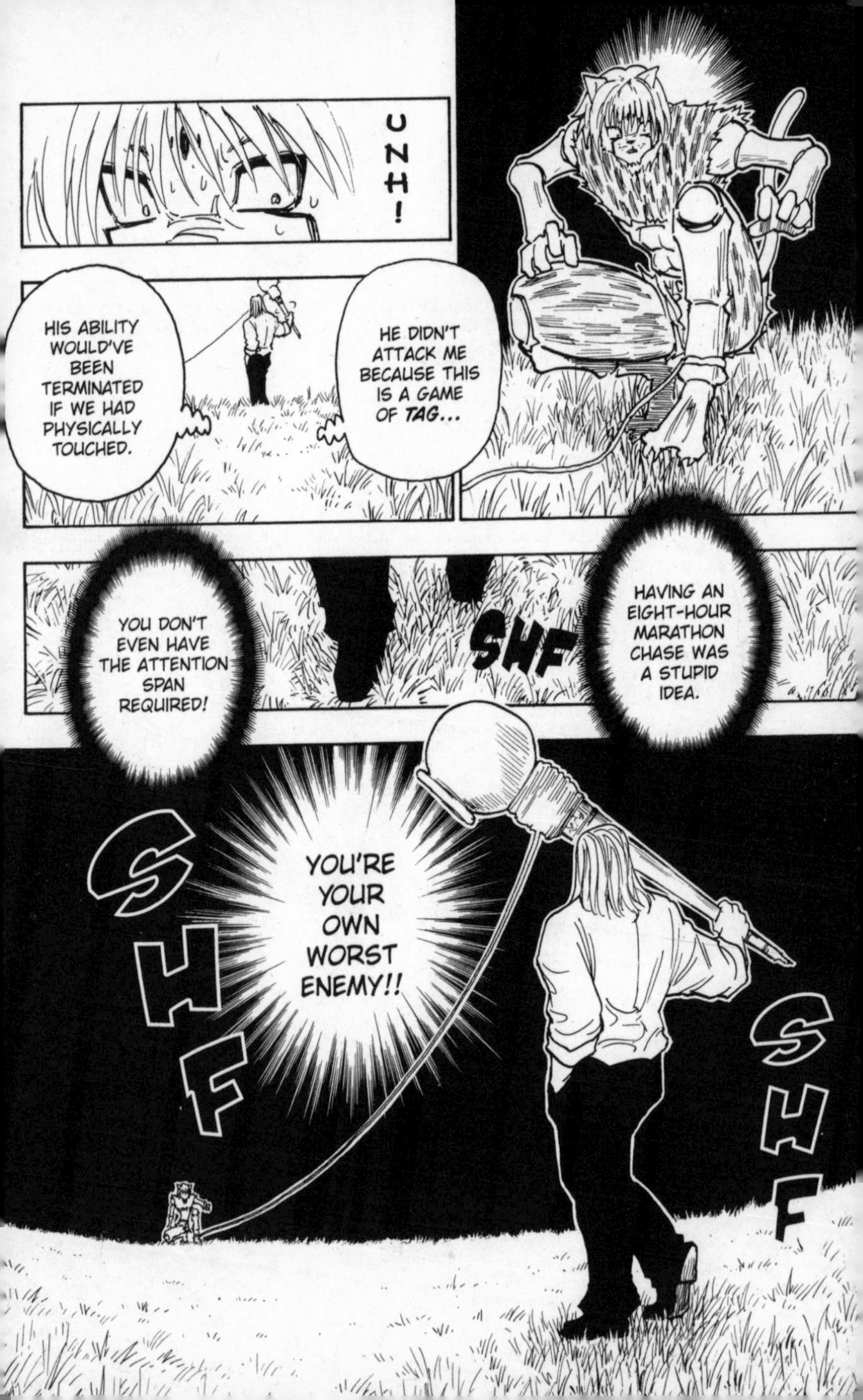
UNH!
HE DIDN'T ATTACK ME BECAUSE THIS IS A GAME OF *TAG*...
HIS ABILITY WOULD'VE BEEN TERMINATED IF WE HAD PHYSICALLY TOUCHED.
HAVING AN EIGHT-HOUR MARATHON CHASE WAS A STUPID IDEA.
SHF
YOU DON'T EVEN HAVE THE ATTENTION SPAN REQUIRED!
YOU'RE YOUR OWN WORST ENEMY!!
SHHF
SHHF

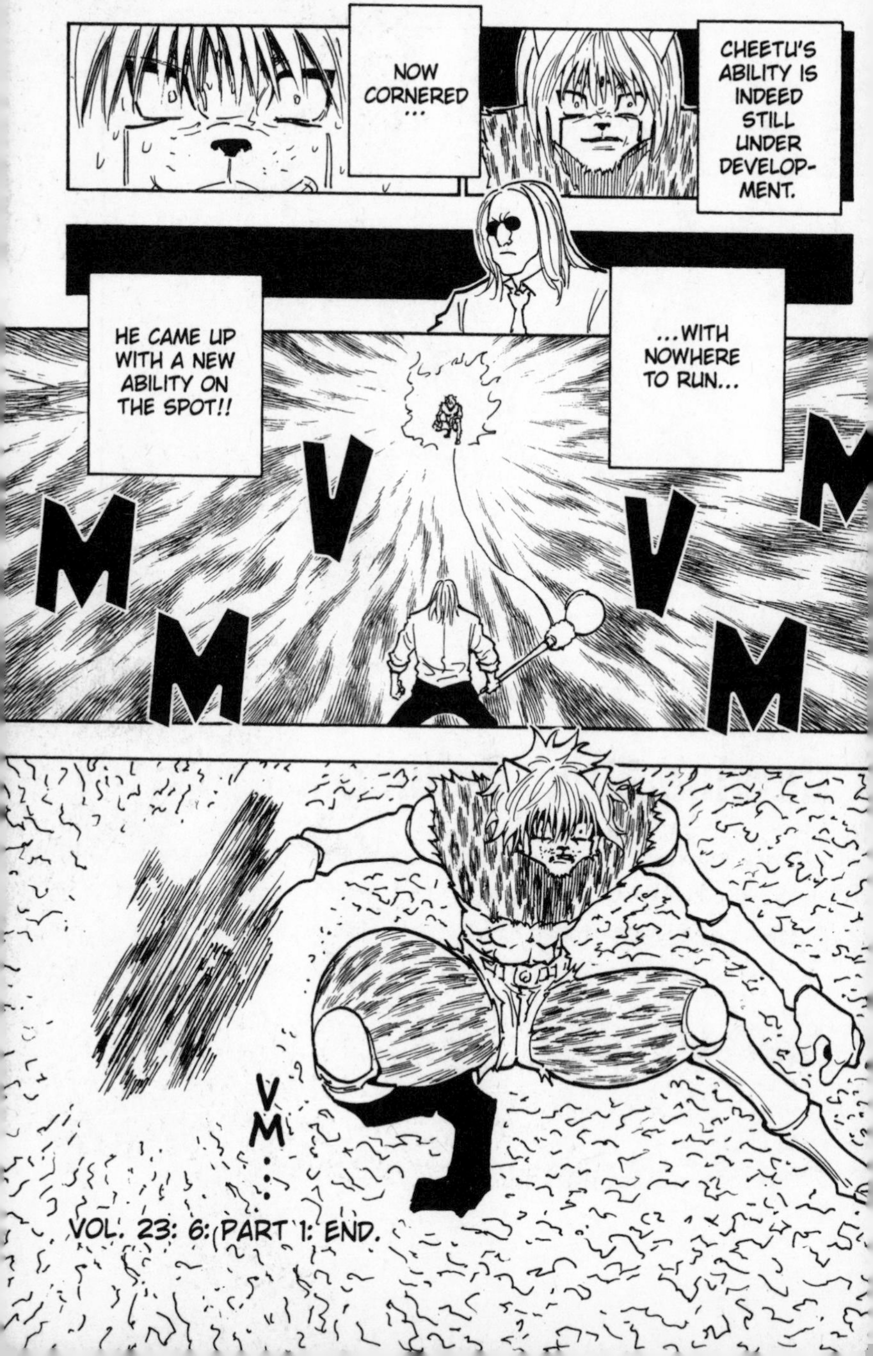
CHEETU'S ABILITY IS INDEED STILL UNDER DEVELOP-MENT.
NOW CORNERED...
...WITH NOWHERE TO RUN...
HE CAME UP WITH A NEW ABILITY ON THE SPOT!!
MVM
VMM
VM...
VOL. 23: 6: PART 1: END.

Coming Next Volume...

With the King engrossed in the game of Gungi, his soldier Ants are out battling the Hunters that are closing in for the kill. When an unforeseen accident causes Neferpitou to turn off his En that protects the King and his palace, the Hunters use this opportunity to invite themselves in!

Available now!

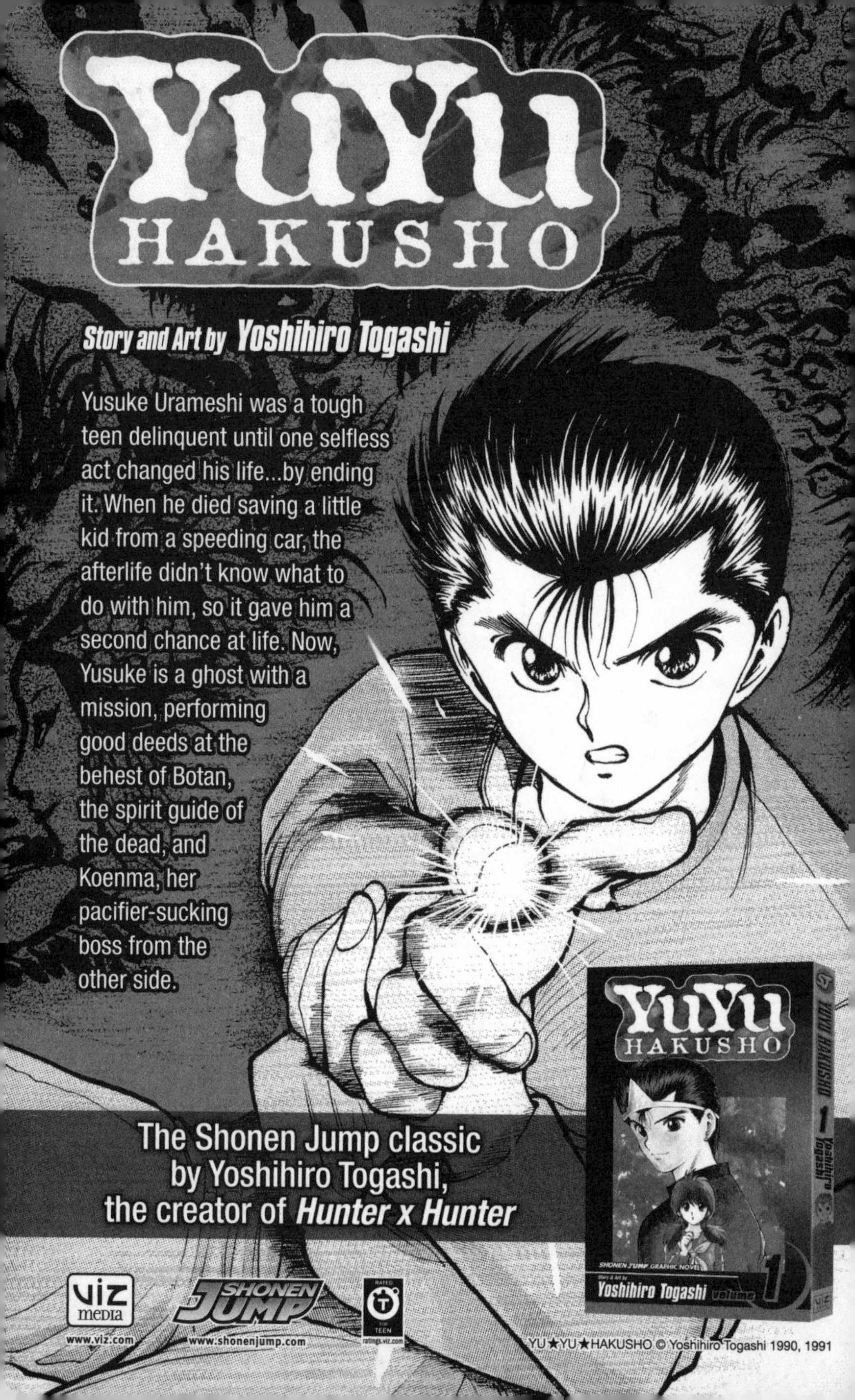
YuYu
HAKUSHO
Story and Art by Yoshihiro Togashi
Yusuke Urameshi was a tough teen delinquent until one selfless act changed his life...by ending it. When he died saving a little kid from a speeding car, the afterlife didn't know what to do with him, so it gave him a second chance at life. Now, Yusuke is a ghost with a mission, performing good deeds at the behest of Botan, the spirit guide of the dead, and Koenma, her pacifier-sucking boss from the other side.
YuYu
HAKUSHO
1
SHONEN JUMP GRAPHIC NOVEL
Yoshihiro Togashi volume 1
The Shonen Jump classic by Yoshihiro Togashi, the creator of *Hunter x Hunter*
viz media
www.viz.com
SHONEN JUMP
www.shonenjump.com
RATED
T
TEEN
ratings.viz.com
YU★YU★HAKUSHO © Yoshihiro Togashi 1990, 1991

You're Reading in the Wrong Direction!!

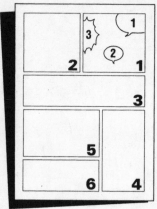

Whoops! Guess what? You're starting at the wrong end of the comic!

…It's true! In keeping with the original Japanese format, **Hunter x Hunter** is meant to be read from right to left, starting in the upper-right corner.

Unlike English, which is read from left to right, Japanese is read from right to left, meaning that action, sound effects and word-balloon order are completely reversed… something which can make readers unfamiliar with Japanese feel pretty backwards themselves. For this reason, manga or Japanese comics published in the U.S. in English have sometimes been published "flopped"– that is, printed in exact reverse order, as though seen from the other side of a mirror.

By flopping pages, U.S. publishers can avoid confusing readers, but the compromise is not without its downside. For one thing, a character in a flopped manga series who once wore in the original Japanese version a T-shirt emblazoned with "M A Y" (as in "the merry month of") now wears one which reads "Y A M"! Additionally, many manga creators in Japan are themselves unhappy with the process, as some feel the mirror-imaging of their art skews their original intentions.

We are proud to bring you Yoshihiro Togashi's **Hunter x Hunter** in the original unflopped format. For now, though, turn to the other side of the book and let the adventure begin…!

—Editor